HISTORY AND STRATEGY

HISTORY AND STRATEGY

Marc Trachtenberg

PRINCETON UNIVERSITY PRESS   PRINCETON, NEW JERSEY

Library of Congress Cataloging-in-Publication Data
Trachtenberg, Marc, 1946–
History and strategy / Marc Trachtenberg.
p. cm.—(Princeton studies in international history and
politics)
Includes bibliographical references and index.
ISBN 0-691-07881-5 (cloth : alk. paper)—ISBN
0-691-02343-3 (pbk. : alk. paper)
1. Strategy. 2. Military history, Modern—20th century.
I. Title. II. Series.
U163.T73   1991
355.4′09′04—dc20   90–21036

This book has been composed in Linotron Sabon

Princeton University Press books are printed
on acid-free paper, and meet the guidelines
for permanence and durability of the Committee
on Production Guidelines for Book Longevity
of the Council on Library Resources

Printed in the United States of America by
Princeton University Press, Princeton, New Jersey

1   3   5   7   9   10   8   6   4   2

1   3   5   7   9   10   8   6   4   2
(Pbk.)

Contents

Preface   vii

Chapter One
Strategic Thought in America, 1952–1966   3

Chapter Two
The Coming of the First World War: A Reassessment   47

Chapter Three
A "Wasting Asset": American Strategy and the Shifting Nuclear
Balance, 1949–1954   100

Chapter Four
The Nuclearization of NATO and U.S.–West European
Relations   153

Chapter Five
The Berlin Crisis   169

Chapter Six
The Influence of Nuclear Weapons in the Cuban Missile Crisis   235

Chapter Seven
Making Sense of the Nuclear Age   261

Appendix
Key to Abbreviations in Chapter Five   287

Index   289

Preface

THE ESSAYS in this volume are concerned with the relationship between history and strategy. They are the product of a historian's attempt to come to terms with the way people from other fields, especially political scientists and economists, think about the problem of war and peace.

This, however, was not something that I had set out originally to do. The project began around 1980 in a more normal way. I wanted to make sense of the whole post–World War II period, to understand it in much the same way that historians try to understand the interwar period, or the period before the First World War. There was a story to be written—not a simple recounting of events, but an account that would convey some sense for what was really driving things. It was obvious that the nuclear revolution played a central role in the story; it was equally obvious that I did not know the first thing about nuclear issues. I wanted to get my bearings in what was for me an entirely new field, and so I began to read the most basic works on nuclear issues, books like Bernard Brodie's *Strategy in the Missile Age* and Thomas Schelling's *Arms and Influence.*

As I began to go through these writings, I was struck both by the extraordinary intellectual power of this body of theory, but also by what was for me its strangeness. These works reflected a way of looking at the world—assumptions about what is important, about what makes for war or for international stability—that was very different from the way I had come to see things. This was not just the result of some personal idiosyncrasy on my part. There really was a gap between the disciplines. Everyone may have been concerned in the final analysis with the same basic problem, the problem of war and peace. But scholars from different fields approached it in quite different ways. It was remarkable that whatever their differences on specific problems of interpretation, all the diplomatic historians I knew and respected shared a common conceptual framework, a common sense for what makes the history of international politics run. But the strategists clearly started from an entirely different set of assumptions.

Perhaps the most striking feature of the strategic literature was the great emphasis it placed on purely military factors in explaining why wars break out: the advantages of getting in the first blow could cause even a relatively minor political dispute to escalate into armed conflict. The clearest example of this was an extraordinary passage in Schelling's very influential article on "The Reciprocal Fear of Surprise Attack":

If surprise carries an advantage, it is worth while to avert it by striking first. Fear that the other may be about to strike in the mistaken belief that we are about to strike gives us a motive for striking, and so justifies the other's motive. But, if the gains from even successful surprise are less desired than no war at all, there is no "fundamental" basis for an attack by either side. Nevertheless, it looks as though a modest temptation on each side to sneak in a first blow—a temptation too small by itself to motivate an attack—might become compounded through a series of interacting expectations, with additional motive for attack being produced by successive cycles of "He thinks we think he thinks we think . . . he thinks we think he'll attack; so he thinks we shall; so he will; so we must."[1]

It would be amazing, I thought, if there had ever been a single statesman who had thought in such terms—who took the analysis, that is, past the first or at most the second cycle. As pure theory, the passage was obviously brilliant. But in the final analysis, wasn't it just a castle in the air? What did it have to do with the way the real world works?

And yet it was also clear that there was *something* real here. The professional diplomatic historians as a rule never paid much attention to the military side of the story. While military power as such was always seen as very important, the coming of a war was never viewed as the product of a dynamic that was largely military in nature. We all took it for granted that war was essentially the outcome of political conflict; it came about as the result of a political process; the key decisions were made for political reasons. Purely military factors, such as the desire to strike before being struck, or (in longer-range terms) before the military balance became unfavorable, were seen as playing at best a very marginal role. We scarcely talked about preemption—at least not in a purely military sense[2]—and traditional diplomatic history rarely took "preventive war" thinking very seriously. Indeed, we tended to shy away from the very notion of "aggression" as reflecting a rather simplistic approach to the problem of war causation. Political conflict—the very term reflected an aversion to making any judgment about who was right and who was wrong— was seen as fundamental; the workings of the military system were of

---

[1] Thomas Schelling, *The Strategy of Conflict* (Cambridge, Mass., 1960), p. 207.

[2] More broadly defined, however, the concept does play a certain role in historical analysis. Note, for example, the discussion of preemptive expansion by the European powers in Asia and Africa in D. K. Fieldhouse, *Economics and Empire, 1830–1914* (Ithaca, N.Y., 1973), pp. 146, 172, 198, 258. The analysis of the pre-1914 Austro-Russian conflict over southeastern Europe in Raymond Sontag, *European Diplomatic History, 1871–1932* (New York, 1933), p. 162, reflects a kind of "security dilemma" approach to the subject. Other examples could be cited, but even in this broader sense—i.e., a sense that refers to political as well as military moves—historians only rarely emphasize the dynamic of preemptive action.

purely secondary importance. There were of course exceptions, but on the whole all this was simply taken for granted by mainstream diplomatic history. Bernadotte Schmitt, for example, remarked in his classic analysis of the coming of the First World War that once either the French or the German government "had made up its mind to fight rather than accept diplomatic defeat at the hands of the other, the details of military preparations are of small consequence."[3] This final phrase essentially captured the attitude of our whole profession.

But was it possible that our traditional approach had been too narrow? The "strategists" were certainly not stupid. Their historical arguments often tended to be amateurish, but still they might be on to something. It was therefore worth taking their ideas seriously. Even if they turned out to be wrong, they might be wrong in such interesting ways that the whole process of coming to grips with their arguments might lead to some real insights. And there was always the possibility that the diplomatic historians had missed something crucial. This, it seemed, was most likely for the nuclear period, where serious research was just beginning, but it also might be the case for earlier periods as well. Perhaps the strategists had been able to intuit things through the pure power of their intellect that we historians, immersed in our documents, had somehow simply missed.

The sort of thinking that had emerged in the 1950s and 1960s as people tried to grapple with the implications of the nuclear revolution was, in any case, interesting in its own right as a historical phenomenon. These ideas had clearly played a certain political role in the United States, especially during the Kennedy period. It therefore seemed to me that doing an intellectual history—a study of how this body of thought took shape— would be a good way of getting a handle on this set of problems. It might also shed some light on the evolution of policy. And finally, doing this sort of history was a means of putting some distance between oneself and ideas that one might otherwise tend to accept uncritically. Intellectual history, as Brodie himself pointed out, is a form of intellectual liberation: ideas that one might regard "as natural and inevitable" turn out to be the product of a specific historical process, and by tracing their evolution, one can "glimpse the arbitrariness of views which we previously regarded as laws of nature."[4]

So I spent over a year studying the American nuclear strategists, or more accurately, the small group of civilians who created the body of thought that came to dominate the discussion of nuclear issues in the

---

[3] Bernadotte Schmitt, *The Coming of the War, 1914* (New York, 1930), vol. 2, p. 20. In reality, of course, it was necessary that both make up their minds to fight rather than accept diplomatic defeat for there to be a war, but this point is of small importance in the present context.

[4] Bernard Brodie, *Strategy in the Missile Age* (Princeton, 1959), p. 19.

United States. The result was the paper on "Strategic Thought in America, 1952–1966." The aim here was to try to understand why strategy hit a dead end intellectually by the late 1960s. This is explained in terms of the distinctive form that this body of thought had taken, which in turn is to be understood in terms of the professional background of the handful of people who had shaped these ideas. A large part of the problem was that the strategic literature was apolitical, and the paper concludes with the argument that it was apolitical in substance in large part because it was ahistorical in method. The programmatic point was implicit: the way to revive the field intellectually is to historicize it—to give the ideas real historical content, to use history for more than just ornamental purposes, to test theoretical ideas systematically against the historical evidence.

These programmatic themes are sounded in most of the articles here. The papers on the Cuban Missile Crisis, on American strategy in the 1949–54 period, and on the coming of the First World War, provide concrete examples of how basic theoretical issues emerging from the strategic literature can be brought into focus, and to a certain extent even resolved, through close study of the historical evidence. The method in all these cases is quite straightforward: one looks at the claims people make, and then looks at the documentary evidence to see how well they are supported. So simple a technique can scarcely be called methodologically interesting, but it is surprising how rarely it is used. With regard to the missile crisis, for example, people for years had been content to study it on the basis of a standard corpus of published materials—and this, in spite of the fact that important archival material had been open since at least 1978. And even when people read the documents, they were often so blinded by preconception that the real meaning of the evidence just passed them by. It perhaps takes a certain effort to approach these issues with an open mind—to define the questions so that the answers are not all known in advance, but depend in some meaningful way on the sort of evidence that turns up. But the result of such an effort can be quite revealing.

The "Wasting Asset" article is a good case in point. Over the years, I had gotten into many arguments with my political scientist friends about the importance of shifts in the military balance—that is, about the meaning of the opening and closing of "windows of opportunity" and "windows of vulnerability," and indeed about the general issue of preventive war. It was hard for me to believe that preventive war thinking had ever carried important political weight, or that "window" thinking had ever played a major role in shaping policy. But I thought it might be easy to test the issue. If there was anything to the argument at all, a study of the 1949–54 period should bring it out. There had never been anything like the revolution in military affairs then taking place, but what political effect did it have? How did people deal with the loss of the American nuclear monopoly, and with the coming of thermonuclear weapons? I fully expected to find that the sort of thinking that emerged as people tried to come to terms with this set of problems was of marginal historical importance. But there was no arguing with the evidence: it turned out that I had been wrong and that the political scientists had been right. These concerns about trends in the military balance played a central role in shaping policy at the time; and to understand why people felt the way they did, one had to go into the military side of the story in some depth.

The articles on the nuclearization of NATO and on the Berlin crisis are cut from a different cloth. The first of these is essentially a sketch, and the second attempts a more far-reaching analysis, but each is in its way a more or less normal work of history. The idea in both cases was to treat the 1950s the same way any earlier period in great power politics would be treated, and build the analysis basically on what turned up in the archives. But each of these papers was strongly influenced by my exposure to the literature on nuclear strategy. If I had tried, for example, to write something on the Berlin crisis ten years ago, I probably would have ignored the military side of the story, but it plays an important role in the analysis here.

The Berlin crisis article is also in part a reaction to what I saw as a somewhat ahistorical and indeed excessive emphasis on crises as discrete episodes in the political science literature. A crisis is not just something that happens out of the blue, rooted essentially in one side or the other's aggressiveness. A crisis—and this is a point most diplomatic historians simply take for granted—has to be seen in historical context, as rooted in long-term historical processes, and as playing an important role in determining how those processes run their course. Too much attention, I thought, had been devoted to the question of how an aggressor might be deterred in crisis situations, as though crises, as a general rule, are really the result of aggression pure and simple, and not enough to how the process that leads up to a crisis might be managed. But a different way of approaching these issues depended, it seemed, on a more sophisticated understanding of how international politics has worked in the past, especially in the nuclear past.

These two papers, and indeed most of the papers published in this volume, are essentially exercises written as part of a larger project, a more wide-ranging study of international politics from 1945 to 1965, which is still in progress and which will not be completed for many years. The final essay in this volume, "Making Sense of the Nuclear Age," lays out the rationale for a work of this sort, and discusses how a historian goes about attacking a project of this scope. It was originally presented at a conference on nuclear threats held at Columbia University in 1985, and was written mainly for political scientists. My goal was to give them some sense for history as a field with an intellectual personality of its own, for the conceptual core of the discipline, for the fact that historians try to do more than simply dig up and present facts about the past. I wanted to show them how the historical approach can yield insights, even of a general nature, that other approaches are simply unable to capture.

But as the articles in this volume show, strategic theory can also drive historical analysis. The interaction process has to work both ways. Indeed, if there is a single conclusion to be drawn from this collection of essays it is this: we historians can learn by taking the political scientists seriously, and they can learn by approaching our works as something more than just grist for their theoretical mills. The two fields can profit, and I think can profit enormously, by engaging each other intellectually, and by coming to terms with each other's most fundamental point of view.

That, in any case, was my experience in writing these pieces. I learned so much from so many individuals that I scarcely know how to begin to express my gratitude for all the help I received. A simple list of names hardly does justice to all the people who helped me understand the issues this book is concerned with. But I do want to thank Thomas Schelling and Albert Wohlstetter, Robert Bowie, McGeorge Bundy, Jack Ruina, and above all Carl Kaysen, whose assistance and generosity went far beyond what I had any right to expect. I am deeply indebted to a number of historians and political scientists for friendship and intellectual support over the years: Thomas Childers, Alan Kors, Bruce Kuklick, Robert Powell, Steven Miller, Jack Snyder, Stephen Schuker, and especially Robert Jervis, David Rosenberg, John Mearsheimer, and Stephen Van Evera. Their influence, individually but also collectively, can be felt on practically every page of this book. Finally, I want to thank the Guggenheim and MacArthur Foundations, the RAND Corporation, the University of Pennsylvania, and the Massachusetts Institute of Technology, for supporting or otherwise facilitating the research on which these articles are based. To all these institutions, and to all these people, I am very grateful.

HISTORY AND STRATEGY

CHAPTER ONE

Strategic Thought in America, 1952–1966

IN the 1950s, strategy emerged in the United States as a new field with a distinct intellectual personality. A small group of men—Bernard Brodie, Thomas Schelling, Albert Wohlstetter, and a handful of others—working mainly at the RAND Corporation, had moved into an intellectually barren "no-man's-land" traditionally neglected by both military officers and students of international politics.[1] The body of thought they created was very different from anything that had come before. Their ideas would prove to be enormously influential, and their style of analysis in large measure became the sophisticated way of approaching nuclear issues in the United States.

The aim here is not simply to offer yet another description of this body of thought. The real goal is to try to give some sense for how this intellectual tradition took the shape it did—what caused it to emerge, how the central ideas developed, and why, after an extraordinary period of intellectual productivity, these ideas by around 1966 or so seemed to have played themselves out. Why, in other words, did strategy hit something of a dead end in the late 1960s?

The focus will be on the basic tension that dominated the development of this set of ideas. It was as though the coming of the hydrogen bomb in 1952 had released two great shock waves in the world of strategic thought. There was on the one hand the fundamental point that when both the United States and the Soviet Union had obtained survivable and deliverable strategic forces, all-out war between these two powers would

This paper is based in part on research in classified material. Under the terms of the "limited security access" that the U.S. Air Force grants to scholars, I was able to see certain older documents up to the level of "secret"; the RAND Corporation also generously allowed me to see many of their documents from the period covered in this study. As part of the agreement authorizing access to these materials, the final manuscript had to be cleared for publication by both of these organizations. But it should be noted that no changes of any substance were required by either RAND or the Air Force, and at no point did I ever feel that my freedom as a scholar was being constrained in any way. An abridged version of this article appeared in the summer 1989 issue of the *Political Science Quarterly*, and many of the articles and papers cited here have been published in Marc Trachtenberg, ed., *The Development of American Strategic Thought*, 6 vols. (New York, 1988).

[1] Bernard Brodie, *Strategy in the Missile Age* (Princeton, 1959), p. 7; see also Thomas Schelling, "The Retarded Science of International Strategy," in his *The Strategy of Conflict* (Cambridge, Mass., 1960).

become an absurdity: with thermonuclear weapons, the overriding goal had to be to limit war—and in particular to reduce to a minimum the risk that the nuclear powers would launch massive attacks on each other's cities. On the other hand, there was the equally basic notion that the threat of nuclear war could be used for political purposes that went well beyond deterring the use of nuclear weapons by an adversary. The idea that one could exploit the threat of escalation was a product of the early atomic age. But it was the coming of the hydrogen bomb that brought this problem into focus. Indeed, the way strategic thought developed— the very distinctive shape it came to have—was very much a product of the thermonuclear revolution.

It was not that separate factions rallied around each of these two poles: the history of American strategic thought during this period cannot be summed up as a dispute between those who believed in "simple deterrence" and those who wanted nuclear forces to play a more far-reaching political role. Strategic discourse during this period was not sectarian or doctrinaire: the striking thing was that the same people were attracted to both approaches, often at the same time. But these two basic ways of approaching strategy were in obvious conflict with each other. The fundamental question was whether there was any way this conflict could be resolved.

THE THERMONUCLEAR REVOLUTION

It is perhaps odd that the most important work on strategic issues was done in the 1950s and early 1960s—or, more precisely, in the period from 1952 to 1966. One might have thought that the coming of the atomic bomb in 1945 would have marked the watershed. But even as late as 1950 or 1951, concepts of strategic bombing that had emerged before and during the Second World War continued to provide an adequate framework for thinking about how an atomic war would be fought. The early atomic bombs were not so powerful that numbers and accuracy were no longer important. Defense against bombers could still make a difference; base location would remain important because of its effect on the intensity with which the bombing campaign could be carried out; and armies and navies would continue to play a significant role in defending those bases and perhaps in blunting an enemy counterattack. A new war, it was assumed, would be a war of attrition, a war of endurance. Thus, mobilization was still meaningful; it therefore still made sense militarily to try to destroy the enemy's war-making capability by destroying his economy. In other words, the atomic bomb, as important as it was, had not rendered the existing conceptual framework obsolete, and this was true even after the Soviet Union had begun in 1949 to amass atomic forces of its own.[2]

In the early 1950s, however, the situation was to change dramatically. By the beginning of 1952, it had become clear to those in the know that a thermonuclear weapon with an explosive force a thousand times as great as the bombs dropped on Japan "was soon to be tested and that success was virtually certain."[3] Viewed in a somewhat broader context, the hydrogen bomb can be seen as simply the most awesome of a whole series of developments in nuclear weapons technology that were reaching a climax at the beginning of the 1950s. Fission bombs had by this time become smaller, lighter, mass-producible and more efficient in their use of fissionable material. Maximum yields of even pure fission weapons had

---

[2] On military planning during this period, see Kenneth Condit et al., *History of the Joint Chiefs of Staff*, vol. 2 (1947–1949), 293–98; David A. Rosenberg, "American Atomic Strategy and the Hydrogen Bomb Decision," *Journal of American History*, vol. 61 (June 1979); Richard Rowe, "American Nuclear Strategy and the Korean War," M.A. thesis, University of Pennsylvania (1984), pp. 5–36; and Samuel Williamson, Jr. (with Steven Rearden), "The View from Above: High-Level Decisions and the Soviet-American Strategic Arms Competition, 1945–1950," October 1975, available from the Office of the Secretary of Defense, Freedom of Information Office. There is a wealth of relevant information in the volumes on National Security Affairs for this period in the State Department's *Foreign Relations of the United States* series.

What emerges from these sources is a sense that the atomic offensive, while clearly of tremendous importance, was nevertheless not viewed at this time as decisive in itself; only a small number of fission bombs had been produced. Instead, the feeling was that a new war would be long; there would thus be time for mobilization; it therefore made sense to assume that the enemy economy would be the main target of the air offensive. These general assumptions were reflected in the RAND documents from the pre-H-bomb period. See, for example, R. T. Nichols, "STRAP: Summary of Economic Panel Discussions," RAND Research Memorandum RM-257 (October 1949; limited distribution), esp. p. 4.

Some of the best writings from this period were written in reaction to the British physicist P.M.S. Blackett's well-known book, *The Military and Political Consequences of Atomic Energy* (London, 1948), which sought to denigrate the military effectiveness of atomic warfare. See especially Joseph E. Loftus, "Strategy, Economics and the Bomb," *Scientific Monthly*, May 1949, pp. 310–20, and Carl Kaysen, "Professor Blackett and the Bomb," *Social Research*, vol. 16, no. 3 (September 1949), pp. 336–81. Blackett may have been wrong in claiming that atomic explosives were of marginal importance, but neither Loftus nor Kaysen wanted to argue that the bomb was an "absolute weapon." Kaysen, in fact, pointed out that the great air raids on Hamburg in the summer of 1943 were "the equivalent of at least two or three atomic bombs, by any standards of damage, including damage to persons"; but production had been able to recover rapidly. "Atomic Bombs in the ETO," RAND Research Memorandum RM-231 (August 30, 1949; limited distribution), p. 5. The article by Loftus, incidentally, played an important part in Loftus's own career, and led eventually to his appointment as the civilian director of target intelligence for the Air Force about a year later.

[3] Bernard Brodie, introduction to "Towards a New Defense for NATO: The Case for Tactical Nuclear Weapons," National Strategy Information Center, Agenda Paper No. 5 (New York, 1976), p. 1.

increased dramatically, rising from the twelve kilotons of the Hiroshima bomb to a half-megaton in 1952. "Boosted" weapons, where part of the explosive power derived from a fusion reaction, and which were being developed at the same time, produced a yield in the one-megaton range.[4] The result was that even if true thermonuclear weapons had never been deployed, the traditional basis for thinking about air warfare would in all probability eventually have been undermined.

In the minds of people at the time, however, the great revolution in military technology was dominated and symbolized by the huge thermonuclear explosives first tested in 1952. It is for this reason that the new conditions of warfare that were emerging in the early 1950s will be referred to here as the "thermonuclear revolution." Certainly, for the small group of civilians at the RAND Corporation who had begun to think seriously about basic problems of nuclear strategy, it was the hydrogen bomb that marked the decisive break with the past.

Charles Hitch, for example, was at this time one of the leading figures at RAND, and in the summer of 1952 he and William Capron prepared a report on the implications of the new weapon. "We may," they wrote, "be able to absorb a large number of A-bombs and recover, particularly if the targets selected are not optimal or if bombing accuracy is poor; we cannot stand fifty 25-MT bombs if they are well-placed and the results are not very sensitive to the placing."[5]

Bernard Brodie, then also at RAND, was by this time arguing along similar lines. The ordinary atomic bomb, he said in a talk at the Air War College, was "not so absolute a weapon that we can disregard the limits of its destructive power." One still had to be concerned with bombing accuracy and with the physical vulnerability of the target. But with the H-bomb, concerns of this sort would count for "astonishingly little."[6] What, however, did this imply about strategy? Simply that the basic aim had to be deterrence—that the overriding goal had to be to prevent war through the threat of retaliation? The problem was that such a threat could carry weight only if one were prepared to follow through on it. Peace would depend, Brodie had argued even in the late 1940s, on a uni-

---

[4] These developments are summarized in David Rosenberg, "The Origins of Overkill: Nuclear Weapons and American Strategy, 1945–1960," *International Security*, vol. 7, no. 4 (Spring 1983), p. 24. This article is by far the best study of American nuclear weapons policy during this period. See also Herbert York, "The Debate over the Hydrogen Bomb," *Scientific American*, October 1975, pp. 110–11.

[5] C. J. Hitch and W. M. Capron, "Implications of Potential Weapon Developments for Strategic Bombing and Air Defense: A Preliminary Study," RAND Research Memorandum RM-868 (July 10, 1952), p. 28.

[6] Bernard Brodie, "Changing Capabilities and War Objectives," pp. 10–11, 18–19, Bernard Brodie Papers, Box 12, UCLA Library. This is the text of a lecture given to the Air War College on April 17, 1952, and was originally classified "top secret."

versal conviction "that war is far too horrible even to be contemplated. And the great dilemma is that that conviction can be sustained only by our making every possible effort to prepare for war and thus to engage in it if need be."[7]

The problem of deterrence could therefore not be divorced from the problem of use. What made this issue so difficult, Brodie stressed in 1952, was the realization that an atomic war would inevitably be a "two-way affair," and an all-out war with thermonuclear weapons might well be tantamount to national suicide. It was obvious "that national objectives could not be consonant with national suicide." Brodie had earlier thought that Clausewitz, with his insistence on the close linkage between political objectives and military means, had become obsolete: even the early atomic weapons were too destructive to be harnessed to rational political goals. But he had since come to see that Clausewitz had been "saying something very profound." He had been saying that "war is violence—to be sure, gigantic violence—but it is planned violence and therefore controlled. And since the objective should be rational, the procedure for accomplishing that objective should also be rational, which is to say that the procedure and the objective must be in some measure appropriate to each other." Brodie's views had been moving in this direction even in 1949 and 1950. But the imminent arrival of the hydrogen bomb had made this sort of thinking particularly salient: a suicidal strategy could never be an appropriate means of supporting rational, political goals. It followed that one had to think about strategies that were not suicidal— that the means of violence had to be controlled and limited.[8]

Brodie's problem in the early 1950s was to think out how the atomic bombs should actually be used in war, and in particular how the "threat value" of nuclear weapons could be exploited.[9] What he objected to was the assumption that the bombing attack should be as swift, as concentrated and as massive as possible. The general idea that there might be a better way to use nuclear weapons than simply launching the kind of concentrated "atomic blitz" called for in the war plans had been actively

[7] "New Techniques of War and National Policies," in William Ogburn, *Technology and International Relations* (Chicago, 1949), p. 167.

[8] Brodie, "Changing Capabilities," pp. 3–4, 21–22. For a similar argument, see also his "Political Consequences of the H-Bomb," Nov. 7, 1952, and "A Slightly Revised Proposal for the Underemployment of SAC in an H-Bomb Era," Jan. 23, 1953, unpublished RAND working papers. On Clausewitz: see Brodie's 1946 Harris Foundation lecture, "The Security Problem in the Light of Atomic Energy," in Quincy Wright, ed., *A Foreign Policy for the United States* (Chicago, 1947), p. 89.

[9] Fred Kaplan, *The Wizards of Armageddon* (New York, 1983), pp. 46–48; Bernard Brodie to David Rosenberg, August 22, 1977, Brodie Papers, Box 9. See also Barry Steiner, "Using the Absolute Weapon: Early Ideas of Bernard Brodie on Atomic Strategy," UCLA Center for International and Strategic Affairs, ACIS Working Paper No. 44, January 1984.

discussed at RAND even in the late 1940s.[10] But it was Brodie who gave the idea written expression; it was in fact to become a major theme in his writings. He laid out the argument, for example, in his paper, "Must We Shoot from the Hip?" which he wrote at RAND in late 1951. The aim, he said, should be to continue to exert pressure—and by that he meant political and psychological pressure—until the war reached a conclusion. But existing policy would make this impossible: "Under present conceptions, it is not too much to say that we shoot our bolt and then wait for something to happen, being then quite unable to affect what will happen."[11]

This was, however, more an argument that the level of violence should be *controlled* than that it should be *limited*. Brodie was not arguing at this point that urban-industrial targets should not be attacked except in retaliation for a similar attack on our own cities. He was simply arguing against what came to be called a "spasm" attack: the atomic offensive had to be conducted in a more deliberate way in order to serve basic political goals.

What exactly was new here? Limited war thinking, of course, had certain precursors in the late 1940s: there were various proposals aired at the time for outlawing the use of nuclear weapons, or at least for ruling out attacks on cities. But whatever appeal these simple limited war arguments had, the problem was that strategic bombing had emerged during the immediate postwar period as the dominant form of great power warfare. Given the technology of the late 1940s, and the resources that could be mobilized at the time, an air-atomic war was actually fightable: the devastation would be terrible, but the war could in theory be won and societies could survive even an unrestrained conflict of this sort. With the tremendous increase in the destructiveness of nuclear weaponry, however, the strategy of massive air bombardment of urban-industrial areas became, or was certainly well on the way to becoming, a victim of its own technical success. What was new, in other words, was the sense that in the very near future the level of devastation would be so incredibly great that unrestrained warfare no longer made any sense at all: there had to be some limit on the level of violence.

For Brodie in particular, the thermonuclear revolution marked an important watershed. In the early atomic age, he had not argued that we should hold back from using nuclear weapons—in general, or simply against an enemy's cities—provided the enemy respected a similar set of restraints. Nor had he argued for major limited war-fighting capabilities.

[10] Interview with Andrew Marshall, March 19, 1987. One product of this sort of thinking was the "Warning and Bombing" or "Warbo" study of 1949–50.

[11] "Must We Shoot from the Hip?" RAND working paper, September 4, 1951, pp. 14, 16.

In his writings at the time, military efficiency was the main concern: the assumption was that if war came, one would use whatever one had. In 1948 he in fact made exactly the kind of argument that just a few years later he was to view as the height of unwisdom. "We cannot," he said, "forever go on planning for two drastically different kinds of large-scale war. Considerations of economy and of getting the most possible fighting strength out of our military resources will dictate that we make up our minds at an early date whether or not we will use the bombs in war and adjust accordingly. There is not much doubt about what that decision will be, especially since the general expectation is that—failing the setting-up of an effective international control system—our major rival will begin to make atomic bombs within the next ten to twenty years."[12] It was only the imminent arrival of thermonuclear weapons that forced him to consider whether there should be any limitation on the level of violence: it was the revolution in the means of warfare that brought about his break with the past. Objectives had to be limited, he said, because the means of warfare had to be limited, "and not the other way around."[13]

But these two arguments—for war limitation, and for using the nuclear threat to support basic political goals—almost at once began to pull in opposite directions. Strategy, Brodie wrote in early 1952, should be concerned with "determining what *not* to hit as well as what to hit"; the central goal now was to figure out what could "be achieved by war, and in what way, other than by unloosing destruction on an unlimited basis."[14] But was the aim to determine what not to attack *initially*, so that

[12] Brodie, "New Techniques," p. 163.

[13] Bernard Brodie, "The Meaning of Limited War," RAND Paper P-1222 (June 10, 1958), pp. 7–8. Brodie frequently referred to this knowledge as marking a watershed in his own thinking. See his "More About Limited War," *World Politics*, vol. 10 (October 1957), pp. 112–13, or his *War and Politics* (New York, 1973), p. 394.

As a basis for comparison, it is interesting to note in this connection the early analysis of the impact of thermonuclear weapons done by the American military: Joint Chiefs of Staff memo, January 13, 1950, *Foreign Relations of the United States*, 1950, vol. 1, pp. 503–11; Defense Department memo, "The Military Implications of Thermonuclear Weapons," enclosed in the "Report by the Special Committee of the National Security Council to the President," January 31, 1950, ibid., pp. 517–23. What was missing from these analyses was any sense that the threat of retaliation might lead to an extreme reluctance, even in the event of a major war, to launch an unrestricted thermonuclear attack. "What effect," the JCS memo asked, "would fear of the use of a super bomb by an enemy have upon the United States?" Here, in its entirety, is their answer to this basic question: "One effect most certainly would be that those persons who really fear the use by an enemy of a super bomb on the United States would bring a tremendous pressure to bear to provide a maximum defense for each locality in which they happened to live and work. As a result of such pressures and demands, the strategic resources of the United States could be so diverted to defensive requirements that the United States would find itself unable to generate sufficient offensive power to gain victory." Ibid., p. 509.

[14] Naval War College lecture, March 17, 1952, Brodie Papers, Box 10.

the threat of further destruction could be exploited for political purposes—that is, used to bring about an acceptable end to the war? One would in that case have to be ready to escalate the war eventually—to use nuclear forces against an enemy's homeland, and even against his cities, even if he refrained from attacking American cities first. Or was the fundamental goal to decide what not to attack *ever*, or at least as long as the enemy abided by a similar set of restraints? In both cases, the massive, concentrated attack was rejected as a strategy. But the fact that both approaches were linked to a critique of the strategy of the single, massive, all-out strike simply obscured the fact that these two lines of argument represented two very different, and ultimately contradictory, approaches to the nuclear question.

This central tension was already apparent in Brodie's April 1952 talk to the Air War College. Nuclear forces, he argued, provided they could survive an enemy attack, would in general be a "very good deterrent." But what if deterrence broke down and we got involved in a full-scale war?

> I've been toying with an idea about that. If I had heard it from anyone else I should have called it a crackpot idea, but I offer it to you for what it may be worth. The atomic bomb thus far has achieved really great successes; it helped end the Pacific War, and it has so far deterred the Soviet Union from aggression. At least, there is nothing else visible to us, that is, nothing physical, that has deterred the Soviet Union from aggression. Notice that the deterrent value has resulted from the threat value. I submit that even the ending of the Pacific War resulted not from the two cities we destroyed, but rather from the threat value of the nonexistent additional bombs which the Japanese didn't know we didn't have—from the threat of more to come. According to our present concepts, this threat value of the atomic bomb is the first thing we plan to throw away the moment that hostilities open. A bomb which has been used no longer has threat value. A city which has been destroyed is no longer worth entering into surrender negotiations for the sake of preserving it. I submit that if we decide through intensive study of the situation that our nuclear weapons would actually enable us to break and burn the Soviet armies on the ground wherever they might commit aggression, we might decide that it was possible to secure our objectives without bombing enemy cities. And provided we communicated that idea in advance and provided we retained a powerful and invulnerable SAC to lay down the ground rules and make sure that they were observed, we could say, "We will not bomb your cities except in retaliation." This, of course, would be sacrificing the prospect of total victory, but for the future that might be a small price to pay for the sake of avoiding total war.[15]

[15] Brodie, "Changing Capabilities," pp. 28–29.

But note how two very different arguments are brought together here: the argument about exploiting the "threat value" of nuclear weapons—the threat of destroying cities if the enemy does not accommodate us—which had been taking shape in Brodie's mind during the previous few years, and the new argument about limited war, about not bombing enemy cities except in retaliation for an attack on our own cities, which was essentially a product of the thermonuclear revolution.

The tension between the two lines of argument was fundamental. It was as though two poles had emerged that were to give the strategic debate its basic structure. Do we want to exploit the risk of escalation, even for essentially defensive purposes, or should our central goal be to minimize it? Should nuclear forces simply cancel each other out, or do they have a broader political function to play? War between the United States and the Soviet Union was not impossible, and if it did break out, there was no guarantee that nuclear weapons would not be used. It was thus important to think about how they might be used, about what might happen "if deterrence failed." But the way we planned to use them might have a major influence on the kind of political effect they had, even before war broke out—if only because of the effect these plans had on the kinds of forces that were created. The question of deterrence could not be divorced from the question of use. The problem of target selection was therefore of fundamental importance.

These problems were all very new, but already in 1952 one thing was clear: the targeting philosophy that had developed before and during the Second World War was becoming increasingly problematic. Indeed, the basic point about the absurdity of all-out war when each side had developed the means of utterly devastating the other must have been tremendously disorienting for professional military officers. It was clear, to the more discerning officers at any rate, that there were very basic and difficult problems here and that no one as yet had any really satisfactory answers. General John A. Samford, for example, the Air Force Director of Intelligence, wrote in 1952 that existing ideas on air power were inadequate and rested on "too narrow a base"; he therefore asked the President of RAND to allow Brodie, whose work he liked and with whom he had been in contact, to "produce a basic treatise on air power in war." Since RAND was under contract to the Air Force, this was in effect the authorization that enabled Brodie to do the work that culminated in his important 1959 book, *Strategy in the Missile Age*.[16]

Brodie and the other civilian strategists were not awed by the expertise of professional military officers. There was a sense that nuclear weapons

[16] Samford to Collbohm, April 18, 1952, and Brodie to Samford, August 20, 1959, Brodie Papers, Box 2. See also Brodie to Rosenberg, August 22, 1977, Brodie Papers, Box 9.

had wiped the slate clean, that the field was wide open, and that no specific form of credentialing was needed for one's ideas to be taken seriously. If anything, there was a certain bias against the military, which was condemned for its excessive offense-mindedness and its consequent neglect of the importance of defense, especially the defense of nuclear forces; the armed forces were viewed as too conservative, incapable of adjusting swiftly to technological change; and the services were blamed also for not taking strategy seriously enough, for viewing it, when they thought about it at all, as essentially tactics writ large, more technical than political in nature.[17]

There was one other profession whose function in the area of strategy was dramatically affected by the coming of thermonuclear weapons. Beginning with the Second World War, the economists had played a central role in strategic bombing. In a bombing campaign, target selection was crucial; but the problem of maximizing the impact of the attack on the enemy's war-making potential was in essence an economic problem—and thus the kind of problem that professional economists were best equipped to deal with. It was in this way that a number of economists, people like Carl Kaysen and Charles Hitch, first became involved with air strategy. The insights and body of lore accumulated during the war were still applicable in the early atomic age, but after 1952 all of this was obsolete: the problem was no longer how to maximize the amount of devastation that bombers could inflict. It was "all too easy" to destroy an enemy's cities. But by the same token it would not be difficult for the enemy to destroy America's cities as well.[18]

[17] These were common themes in Brodie's writings. He was particularly blunt in unpublished memoranda and correspondence; see especially Brodie to Hans Speier, November 23, 1954, Brodie Papers, Box 4, file "Washington Office," where he sets out his views about the military. Note also Brodie's "Commentary on the Force Employment Study," unpublished RAND working paper, January 9, 1953, esp. the last page, or, many years later, his comments on the lessons he drew from his experience working for the Air Force in 1951: "The experience was certainly a shocking one with respect to what I observed as sheer frivolousness and stupidity with respect to the treatment of the No. 1 strategic problem confronting the U.S. at the time. It also made me skeptical of the net utility of the intense secrecy which served as a shield for the perpetration of such blunders." Brodie to Rosenberg, August 22, 1977, p. 4.

[18] On the role of the economists, see, for example, Bernard Brodie, "The American Scientific Strategists," RAND Paper P-2979 (October 1964), pp. 20–22; this was different from his chapter on "The Scientific Strategists" in Robert Gilpin and Christopher Wright, *Scientists and National Policy Making* (New York, 1964), but was published in French in *La Guerre Nucléaire*, a book Brodie edited, although much to his annoyance this fact was not noted on the title page. Brodie had stressed the importance of economics in his article "Strategy as a Science" which appeared in the first volume of *World Politics* in 1949, but by the mid-1960's, he was almost sorry he had taken this line. By 1966, he wrote, he tended "to downgrade the credit I have in the past given economists," the "great majority" of whom

In this kind of world the economists still had a role to play, a very basic role in fact. It was not their skill in handling quantitative data that proved to be crucial. As Hitch himself pointed out, their basic contribution "turned out to be the far more critical one of helping to formulate the problems themselves—as economic problems—and to design analyses to solve them." His main example had to do with what he called "widespread" but (to the economists) "incredible" misconceptions about the "nature of costs." People often assumed that costs should not matter: "military requirements" alone should determine the size of the effort. On the other hand, it was also frequently taken for granted that costs were "simply a constraint." But both approaches really missed the point: requirements were not absolute; they depended on costs; and in "choosing among alternatives," costs were therefore "as essential as objectives."[19]

To an economist, or to someone who has had some training in economics, all of this is quite obvious. But since it was far from obvious to many other people, the economists enjoyed a certain comparative advantage: they had a way of getting a handle on an important class of strategic problems—those that were more than just technical yet not quite political in nature—and this meant that they would play a central role in the whole area of military policy.

What made all this particularly important was a certain shift in perspective that took place in the 1950s. In the immediate postwar period, and even in the early 1950s, there was a very widespread sense that a nuclearized world was inherently unstable—that a policy of drift and an unconstrained nuclear arms race would almost inevitably lead to disaster. This led to a certain willingness, even among some of the RAND strategists during this period, to consider such extreme solutions as preventive war.[20] With the passage of time, these basic anxieties began to fade: it was gradually becoming evident that the world could live with nuclear weapons. There were terrible dangers of course, but there were advan-

---

"show an astonishing lack of political sense" (Brodie to K. Archibald, May 10, 1966, Brodie Papers, Box 1). See also *War and Politics*, pp. 474–75, and esp. p. 475n.

[19] Charles S. Hitch, "The Uses of Economics," RAND Paper P-2179-RC (November 17, 1960), pp. 3, 21; this was also published in *Research for Public Policy* (Washington, 1961). See also his "Economics and Military Operations Research," *Review of Economics and Statistics*, vol. 40, no. 3 (1958), esp. pp. 200, 202, 203–8. Hitch had been arguing along these lines since the early 1950s. See his "Economic Aspects of Military Planning," June 1, 1951, RAND S-5 [limited distribution], and his "Adequate Air Power at Minimum Cost," November 16, 1956, RAND S-44 [limited distribution]. See also Brodie, *Strategy in the Missile Age*, chapter 10, and two articles by the RAND strategist (and economist by training) Malcolm Hoag: "The Relevance of Costs," in E. S. Quade, ed., *Analysis for Military Decisions* (Chicago, 1967), and "Some Complexities in Military Planning," *World Politics*, vol. 11 (July 1959), pp. 553–76.

[20] See n. 40 below.

tages as well, and—especially when one considered the alternatives—the situation on balance was by no means intolerable. Very serious problems remained, but the sense began to take hold that the United States and the Soviet Union were settling into a long-term rivalry. As a result, U.S.-Soviet relations came to be perceived increasingly in interactive terms: if we did something, they would have time to respond, and the nature (and relative cost) of their response should therefore rationally be factored into our original calculations. Thus the gamelike aspects of military policy became increasingly salient, and this way of thinking was clearly linked both to the presence of formal game theory as part of the intellectual culture at RAND, and to the great interest people at RAND took in many forms of gaming.[21]

Finally, there was a special shift in the political environment during this decade that had a great effect on both strategic thought and military policy. At the beginning of the 1950s, the Korean War was on everyone's mind, and the Eisenhower administration's emphasis on nuclear weapons probably had a good deal to do with the lessons it drew from the Korean conflict.[22] But by the end of the decade, the Berlin Crisis was at the center of international politics, and the problem of the defense of Berlin was a matter of great concern. In this case, for all the obvious reasons—the local indefensibility of the city, and the great importance of Europe in compar-

---

[21] This, of course, is a far cry from the idea that the mathematical theory of games, for example, was a major force in shaping American strategic thought. This argument, sometimes made by critics of nuclear strategy, simply cannot be sustained by the evidence. Schelling, for example, who was clearly more interested in both game theory and "gaming" than any of the other leading strategists, had no trouble destroying this claim in a long review of Anatol Rapoport's *Strategy and Conscience* that he published in the *American Economic Review* in December 1964 (pp. 1082–88). On the other points made above, see especially Thomas Schelling, "Assumptions about Enemy Behavior," in Quade, *Analysis for Military Decisions*; the articles in this book were based on lectures originally given in 1955 and 1959. Note also William Capron, "A Note on the Rehabilitation of the Concept of 'Economic War Potential,'" unpublished RAND working paper, September 23, 1959, esp. pp. 4–6; Garry Brewer and Martin Shubik, *The War Game: A Critique of Military Problem Solving* (Cambridge, Mass., 1979), esp. chapter 6.

[22] The standard accounts of the New Look stress the administration's fiscal conservatism and the set of general and fairly abstract ideas about strategy with which they were linked; the specific historical context rarely gets much attention. One suspects, however, that the emergence of the New Look was to some extent related to the Korean War—to assumptions about the way the war should have been fought, to lessons drawn about the role that nuclear threats played in ending it, to the conclusion that the United States was not going to be, in Richard Nixon's memorable phrase, "nickeled and dimed to death" by Korea-style aggression in the future. Some of the newly declassified material suggests a certain connection: see, for example, Radford to Dulles, October 13, 1953, in Declassified Documents Collection, 1979/378B. Note also Brodie's comments in *Strategy in the Missile Age*, pp. 250–51, and Congressman Mahon's remarks in U.S. Congress, House Appropriations Committee, *Department of Defense Appropriations for 1964*, Part 1 (Washington, 1963), p. 222.

ison with most other regions of the world—normal, military, war-fighting considerations simply did not apply. The effect was thus to highlight the "war of nerves" aspect of international conflict.

Putting all these things together, what the argument boils down to is this: there was an intellectual vacuum in the whole national security area. The economists, and people heavily influenced by their style of thinking, were for a variety of reasons drawn into this vacuum. What they had was something very general, a way of approaching issues, rather than anything that in itself suggested substantive answers that went right to the heart of the strategic problem. But this meant that a constituency existed—in their own terms, a market existed—for ideas from economics that would have some substantive bearing on the very new problems of strategy that were to emerge in the 1950s.

THE MANIPULATION OF RISK

It was a question of intellectual ecology: a niche had taken shape, and then Thomas Schelling came along. The ideas in question were the notions about bargaining that had developed mainly out of the theory of imperfect competition. Schelling's "Essay on Bargaining," which appeared in the *American Economic Review* in June 1956, was in large measure based on the theory of oligopoly, as represented most notably by William Fellner's *Competition Among the Few*.[23] This way of thinking was to mesh perfectly with the notions about war limitation and the "threat value" of nuclear weapons that Brodie, as he put it, had been "toying with" since the early 1950s.

Once again, the thermonuclear revolution plays an important role in the story. A war with hydrogen weapons would be short, much shorter than the kinds of wars that were possible even in the early atomic age. Industrial mobilization could therefore not have anything like the importance it previously had. In World War II, Brodie pointed out, strategic bombing was militarily meaningful only because a ground war was going on at the same time: the bombing served to deprive the Germans of commodities "which the ground battles were using up." In a future world war, "there wasn't going to be a ground battle." What was the point, therefore, of attacking the enemy's industrial base?[24]

[23] Schelling's interest in bargaining also had a good deal to do with his experience with the Marshall Plan administration. "An Essay on Bargaining" was also republished as the second chapter in *The Strategy of Conflict* (Cambridge, Mass., 1960). See also Schelling's "Bargaining, Communication and Limited War," *Journal of Conflict Resolution*, vol. 2, no. 3 (September 1958), republished as the third chapter in *The Strategy of Conflict*.

[24] Brodie, "Changing Capabilities," pp. 12–13.

In other words, if there was no urgent military need to destroy industrial targets, the destruction of cities no longer made sense in traditional military terms. If mobilization essentially does not matter, what was the point of still trying to destroy the enemy's industrial base? For those few individuals who really grasped the fundamental point—it certainly was never reflected in the war plans—what this implied was that the real function of counter-city targeting was punitive and coercive, and not military in the traditional sense, and therefore had to be analyzed explicitly in those terms. For Schelling in particular, the threat of inflicting pain lay at the heart of nuclear strategy: the point was repellent, but it was important to face the fact that this was what the targeting of cities was all about. The whole issue of threat manipulation—of the efficient exploitation of nuclear risk—therefore came to be treated in a much more overt and straightforward way. Schelling quite explicitly set out to analyze how the "power to hurt" could be exploited for political purposes.

Brodie had assumed at the beginning of the 1950s that an enemy might be coerced by the threat of a *deliberate* escalation of the war. But a deliberate escalation was something that Schelling, who came on the scene toward the end of the decade, found hard to imagine. His problem, he wrote, was to explain how it could be, "when almost nothing that ever arises is really worth a general war," that "strategic forces [could] have any influence on decisions." The answer he came up with was "the threat that leaves something to chance": one needed some mechanism, "involving uncertainty and unpredictability, of a potential progressive loss of control over the situation by both sides—in order to make any connection between the strategic background and the local foreground."[25] It might be absurd for anyone "coolly and deliberately" to order an all-out attack "in response to some enemy transgression"; but one could plausibly threaten actions that might set off a semi-uncontrollable chain of events that just might culminate in a thermonuclear holocaust. The threat value of nuclear weapons could thus be exploited even in a situation where, because of the prospect of retaliation, a deliberate attack on an enemy might be totally irrational.

The assumption was that the degree of risk could be manipulated, and Schelling in fact at one point spoke of the "controlled loss of control."[26] But these methods could be used by both sides in a conflict. International politics, in time of crisis or especially after the outbreak of hostilities, would then be a "competition in risk taking, characterized not so much

[25] Schelling to Brodie, February 22, 1965, Brodie Papers, Box 2, file "Schelling." Note also Thomas Schelling, "Nuclear Strategy in Europe," *World Politics*, vol. 14 (April 1962), p. 422.

[26] Thomas C. Schelling, "The Role of Theory in the Study of Conflict," RAND Research Memorandum RM-2515-PR (January 13, 1960), p. 28.

by tests of force as by tests of nerve."[27] This, of course, was not a world of certainty, or predictability and of near-perfect rationality, where the level of violence could be easily controlled, although deterrence theory is often caricatured in this way.[28] It was rather the existence of uncertainty that created risk, and risk, for Schelling especially, was what made it possible for nuclear forces to play a political role.

This whole approach to strategy was in fact very new, and differed dramatically from more conventional ways of dealing with military problems. To those in the armed forces especially, it had been natural to assume that what happened on the battlefield was of prime importance, that military action should be "decisive," that control and initiative are desirable in themselves. But now it seemed that everything was being turned on its head. The manipulation of risk was much more important, Schelling insisted, than securing tactical advantage on the battlefield; military action was seen in terms of a bargaining process, and would therefore have to be limited, rather than "decisive," in nature; and, most perplexing of all, there was the argument that perhaps too much control might not be a good idea—there were advantages in making sure that one's choices were limited and that the enemy was the one who had to make the really difficult decisions.

For Schelling, the concept of risk was central. His whole argument was built on the insight that a general war need not result from a deliberate and cold-blooded decision. Events, that is, might have a momentum of their own, quite apart from the conscious intent of political leaders. This line of reasoning, therefore, led to an intense interest in the logic of escalation: why exactly was there, in certain circumstances, a serious risk that matters might get out of hand?

THE LOGIC OF PREEMPTION

It was at this point that the intellectual tradition represented by Brodie and Schelling merged with a rather distinct line of thought, also associated with RAND; the most prominent figure here was Albert Wohlstetter. In the early 1950s, Wohlstetter had been asked to work on the problem of base selection, and this led him and his associates into a detailed, quan-

---

[27] Thomas Schelling, *Arms and Influence* (New Haven, Conn., 1966), p. 94.

[28] This is a common criticism leveled against this group of strategists. But it is hard to imagine how Schelling, at least, could have been more explicit about these matters: see esp. *Arms and Influence*, pp. 92–93. Brodie and Wohlstetter in their writings also took it for granted that a war could easily get out of control. See, for example, Bernard Brodie, *Strategy in the Missile Age* (Princeton, 1959), p. 355, and Albert Wohlstetter, "Nuclear Sharing: NATO and the N + 1 Country," *Foreign Affairs*, vol. 39 (April 1961), pp. 378–79.

titative analysis of what might happen in an air war.[29] The Wohlstetter approach, by its very nature, assumed that numbers mattered: the atomic bomb was not an "absolute weapon"; if its effects were measurable, they were finite and thus limited; it therefore made an important difference how such a war was fought, and especially how well America's nuclear forces would be able to survive a surprise enemy attack.

Again, what exactly was new here? The general point about the importance of defending America's strategic forces had been made before. Brodie, in particular, had argued repeatedly in 1946 (in *The Absolute Weapon*) that it was crucial to make sure that the United States would be able to retaliate in kind—that it was necessary "to explore all conceivable situations where the aggressor's fear of retaliation will be at a minimum and to seek to eliminate them."[30] It was clear also that Brodie was thinking in terms of what would be left after a surprise attack: "our most urgent military problem is to reorganize ourselves to survive a vastly more destructive 'Pearl Harbor' than occurred in 1941."[31] He even speculated on how the ability to strike back could be guaranteed: the nuclear retaliatory force, he said, should be "spread over a large number of widely dispersed reservations, each of considerable area, in which the bombs and their carriers are secreted and as far as possible protected by storage underground."[32]

Thus, Brodie in 1946 clearly understood that nuclear weapons might be used against an enemy's strategic forces; indeed, another passage even touched on the idea of tactical use on the battlefield.[33] But Brodie was terribly inconsistent in this book; at other points he simply took it for granted that the bomb would only be used against cities, that it was "inevitably a weapon of indiscriminate destruction."[34] One has the sense that at this point he had really not yet come to grips with these issues.

Wohlstetter's approach was very different. The most important thing about it was its empirical depth and sensitivity to operational detail. Wohlstetter went to the SAC bases to get as much information as he could on force readiness, on warning time, on all those things that would bear on the ability of the strategic forces to survive a surprise attack and conduct a retaliatory strike. What was distinctive about his analysis was that

---

[29] On Wohlstetter's work, see, for example, Bruce Smith, "Strategic Expertise and National Security Policy: A Case Study," *Public Policy*, vol. 13 (1964), and E. S. Quade, "The Selection and Use of Strategic Air Bases: A Case History," in Quade, *Analysis for Military Decisions*.

[30] Bernard Brodie et al., *The Absolute Weapon* (New York, 1946), p. 77.

[31] Ibid., pp. 87–88.

[32] Ibid., p. 91.

[33] Ibid., p. 83.

[34] Ibid., pp. 46–47.

instead of assuming that enemy attacks would be massive (and that a degree of warning would thus probably be available), Wohlstetter paid a good deal of attention to attacks that were small in scale, unconventional in nature, and focused on a discrete range of targets—especially on air bases. The assumption, in other words, was that the enemy was intelligent, and would (if he attacked at all) try to exploit those areas where America's defenses were weak. It was extraordinary for a civilian to proceed in this way. It gave Wohlstetter's work a cogency and a power that those who argued along more casual lines were just not able to achieve.

Brodie, for example, was by this time thinking along parallel lines. He argued strongly for "reducing the almost comic opera vulnerability of our military structure." It was absurd, he said, for SAC aircraft to be concentrated on only about sixteen airfields in the continental United States. He could not understand why America's nuclear weapons "should be stored in only three or four sites, the locations of these being very well known to the enemy and each individually being very slightly guarded." He had recently heard, in fact, with regard to one of these sites, that an airline "which flew over that area used to point out the storage site to the passengers as one of the sights along the way."[35]

The problem was that casual argument of this sort simply did not cut very deep. Wohlstetter was able to show in much greater detail just how vulnerable America's strategic forces were. But for present purposes, the more important point is that thinking these issues through at that level of detail led to certain general conclusions about strategy—conclusions that were to be enormously influential.

Then as now there were those who argued that it hardly mattered if the enemy was able to destroy the great bulk of the American retaliatory force in a surprise attack. What difference would it make if even 85 percent of SAC was wiped out? The remaining 15 percent, for the period Wohlstetter considered, "could still have destroyed roughly 600 targets," and this was more than enough for deterrence.[36]

But one of the basic conclusions Wohlstetter reached was that this kind

[35] Brodie, "Changing Capabilities," p. 27.

[36] The quotations are from Kaplan, *Wizards of Armageddon*, pp. 108–9, but arguments of this sort were very common in the 1950s as well. According to Kaplan, the 85 percent figure represented Wohlstetter's "worst case," but it should be noted that this was not exactly what Wohlstetter had said in the text. This figure referred to the result of a "single, high-altitude mass Russian strike against U.S. targets," and Wohlstetter had been careful to note that a mass raid would not necessarily be the worst case. A "sneak attack," involving relatively few aircraft, "might result in substantially higher damage to our strategic force." Albert Wohlstetter et al., "Selection and Use of Strategic Air Bases," RAND Report R-266 (April 1954), pp. xxiii, 233. Note also Wohlstetter's later comment that this report, and related studies, "deliberately understated the vulnerability" of America's strategic forces. Wohlstetter to Michael Howard, November 6, 1968, pp. 37–38 (provided to author).

of approach was fundamentally flawed. Indeed, as soon as one began to think in operational terms, one could see what the problems were. It was one thing to say that 15 percent of the bombers would survive an enemy's first strike, and quite another to say that they would all be able to destroy their targets. There was the problem of getting through fully alerted defenses, and the related problem of coordinating the retaliatory strike when command and control facilities were in a state of complete disarray. How would a commander know which targets to hit, when and how to attack, or even whether to strike at all? It was obviously impossible to know in advance which aircraft would survive, so contingency planning would always be inadequate. The simple "minimum deterrence" approach ignored problems of this sort, but when one began to think about them at the operational level, the overall issue took on a very different cast.

To Wohlstetter, the fundamental point to emerge from the empirical analysis was that the mere possession of significant numbers of thermonuclear weapons by both sides did not in itself create a stable balance of terror. The weaponry did not necessarily create a "stalemate" which would make general nuclear war "impossible." Mutual deterrence was not automatic; the nuclear balance was therefore "delicate," and it would take a serious and continuing effort to sustain it. These fundamental conclusions grew out of the operationally oriented work Wohlstetter did in the 1950s, and came to be shared very widely at RAND. At the end of the decade, Wohlstetter laid out these basic ideas in "The Delicate Balance of Terror," probably the single most important article in the history of American strategic thought.[37]

What made the argument about vulnerability so powerful was the related assumption that vulnerability might in itself be a primary *cause*—perhaps *the* primary cause—of war. This assumption was rooted in several distinct lines of argument. There was first the idea that their Bolshevik ideology would compel the Soviets to strike if American forces were vulnerable. "If the Soviet leaders," Brodie asked, "should ever decide that by a surprise attack they could confidently count on destroying our strategic retaliatory force, whose very purpose it is constantly to threaten their existence, would it not be their duty as good Bolsheviks to launch that attack?"[38] Brodie made this point frequently in the 1950s; this argument was based explicitly on the work of his friend Nathan Leites, one of the leading Kremlinologists at RAND.[39] This was, incidentally, one of

---

[37] "The Delicate Balance" appeared in *Foreign Affairs* in January 1959; an earlier and more complete version, dated December 1958, is available as RAND Paper P-1472.

[38] Brodie, *Strategy in the Missile Age*, p. 355.

[39] Ibid., p. 355n. See also his "More About Limited War," *World Politics*, vol. 10, p. 121;

the very few cases where the work of the Soviet specialists had a direct impact on mainstream strategic thought.

The point about the danger of a Soviet strike was undoubtedly related to the fact that in the late 1940s and early 1950s preventive war thinking was surprisingly common on the American side. Brodie, for example, frequently came into contact with it at RAND and during his visits to the Air War College, where it was, as he put it, for several years the "prevailing philosophy."[40] Nor was the idea limited to RAND and military circles. The famous physicist Leo Szilard evidently had made a preventive war argument at the very beginning of the atomic age: it was "from the lips of Leo Szilard," Brodie wrote, that he had "heard, in October of 1945, the first outright advocacy in my experience of preventive war."[41] The fact that this kind of thinking was not limited to the lunatic fringe had important implications, and chief among them was the idea that if serious Americans supported the strategy, then the Soviets, if they were in a position to pull it off, might also find a preventive war policy very attractive.[42]

In the development of American strategic thought, however, there was a far more important argument that had nothing to do with ideology or preventive war, but focused instead on the "logic of preemption." Here once again Wohlstetter played a central role. The vulnerability of strate-

---

and Brodie, Hitch, and Marshall, "The Next Ten Years," unpublished RAND working paper, December 30, 1954, p. 17.

[40] Bernard Brodie, "A Commentary on the Preventive-War Doctrine," unpublished RAND paper, June 11, 1953, p. 1. The mathematician John Williams, then one of the leading figures at RAND, was in the early 1950s the principal champion there of a preventive war strategy. He and Brodie had a very interesting memorandum debate on the issue in 1953 and 1954, in which Victor Hunt, another major participant in these discussions of basic strategy, later joined. See John Williams, "In Response to Paxson's Memo on the Probability of War," February 3, 1953, and his "Regarding the Preventive War Doctrine," July 27, 1953, unpublished RAND working papers. The memoranda Brodie, Williams, and Hunt exchanged on the question are in the folder "Strategic Objectives Committee," in James Digby's personal files at RAND; I am grateful to Mr. Digby for allowing me to consult them. On the Air War College, see Brodie's "Commentary on the Preventive-War Doctrine," unpublished working RAND paper, June 11, 1953, p. 1, and his "Changing Capabilities" speech, p. 23ff. All of this, incidentally, explains the amount of attention Brodie gave to the preventive war questions in *Strategy in the Missile Age*: he spent fourteen pages (pp. 227–41) discussing the issue, not to mention another eight pages devoted to preemptive attack, which he defined as a "variant of the preventive war idea."

[41] Brodie's recollection is in Brodie to Schelling, January 8, 1965, enclosure, Brodie Papers, Box 2. See also the last paragraph of Szilard to Bush, January 14, 1944, in Gertrude Weiss Szilard and Spencer Weart, eds., *Leo Szilard: His Version of the Facts* (Cambridge, Mass., 1978), p. 163, and also Szilard's article, "Calling for a Crusade," *Bulletin of the Atomic Scientists*, April 1947, p. 103.

[42] As Brodie put the point, one reason for considering the preventive war issue was that the discussion might "help sensitize us to the factors that could cause it to become Soviet policy." *Strategy in the Missile Age*, pp. 228–29.

gic forces had been a great source of concern to him even before the thermonuclear revolution. But with the coming of the hydrogen bomb, it was clear that counterforce would play an increasingly important role. On the one hand, since there was no really effective defense against an unrestrained thermonuclear attack once it was launched, the only way to survive an all-out war was to destroy the enemy's forces before they left the ground. On the other hand, because these new weapons were so powerful, and because industry was concentrated in a relatively limited number of cities, only a fairly small number of hydrogen weapons had to be allocated to urban-industrial targets; the rest of the expanding stockpile would be targeted on the enemy's military forces. It was simply a question of numbers: in the natural course of things, military targets, and especially counterforce targets, would, as Wohlstetter and Fred Hoffman predicted in early 1954, come to dominate the plan for general war.[43] And if this was true for the United States, it would, within a relatively short period of time, be true for the Soviet Union as well.

The effect of this line of argument was thus simply to underscore the fundamental importance of protecting strategic forces, and throughout the 1950s, Wohlstetter conducted what amounted to a campaign on the vulnerability issue. In the process, he developed many arguments, but one in particular was quite distinctive. This was the point that our vulnerability was not only dangerous to us, but was dangerous to our adversaries as well, since it might lead us to preempt—that is, to strike first in a crisis. If our strategic forces became vulnerable to an ICBM attack, he and Hoffman argued in early 1954,

> then our advertised capability for retaliation will be fictitious. We could not
> expect to hurt the Russians very much, unless we could be sure to strike the
> first blows. This should make us rather trigger happy, particularly if we were
> to couple this fragile strategic capability with an announced policy of relying
> mainly on a threat of major strategic atomic attack to deter even minor war.
> It would appear also to make the Russians equally trigger happy. Because in
> this case striking the first blow is the only means of defense, any delay in
> striking the first blow by either side risks the chance that the enemy will be
> the one to have this prerogative. With a defense of SAC against the I[C]BM and
> any other likely menace, on the other hand, we can assure ourselves and
> Russia that whether we strike first or second we can lay waste a large proportion of the Russian economy and the Russian population. This will make
> a decision to strike the first blow extremely unpleasant for the decision-
> maker as well as for the recipient of the blow.[44]

[43] Albert Wohlstetter and Fred Hoffman, "Defending a Strategic Force after 1960," unpublished RAND working paper, February 1, 1954, p. 18.
[44] Ibid., p. 3.

It followed (although Wohlstetter did not make this argument at the time) that by the same token *their* vulnerability would be dangerous for *us*. But he did, in "The Delicate Balance of Terror," consider the extreme but symmetrical case where

> both the United States and the Soviet Union had the power to destroy each other's retaliatory forces and society, given the opportunity to administer the opening blow. The situation would then be something like the old-fashioned Western gun duel. It would be extraordinarily risky for one side *not* to attempt to destroy the other, or to delay doing so, since it not only can emerge unscathed by striking first but this is the sole way it can reasonably hope to emerge at all. Evidently such a situation is extremely unstable. On the other hand, if it is clear that the aggressor too will suffer catastrophic damage in the event of his aggression, he then has strong reason not to attack, even though he can administer great damage. A protected retaliatory capability has a stabilizing influence not only in deterring rational attack, but also in offering every inducement to both powers to reduce the chance of accidental war.[45]

A draft of the "Delicate Balance" was circulated among the American experts preparing for the 1958 Geneva Surprise Attack Conference, and that was how Schelling first heard of the idea.[46] He in fact became fascinated by the logic of preemption—that is, with the problem of "accidental war" resulting from the "reciprocal fear of surprise attack." This was how war could come without a "cool and deliberate" decision to launch an attack "in response to some enemy transgression." This was what generated the nuclear risk, whose "manipulation" was for Schelling what strategy was all about.[47]

"The premium on haste," Schelling wrote, was "the greatest source of danger" that peace would "explode into all-out war." "The whole idea of accidental or inadvertent war" rested on the "crucial premise" that there was a great advantage to striking quickly: "It is hard to imagine how anybody would be precipitated into full-scale war by accident, false alarm, mischief, or momentary panic, if it were not for such urgency to get in quick."[48] The process of escalation might be very complex; but what does seem clear is that for Schelling the fear of losing the enormous

---

[45] Albert Wohlstetter, "The Delicate Balance of Terror," *Foreign Affairs*, vol. 37, no. 2 (January 1959), p. 230. Note also Schelling's use of the Old West metaphor in "Surprise Attack and Disarmament," *Bulletin of the Atomic Scientists*, December 1959, p. 414, and Brodie's use of it even earlier in "Unlimited Weapons and Limited War," *The Reporter*, November 18, 1954, p. 18.

[46] Interview with Thomas Schelling, Cambridge, Mass., October 3, 1983.

[47] Schelling, *Arms and Influence*, chapter 3, especially p. 97.

[48] Ibid., p. 227.

advantages of getting in the first blow would lie at the heart of the esca-
latory process, especially if one knew one's adversary were subject to the
same pressures, and that he knew that you were tempted to preempt for
these reasons. This logic could be sufficient in itself: there was no need
for a ' "fundamental' basis"—that is, a real political cause—for the war.[49]
A situation of this sort was thus more unstable, in the sense that things
could more easily get out of hand, than a situation where retaliatory
forces were secure and where there was thus no incentive to preempt. The
"delicacy" of the balance was therefore the source of instability; a war
might come essentially because strategic forces were vulnerable to enemy
attack.

The result was that a theory of war causation took hold in which military factors loomed very large. The assumption was, as William Kaufmann, another member of the RAND group, put it in 1958, that deterrence
"has become essentially unstable," that "increasingly military conditions
are becoming such that catastrophe can descend on us as a bolt from the
blue."[50] It was clear, therefore, that American forces had to be made more
secure.

But beyond that—and here is where the argument really began to break
new ground—it seemed to follow that Soviet forces should perhaps not
even be targeted, and maybe American cities should not be defended, even
if a defense of populations some day became feasible. For if the vulnerability of our forces made us more trigger happy and was thus a danger to
them, then by the same logic their vulnerability was a danger to us: we
should therefore not threaten their strategic forces, either directly, by targeting them, or indirectly, by defending our cities and thus effectively neu-

[49] Schelling, "The Reciprocal Fear of Surprise Attack," *The Strategy of Conflict*, p. 207.

[50] William Kaufmann, "The Evolution of Deterrence," unpublished RAND working paper,
October 2, 1958, pp. 26, 28. Eisenhower and Dulles, however, did not at all share this set
of anxieties: they simply did not believe that a "bolt from the blue" was a real possibility.
Dulles, for example, gave Eisenhower his reaction to a briefing from the Gaither committee
in 1957. "The possibility considered," he wrote, "was that in a time of relative tranquillity
and a reduction of international tension there would be mounted a massive surprise attack
against the United States and simultaneously against all our important bases." He told the
President that he thought "such an attack without provocation involving casualties of perhaps one hundred million would be so abhorrent to all who survived in any part of the
world that I did not think that even the Soviet rulers would dare to accept the consequences." John Foster Dulles, "Memorandum of Conversation with the President," November 7, 1957, John Foster Dulles Papers, 1952–59, White House Memoranda Series, Box 5,
Eisenhower Library, Abilene; also in the Seeley G. Mudd Library, Princeton University, and
the Declassified Documents Collection, 1985/1630. The briefing in question is recorded in
A. J. Goodpaster, "Memorandum of Conference with the President," November 7, 1957,
Dwight D. Eisenhower Papers as President of the United States, 1953–61 (Ann Whitman
File), DDE Diaries, Box 17, folder "November 1957 Staff Notes," Eisenhower Library, Ab-
ilene; also in the Declassified Documents Collection, 1979/331A.

tralizing them. Such was the essence of the doctrine of "strategic stability," or "mutual assured destruction," as it has bizarrely come to be called, that emerged with great force and suddenness at the end of the 1950s. Wohlstetter himself never really accepted it, but others embraced the doctrine enthusiastically, and in particular it came to provide the conceptual basis for American thinking on arms control: by mutual agreement, one might be able to achieve a world where each side's strategic forces were secure. Schelling, using this idea as a point of departure, coauthored a seminal work on arms control in 1961; the two other important books on the subject that appeared that year were also, to one extent or another, inspired by the same idea.[51]

The stability doctrine thus developed in a fairly natural way out of the body of thought that had been concerned primarily with strategic vulnerability. It did *not* emerge as the by-product of shifting political views: a "stable" strategic relationship was not sought originally as the military counterpart to political détente. In fact, one of the most striking features of this body of thought is the apolitical and often abstract nature of its approach to strategy. Military problems were only remotely connected to the world of international politics: if a crisis came up, or a war broke out, decisions about military policy would of course be relevant. But it was as though they had little bearing on the normal dynamics of international political life. They certainly were not analyzed in those terms. It might be admitted in theory that war is the outcome of a political conflict that unfolds over a long period of time; but it was not taken for granted that the primary purpose of military policy was to influence the course of that conflict. To gain this kind of leverage, military policy would have to be made to depend, at least in some important way, on the political behavior of one's adversary. But in this body of thought, basic problems were defined in general and hypothetical terms, and the relevant data were technical and essentially military in nature; political considerations, beyond those captured by the basic notion of "deterrence," were thus simply factored out of the analysis.

NUCLEAR WAR-FIGHTING

There was of course more to strategy than assuring the survival of strategic forces. Once the forces were able to ride out an attack, one would still have to face the question of how they should be used. If forces were

---

[51] Thomas Schelling and Morton Halperin, *Strategy and Arms Control* (New York, 1961); Hedley Bull, *The Control of the Arms Race* (London, 1961); and Donald Brennan, ed., *Arms Control, Disarmament and National Security* (New York, 1961).

survivable, there would be less pressure to launch an all-out attack at once; they could, in theory at least, be used in a more controlled way.[52] Moreover, if a general war was going to be preeminently a counterforce war, it made sense, especially for people working for an organization like RAND, to be concerned with how this strategy could be rationalized—that is, with what the most rational way to fight a counterforce war was. In any case, the nuclear threat lay at the heart of American foreign policy; if Europe was to be defended, it was important that nuclear forces do more than simply cancel each other out. Given assumptions about a more or less permanent Soviet conventional superiority, it was vital that they cast a broader political shadow, and this was possible only because there was a risk that in some situations they might be used. Indeed, the kind of political effect might depend on the sort of employment strategy that was adopted, and in particular on how rational and therefore how credible it was. Operational strategy might also have an important impact on how a war actually ran its course—on what would happen "if deterrence failed."

The basic idea to emerge out of this kind of thinking was the notion that if nuclear weapons had to be used, they should be used in a controlled way; the attack should never be indiscriminate or spasmodic. It was not that the people at RAND in the 1950s or early 1960s were under any illusions about how easy it would be to effect this sort of control.[53] It was simply that the alternative of just throwing up one's hands and settling for a single, massive, all-out attack as the country's only general

[52] See, for example, Albert Wohlstetter, "Analysis and Design of Conflict Systems," in Quade, *Analysis*, p. 127, and Thomas Schelling, "Les armements nucléaires, l'OTAN et la 'nouvelle stratégie,' " *Politique Etrangère*, summer 1963, p. 136.

[53] Note, for example, William Kaufmann's discussion of the problem of escalation, on p. 18 in Charles Hitch et al., "The Crisis in National Security," unpublished RAND working paper, April 18, 1958—this collection of talks comes as close to summing up the mainstream RAND position on security issues as any single document I was able to see. Kaufmann was concerned with the question of whether theater nuclear warfare was more likely than conventional warfare to "develop into a thermonuclear exchange between the United States and the Soviet Union." This was a "terribly difficult" question, but, he said, "there are several features unique to nuclear engagements, as we now understand them, which suggest that they might prove very hard to control. Their tempo is likely to be much more rapid than in the case of wars fought with traditional means. Decisions will seem novel, complex, and portentous. And they will have to be made hastily, under the pressure of events, with very little foreknowledge of their consequences. Control over the operational use of atomic weapons will almost certainly have to be decentralized to the theater; and the local commanders will probably have to be allowed some discretion in the selection of targets in order to cope with rapidly changing situations. In addition, there will be very great pressure and a very real need to try and fight the air battle by knocking out the enemy's bases. Considering the distances from which modern airpower armed with nuclear weapons can be effective, this battle could quickly reach the brink of a Soviet-American thermonuclear exchange."

war-fighting option was patently unacceptable. By the end of the 1950s, this sort of thinking had begun to revolve around the idea of city-avoiding counterforce warfare.

Ideas of this sort were of course closely related to Brodie's earlier notions about "threat value" and preserving cities as hostages, and later with Schelling's ideas about the "manipulation of risk." This line of thought had a noticeable effect even though neither Brodie nor Schelling was ever particularly keen about the idea of counterforce.[54] For most of the 1950s, however, they were simply ideas—part of the intellectual culture at RAND, arguments that deserved to be taken into account, but which by no means automatically added up to an argument for a "no-cities" counterforce strategy. Things were still in a state of flux; ideas had not hardened into strategic dogmas. The risk manipulation approach could coexist and freely interact with the more straightforward counter-force/nuclear war–fighting strategy. The difference between the two was more one of emphasis than anything else: how important in a war were such things as resolve and signaling as opposed to the shifting balance of military forces? Later, the lines would become more clearly drawn. The different approaches would come to be seen as alternative strategies; but, in 1960, all of this was still very much in the future.

One of the most striking things about this period, in fact, is a real intellectual openness, an absence of doctrinal rigidity. It is important to note, for example, that there had been no headlong rush to counterforce at RAND in the 1950s. Reading the RAND documents from the first half of

[54] See Brodie to S. Jones, February 25, 1955, Brodie Papers, Box 1, and Schelling to Brodie, Feb. 22, 1965, Brodie Papers, Box 2. It was not obvious from Schelling's writings—for example, from the fifth chapter of *Arms and Influence*—that he was opposed to a "really vigorous" counterforce strategy. Indeed, the first few pages of that chapter might have suggested to the casual reader that he was a supporter of the "no-cities" version of counterforce. This was, however, no accident: his hostility to counterforce, he explained to Brodie in the letter just cited, was "a strong prejudice which I tried to damp somewhat [in a draft of that chapter] in order not to alienate people who are of a quite different opinion and in particular who may know more than I do about present day target intelligence, weapons accuracy and so forth." The odd thing here is that his skepticism about counterforce did not prevent him from assuming, as he did in this letter, that "American strategic superiority" could be meaningful in a crisis.

The evidence on the kind of cross-fertilization referred to in the text is abundant. Wohlstetter, for example, cited Brodie's "Must We Shoot from the Hip?" in one of his earliest RAND papers; and in January 1955 he told RAND's Strategic Objectives Committee that one of the things he was studying in his work was the feasibility of the "Brodie Rule" (which evidently referred to a strategy of either withholding attacks on cities, or of not striking Soviet territory at all). Wohlstetter and Rowen, "Economic and Strategic Considerations in Air Base Location: A Preliminary Review," unpublished RAND working paper, December 19, 1951, p. 17; minutes of Strategic Objectives Committee, January 21, 1955, in James Digby's files.

the decade, what comes across is a certain skepticism about counterforce. The Wohlstetter basing study, for example, was primarily concerned with the ability of SAC to carry out an attack on urban-industrial targets; the "counterair" or "blunting" mission was discussed only briefly and pessimistically at the end of the report. (The skepticism was in large part rooted in the assumption that American target intelligence was not only inadequate for counterforce purposes, but was probably even getting worse.) One might have thought that a concern with American vulnerability would have been linked to an interest in exploiting Soviet vulnerability, but Wohlstetter deliberately chose not to develop the argument in that direction. The protection of the retaliatory force was so basic that all other considerations paled in comparison: Wohlstetter did not want to distract attention from the great need to assure an American "second strike capability."[55]

The same general point is true of another important RAND document from this period, "The Next Ten Years," written at the end of 1954 by Brodie, Hitch, and Andrew Marshall. Far from being an argument for counterforce,[56] or for controlled nuclear war–fighting, this document was essentially a *tour d'horizon*—a survey of a wide range of possible American strategies.[57] A "counter-force" strategy was discussed, and it included a "no-cities" component. It was recognized that the strategy had certain attractive features, but the authors seemed more interested in talking about all the problems with this policy. As in Wohlstetter's case, one of the greatest problems had to do with the (supposed) inadequacy of target intelligence.[58]

It is not surprising, therefore, that when new information about strategic intelligence began to filter into RAND beginning in 1955, attitudes toward counterforce—and in particular toward city-avoiding counterforce—began to shift. The key person here was Joseph Loftus, who during the Korean War had been the chief civilian target analyst for the Air Force. He eventually took a position with RAND, working for a while out of RAND's Washington office. It was there that he read "The Next Ten Years," and was struck by the very pessimistic attitude about target intelligence which prevailed at RAND in the early 1950s and was reflected in that document. These people, he thought, simply did not know what they were talking about. The Air Force had much better information about Soviet strategic targets—that is, counterforce targets—than the people at RAND seemed to realize.

[55] See esp. A. J. Wohlstetter et al., "Selection and Use of Strategic Air Bases," pp. 365–69, and Wohlstetter to the author, October 23, 1984, commenting on this passage.

[56] As implied by Kaplan, *Wizards of Armageddon*, p. 207.

[57] "The Next Ten Years" has recently been declassified.

[58] Brodie, Hitch, and Marshall, "The Next Ten Years," pp. 13–14, 24–26, 30.

Loftus reacted by writing a short paper called "Ten Minutes on the Next Ten Years," which implied that maybe the counterforce mission was not quite as hopeless as Brodie, Hitch, and Marshall had assumed. Perhaps for internal bureaucratic or political reasons the Soviets had structured their forces in such a way as to make their strategic forces more vulnerable than they otherwise might be. After all, he said (pointing to the McMahon Act), even the Americans had been reluctant to put nuclear weapons directly in the hands of the military. The same sort of thing might be going on with the Soviets, perhaps with even greater effect. Their tendency to overcentralize control might have some bearing on the vulnerability of their strategic forces.[59]

Marshall had worked on target intelligence in the past, and now he, together with Loftus, began to study these issues in much greater depth. Their collaboration was to last for nearly a decade. Perhaps the most striking thing to emerge from their work was the extraordinary vulnerability of the Soviet Air Force. The "irrationality" of Soviet basing, Marshall told a small group in 1960, was "fantastic." "It takes six to eight hours to load the planes," he said. "In those circumstances, they are just sitting ducks."[60] This may not have been the only channel through which information about intelligence was affecting attitudes toward counterforce, but what does seem clear is that information of this sort played a pivotal role: counterforce was not nearly as hopeless as had earlier been assumed. And indeed with good intelligence, targets could be pinpointed and yields could be reduced dramatically; a strategy that aimed at minimizing collateral damage might therefore be feasible.

To digress briefly, it is interesting to note that this information on Soviet vulnerability had a significant effect in an entirely different area. It was intimately related to the rise of the bureaucratic politics paradigm, which eventually was to have an important influence on the structure of the nuclear debate. Already in 1955—in fact, even earlier—Loftus had come to interpret the inefficiencies of the Soviet system in internal bureaucratic terms, and by 1963, he and Marshall had developed the argument in some detail. The Soviets, it appeared from their work, had been very reluctant to marry nuclear warheads to their delivery vehicles. Warheads were generally kept isolated from missiles—for MRBMs, the storage sites were fifty miles away on the average. Of the five main Soviet bomber bases, only three were defended by SA-1 batteries, and even they were not deployed for quick reaction. The Soviets, moreover, did not go in for the

[59] Joseph Loftus, "Ten Minutes on the Next Ten Years," unpublished RAND working paper, February 14, 1955.

[60] Quoted in Daniel Ellsberg and Paul Kecskemeti, "Minutes of the Monterey Seminar on Active and Passive Defense," July 19–21, 1960, unpublished RAND working paper, vol. 2, p. 20.

kind of alert measures that were common practice in the American Air Force, and the situation evidently did not change much even during times of crisis. With regard to their ICBM force, the kinds of missiles they built and the sorts of systems that supported them suggested that this force had not been designed for quick reaction.

How was the astonishing vulnerability of the Soviet nuclear force to be explained? The Soviet intercontinental force had evidently been starved for resources; the odd thing here was that the Soviets had spent more, by American estimates, on antiaircraft artillery alone since 1945 than on their strategic forces—heavy bombers, missile submarines, and ICBMs. The explanation for this bizarre behavior, Loftus and Marshall argued, had to do with established patterns of resource allocation rooted in the balance of bureaucratic power within the Soviet military establishment.

The "bureaucratic politics" argument became an important theme in Marshall's writings, and in the work done by other people at RAND.[61] Of course, the argument that bureaucratic interest went a long way toward explaining government behavior had been made many times before, and the general point had no doubt occurred to a great many people who at one time or another had served in some official capacity. But the case of Soviet military policy was so striking that it suggested in itself that the bureaucratic politics approach could really be developed into a central explanatory model. And it does seem that Marshall played a direct role in the emergence of the paradigm: in the mid-1960s, he was a major influence in the "May Group," a seminar led by the Harvard historian Ernest May; Morton Halperin and Graham Allison, who were to play leading roles in the articulation of the bureaucratic politics paradigm, also took part.[62]

All this is worth talking about only because of the effect it had. The rise of the bureaucratic politics model had an important influence on the way the debate on military policy was structured. There was on one side the rather straightforward theory that the strategic arms competition was dominated by an "action-reaction mechanism," where each power was reacting rationally to moves made by its opponent. The bureaucratic politics approach took issue with that interpretation: the interaction process

[61] See especially A. W. Marshall, "Bureaucratic Behavior and the Strategic Arms Competition," Southern California Arms Control and Foreign Policy Seminar, October 1971; and James Schlesinger, "Arms Interactions and Arms Control," RAND Paper P-3881, September 1968. Schlesinger had been tempted to entitle this paper "Budgets, Bureaucracies and Blindness: The Three Hidden Weapons of Arms Control." Marshall's and Schlesinger's interest led to a major and still only partially declassified study, the Department of Defense-sponsored history of the strategic arms competition. Note also Fred Iklé, *Every War Must End* (New York, 1971).

[62] Note also the references to Marshall in Graham Allison, *Essence of Decision* (Boston, 1971), pp. ix, x, 98, 301 n. 44, 315 n. 59; see also Morton Halperin, *Bureaucratic Politics and Foreign Policy* (Washington, 1974), p. xxi.

was not nearly as smooth or as governed by rational strategic calculation as simple models of the arms race would have it. It was in this way that the parameters of the debate became established: an externalist interpretation, the "action-reaction mechanism," battled an internalist explanation, the bureaucratic politics model.[63] In a debate of this sort, an interpretation of the military competition in terms of the ebb and flow of international political conflict simply had no place.

STABILITY VERSUS COUNTERFORCE

By the end of the 1950s the civilian strategists, working mainly at RAND, had developed two distinct sets of ideas, two radically different ways of looking at nuclear issues. On the one hand, there was the stability doctrine. At the heart of this doctrine was the idea that the vulnerability of strategic forces was destabilizing because of the premium it would place on preemption. The doctrine, however, was by no means limited to this basic idea: a whole conceptual superstructure had been built on this fundamental concept.

From the point of view of the stability doctrine, the risk of nuclear war was the central danger. This risk derived essentially from the vulnerability of strategic forces—not just American, but Soviet forces as well. The basic goal therefore was to reduce this vulnerability, and this implied, among other things, that counterforce targeting was to be avoided, above all if it was massive enough to make a meaningful difference in the amount of damage that would be suffered in the event of an all-out war. "Strategic superiority," which implied a strong counterforce capability, was therefore not to be sought—especially since negotiated arms control might be an important way of assuring stability, and negotiated agreements could be reached only on the basis of a kind of rough parity. But all this implied that it would be difficult to rely on the threat of nuclear war, overt or implicit, as the ultimate basis of policy.

On the other hand, there was the new concept of "controlled and discriminate general war." The aim in such a war would be to destroy military targets and spare civilian populations, preserving them in fact for their hostage value. This would be a war of coercion and bargaining, not of pure destructiveness or mindless violence. The outcome of the war would be governed in part by the shifting strategic balance resulting from the counterforce campaign, and in part by the sheer terror that such a war

---

[63] See, for example, Graham Allison, "Questions about the Arms Race: Who's Racing Whom? A Bureaucratic Perspective," in Robert Pfaltzgraff, Jr., ed., *Contrasting Approaches to Strategic Arms Control* (Lexington, Mass., 1974). Marshall, it should be noted, later placed increased emphasis on other factors, especially the distinct Soviet way of looking at the world.

would inevitably generate. With a strategy of this sort, a nuclear war would not necessarily be tantamount to national suicide; nuclear forces would therefore carry more political weight—perhaps a good deal more—than they otherwise might.

One obviously could not have it both ways: the two lines of argument were fundamentally inconsistent. But from the very beginning, people were drawn in both directions. On the one hand, there was a sense that a general nuclear war might well be virtually tantamount to mutual suicide, that the risk of things getting out of control was so great and the destructive power of the weapon so enormous that it did not much matter exactly how such a war would be fought. The important thing, from his point of view, was to prevent a nuclear conflict, and thus to keep the lid on any wars that were fought. And this implied that it was dangerous to try to use nuclear threats to support general political goals.

On the other hand, however, if the possibility of armed conflict between nuclear powers could not be ruled out completely, and if there was an ultimately irreducible risk that a major conventional war could get out of hand and lead to a nuclear exchange, it was important to think through just how a nuclear war might war might be waged. Escalation, after all, need not be totally automatic, and how such a war might be fought could make a big difference. The strategic balance might then be politically meaningful; nuclear forces could serve purposes beyond merely deterring their use by others.

The tension was fundamental: one is struck by how pervasive and how persistent it was, and by how ambivalent people's feelings were on these issues. Take for example the first serious examination of the implications of the atomic bomb, Brodie's two chapters in *The Absolute Weapon*. The first chapter reflected the assumption that there was no meaningful defense against the bomb, that the weapon would be used mainly against cities, that because the bomb was relatively cheap to produce and deliver, any world power possessing a nuclear arsenal could destroy the cities of its enemy. Under such circumstances, numbers of bombs, or even gross disparities in delivery systems, would not matter greatly; in fact, it did not particularly matter how such a war would be fought, and so strategy as such no longer existed.[64] But in his second chapter, he took a completely opposite line: numbers here do matter, defense can make a difference, superiority is still a meaningful concept—and the bulk of the chapter is devoted to a discussion of how an atomic war should be fought.

By 1959, when *Strategy in the Missile Age* was published, Brodie had been thinking about these issues full-time for many years. But again he failed to take a clear line. If all we sought was to maximize the prewar

[64] Note also his remarks in "The Security Problem in the Light of Atomic Energy," in Quincy Wright, ed., *A Foreign Policy for the United States* (Chicago, 1947), pp. 89, 101.

deterrent effect, he wrote, we should "assign the hard-core elements in our retaliatory force to the enemy's major cities, provide for the maximum automaticity as well as certainty of response, and lose no opportunity to let the enemy know that we have done these things." The problem was that "what looks like the most rational *deterrence* policy involves commitment to a strategy which, if we ever had to execute it, might then look very foolish." "For the sake of deterrence before hostilities," he argued, "the enemy must expect us to be vindictive and irrational if he attacks us"—even if his attack took care to spare our populations and successfully destroyed much of our retaliatory force; but "a reasonable opposing view" was "that no matter how difficult it may be to retain control of events in nuclear total war, one should never deliberately abandon control,"[65]

Brodie understood that the basic issue in nuclear strategy was target selection, and the central problem here was whether the attack should focus on destroying the enemy's retaliatory force, sparing, to the maximum extent possible, the enemy's population, in order to preserve its hostage value—or whether the enemy's strategic forces should not be targeted at all, since the ability to destroy them might lead the enemy to preempt and thus be "destabilizing." Brodie simply laid out both sets of arguments and made no serious attempt to resolve the issue: he had "given relatively little space," he said in his conclusion, "to the matter of how to fight a general war if it should come," because "the strategy of a total war is like an earthquake in that all the forces which determine its occurrence and its character have been building up over time, as have almost all the factors which determine how it runs its course."[66] The implication here was that rational analysis could make no real difference. And similarly on the basic issue of limited war strategy—the question of tactical nuclear weapons—Brodie again simply laid out the pros and cons and drew back in this book from taking a position on the issue himself.[67]

[65] *Strategy in the Missile Age*, pp. 291–93. Compare also his skepticism about counterforce/"no-cities" on pp. 155–56 with his comment on p. 310 that "It is certainly conceivable that strategic bombing could be carried on in a restrained and discriminatory fashion; one could argue it *ought* to be, for strategic as well as moral reasons, if carried on at all!"

[66] Ibid., pp. 156, 289, 292–93, 303, 310, 401–2.

[67] Ibid., esp. pp. 329–30. Since Brodie's views in the 1950s on tactical nuclear weapons were somewhat equivocal, it was easy to misinterpret his position and label him as either a supporter or an opponent of a strategy based on these weapons. Gregg Herken, for example, portrays Brodie as a champion of the strategy based on tactical nuclear weapons, even in the late 1950s, while Lawrence Freedman assumes that Brodie had by that time become hostile to the general idea. Gregg Herken, *Counsels of War* (New York, 1985), pp. 84–87, 100; Lawrence Freedman, *The Evolution of Nuclear Strategy* (London, 1981), pp. 115–16. It is also very common for people to claim that there was a dramatic shift in Brodie's views on the subject from the late 1950s to the early 1960s. This shift is most often explained in personal terms—that is, in terms of Brodie's resentment of the increasing prestige and influence of Albert Wohlstetter and his followers in the early 1960s, as against his own exclusion

Wohlstetter at this time was also fully aware of the problem, but unlike Brodie he actually tried to come up with an answer. His solution was "second-strike counterforce." In 1959, in response to a request from General Thomas White, the Air Force Chief of Staff, he and his RAND colleague Henry Rowen outlined some of their basic ideas on strategy.[68] Counterforce, they argued, was desirable as a form of insurance. It was

---

from policy-making circles. Brodie's position did shift in the 1960s, not so much in substance as in emphasis, and this shift undoubtedly had a good deal to do with personal jealousies. In the Brodie papers, there are some quite extraordinary examples of his personal touchiness. See expecially his correspondence with Henry Kissinger ànd William Kaufmann in Box 1. But this is hardly the whole story. A good deal of the explanation has to do with what Brodie himself recognized as a certain perverseness of disposition—see, for example, the preface to *Strategy in the Missile Age*—which led him always to lean against the prevailing wisdom. From his point of view, the pendulum was always shifting too far in one direction or another, and he wanted to redress the balance. This particular faculty meant that he was a superb critic, able always to see the flaws in other people's arguments. But by the same token, he could never be a system-builder; it was much harder for him to construct positive arguments of his own. One should also note that there was a technical factor bearing on this shift. With the deployment of Polaris and Minuteman missiles in the early 1960s, there was a striking change in the "stability" of the nuclear balance: these survivable systems vastly decreased the risk of "accidental war." The increasing stability of the balance was for Brodie a kind of license sanctioning the use of tactical nuclear weapons. Brodie made this argument frequently. See especially his "A Critique of the Doctrine of Conventional War in Europe (CWE)," RAND paper, September 24, 1962, p. 18, and "The Missing Middle—Tactical Nuclear War," RAND working paper, May 8, 1964, pp. 5–6.

Note finally Schelling's very interesting interpretation in 1964 of the course of the debate on the defense of Europe. He was criticizing an early draft of what was to become *Escalation and the Nuclear Option*, the book where Brodie dealt with these questions most directly. "Let me tell you what really bothers me," he wrote Brodie. "I have believed for a couple of years that some of my friends, and I prefer not to name them, got concerned about a lazy tendency to rely on nuclear weapons, and an evasive tendency to pretend that nuclears actually would be used with ease, and began to resist these tendencies with an argument that became progressively more extreme, more alarmist, and eventually terribly enthusiastic about doing almost the whole job in Europe with conventional weapons, come what might. By overstating their case, and perhaps somewhat persuading themselves in the process, they alarmed a lot of Europeans, who I believe came to mistrust American intentions and even to lose a little respect for the analytical balance of American strategists. I believe many of them got so carried away in their arguments that, by holding out for doctrinal victory, they missed an opportunity for healthy compromise not only with the Europeans but with some of our own armed services. Every time I speak at a War College I get questions that imply that the guiding doctrine of this Administration is more extremely anti-nuclear than in my judgment it has ever been. But I cannot be sure, and often worry that people may have swallowed too much of their own propaganda. Now I worry that people like yourself, to redress the balance, may repeat the process at the other extreme, either winning an exaggerated argument that would err in the opposite direction, or losing the argument and only hardening the position that they oppose." Schelling to Brodie, September 30, 1964, Brodie Papers, Box 2.

[68] Albert Wohlstetter and Henry Rowen, "Objectives of the United States Military Posture," unpublished RAND working paper, May 1, 1959, p. 15.

unlikely that a rational enemy who chose to attack would use anything more than a small portion of his total force in the first wave. This was because, first, he would seek to "avoid giving warning," and second, because "a rational strategy, both for ourselves and for the enemy, requires the ability to pose a military threat not only before the opening strike but after it." Hence strategic forces would be reserved, and there would be something meaningful to counter. If the enemy had a complete "free ride," the country might be literally wiped out in the course of the war; but the kind of counterforce and defense capabilities Wohlstetter and Rowen had in mind might "make a significant difference in the size of the disaster suffered by our population." "By 'significant,'" they added, "is meant the difference, for example, between 60 and 160 million dead, and an even greater difference in damage to structures, equipment and stocks."[69]

This argument, Wohlstetter and Rowen insisted, was "quite different" from the usual one put forth by defenders of counterforce. They did not want anything like a full counterforce capability. Both counterforce and city defense carried with them "some danger of destabilizing the deterrent balance." Measures of this sort, while valuable as insurance "in case deterrence fails," nevertheless would place "an extra burden on the deterrent itself." The argument was that as long as these capabilities were limited—as long as counterforce and strategic defense capabilities did not "remove [the enemy's] power to deter us"—the stability problem would be manageable: "If the counterforce capability and a hardened defense might make the difference between 40 and 160 million dead, the answer to the question of destabilization is that the lower limit to which we might aspire is still a catastrophe so large that we would hardly undertake it lightly. If so, then the amount of instability introduced by the counterforce and by city defenses appears no more than tolerable."[70]

As for Schelling, he too was being pulled in both directions. In a paper dated April 1960, he argued for the "no-cities"/counterforce strategy, but just a few months later he was making a case, in a small meeting in Monterey, for a strategy of controlled counter-city warfare—a strategy which "consciously eschews counterforce capabilities."[71] Soviet vulnerability,

---

[69] Ibid., p. 13. The next few sentences reflected a certain sensitivity to the criticism that might be directed against this line of argument: "Such differences may seem much too modest to impress some readers. Just what, it may be asked, is the difference between two such unimaginable disasters as 60 and 160 Americans dead? The only answer to that is, '100 million.' Starting from the smaller losses, it would be possible to recover the industrial and political power of the Untied States."

[70] Ibid., pp. 15, 17.

[71] Thomas Schelling, "Reflections on Active Defense in the Missile Age," unpublished RAND working paper, April 8, 1960 and "Les armaments nucléaires," p. 134; note also the related argument in his "Dispersal, Deterrence, and Damage," *Operations Research*, vol. 9

which Marshall had been describing at this meeting, was for Schelling not an opportunity but a problem. "We can tell them," he said, "that we are scared by their vulverability." What he wanted was a strategy that would make it possible to bargain with the enemy, something that would allow each side to generate fears and thus to put pressure on its adversary while keeping the door open to a negotiated end to the war. Paul Nitze asked him whether counterforce could be used for purposes of demonstration and bargaining. A counterforce strategy, he replied, "would force the tempo of the war and obliterate the environment in which bargaining can take place."[72]

Actually, what Schelling really objected to was a full counterforce capability. A limited counterforce capability might be an important way to manipulate risk and engage in a strategy of bargaining: "We want to reduce the urgency of striking, the feeling that one must use his strategic force lest it be wiped out. The main thing is not to aim at *complete* counterforce success. One can mount counterforce missions on various levels; the important thing is to preserve the character of limited war."[73]

What created a special problem for Schelling was the key role that the manipulation of risk, and the "threat that leaves something to chance," played in his system. For Schelling, the suffering inflicted on civilian populations was important not so in itself. It was the specter it raised of more agony, of pain on an even greater scale, that would generate the emotional forces governing the outcome of the war. The pain, he stressed, did not have to be inflicted directly: it could come "in the guise of 'military tactics.'" Indeed, it might come into being not as a result of design but as an unavoidable by-product of the "more 'tactical' kind of war."[74] Nevertheless, it was the civilian suffering and not the damage sustained by the military forces that was crucial.

The basic problem here, however, was whether such tactics would be employed even if they did not make military sense—that is, to take the most important example, if counterforce attacks did not make a meaningful difference in the size of the enemy's nuclear forces. If in fact there was no real military logic at work, then there would be no semiautomatic mechanism that would create a risk of things getting out of control. The strategy of inflicting pain would in that case have to be carried out "coolly and deliberately": this would be a simple, although obviously terrifying,

(May–June 1961), pp. 363–70. Ellsberg and Kecskemeti, "Minutes of the Monterey Seminar," 1, pp. 3–14.

[72] Ellsberg and Kecskemeti, 1, pp. 16.

[73] Ibid., p. 17.

[74] In Klaus Knorr and Thornton Read, eds., *Limited Strategic War* (New York, 1962), p. 255; Schelling, *Arms and Influence*, pp. 181–82, 194.

war of endurance, and not the kind of risk manipulation that Schelling had consisted so vital in the third chapter of *Arms and Influence.*

The problem seemed inherent in the nature of strategic nuclear warfare. The level of risk could not be finely calibrated for bargaining purposes. The military mechanism, and especially the desire to strike before being struck, which for Schelling was the great generator of risk, had a kind of all-or-nothing character: if the mechanism counted for anything at all, it might be too spring-loaded, and once set off might quickly take things to their ultimate limit.

This problem emerged as soon as people began to consider the operational implications of these war-fighting strategies. If the counterforce campaign was to have a meaningful impact on the other side's military capabilities, then large numbers of people might be killed and enemy command and control facilities might be destroyed. Everyone knew that there were serious problems with America's command and control system. Hitch in 1960 called it the "weakest point" in America's "capability for waging actual war"—it was "hardly capable," he said, "of giving a 'go' order."[75] In their report for General White, Wohlstetter and Rowen viewed the problem as very serious and discussed it at some length, and Schelling in 1960 also stressed the need for studying "the requirements for reconnaissance, communication and control in bringing the war to any kind of close other than through the sheer exhaustion of weapons on both sides."[76] But there just did not seem any way to control a full-scale counterforce war. The tempo would be too fast, the command facilities on both sides were too fragile. "A really vigorous counter-force campaign," Schelling wrote Brodie in 1965, "may just make it impossible to observe the restraint and targeting care and so forth that would be needed to make the 'no-cities' strategy work."[77]

Schelling therefore turned to the strategy of controlled counter-city

[75] Ellsberg and Kecskemeti, 1, p. 11. It is worth nothing in this context that, according to one official historical study, "no subject consumed more time and effort in the highest levels of the government, within the DOD, USAF and SAC during 1961 than command and control of US nuclear forces." But even with these efforts, the best that could be done with any real confidence was to assure that a simple "go-code" would be executed. As another official study put it diplomatically: due to the changes that took place in the early 1960s, there was "little doubt about force execution despite the inroads of the ICBM," but "less certainty about continuous control of the force during a true thermonuclear, post-attack environment." *History of Headquarters Strategic Air Command 1961*, p. 24, SAC Historical Study No. 69, and *Strategic Command Control Communications (1959–1964)*, p. 3, SAC Historical Study No. 98, both at the Office of Air Force History, Bolling Air Force Base, Washington, D.C.

[76] Wohlstetter and Rowen, "Objectives of the United States Military Posture," pp. 20–21, 29–32, 36–37; Schelling, "Reflections on Active Defense," p. 30.

[77] Schelling to Brodie, February 22, 1965, p. 4, Brodie Papers, Box 2.

warfare—to a strategy of "pure coercion" and "pure pain."[78] If a general nuclear war had to be fought, this was the way to fight it. Maybe it seemed cruel to deliberately inflict pain for political ends, but was the policy of massive retaliation any better? A single all-out attack, he said, "may seem less cruel because it does not have a cruel purpose—it is merely purposeless—compared with deliberate, measured violence that carries the threat of more." But "a purely destructive war" was "neither clean nor heroic," and it was irresponsible for violence to be purposeless, since "coercion is the business of war."[79]

What did all this amount to? Here were some of the brightest people in America spending years wrestling it the most basic problems of strategy in the nuclear age, and yet what they finally came up with was not terribly satisfactory. Brodie, on the most central issues, did not even pretend to give answers. Schelling, on the other hand, embraced the strategy of controlled counter-population warfare, which he knew struck many people as cruel or bizarre.[80] As for the approach that Wohlstetter had settled on in 1959, the whole notion of second-strike counterforce seemed to raise as many problems as it solved. The first wave of an enemy attack might be limited, as Wohlstetter argued, in order to preserve the advantages of surprise, but a strong second-strike counterforce capability might simply convince an enemy to launch a more massive and more rapid follow-up attack than he otherwise might—that is, to use the forces he was holding in reserve before they were destroyed. This might force an enemy to make "all-or-nothing" choices, and thus, in the usual fashion, to contribute to deterrence: the "all" being virtually suicidal, "nothing" would emerge as the preferred choice. But from the point of view of actual war-fighting, second-strike counterforce made less sense: would the enemy attack in the first place unless he knew, with a high degree of confidence, that the strategic balance at the end of the exchange would be very lopsided and very favorable to him? It is hard to see how following such an attack the United States would be in a position to pursue any sort of successful military strategy. If, on the other hand, the United States was so strong that even after absorbing an enemy attack it would be able to pursue a counterforce strategy able to support its political goals, then what would this imply about its first-strike capabilities? If America were able to hold fatalities down to 40 million even if the enemy struck first, the same capabilities might enable the United States to keep damages at much lower levels if it were to strike the first blow, thus again raising the problem of "stability."

[78] Schelling, *Arms and Influence*, pp. 199, 201.
[79] Ibid., pp. 202, 216.
[80] Thus the defensive tone of the passages where the idea is discussed: ibid., pp. 177, 178, 202–3, 215–16.

It was as though whichever way one turned the problems were unavoidable. And of course the leading civilian strategists were all fully aware of these difficulties. This comes out above all in the tone they took in their writings. The strategists are often criticized for being too blasé or cavalier in their approach to nuclear war—for being too ready to assume that nuclear war is controllable, or that such a war could be fought rationally. Herman Kahn was, I think, the only strategist in the RAND group who ever took anything like a "nonchalant" tone when dealing with these questions.[81] But the strategists as a whole never approached these nuclear issues light-heartedly. All of the different possible strategies had problems, of which everyone was aware. It was as though one settled on a preferred strategy by a process of elimination—not because one would ever want to execute it, or because there was any great enthusiasm for it, but because the alternatives had been even more discredited. James Schlesinger, for example, in a 1968 RAND document heavily influenced by Schelling's ideas, laid out the rationale for a flexible nuclear war-fighting strategy—for what were eventually to be called, during his tenure as Secretary of Defense, "limited nuclear options." "The argument for sub-SIOP options"—that is, options more limited than those spelled out in the Single Integrated Operational Plan, the basic American plan for a massive nuclear attack on the Soviet bloc—"is not that they are especially appealing," Schlesinger wrote, "but only that such options may be less miserable than the other alternatives under given circumstances. The sub-SIOP option may be compared to playing Russian roulette with three

---

[81] It is hard to know what exactly to make of Kahn, or how to assess his importance. On the one hand, his writings do not have anything like the intellectual distinction or rhetorical elegance that, for example, characterize practically all of Schelling's work. The basic problem with Kahn's writings, to my mind, is that they were almost totally devoid of political sense. Kahn's work clearly had a certain shock value, and forced people to think; but the way he approached these issues tended to discredit the civilian strategists as a group. One might think, therefore, that the more serious strategists would have turned against him. Wohlstetter, in fact, made fun of one of Kahn's more outrageous hypotheses in a footnote: Kahn's assumption that the Russians, "'simply to demonstrate their strength and resolve,' wipe out London, Berlin, Rome, Paris and Bonn," had to be "the classic case for all time of simply flexing muscles" ("Nuclear Sharing," p. 381n.). And Brodie, for his part, did not mince words. In a letter to Kahn, he criticized him for lapsing "into levity": "You are discussing a serious and terrible subject, and you do nothing to enhance the acceptability of your work by being occasionally (even if most infrequently) flippant." Brodie to Kahn, January 31, 1962, Brodie Papers, Box 4, File "Kahn, Herman." Note also Brodie's capsule description of Kahn in *La Guerre nucléaire* (Paris, 1965), pp. 49–50. On the other hand, I was struck by what can only be called a fondness and even respect people still have for Kahn—an insistence on his importance, an aversion to denigrating his work shared by even the most important people in the field. The conclusion seems inescapable: there must have been something about Kahn—as a fountain of ideas and constant source of intellectual stimulation—that came out in informal, personal contacts, but just did not transfer well to the printed page.

chambers filled, hardly an enticing prospect for decisionmaking." But executing the full SIOP—that is, launching a massive attack—would be like playing with all six chambers filled.[82]

STRATEGY HITS A DEAD END

The nuclear debate in the 1950s and early 1960s was lively and exciting because the problems themselves were so hard to resolve. It was common for people to talk about "paradoxes" and "dilemmas"; the answers were not easy or obvious. It was for this reason that the ideas that emerged at this time, especially at RAND, hardly amounted to a dogma. Instead, people felt themselves to be grappling, as Brodie put it, with "problems of terrible intellectual difficulty,"[83] and the mark of sophistication was a sense for what those difficulties were. It was easy to criticize those, both on the right and on the left, who thought that the answers were simple. In fact, it was the campaign against the official policy of the 1950s—the strategy of "massive retaliation"—that gave this body of thought its focal point, its political identity and intellectual coherence.

But as the 1950s progressed, the strategy of massive retaliation was viewed increasingly as bankrupt—even at the highest levels of the administration, although a certain effort was made to conceal this from the outside world. At the beginning of 1954, Secretary of State John Foster Dulles gave his famous speech setting out the new doctrine. But by the end of that year Dulles was already questioning, in a letter to President Eisenhower, whether America was "prepared to deal adequately with the possible 'little wars' which might call for punishment related to the degree and locality of the offense, but which would not justify a massive retaliation against the Soviet Union itself."[84] During the mid- and late-1950s, the doctrine was in constant retreat, as one can see, for example, by reading the series of annual Basic National Security Policy papers—documents that were taken quite seriously during the Eisenhower period.[85]

[82] James Schlesinger, "Rationale for NU-OPTS," RAND Report R-1608-PR [limited distribution]; the references to Schelling are on pp. 18 and 22; the passage quoted is on p. 5.

[83] Asilomar talk, April 29, 1960, Brodie Papers, Box 17.

[84] Dulles memo of December 22, 1954, John Foster Dulles Files, Eisenhower Library, White House Memoranda Series, Box 1, file "Meetings with the President." Copies are available at the J. F. Dulles Papers, Seeley Mudd Library, Princeton University. See also Memo, ExecSecy, NSC, to NSC, "Review of Basic National Security Policy," November 17, 1954, JCS 2101/172, November 18, 1954, CCS 381 US (1–31–50) sec 48, R. G. 218, US National Archives, cited in Robert J. Watson, *The Joint Chiefs of Staff and National Policy, 1953–1954* (Washington, 1986), p. 50.

[85] The following BNSP papers are available at the National Archives: NSC 162/2, 5422/2,

By 1958 Dulles was in fact leaning toward finite deterrence: the United States, he told the National Security Council, "should not attempt to be the greatest military power in the world, although most discussions in the Council seemed to suggest that we should have the most and the best of everything. Was there no group in the government which ever thought of the right kind of ceiling on our military capabilities?"[86] On the question of limited war, Dulles simply felt that it was dangerous to permit any

> doubt as to the willingness of the United States to resort to massive nuclear retaliation until such time as we have something to take its place. The massive nuclear deterrent was running its course as the principal element in our military arsenal, and very great emphasis must be placed on the elements which in the next two or three years can replace the massive nuclear retaliatory capability. In short, the United States must be in a position to fight defensive wars which do not involve the total defeat of the enemy. . . . If we have to keep our basic policy paper in the form and language that it presently has in order to avoid showing our hand, this was ok with Secretary Dulles. But we must do everything that is necessary in order to develop the supplementary strategy of which he had spoken.[87]

And indeed by the time the administration left office at the beginning of 1961, the outgoing Secretary of Defense, Thomas Gates, felt very confident about America's "limited war capabilities."[88] One has the sense in

---

5501, 5708/8, 5810/1. The BNSP Papers have also been published in Trachtenberg, ed., *The Development of American Strategic Thought*, vol. 1.

[86] "Discussion at the 363rd Meeting of the National Security Council, April 24, 1958," in Eisenhower: Papers, 1953–1961 (Ann Whitman File), NSC Series, Box 10, Eisenhower Library; also in Declassified Documents Collection, 1980/384B.

[87] "Discussion at the 364th Meeting of the National Security Council, Thursday, May 1, 1958," in same file as last document cited; also in Declassified Documents Collection, 1980/384C. Note also the antinuclear thrust of a paper he wrote on the nuclear issue dated January 22, 1956, in John Foster Dulles Papers, Subject Series, Box 4, Seeley Mudd Library, Princeton; also in Declassified Documents Collection, 1982/802.

[88] Clifford to JFK, January 24, 1961, President's Office Files, Box 29a, folder "Eisenhower, D.D. 1/17/61–10/9/61," JFK Library. Note also the McNamara "Appraisal of Capabilities of Conventional Forces." This document was dated May 12, 1961, and thus reflected the situation that had been reached at the very end of the Eisenhower period. The document argued that "we have a substantial capability for waging non-nuclear warfare"— that conventional combat in any one locality could be sustained at the level of "250,000–300,000 U.S. personnel" which was the "threshold of a combat environment indicating the employment of nuclear weapons." "It is my belief," McNamara therefore concluded, "that the overall force strength" described in the document "is appropriate at this time and should not be significantly expanded." President's Office Files, Box 77, JFK Library. McNamara is identified as the author in Theodore Sorensen, "Memorandum to the President," July 17, 1961, President's Office Files, Box 116a, folder/"Germany. General. 7/61," JFK Library. According to McNamara, this was not a mature reflection of his personal views, but simply reflected the Army line at the time.

fact that by this point, massive retaliation would only be considered in the context of a major U.S.-Soviet war in Europe—as an initial response only to a massive attack on Western Europe, or, even more remotely, an attack on America itself—and Brodie, one should note, more or less accepted massive retaliation as the proper strategy for such extreme cases.[89]

Reading the documents, one sometimes gets the sense that Eisenhower himself was one of the last true believers. To him, even as late as 1960, a major U.S.-Soviet limited war was an absurdity.[90] His "basic philosophy," he said during the Berlin Crisis in 1959, was that America had "to be willing to 'push its whole stack of chips into the pot' when such became necessary. . . . He expressed the conviction that the actual decision to go to all-out war will not come, but if it does come, we must have the crust to follow through."[91] Eisenhower could on occasion be extremely assertive, but on many issues he was also willing to allow his government to take its own course. He might comment, sometimes in a sharp and antagonistic manner, on the way things were moving, but would still be reluctant to assert his authority directly.[92] It thus seems that he acquiesced in the drift away from massive retaliation, but in his heart remained skeptical: as awful as it was, there was no getting away from the massive strike

[89] Brodie, *Strategy in the Missile Age*, pp. 341, 354–55. Note also the famous article by William Kaufmann, "The Requirements of Deterrence," in W. Kaufmann, ed., *Military Policy and National Security* (Princeton, 1956), pp. 26–27.

[90] George Kistiakowsky, *A Scientist at the White House* (Cambridge, Mass. 1976), p. 400. Note also General Goodpaster's "Memorandum of Conference with the President," August 16, 1960, declassified in November 1986. Eisenhower was reacting to Robert Bowie's ideas about the future of NATO: "The President said he agreed that we are not going to have a tactical nuclear war in Western Europe. In fact, he said he cannot see any chance of keeping any war in Europe from becoming a general war. For this reason he thought we must be ready to throw the book at the Russians should they jump us. He did not see how there could be such a thing as a limited war in Europe, and thought we would be fooling ourselves and our European friends if we said we could fight such a war without recourse to nuclear weapons." Declassified Documents Collection 1987/1139.

[91] "Memorandum of Conference with the President," March 8, 1959, in Declassified Documents Collection, 1981/598A.

[92] For an extraordinary example of the President as "kibbitzer in chief," see "Discussion at the 363rd Meeting of the National Security Council, Thursday, April 24, 1958," Eisenhower Papers, 1953–61 (Ann Whitman file), NSC Series, Box 10, where the President severely criticized, but nevertheless approved, an important Defense Department proposal on IRBMs. This is also in the Declassified Documents Collection: 1980/384B. Note also A. J. Goodpaster, "Memorandum of Conference with the President," August 8, 1960: the President had "become very dissatisfied regarding our relationships with our allies in the matter of atomic weapons and missiles. The US Government seems to be taking the attitude that we will call the tune, and that they have inferior status in the alliance." It is as though we were criticizing someone else's administration. This document is in the White House Office, Office of the Staff Secretary: Records, 1952–61, International Trips and Meetings Series, Box 5, folder "NATO (4)," Eisenhower Library; also in Declassified Documents Collection, 1978/451D.

as the ultimate basis of policy, and it was just self-deception to pretend otherwise.

In the 1950s, when "massive retaliation" was the country's official policy the strategists had new and important things to say. Eisenhower had given these people something to react to, a target for their fire. But in 1961 the situation changed dramatically. Under Kennedy, the strategy of massive retaliation was explicitly rejected; although the change in the formal war plans was not nearly as great as the shift in doctrine seemed to imply, it was clear that the Kennedy administration generally shared most of the ambivalences of the strategists on nuclear issues. Indeed, many of the strategists who had worked at RAND in the 1950s played a key role in shaping the military policy of the new administration.[93] But what this ultimately meant was that the theorists were losing their target, which was a lot fuzzier now than it had been during the Eisenhower period. And with the Vietnam War in the late 1960s, they began to lose their self-confidence as well.

The role that the ideas developed by the nuclear strategists, especially Schelling, played in shaping American policy in Vietnam, can easily be exaggerated.[94] It is clear that ideas about signaling through military action, and warfare as a kind of bargaining process, played a certain role; but the American bombing policy, for example, was not based on generating a sense that matters were getting out of control—on exploiting a threat "that leaves something to chance." In fact, one of the most striking things to emerge from the study of the American air war is the way proposals for a relentless and ominous increase in the destructiveness of the air war were rejected when the bombing policy was worked out.[95] But

[93] See especially Bernard Brodie, "The McNamara Phenomenon," *World Politics*, vol. 17 (July 1965); Desmond Ball, *Politics and Force Levels: The Strategic Missile Program of the Kennedy Administration* (Berkeley and Los Angeles, 1980), pp. 31–34; and Kaplan, *Wizards of Armageddon*, esp. chaps. 15–18.

[94] Kaplan, for example, claims (on p. 332) that Schelling's "concept of coercive warfare" shaped American strategy in Southeast Asia.

[95] See Wallace Thies, *When Governments Collide: Coercion and Diplomacy in the Vietnam Conflict, 1964–1968* (Berkeley and Los Angeles, 1980), pp. 2 (esp. n. 5), 3, 85–86, 88, 93. See also Michael Nacht, "The War in Vietnam: The Influence of Concepts on Policy," UCLA Center for International and Strategic Affairs, July 1980, p. 12 and n. 16. A truly coercive policy, however, would have needed to create the sense that the level of suffering might escalate dramatically, that events were acquiring a certain momentum and that it might be too dangerous to try to ride out the storm. A highly controlled policy could scarcely create a feeling that things were moving out of control; and the American government—to its credit, I think, given the circumstances—could scarcely bring itself to engage in a full-fledged strategy of pain infliction. And of course Schelling would not have wanted it to: an analysis of how military power can be effective is not in itself an argument that power should be used in these ways in all circumstances. That it sometimes sounded that way had to do mostly with the abstract and apolitical character of the analysis—it often

clearly something had changed after Vietnam. It was not so much that the logic had been revealed as defective, it was the relevance of this body of thought that now came to be questioned. There was a sense that it was somehow out of touch with reality.

For Brodie especially, there was a great shift in perspective. The military problems and strategists had focused on, he now came to feel, were really of secondary importance. The strategists as a group had vastly overestimated the extent to which war could result from essentially military factors: the problem of "strategic instability" had been greatly exaggerated. He even went so far as to claim that he had never believed in the "delicacy" of the balance, although this was certainly untrue.[96] The whole concept of an "accidental" nuclear war, which had played such an important role in the arguments about preemption and stability circa 1960, he now dismissed as "ludicrous."[97]

Looking back at this body of thought as a whole, it is clear that the publication of Schelling's *Arms and Influence* in 1966 marked something of a climax. After 1966 the field went into a period of decline: the well seemed to have run dry, the ideas were by and large no longer fresh or exciting, or, to use a phrase that Brodie had himself used in a different context in 1955, strategy had hit a dead end.

Was this to be attributed simply to the way the world was changing in the 1960s—to the shift in nuclear strategy under Kennedy and to the Vietnam War? The problem in fact had deeper roots. The most basic issues were analyzed on a very abstract level. One could work out in general terms the argument for "strategic stability," or for various nuclear war–fighting strategies. But at this level of abstraction there were no final answers—at this highly abstract level of conceptualization the most basic intellectual tensions could not be resolved.

What, therefore, had this body of thought amounted to? On the one hand, the strategists had developed a way of thinking about nuclear issues—not a technique for processing hard, and especially quantitative,

---

sounded like a manual on how to prevail in a conflict. Once again, Brodie is worth quoting in this context: "When we recall how we discussed methods of demonstrating 'our superior resolve,' without ever questioning whether we would indeed have or deserve to have superiority in that commodity, we realize how puerile was our whole approach to our art." Bernard Brodie, "Why Were We So (Strategically) Wrong?" *Foreign Policy* no. 5 (Winter 1971–72), p. 161.

[96] Bernard Brodie, "The Development of Nuclear Strategy," *International Security*, vol. 2 (Spring 1978), p. 69. Compare this, for example, with the final paragraph of his "The Anatomy of Deterrence," *World Politics*, vol. 11 (January 1959), and especially with his "Strategic Objectives and the Determination of Force Composition," unpublished RAND working paper, June 9, 1959, p. 11.

[97] Bernard Brodie, "How Much is Enough? Guns Versus Butter Revisited," California Seminar on Arms Control and Foreign Policy, August 1975, p. 20.

information, and mechanically grinding out answers, for it was universally recognized that the really interesting questions were those with a political dimension, the kind that did not lend themselves to a purely technical analysis. In fact, the particular answers that were given were not especially important in themselves: to someone like Brodie, it was not even clear whether there were any right answers, although there were certainly plenty of wrong ones. What was important was the often counterintuitive nature of the argument, the questions it raised, and the depth of insight it made possible.

On the other hand, there was something strange about this intellectual tradition. For Schelling especially, but to a certain degree for the others as well, the emphasis on risk meant that the manipulation of risk became perhaps *the* central concern of strategy. Ironically, given the hostility of these strategists to the military policies associated with Eisenhower and Dulles, the bottom line here was a defense of "brinkmanship." "Until we can manipulate the risk of general war and engage in competitive risk-taking with the Soviets," Schelling said in 1963, "I don't think we are going to learn to take care of Berlin, much less to take care of Indonesia and Finland when the time comes."[98]

The effect, at least, in Schelling's case, was to transform strategy once again into tactics writ large—not military tactics this time, but bargaining tactics; for the group as a whole, the great problem of international politics, the problem of war and peace, was reduced to the problem of behavior during times of crisis and after the outbreak of hostilities. The purely military side of war causation, as Brodie later complained, became the focus of analysis, as though war itself were not in essence a political artifact—as though the basic insight of Clausewitz, whom they all respected, was somehow obsolete. It was not that the issues they focused on were meaningless or irrelevant. The problem, for example, of "accidental war" resulting from the "reciprocal fear of surprise attack" was ceratainly worth thinking about. It was simply a question of balance, of not allowing the tail to wag the dog, and this depended on the sophistication of one's theory of war causation.

"Strategy," Brodie wrote, "is a 'how to do it' study, a guide for accomplishing something and doing it efficiently."[99] It was concerned above all with certain hypothetical situations: if war breaks out, what should we do? If Soviet armies attack Western Europe, or cut off West Berlin, how should be respond? If we get involved in a crisis, how should we handle it? The central issues of military policy were analyzed in this context:

[98] David Abshire and Richard Allen, eds., *National Security: Political, Military and Economic Strategies in the Decade Ahead* (New York, 1963), p. 646.
[99] Brodie, "Why Were We So (Strategically) Wrong?" p. 151.

what sort of military policy would put us in the best position for dealing with these situations once they arose? The focus was not on war, or even crisis, as the outcome of a historical process unfolding over a period of years. Policy was therefore not analyzed in terms of the manipulation of that process—the shaping of hopes and anxieties so as to influence the course of great power politics. It was as though a whole dimension of strategy had somehow disappeared. A broad range of strategic issues, having to do with the way the political and military spheres interact with each other, not just in time of war or crisis, but in more normal times as well, was never really closely examined by mainstream American strategic thought.

These, in any case, are the kind of reflections which suggest themselves to someone trained to think in terms of traditional European great power politics. None of the strategists of the 1950s and 1960s came from that tradition. The small group of men who dominated the field were not people who had been thinking for years about how the international system operated, about what made for war or about the role that military power played in international politics. Even Brodie, the most politically minded individual in the group, was an isolated, and to some extent an alienated, figure in American political science: he was much more a student of military issues than of international politics in general. Given where they did come from intellectually, it was natural that their thinking on these basic issues should take place on a fairly abstract and apolitical level.

And it was apolitical in substance, I think, in large part because it was ahistorical in method. History, for the strategists, when they used it at all, was more a source of illustration than of insight. Brodie himself, a partial exception to this general rule, realized that this was a basic problem. "One of the distinctive weaknesses," he said, "of the otherwise spectacular kind of strategic analysis that has developed especially in the United States is that it often seems to be conspicuously lacking in something that I can only call historic sense or sensitivity."[100] But if the diagnosis is sound, the prescription seems inescapable: historical analysis has to move into the mainstream of strategic studies. History, as a scholarly discipline, has a basic role to play in the intellectual reinvigoration of the field.

[100] "Nuclear Strategy in its Political Context," February 1968, folder "Munich Conference," Brodie Papers, Box 20, p. 2. See also his comments in "The American Scientific Strategists," pp. 21–22, deploring the absence of historians from the field. But note that Brodie was talking about military and not diplomatic historians, which is odd for someone who thought it was more important to figure out how to avoid wars than how they should be fought.

CHAPTER TWO

The Coming of the First World War:
A Reassessment

THE IDEA that a great war need not be the product of deliberate decision—that it can come because statesmen "lose control" of events—is one of the most basic and most common notions in contemporary American strategic thought. A crisis, it is widely assumed, might unleash forces of an essentially military nature that overwhelm the political process and bring on a war that nobody wants. Many important conclusions, about the risk of nuclear war and thus about the political meaning of nuclear forces, rest on this fundamental idea.[1]

This theory of "inadvertent war" is in turn rooted, to a quite extraordinary degree, in a specific interpretation of a single historical episode: the coming of the First World War during the July Crisis in 1914.[2] It is often taken for granted that the sort of military system that existed in Europe at the time, a system of interlocking mobilizations and of war plans that placed a great emphasis on rapid offensive action, directly led to a conflict that might otherwise have been avoided. "The war systems of the day," Paul Bracken says, "stimulated each other into a frenzy. Political leaders lost control of the tremendous momentum built up when their armies went on alert."[3] It was as though an enormous, uncontrol-

Part of this chapter appeared in *International Security*, vol. 15, no. 3 (Winter 1990–91). The author is grateful to the editors of that journal and to MIT Press for permission to republish it here.

[1] For a penetrating analysis of the question of "loss of control," see Robert Powell, "The Theoretical Foundations of Strategic Nuclear Deterrence," *Political Science Quarterly*, vol. 100, no. 1 (Spring 1985), esp. pp. 83–92.

[2] See, for example: Thomas Schelling, *Arms and Influence* (New Haven, Conn., 1966), pp. 221–25; Graham Allison, Albert Carnesale, and Joseph Nye, eds., *Hawks, Doves, and Owls: An Agenda for Avoiding Nuclear War* (New York, 1985), pp. 17–18, 30, 43, 210, 217; Richard Ned Lebow, *Nuclear Crisis Management: A Dangerous Illusion* (Ithaca, N.Y., 1987), pp. 24–26, 32–35, 59–60, 109–13, 122–23. Note also the rather extreme argument in Paul Bracken's *The Command and Control of Nuclear Forces* (New Haven, Conn., 1983). This book is laced with references to the July Crisis; see esp. p. 65 where Bracken admits that his argument about how a nuclear war could begin might sound a bit extreme "were it not for the history of the outbreak of World War I." A certain interpretation of the Cuban Missile Crisis is also frequently used to support the inadvertent war theory. For an analysis of that interpretation, see Marc Trachtenberg, "New Light on the Cuban Missile Crisis?" *Diplomatic History*, vol. 14, no. 2 (Spring 1990).

[3] Bracken, *Command and Control*, p. 53.

lable machine had begun to move. There was, Thomas Schelling writes, "a great starting of engines, a clutching and gearing and releasing of brakes and gathering momentum until the machines were on collision course."[4] "Armies," says Michael Howard, "were juggernauts which even their own generals could hardly control."[5]

This basic problem, the argument runs, was compounded by a whole series of other factors. Because of the complexity of the mobilization process, the war plans had to be worked out in advance down to the last detail. This meant that the plans were extraordinarily rigid, and could not be adjusted to changing political circumstance. In the planning process itself, political considerations were never really taken into account; the plans were elaborated instead essentially on the basis of technical, military considerations. "The German Army's almost total autonomy," according to Ned Lebow, "enabled it to plan for war in a political vacuum. When the July Crisis came, Germany's political leaders were confronted with a military plan that had been formulated solely with reference to narrow organizational criteria and requirements."[6] The political leadership, it is further argued, was abysmally ignorant, both of the plans themselves and especially of their implications. "The bland ignorance," Howard wrote in 1964, "among national leaders of the simple mechanics of the system on which they relied for the preservation of national security would astonish us rather more if so many horrifying parallels did not come to light whenever British politicians give their views on defence policy to-day."[7] The failure to understand what mobilization meant was the basis for a series of disastrous miscalculations on the eve of the war, when this measure was ordered by statesmen who simply had no real understanding of how extremely dangerous it in fact was.

The term "inadvertent war" can have many meanings. It might bring to mind the full range of factors that can lead to a war that nobody wants or expects at the beginning of a crisis—miscalculation, misapprehension, and misjudgment; the impulsiveness of statesmen and the deviousness of ambassadors; the sheer momentum of a mounting crisis, the difficulty of backing down from positions taken, the need for toughness in order to force the adversary to give way. The term, however, is frequently used in a much narrower sense: a war is often said to be inadvertent if it breaks out because statesmen are overpowered by the workings of the military system.

The main purpose of this article is to examine the idea that World War I was in this sense an inadvertent war. Before this analysis can begin, however, there is one major issue that first has to be cleared up. It is necessary

[4] Schelling, *Arms and Influence*, p. 221.
[5] Michael Howard, "Lest We Forget," *Encounter* (January 1964), p. 65.
[6] Lebow, *Nuclear Crisis Management*, p. 78.
[7] Howard, "Lest We Forget," p. 65.

at the outset to examine the claim that Germany deliberately set out from the very start of the crisis to provoke a European conflict. For if World War I were in essence a war of German aggression, one could hardly claim that it came about because a political process, which might otherwise have brought about a peaceful settlement, had been swamped by forces from within the military sphere. It turns out that the argument that Germany contrived throughout the crisis to bring on a great war is quite weak, but this in itself does not mean that the European nations simply stumbled into the conflict. A positive case has to be made if the "inadvertent war" thesis is to be accepted. To test this theory, the specific arguments on which it rests therefore have to be examined, and the most important of these arguments will be analyzed here: claims about the rigidity of military plans, about the "cult of the offensive," and, most importantly, about preemption and interlocking mobilizations. What this analysis will show is that this theory, broadly speaking, is not supported by the evidence. The war did not break out in 1914 because events had "slipped out of control"—because statesmen had been overwhelmed by forces that brought on a conflict that all the governments had been trying to avoid.

THE FISCHER THESIS

In the early 1960s, the German historian Fritz Fischer set off a storm of controversy by arguing that the German government decided to seize the opportunity created by the assassination of the Austrian Archduke Franz Ferdinand on June 28, 1914, and adopted a policy designed to lead to a European war. This thesis was first laid out, rather obliquely, in a chapter in Fischer's *Griff nach der Weltmacht* ("Grab for World Power"), translated into English as *Germany's Aims in the First World War*.[8] In his sequel, *War of Illusions*, the argument was made explicit. The First World War, Fischer repeatedly claimed, had been "started" by German politicians; their goal had been "to defeat the enemy powers before they became too strong" and thus bring about "German hegemony over Europe." The decision to start a war with Russia and France—although not with Britain—had been taken at the beginning of July. The plan had been "to use the favorable opportunity of the murder at Sarajevo for the start

[8] Fritz Fischer, *Germany's Aims in the First World War* (New York, 1967). The message, however, was never far below the surface, and as Fischer himself later pointed out, his thesis in that book was that Germany saw "the murder at Sarajevo as a golden opportunity to declare war." Fritz Fischer, *World Power or Decline: The Controversy over Germany's Aims in the First World War* (New York, 1974), p. 95. See also Imanuel Geiss, ed., *July 1914: The Outbreak of the First World War. Selected Documents* (New York, 1967), p. 370.

of the continental war." This plan, he says, was in fact "carried out successfully."[9]

A number of Fischer's students and followers, most notably Imanuel Geiss and John Röhl, also published a number of books and articles in this vein. Fischer's followers soon began to claim victory. His originally controversial views, it was said, had now been generally accepted. As one of Fischer's supporters put it in a survey of the Fischer debate: "No serious German historian today can venture to pit himself against the evidence compiled by the Fischer school."[10]

It is certainly not true, however, that the views of the Fischer school have come to be almost universally shared, either inside Germany or out. The older interpretations of people like Pierre Renouvin, Bernadotte Schmitt, and Luigi Albertini—which, while quite critical of Germany, never went so far as to claim that the German government deliberately set out to provoke a general war—are still very widely accepted.[11] Albertini's massive account, *The Origins of the War of 1914*, which was published in Italy in the middle of World War II, is the most impressive of these works. Regardless of what one thinks of certain of his conclusions, the work itself must be regarded as monumental. Because of the completeness of the documentation, and the intelligence and honesty of the author, this study is still the point of departure for all serious work on 1914.[12]

Fischer's followers claim that their views fall within this older tradition. Geiss, for example, said that in his chapters on the origins of the war in *Griff nach der Weltmacht*, Fischer "did nothing more than introduce Albertini's results into Germany for the first time."[13] But on the central issue, Albertini's and Fischer's views were diametrically opposed—"it is undeniable," Albertini wrote, "that in 1914 neither the Kaiser nor his Chancellor wanted a European war"[14]—and the claim that the German

---

[9] Fritz Fischer, *War of Illusions: German Policies from 1911 to 1914* (New York, 1975), pp. 470, 473, 480, 494, 515.

[10] John Moses, *The Politics of Illusion* (London, 1975), p. 127. See also John Röhl, *1914: Delusion or Design? The Testimony of Two German Diplomats* (London, 1973), p. 21.

[11] See Jacques Droz, *Les Causes de la Première Guerre Mondiale: Essai d'historiographie* (Paris, 1973). This, in my opinion, is the best discussion of the Fischer debate and related issues. Note also Droz's "Bulletin historique," in the *Revue historique*, no. 552 (October–December 1984), pp. 512–20.

[12] Luigi Albertini, *The Origins of the War of 1914*, 3 vols. (London, 1952–57), a translation of his *Le origini della guerra del 1914*, 3 vols. (Milan, 1942–43). The two other works mentioned are somewhat older and more limited in their use of sources: Pierre Renouvin, *Les Origines immédiates de la guerre* (Paris, 1927); and Bernadotte Schmitt, *The Coming of War 1914*, 2 vols. (New York, 1930).

[13] Geiss, *July 1914*, p. 11.

[14] Albertini, *Origins*, vol. 3, p. 252.

political leadership deliberately engineered the conflict represented a radical departure from this older interpretation.

Albertini had stressed the role of miscalculation and bungling in bringing on the conflict. Given that no one wanted a great war, it was a "source of amazement" that it came about anyway. To be sure, Germany had wanted Austria to go to war against Serbia; she had encouraged Austria to strike and had sabotaged all attempts at mediation. But this was all with the hope that the war in the Balkans could be kept from escalating, and this turned out to be a terrible misjudgment. The political leaders had no real understanding of military realities, and this also helps explain why moves were made that set off the avalanche. Beneath it all was an "utter lack of political horse-sense," "the main cause," according to Albertini, "of European disorders and upheavals."[15]

Had Albertini, however, missed the point? Maybe it was not just a case of blundering; maybe Germany, as Fischer claimed, had actually set out to provoke a continental war. Whether Fischer's argument on this key issue stands or falls is ultimately a function of the adequacy of the evidence on which it rests. Does he prove that right after Sarajevo the German leadership adopted a plan to engineer a war with Russia and France? The evidence, if it exists, should appear in his section in *War of Illusions* on the initial phase of the crisis, a section entitled "The Occasion is Propitious—the first Week in July."[16] But he gives no real evidence here of a decision by the German government to provoke such a conflict. The material in this section only shows that the German government was aware that a tough line on the Serbian question might lead to European complications, but this in itself hardly proves that the Germans had decided to use the occasion to bring about a great European war.[17]

It is true that at two points in Fischer's account the Emperor William II is made to appear bellicose at this phase of the crisis, but this impression results from a simple twisting of the evidence. The very first document Fischer cites in this section is a report of a conversation that the well-connected German publicist Victor Naumann had with a top Austrian Foreign Ministry official on July 1. Naumann was sure, according to Fischer's summary, that in Germany, "unlike the year before not only the military but also the Foreign Ministry *and the Emperor* no longer objected to a preventive war against Russia."[18] The original document, however, had said nothing at all about the emperor in this context, and indeed all Naumann had said was that in the military and in the foreign ministry, "the idea of a preventive war against Russia was regarded with

[15] Ibid., pp. 252–53.
[16] Fischer, *War of Illusions*, p. 473.
[17] Ibid., pp. 473–80.
[18] Ibid., p. 473. Emphasis added.

less disfavor than a year ago," which itself was considerably weaker than Fischer's paraphrase.[19] Two pages later Fischer writes that a certain official had been wrong to assume that William II wanted to avoid a European war, and his proof is the emperor's famous marginal comment on a dispatch from the German ambassador in Vienna, "Now or never," which Fischer had in fact used as the subtitle of the chapter. But again this is misleading: the "now or never" referred not to a great war with Russia and France, as Fischer had implied, but to a "final and fundamental reckoning" between Austria-Hungary and Serbia.[20] Certainly the German leadership wanted Austria to bring matters to a head with Serbia, and it is also clear that elements within the German government, especially in the army, thought the time was right for a European war. Fischer, however, gives no direct evidence that the top political leadership, the people who were really making German policy at this point, consciously decided to use the assassination to provoke a crisis that would lead to a great war.

If a case is to be made at all, it has to rest on indirect reasoning. To go from the correct point that the German government encouraged Austria to move against Serbia to the conclusion that Germany was trying to engineer a continental war, Fischer and his followers therefore have to argue that a local war between Austria and Serbia, with all the other powers remaining on the sidelines, was a political impossibility—that what was called "localization" was never in the cards—and that the German government knew it. "As innumerable documents show," Fischer writes, "Germany knew that Russia would never allow Austria-Hungary to act in the Balkans unopposed."[21] And Geiss says: "Berlin was well aware that Russia would be forced to intervene, making world war inevitable."[22]

Was it in fact a foregone conclusion that Russia would intervene militarily in the event that Austria attacked Serbia? The original Russian policy during the July Crisis had been to advise the Serbs not to resist an

[19] "Hoyos' Conversation with Victor Naumann," July 1, 1914, republished in Geiss, *July 1914*, pp. 65–66. Fischer also claimed on p. 473 of *War of Illusions* that "Naumann warned that if Austria-Hungary failed to use this opportunity Germany would drop Austria as an ally," but in fact no such threat was reported in the document. The closest Naumann came was to point out that "Austria-Hungary will be finished as a Monarchy and as a Great Power if she does not take advantage of this moment," which was a comment that many Habsburg leaders would have agreed with. On the role of Austria during the crisis, see Samuel Williamson, "Vienna and July 1914: The Origins of the Great War Once More," in Samuel Williamson and Peter Pastor, *Essays on World War I: Origins and Prisoners of War* (New York, 1983).
[20] For William II's marginalia, see Tschirschky to Bethmann Hollweg, June 30, 1914, in Geiss, *July 1914*, pp. 64–65.
[21] Fischer, *Germany's Aims*, p. 63.
[22] Geiss, *July 1914*, p. 364.

Austrian invasion and to "entrust her fate to the judgment of the Great Powers."[23] One of the major determinants of Russian policy in this matter, moreover, was the attitude of the western powers, and the British especially were by no means eager for war over the Serbian question. As late as July 25, the Russian foreign minister, S. D. Sazonov, referred to the fact that, except for the London *Times*, "nearly the whole of the British press was on the side of Austria."[24]

Whatever the reality, however, did the German government calculate that Russian intervention was inevitable? Are there "innumerable documents" which prove that for the German government "localization" was simply a sham? Fischer gives no evidence to prove that the top German leadership thought that Russia was bound to intervene if Austria attacked Serbia.[25] All that Fischer shows is that the German government under-

[23] Special Journal of the Russian Council of Ministers, July 24, 1914, and Sazonov to Strandtmann, July 24, 1914, in Geiss, *July 1914*, pp. 186–88.

[24] Albertini, *Origins*, vol 2, p. 307. Sazonov's characterization of British attitudes was somewhat exaggerated, but a good part of British, and especially Liberal, opinion was pro-Austrian, and the Liberals were of course the governing party. See D. C. Watt, "The British Reactions to the Assassination at Sarajevo," *European Studies Review*, vol. 1, no. 3 (July 1971), pp. 233–47.

[25] Geiss says that Bethmann "originally expected" intervention, but the one document he cites to support this claim had said nothing about the chancellor, and had simply reported the views of unidentified officials at the foreign office. Geiss, *July 1914*, pp. 61, 68, 365. In another book, however, he reprints a letter from Bethmann to Austrian foreign minister Berchtold of February 10, 1913, pointing out that Russia "will hardly be able to observe passively any military action by Austria-Hungary against Serbia without a tremendous loss of face," and that a full-scale war between the Triple Alliance and the Triple Entente would be the likely result. Imanuel Geiss, *German Foreign Policy, 1871–1914* (London, 1976), p. 205. But an argument developed for dissuasive effect in 1913 does not necessarily reflect Bethmann's real views in 1914. Indeed, since the Fischer school argues that Bethmann in July 1914 was counting on British neutrality in a continental war, and since Bethmann here takes British intervention for granted, it would presumably accept the conclusion that the Chancellor was taking an exaggeratedly somber line in 1913, presumably to keep the Austrians under control. In more recent writings, Fischer and his followers cite evidence that Zimmermann, the number two man in the German Foreign Office, allegedly told the Austrian representative Hoyos early on in the crisis that an Austrian attack on Serbia would lead "with 90 percent probability to a European war." If true, this would be important evidence, even though Zimmermann's views were generally more extreme than those of Bethmann. (Fischer, for example, refers to him as a "strongly pan-German oriented diplomat.") But this piece of evidence cannot be accepted uncritically. It comes from a memorandum that Hoyos wrote after the war, and Fritz Fellner, who discovered and analyzed the document, situates it in the context of post-1914 attempts by Austria and Germany to blame each other for precipitating the conflict. Moreover, if Zimmermann had actually said something of this sort at the time, one would expect this very important fact to have been reported to the highest authorities in Vienna, and to have been reflected in at least some other sources, but there is no evidence that it was. Finally, it is simply not plausible that if Fischer's general theory is correct, and Zimmermann in particular really wanted to bring on a European war, that he would have revealed this calculation to the Austrians. This would

stood there was a certain chance that Russia and France would come in.[26] Its goal, in fact, was to reduce this chance to a minimum by adopting a forceful policy: "the more determined Austria shows herself, the more energetically we support her, so much the more quiet will Russia remain."[27]

This quotation is from a letter that the German foreign secretary, Gottlieb von Jagow, sent to Prince Lichnowsky, the German ambassador in London, laying out the basic thinking underlying German policy in the crisis. Fischer himself says that this document sums up Germany's attitude "in a nutshell."[28] In it Jagow took localization seriously and viewed it as a real possibility: "I still hope and believe, even today, that the conflict can be localised." The basis for Jagow's hope—and in this he was by no means atypical—was his conviction that Russia was not ready for war in 1914, and that she would be much better prepared to fight a few years later. Fischer, however, turns this point on its head: Jagow's argument that war with Russia could be avoided in 1914 is, through the use of some creative paraphrasing, transformed into an argument for provoking a war with Russia before she became too strong.[29]

The German government thought until very late in the crisis that Austria might be able to have her war with Serbia without having to face Russia as well. Indeed, the whole point of pressing Austria to act quickly

---

run the risk of frightening them off, and according to the Fischer school, the Germans were quite worried as it was that Austria was too prone to hesitate. For all these reasons, the whole story has to be taken with a grain of salt. Fritz Fellner, "Die Mission Hoyos," in W. Alff, ed., *Deutschlands Sonderung von Europa 1862–1945* (Frankfurt, 1984), pp. 292–96 and n. 32; Hartmut Pogge von Strandmann, "Germany and the Coming of War," in R.J.W. Evans and H. P. von Strandmann, eds., *The Coming of the First World War* (Oxford, 1988), p. 115, and Fritz Fischer, "The Miscalculation of English Neutrality: An Aspect of German Foreign Policy on the Eve of World War I," p. 371, in Solomon Wank et al., *The Mirror of History: Essays in Honor of Fritz Fellner* (Santa Barbara, 1988).

[26] Fischer, *Germany's Aims*, pp. 63–64.

[27] Jagow to Lichnowsky, July 18, 1914, in Geiss, *July 1914*, p. 123. For the original text, see Karl Kautsky, comp., *Die deutschen Dokumente zum Kriegsausbruch*, 4 vols. in 2 (Charlottenburg, 1919), doc. 72, translated into English as *Outbreak of the World War: German Documents Collected by Karl Kautsky* (New York, 1924).

[28] Fischer, *Germany's Aims*, p. 60.

[29] "The struggle between Teuton and Slav," he paraphrases Jagow as saying, "was bound to come . . . which being so, the present was the best moment for Germany, for 'in a few years Russia . . . will be ready.' " Fischer, *Germany's Aims*, p. 59. But in the original text, there is no reference to a "struggle between Teuton and Slav," let alone to its inevitability. All Jagow did was comment that in Russia "the feeling of the Slavic element is becoming more and more hostile to Germany." Geiss, *July 1914*, pp. 122–24. Nor is this an artifact of mistranslation. For the German originals: Fritz Fischer, *Griff nach der Weltmacht: Die Kriegszielpolitik des kaiserlichen Deutschland 1914/18*, 3d ed. (Düsseldorf, 1964), pp. 69–70; Kautsky, *Deutschen Dokumente*, vol. 1, no. 72.

was to minimize the risk of third power intervention.[30] The strategy of "localization" may not have worked, but it was not a sham. So the indirect argument, which is based on the contention that the German government knew from the very outset that localization was impossible, also fails.

If, however, there is little basis for the extreme Fischer view that Germany set out deliberately to provoke a war with Russia and France, this does not mean that more moderate versions of the thesis do not capture the essence of what was going on. Germany, for example, may not have wanted a European war in 1914, but she might have been prepared to accept one if Austria felt she could not compromise on the Serbian question. Such an attitude, in turn, might have been strongly influenced by the idea that if war broke out that year, this would not be the worst thing that could happen: Germany could then still fight such a war with some hope of success, whereas in a few years this would no longer be possible.

One can, in fact, imagine a spectrum of possible interpretations of the July Crisis:

  1. The extreme Fischerite view that Germany was deliberately trying to bring about war with Russia and France.

  2. A more moderate view that still emphasizes volition. Maybe no one wanted war. But the Germans and Austrians were intent on crushing Serbia, even if this meant a European conflagration, and Russia, supported by France, was determined to prevent this, regardless of the consequences. The war, in this case, would be the product of a simple political conflict. If one assumes that Germany and Austria took an extreme and uncompromising position with the full knowledge that this policy would probably lead to war with Russia and France, and if one assumes further that such an attitude was rooted in a deep-seated sense that maybe it would not be so bad if war broke out in 1914, then this view merges into the more moderate versions of the Fischer interpretation.

  3. An approach that emphasizes non-volitional factors. Here the war is not seen as the product of a simple clash of wills. What happened during the crisis itself is viewed as very important. This interpretation stresses the role of miscalculation, misperception, and misunderstanding, and also emphasizes the sheer dynamics of the crisis situation, the way a developing crisis tends to take on a life of its own. Each side was drawn in deeper and deeper; as the stakes rose, it became increasingly difficult for either side to draw back.

[30] See, for example, Szögyény to Berchtold, July 25, 1914, in Geiss, *July Crisis*, pp. 200–201. See also the extracts from the diary of General von Plessen, the Kaiser's military adjutant, in the editor's introduction to August Bach, *Deutsche Gesandtschaftsberichte zum Kriegsausbruch 1914* (Berlin, 1937), summarized in G. P. Gooch, *Recent Revelations of European Diplomacy* (London, 1940), p. 5.

The result is that the different parties to the conflict may have ended up taking positions that none of them would have taken if they had been able at the outset to see how things were going to develop.

4. Finally, the "inadvertent war" interpretation, which focuses on one special set of non-volitional factors, those that relate to the nature of the military system that was in place in 1914. The rigidity of the war plans, the heavy emphasis on offense, and the pressure to mobilize first, are all viewed as playing an important role in bringing on the war. The assumption is that if it had not been for factors of this sort, an armed conflict might well have been avoided.

My own view falls about midway between (2) and (3). In general, historians of the war origins question today attribute greater weight to the factor of intentionality than they did in the past. This has partly been the result of new evidence that has come to light on international politics, and especially on German foreign policy, in the pre-1914 period.[31] But it is also a product of a new way of thinking about the problem, and here Fischer certainly played a leading role. The attitudes of different elements in German society can be studied; knowing the structure of power within that country, inferences can be drawn about how much weight those views probably carried. There was certainly a good deal of aggressiveness in German political culture before 1914; even the preventive war strategy had considerable support within Germany, especially in military circles. It is reasonable to assume that all this had some impact on the way events in July 1914 ran their course.

The point, however, cannot be taken too far. Bellicose rhetoric may have been common in Germany before 1914, and the emperor himself often expressed extreme views. But this does not in itself mean that the political leadership during the crisis pursued an aggressive policy on the Serbian question with its eyes open, fully aware that this was likely to lead to a European war which could be accepted "with equanimity." If the chancellor, Bethmann Hollweg, and the other key German policymakers had been able to see in early July that their policy would lead Germany into a world war, or even into a great continental war, it is hard to believe that events would have unfolded more or less as they did. On the other hand, it is also clear that the German leadership had not rejected the "preventive war" arguments out of hand. Bethmann in particular

---

[31] On Germany, see especially Paul Kennedy, *The Rise of the Anglo-German Antagonism, 1860–1914* (London, 1980); Peter Winzen, *Bülows Weltmachtkonzept* (Boppard a. R., 1977). See also David Kaiser, "Germany and the Origins of the First World War," *Journal of Modern History*, vol. 55 (September 1983). On Austria, see Williamson, "Vienna and July 1914," and on Russia, see D.C.B. Lieven, *Russia and the Origins of the First World War* (New York, 1983), chap. 5, esp. pp. 141–43.

thought that these arguments had a certain force, and recognized that eventually he might have to take the plunge.[32] But the choice was difficult and could be put off until it became inescapable. A young man like his assistant Kurt Riezler might be drawn to war, attracted, he thought, by the "lure of the uncertain." For Bethmann himself, however, Riezler wrote in mid-July, a decision for war was a "leap into the dark." He might someday have to choose war. But such a decision would be his most difficult responsibility.[33]

There is no need, however, to resolve the war origins question here. It is sufficient to note that a whole range of interpretations is possible, and that therefore one does not have to take a particularly dark view of German intentions in 1914 in order to question the "inadvertent war" theory.

THE RIGIDITY OF MILITARY PLANS

The argument that the German government consciously and systematically engineered a European war in 1914 is quite weak. If the war, however, cannot be attributed simply to German aggression, it does not automatically follow from this that it came about because statesmen "lost control" of events, and were overwhelmed by forces of a military nature. A positive argument has to be made, and indeed the "inadvertent war" theory rests on a series of claims which purport to lay out what those forces are—that is, what these mechanisms were that led to a war that otherwise might well have been avoided. To test the theory, these claims therefore need to be examined systematically.

The first of these arguments focuses on the nature of military planning in the period before 1914. It is often alleged that the "inflexibility" of operational thinking and the "rigidity" of war and mobilization plans played a very important role in bringing on the war.[34] The war plans

[32] See, for example, the sources cited in Stephen Van Evera, "The Cult of the Offensive and the Origins of the First World War," *International Security*, vol. 9, no. 1 (Summer 1984), pp. 80–81.

[33] Riezler diary entry for July 14, 1914, K. D. Erdmann, ed., *Kurt Riezler: Tagebücher, Aufsätze, Dokumente* (Göttingen, 1972), p. 185.

[34] See, for example: Bernard Brodie, "Unlimited Weapons and Limited War," *The Reporter*, November 18, 1954, p. 21; Howard, "Lest We Forget," p. 65; Gordon Craig, *The Politics of the Prussian Army* (New York, 1964), p. 295. For the most influential account: Barbara Tuchman, *The Guns of August* (New York, 1962), esp. pp. 72, 79, 169. These are, of course, all old, and—from the point of view of many contemporary historians—outdated sources. But they played an important role in shaping beliefs about the meaning of the July crisis in what remain the classic works in the strategic studies literature, and are still frequently cited in that literature. Since the present aim is not simply to report contemporary

themselves, it is said, had a momentum of their own which statesmen were in the end powerless to resist.

In support of this claim, one story is told over and over again. At the very last minute, on August 1, with the storm in its full fury about to break, the German government was told by its ambassador in London that Britain might remain neutral, and might even guarantee French neutrality, if Germany did not attack France and conducted the war only in the east. The emperor was jubilant and wanted to take the British up on this offer and march only against Russia. But General Helmuth von Moltke, the chief of the general staff, explained that Germany had only one war plan—what has come to be called the "Schlieffen Plan" after its architect, General Alfred von Schlieffen, head of the general staff from 1891 to 1905—and this provided only for a massive initial attack on France to be followed after France's defeat by a campaign against Russia. It was too late now, he said, to change that strategy; the plan would have to be carried out. The chancellor and the emperor, Gordon Craig writes— and this is characteristic of the way this story appears in many accounts— "had no answer for this and gave way."[35] It soon turned out that British views had been misunderstood, but Bernard Brodie's comment on the affair is typical of the way this story is interpreted: "The falsity of the initial report saved that particular episode from being utterly grotesque; but the whole situation of which it formed a part reveals a rigidity and a habit of pleading 'military necessity' that made it impossible after a certain point to prevent a war which no one wanted and which was to prove infinitely disastrous to all the nations concerned."[36]

This is certainly a wonderful story. The only problem with it is that it happens to be wrong on the most important point. On the issue of whether the attack on France had to proceed as planned, it was the Kaiser and not Moltke who won. This should have been clear from the most important source on the incident, Moltke's memoirs, written in November 1914 and published posthumously in 1922; Moltke's account is confirmed by a number of other sources, extracts from which appear in the sections on the episode in Albertini's book.[37] It is true that there was a

---

historical opinion, but rather to examine certain traditional views, these older works will be taken seriously here—not because of their intrinsic merit, but simply because they provided the basis for what are still strongly held beliefs about the coming of the war, beliefs which have an important bearing on how the fundamental problem of war and peace is approached today.

[35] Craig, *Politics of the Prussian Army*, p. 294. See also Fischer, *Germany's Aims*, p. 86; Barry Posen (citing Craig), "Inadvertent Nuclear War? Escalation and NATO's Northern Flank," *International Security*, vol. 7, no. 2 (Fall 1982), p. 32; Brodie, "Unlimited Weapons and Limited War," p. 21.

[36] Brodie, "Unlimited Weapons and Limited War," p. 21.

[37] Helmuth von Moltke, *Erinnerungen—Briefe—Dokumente, 1877–1916* (Stuttgart,

violent argument on August 1 between Moltke and the political leadership about whether to accept what appeared to be the British proposal.
Although Moltke succeeded in convincing the emperor that for technical
reasons the concentration in the west would have to "be carried out as
planned," and that only after it was completed could troops be transferred to the east, a basic decision was made to accept the "offer." "In the
course of this scene," Moltke wrote, "I nearly fell into despair." Bethmann then pointed out how important it was, in connection with this
British proposal, that the plan for the occupation of neutral Luxemburg
be suspended. "As I stood there the Kaiser, without asking me," Moltke
went on, "turned to the aide-de-camp on duty and commanded him to
telegraph immediate instructions to the 16th Division at Trier not to
march into Luxemburg. I thought my heart would break." Moltke again
pleaded that the very complicated mobilization plan, "which has to be
worked out down to the smallest details," could not be changed without
disastrous results. It was essential, he said, for Germany to secure control
over the Luxemburg railroads. "I was snubbed with the remark that I
should use other railroads instead. The order must stand. Therewith I was
dismissed. It is impossible to describe the state of mind in which I returned home. I was absolutely broken and shed tears of despair."[38]

This story is of interest not only in itself, but also because it bears on
the general issue of the relationship between strategy and policy in prewar Europe. It is commonly argued that at least in Germany, and perhaps

---

1922); extracts appeared in translation in *Living Age*, January 20, 1923, pp. 131–34. Albertini, *Origins*, vol. 3, pp. 171–81, 380–85. See also Harry Young, "The Misunderstanding of August 1, 1914," *Journal of Modern History*, vol. 48, no. 4 (December 1976), pp.
644–65.

[38] Quoted in Albertini, *Origins*, vol. 3, pp. 172–76. It is sometimes argued that despite
the Kaiser's order, the Luxemburg frontier was violated, and that this shows that the plans
had a momentum of their own, which the political leadership was unable to control. In fact,
an infantry company had moved into Luxemburg before the Kaiser's order had been received, but a little later a second detachment arrived and ordered it out (in accordance, one
assumes, with the Kaiser's instructions). This episode thus scarcely proves that central control over military operations had been lost. The story has been clear since the publication of
the Kautsky documents in 1919, the source Tuchman relies on for her accurate account in
Guns of August, p. 82. Note also the story about the revocation of the Russian general
mobilization order by the Tsar after he had agreed to it the first time on July 29. According
to one account, when the Chief of Staff told him "that it was not possible to stop mobilization, Nicholas had replied: 'Stop it all the same,' " and of course this order was respected.
Albertini, *Origins*, vol. 2, p. 560. See also the excellent analysis and refutation of Conrad's
claim that technical military requirements prevented him from adjusting his strategy to the
new situation created by Russian mobilization in N. Stone, "Moltke and Conrad: Relations
between the Austro-Hungarian and German General Staffs, 1909–1914," in Paul Kennedy,
ed., *The War Plans of the Great Powers, 1880–1914* (London, 1979), pp. 235–41; see also
Stone's chapter on Austria-Hungary in Ernest May, ed., *Knowing One's Enemies: Intelligence Assessment before the Two World Wars* (Princeton, 1984).

in Europe as a whole, there was an almost hermetic separation between military and political concerns. The war plans had been based mainly on technical military considerations; political considerations had been essentially ignored. The plans could not be adjusted to changing political conditions. Governments, on the other hand, had not been able to adjust their foreign policies to these immutable strategic realities, because the military authorities had kept the political leadership in the dark: the civilians were not familiar with the plans, and were thus overwhelmed during the crisis by military imperatives that they had not been able to anticipate.[39]

Had the plans been worked out essentially on the basis of technical military considerations—that is, had political considerations been largely ignored? Germany is held up as the principal case in point: the Schlieffen Plan, according to Gerhard Ritter, was rooted not "in political considerations, but exclusively in military-technical ones."[40] There is, however, a certain basis for skepticism on this issue. The German military leadership was not sealed off from its political counterpart; Schlieffen and Friedrich von Holstein, the leading figure at the Foreign Office in Schlieffen's day, were on particularly intimate terms.[41] The military leadership, as Ritter himself shows, had strong political convictions. The elder Moltke, chief of staff during the Bismarckian period, had, according to Gerhard Ritter, been very much against "territorial conquests in Russia or anywhere else." It is hard to believe that such a view was unrelated to the very conservative military strategy he had opted for.[42] The opposition of his nephew, the younger Moltke, on August 1, 1914, to any change in the German war plan, was based not just on narrow, military considerations, but on his skepticism that France would really keep out of a Russo-German war—that is, on what turned out to be a perfectly realistic *political* judgment.[43]

As for Schlieffen himself, he clearly had strong political beliefs. In

[39] See, for example, Craig, *Politics of the Prussian Army*, p. 295; Howard, "Lest We Forget," p. 65; Albertini, *Origins*, vol. 2, pp. 479–83, 579; and, for a more contemporary example, Richard Ned Lebow, "The Soviet Offensive in Europe: The Schlieffen Plan Revisited?" *International Security* (Spring 1985), p. 69. Some other examples are cited and then criticized in L.C.F. Turner, "The Role of the General Staffs in July 1914," *Australian Journal of Politics and History*, vol. 11, no. 3 (December 1965).

[40] Gerhard Ritter, *The Schlieffen Plan: Critique of a Myth* (London, 1958), p. 97. Note also Fischer's comment on the plan to violate the neutrality of the Low Countries: "The military technician Schlieffen had taken no account of the political implications of such violations of neutrality and it was not really for him to do so." *War of Illusions*, p. 391.

[41] Norman Rich, *Friedrich von Holstein: Politics and Diplomacy in the Era of Bismarck and William II*, vol. 2 (Cambridge, Mass., 1965), p. 698.

[42] Ritter, *Schlieffen Plan*, p. 18.

[43] See the extracts from Moltke's memoir quoted in Albertini, *Origins*, vol. 3, pp. 173–74. On these issues in general, see M. Messerschmidt, *Militär und Politik in der Bismarckzeit und in Wilhelminischen Deutschland* (Darmstadt, 1975).

1905, for example, after Russia's defeat by Japan, he evidently favored a preventive war against France: "We are surrounded by an enormous coalition, we are in the same position as Frederick the Great before the Seven Years War. Now we can escape from the noose. The whole of Russia's west is stripped of troops, it will be years before Russia can take action; now we can settle the account with our bitterest and most dangerous enemy, France, and would be fully justified in doing so." Ritter's comment on this quotation is rather defensive: "Well, why should Schlieffen not have talked on such lines to a friend? It would almost be surprising if he had not entertained such sentiments as a soldier; they are reported of other senior members of the officer corps too. But all this has nothing to do with a political action as Chief of the General Staff." Perhaps not: Schlieffen might never have formally proposed that Germany launch a preventive war. But the comment still reflects a way of looking at the world that may well have helped draw Schlieffen to the strategy of the knockout blow against France—that is, to a strategy that aimed at total victory in a European conflict.[44] Indeed, a new mood had emerged in Germany in the post-Bismarckian period: the nation as a whole was no longer a satiated continental power, and important elements in German society now wanted very much to transform Germany's position in the world. The military shared these aspirations, and it is safe to assume that the Schlieffen strategy was closely related to these new political attitudes.

The German government, moreover, certainly understood in general terms what the plans called for, and was in particular fully aware that Belgium would be invaded in the event of war. Arguments to the contrary, common in the older historical literature, are not supported by the evidence. Craig, for instance, writes that the German General Staff "did not see fit even to inform" the Foreign Office of the Schlieffen Plan "except in the most general and misleading terms."[45] The footnote appended to this very sentence, however, states that "there can be little doubt" that Chancellor Bülow and Holstein "knew of the invasion plan," and gives a reliable source to back this up.[46] Craig then comments simply that "it is less easy to determine how much Bethmann knew." But it is clear that Beth-

---

[44] From Hugo Rochs, *Schlieffen. Ein Lebens- und Charakterbild für das deutsche Volk*, 5th ed. (Berlin, 1940), p. 40, quoted in Fischer, *War of Illusions*, p. 55; Ritter, *Schlieffen Plan*, p. 106. For other countries, the argument that military planning was apolitical is weaker still. In France, for example, the army was interested in attacking Germany through Belgium, and even some of the political leaders were attracted to the idea of a preemptive invasion of that country, but they were all held back for fear of the British reaction. See S. R. Williamson, *The Politics of Grand Strategy* (Cambridge, Mass., 1969), pp. 210–18.

[45] Craig, *Politics of the Prussian Army*, p. 295.

[46] Ibid. Indeed, five pages earlier he had pointed out that Moltke had written to his Austrian counterpart Conrad describing Germany's basic military strategy for a European war, and that the emperor and Bülow had been informed of the contents of this letter. See also Schmitt, *Coming of the War*, vol. 1, pp. 15–16.

mann was familiar with the plan for the invasion of Belgium; and Jagow remarked in his unpublished memoirs that he had been informed of the German campaign plan when he became foreign secretary in January 1913. The basic Schlieffen strategy, in fact, had in 1900 been cleared first with Holstein and then with the chancellor at the time, Prince Hohenlohe. Soon even foreign governments knew in rough terms what Germany intended to do in the event of war; Schlieffen himself, after his retirement, published an article in which he took the invasion of Belgium as self-evident; and the Kaiser in effect even told the Belgian king that if war broke out, Germany would march through his country.[47]

The collaboration between military and political authorities was of course by no means perfect in Germany before 1914.[48] Military strategy was obviously not inspired by a Clausewitzian recognition that political concerns were fundamental.[49] But the divorce between military and political considerations was not total. To the degree that military strategy, however, was an independent element in the story, what difference did it actually make? Is it simply to be taken for granted, as a matter of principle, that rigid plans are a source of danger—that they were, almost by definition, an important cause of the war, and that more flexible military arrangements would have led to greater stability? Since Germany is by far the most important case—the Schlieffen Plan dominated the whole military situation in 1914—this issue turns on the question of the effect a more flexible German strategy would have had.

[47] On Bethmann: see Ritter, *Schlieffen Plan*, p. 94, and Fischer, *War of Illusions*, p. 168, citing a Bethmann note of December 21, 1912. On Jagow: Fischer, *War of Illusions*, p. 390. On these matters in general, see L.C.F. Turner, "The Significance of the Schlieffen Plan," *Australian Journal of Politics and History*, vol. 13, no. 1 (April 1967), pp. 53–55; and Ritter, *Schlieffen Plan*, pp. 91–95. On British knowledge, note especially the extract from Churchill's *The World Crisis*, cited on p. 53 of the Turner article. The French certainly knew about the German strategy well before the outbreak of the war; see Henry Contamine, *La Revanche, 1871–1914* (Paris, 1957), pp. 95–97; France, Ministère de la Guerre, Etat-Major de l'Armée, Service historique, *Les Armées françaises dans la Grande Guerre*, part 1, vol. 1 (Paris, 1936), p. 37; and finally Isvolsky to Sazonov, February 2, 1911, quoted in Friedrich Stieve, *Isvolsky and the World War* (New York, 1926), p. 51. Jan Karl Tanenbaum, "French Estimates of Germany's Operational War Plans," in May, *Knowing One's Enemies*, is the most detailed account. Schlieffen's article, "Der Krieg in der Gegenwart," *Deutsche Revue* (January 1909), created a sensation when it came out and even had diplomatic repercussions. See Ritter, *Schlieffen Plan*, p. 94n. One strongly suspects that the political leadership did not simply accept the need for an invasion of Belgium without asking why it was so necessary, and that in this way became familiar with the basic thinking underlying German military strategy at the time. The military leadership, for its part, had an interest in explaining the strategy so that it could convince the government to provide the funds needed if the plan was to be implemented with some prospect of success; budgetary support was far from automatic.

[48] See n. 155 below.

[49] This point has been made by many writers. See, for example, Ritter, *Schlieffen Plan*, p. 96; Kennedy, *War Plans*, p. 17; Craig, *Politics*, p. 277.

Suppose Germany had been able, if she chose, to implement the strategy of the elder Moltke—that is, to stay on the defensive in the west and concentrate her attack on Russia. The basic effect would have been to improve Germany's general position.[50] If Germany had simply secured her defenses in the west and refrained from invading Belgium, France and Britain would have been much less able to intervene on Russia's behalf in a militarily effective way—if indeed they, or at least Britain, ended up intervening at all. The great bulk of German power could in that case be thrown against Russia. In such circumstances, why should Germany have been less likely to risk war? But if a more flexible German strategy would in principle have strengthened Germany's position, then this can only mean that the rigid Schlieffen strategy was a source of weakness and thus in theory should have served as a brake on German policy. If it failed to do so, this would not be because of the rigidity of the plan, but because the political judgment had been made that in spite of this weakness, Germany should still plunge ahead.

There is also the case of Russia to consider. The rigidity of Russian military planning is sometimes viewed as one of the causes of the disaster. "The Russians," Paul Kennedy writes, "possibly possessed the most inflexible plan of all, and their inability to mobilise separately against Austria-Hungary proved to be one of the most fateful errors of the July crisis."[51] But if an adequate partial mobilization plan had existed, why would events have taken a fundamentally different course? As will be seen, it was the fear that general war was imminent that led the Russians to order general mobilization. Even if a partial mobilization against Austria could have been implemented without difficulty, the Russians would still have felt the same pressure to escalate to full mobilization. Albertini, incidentally, goes a bit further and argues in effect that the Russian plans were if anything insufficiently rigid: the world would have been better off if it had been abundantly clear from the outset that a partial mobilization was impossible, so that it would never have been ordered in the first place.[52] The ruling out of such limited options could have created a kind of "firebreak" that might have helped keep the conflict from escalating.

The war plans certainly determined how the initial campaigns would be fought. But it is hard to see how the inflexibility of these strategies was in any real sense a major cause of the war—that is, why war would have

[50] This is in fact an old argument. See, for example, Winston Churchill, *The World Crisis, 1911–1914* (New York, 1924), pp. 281–82. Note also Jack Snyder, *The Ideology of the Offensive: Military Decision Making and the Disasters of 1914* (Ithaca, N.Y., 1984), pp. 141–45, which brings out the irrationality of Schlieffen's preference for the west-oriented strategy.

[51] Kennedy, *War Plans*, p. 4.

[52] Albertini, *Origins*, vol. 2, p. 294.

been less likely if the European powers had created more military options for themselves.

THE "CULT OF THE OFFENSIVE"

In Europe before 1914, there was a great bias in favor of offensive as opposed to defensive military operations; the attack was glorified, and highly offensive strategies were assumed to be the best way to conduct a war. This "cult of the offensive," it has been argued in recent years, was a root cause of a wide range of dangers that played an important role in bringing on the war.[53]

The point of departure for this body of literature was Robert Jervis's seminal article, "Cooperation under the Security Dilemma," which appeared in *World Politics* in 1978.[54] The term "security dilemma" refers to the idea that in trying to increase their own security, states do things, such as building up their own military power, which tend to diminish the security of other states. What makes this a "dilemma" is the assumption that this is an unintended or even undesired consequence: states might prefer that other powers not feel threatened, and yet, in order to provide for their own safety, they are virtually forced to take measures which will alarm these other states, who will then respond in kind. This sense of mutual threat introduces an element of tension and therefore instability into the situation: the tension goes well beyond what would be warranted by genuine political conflict. Hence the link with the "inadvertent war" argument: war can come in large part because states are, in Jervis's phrase, "trapped by the dynamics of the situation." Because of the security dilemma, the range of choice in certain circumstances may be quite narrow, and unless statesmen are exceptionally able, states might easily be drawn into conflict with each other.

The offense-defense balance, according to this school, is the basic factor that determines how pernicious the security dilemma is.[55] When the

[53] Van Evera, "Cult of the Offensive," esp. pp. 58, 105; see also Jack Snyder, "Civil-Military Relations and the Cult of the Offensive, 1914 and 1984," *International Security*, vol. 9, no. 1 (Summer 1984). Note also Steven Miller's introduction to the issue of *International Security* in which these articles appeared: "The Great War and the Nuclear Age: Sarajevo after Seventy Years," pp. 3–5. The whole issue was republished as Steven Miller, ed., *Military Strategy and the Origins of the First World War* (Princeton, 1985). Note also in this context the section "Deterrence and World War II; Spiral Model and World War I," in Robert Jervis, *Perception and Misperception in International Politics* (Princeton, 1976), pp. 94ff.

[54] Robert Jervis, "Cooperation under the Security Dilemma," *World Politics*, vol. 30, no. 2 (January 1978).

[55] Jervis, "Security Dilemma," p. 186ff; Van Evera, "Cult of the Offensive," pp. 63–66.

balance shifts in favor of the offense, expansion is seen as both easier and more necessary (to deprive an adversary of resources that might serve as the basis for offensive military action against one's own homeland); pre-emption also becomes both more attractive and more necessary. States, moreover, become increasingly sensitive to trends in the military balance, and might even come to think in terms of preventive war. In such a world, even status quo powers are forced to act like aggressors. It follows from this point of view that the pre-1914 "cult of the offensive" could be expected to have had important destabilizing consequences. Indeed, certain claims about the coming of the First World War play a central role in providing a degree of empirical support for this general theory.

Stephen Van Evera in his influential article, "The Cult of the Offensive and the Origins of the First World War," identifies a series of dangers "which helped pull the world to war," and discusses how those dangers were linked to the emphasis on offensive military action.[56] Germany's expansionist policy, first of all, was rooted in a belief that the offense had the advantage. It was this, he says, that "made empire appear both feasible and necessary."[57] The "cult of the offensive," moreover, "magnified the incentive to preempt": the first strike or first mobilization advantage is more valuable in a world where small shifts in force ratios between states lead to major shifts "in their relative capacity to conquer territory." Furthermore, it was this belief in offense-dominance that caused people to be so concerned with impending shifts in the military balance: Germany's "window of opportunity" opened wider, and the "window of vulnerability" which German statesmen saw opening a few years down the road was taken more seriously than it would have been if German leaders had understood that it was the defense that really had the upper hand in land warfare at the time.[58] Indeed, the "cult" was based on an extraordinary misconception: if the military realities of 1914 had been understood, if the actual power of the defense had been recognized, the whole system would have been much more stable, and "in all likelihood, the Austro-Serbian conflict would have been a minor and soon-forgotten disturbance on the periphery of European politics."[59]

What is to be made of these arguments? That a "cult" existed, in the sense of a set of military practices considerably more extreme than what the objective situation truly warranted, seems to me beyond question. Scott Sagan, in criticizing the "cult of the offensive" theorists, argued that it was the political need to support allies and relieve military pressure on them that led states to adopt offensive strategies. Alliance considerations

---

[56] Van Evera, "Cult of the Offensive"; the quotation is on p. 105.
[57] Ibid., p. 68.
[58] Ibid., pp. 64–65, 79ff.
[59] Ibid., p. 105. See also Jervis, "Security Dilemma," pp. 191, 214.

were of course important, but these strategies went well beyond what was needed for such purposes. Sagan, for example, in arguing that the French opted for a more offensive strategy because they were "haunted" by the prospect that if they stayed on the defensive, Germany would be able to defeat her opponents piecemeal, quotes General Joffre, the French chief of staff, as saying that the French increased the emphasis they placed on offensive action in part because they were afraid the Germans might return to the strategy of the elder Moltke for a campaign focusing on the east. It might have been necessary, of course, for France to prepare for offensive action against Germany as soon as there were indications that Germany was returning to the old Moltke strategy. But until she showed signs of doing so, a defensive strategy would have made more sense for the first phase of the war, since, as Sagan himself points out, "it has been generally recognized since Clausewitz that defense is almost always 'easier' in land warfare because of the advantages of cover and the capability to choose and prepare terrain and fortify positions."[60] Joffre's preference for offense at the beginning of the war, before France's allies had a chance to fully generate their own forces, can therefore scarcely be rationalized in terms of alliance considerations.[61]

It is one thing, however, to recognize the existence of a certain degree of irrationality in this area. It is quite another to show that it was in major ways responsible for the coming of the war. How well do the specific arguments about the relationship between the "cult" and the outbreak of the war hold up in the light of the evidence? The weakest claim relates to

[60] Scott Sagan, "1914 Revisited: Allies, Offense and Instability," *International Security*, vol. 11, no. 2 (Fall 1986), pp. 161, 164. See also the correspondence between Sagan and Snyder in *International Security*, vol. 11, no. 3 (Winter 1986–87).

[61] The German emphasis on offense reflects a similar degree of irrationality. In his famous memorandum of December 1905, Schlieffen had outlined a strategy for a one-front war, but even this he thought was "an enterprise for which we are too weak." Over the next decade, Russia recovered her strength, and it became clear that Britain would probably intervene with a sizable expeditionary force. Schlieffen himself, in his writings after his retirement, ignored these factors; he suppressed his own skepticism about the "theory of a decisive battle" in the west; this, he had said in 1905, was "not the way of wars today." One answer was to increase the size of the force the Germans would be able to deploy when the war began; but although there were significant increases in the army budget before the war, the measures taken were by no means adequate to deal with the problem. A massive expansion was resisted in large part because it would have altered the social composition of the officer corps and thus might in the long run have reduced the power of the old Junker elite. But the plans were never adequately adjusted to all these realities. See Ritter, *Schlieffen Plan*, pp. 53, 66–67, 73–74, 77, and Snyder, *Ideology of the Offensive*, pp. 139, 141–45, 153. For a similar point about Austria, see Samuel Williamson, "Military Dimensions of Habsburg-Romanov Relations during the Era of the Balkan Wars," in Bela Kiraly and Dimitrije Djordjevic, eds., *East Central European Society and the Balkan Wars* (Boulder, Colo., 1987), esp. pp. 330–31.

the alleged connection between German expansionism and the belief in offense-dominance. When one looks at such a broadly based phenomenon as German imperialism, it is difficult to see a technical judgment about the balance between offense and defense on the battlefield as a major driving force. Indeed, if such a judgment were the key factor, and physical security against land attack were the fundamental goal, one would expect German expansionism to have focused on adjoining areas in Europe. Instead, the interests Germany most actively pursued lay in Africa and the Near East. In an offense-dominant world, where security is (in Van Evera's term) a "scarce asset,"[62] one would expect a continental power like Germany to concentrate on building a strong land army; instead, resources were diverted into the construction of a great navy. The purpose of the navy was to help Germany acquire an empire. But even if she succeeded in acquiring colonies, this would hardly improve her security position: as the most clear-sighted Entente statesmen occasionally pointed out, German colonies would be hostage to Anglo-French naval power.[63] Whether this policy was successful or not, the whole effort was bound to have an unfavorable effect on Germany's security position: the policy in fact drove Britain onto the side of her enemies, thereby strengthening France and Russia and thus enabling them to pursue more aggressive anti-German policies, first in Morocco and then, with the formation of the Balkan League in 1912, in southeastern Europe as well.[64] Germany's position had been weakened by the policy; but she continued to pursue it, even when it became clear that she was paying such a price, and indeed was taking on Britain, France, and Russia all at the same time. This was hardly a world in which for Germany "security was scarce." Germany was not driven to expand because, in Jervis's phrase, "there seemed no way for [her] merely to retain and safeguard her existing position."[65] If that had been her basic goal, her foreign policy problems would have been quite manageable. As Kiderlen-Wächter, then foreign secretary, pointed out in 1910 in a passage quoted by Van Evera, the British and the French were too committed to peace to ever cause a war, so if Germany did not provoke one, "no one else certainly will do so."[66]

The "cult of the offensive" theorists are on firmer ground when they

[62] Van Evera, "Cult of the Offensive," p. 64.

[63] See especially the remarkable analysis by Jules Cambon, French ambassador in Berlin: Cambon to Pichon, July 8, 1913, *Documents diplomatiques français*, series 3, vol. 7, no. 317, esp. p. 352.

[64] When Poincaré, then prime minister, was shown the text of the basic treaty setting up the Balkan League, he remarked that "it contained the seeds not only of a war against Turkey, but of a war against Austria as well." Quoted in Pierre Renouvin, *La Crise européenne et la première guerre mondiale* (Paris, 1962), p. 173.

[65] Jervis, "Security Dilemma," p. 191.

[66] Quoted in Van Evera, "Cult of the Offensive," p. 69.

turn to factors more purely military in nature. The various war plans, and above all the Schlieffen Plan, placed an extraordinary emphasis on offensive military operations: if a war was to be fought, total victory had to be the goal, and the only way to achieve it was by overwhelming the enemy as quickly as possible, and destroying his power to resist. But while these plans certainly reflected a belief that a heavy emphasis on offense was *necessary*, they did not reflect a belief that offense would be *easy*. The point of departure for the German strategy was Schlieffen's realization that French defenses on the border with Germany made a direct attack out of the question, and indeed the chief of staff was fully aware of the defender's advantages: "We shall find the experience of all earlier conquerors confirmed, that a war of aggression calls for much strength, and also consumes much, that this strength dwindles constantly as the defender's increases, and all this particularly in a country with fortresses."[67]

A strategy of this sort led to a certain interest in preemption. A swift seizure of the Belgian city of Liège became an important part of the German war plan in 1911. The Liège fortress system, Moltke wrote, had to be neutralized at the very beginning of the war: "everything depends on meticulous preparation and surprise."[68] It is not altogether clear, however, what role such considerations played in bringing on the war; the "cult of the offensive" theorists are in any case quite moderate in their claims about preemption.[69] But whatever interest there was in preemption in 1914, it is important to note that it was not rooted in a belief that conquest would be easy. It was because conquest was viewed as so difficult that small advantages, which if seized might just swing the balance, could count for so much on the margin—that is, as long as one was absolutely committed to total victory. Nor is it clear that preemption would have been less likely if the Germans had not opted for the Schlieffen strategy. If they *had* been able to see what the war was going to be like, and had chosen to stay on the defensive in the west and fought the war mainly in the east—that is, the more rational strategy that Van Evera assumes they would have adopted if no "cult of the offensive" had existed[70]—the slowness of the Russian mobilization might still have given the Germans a great incentive to act quickly and attack the Russians before their preparations were complete. Indeed, the elder Moltke's final plan, worked out

---

[67] Quoted in Turner, "Schlieffen Plan," p. 50.

[68] Moltke memorandum, in Ritter, *Schlieffen Plan*, p. 166. On the Liège issue, see n. 161 below.

[69] Van Evera, "Cult of the Offensive," p. 79, says that the war was "in some modest measure preemptive." Snyder does not see preemption as a decisive factor for either Germany or Russia: "Civil-Military Relations," pp. 113–14.

[70] Van Evera, "Cult of the Offensive," p. 90.

in 1888, provided for "the encirclement of the main Russian force behind Warsaw and a surprise attack while it was deploying."[71]

Van Evera's strongest argument relates to "windows" and preventive war. In 1914, victory was still possible; but the balance was moving against Germany, and it is certainly true that many influential people thought that Germany should take advantage of what we would now call this "window of opportunity" before it closed and perhaps deliberately bring about a war.[72] The preventive war argument in its pure form was particularly strong in the army. The views of the political leadership were less extreme. From its point of view, given the way things were moving, there was a good chance that Germany would eventually find herself at war with the Entente; this was especially true if Russia was determined to tighten the noose around the Central Powers; if such a war was inevitable, it was better for Germany that it come sooner rather than later; and the test of its inevitability, the test of Russian intentions, was whether the Russians would now tolerate a tough Austrian policy against Serbia. A policy of annihilating Serbia as an independent factor in European politics was thus for Germany, as Naumann put it at the time, "the touchstone whether Russia meant war or not."[73]

This assessment of how the balance was shifting—this sense that Germany's "window of opportunity" was closing rapidly—was in turn rooted in the sort of strategy that Germany had adopted, the highly offense-oriented strategy embodied in the Schlieffen Plan. This plan depended on the existence of a tactical "window": Germany would be able to attack France with the great mass of her army because the slowness of Russian mobilization meant that Germany's eastern border would not

---

[71] Ritter, *Schlieffen Plan*, p. 20.

[72] On preventive war thinking in Germany before the war, see especially Walter Kloster, *Der deutsche Generalstab und der Präventivkriegsgedanke* (Stuttgart, 1932); Adolf Gasser, "Deutschlands Entschluss zum Präventivkrieg 1913/14," in Marc Sieber, ed., *Discordia concors: Festgabe für Edgar Bonjour*, vol. 1 (Basel, 1968); and Albrecht Moritz, *Das Problem des Präventivkrieges in der deutschen Politik während der ersten Marokkokrise* (Frankfurt, 1974).

[73] Geiss, *July 1914*, p. 66. Some of these considerations are reflected in other documents; see for example Szögyény to Berchtold, July 12, 1914, and Jagow to Lichnowsky, July 18, 1914, both in Geiss, *July 1914*, pp. 110, 123, and also Mérey's comments quoted in Albertini, vol. 2, p. 383. Note also an important letter from Count Hoyos describing his mission to Berlin at the beginning of the crisis (during which the famous "blank check" was issued). The Austrians wanted to know, Hoyos said, how the Germans felt about an Austrian move against Serbia, and in particular, "whether, from a political and a military point of view, it judged the moment as favorable." The chancellor and a top foreign office official replied that "if war should break out, we [that is, the Germans] think that it is better that it should happen now than in one or two years when the Entente will have become stronger." Hoyos to Mérey, July 20, 1917, *Revue d'histoire de la guerre mondiale*, vol. 10, no. 1 (January 1932), pp. 110–11.

have to be heavily defended during the initial phase of the war. But with the construction of Russian strategic railroads and other measures, this tactical "window" was disappearing—indeed, the central purpose of these measures was to close it[74]—and this meant that the Schlieffen Plan would soon become unworkable. In other words, the disappearance of the tactical window meant that Germany's strategic window was also closing.[75] With a more defensive strategy, the "preventive war" arguments would have carried much less weight.

This does not in itself mean, however, that "window" thinking was an important cause of the war. The reason is that these "window" arguments should have had opposite effects on the two sides: Germany's "window of opportunity" was the Entente's "window of vulnerability," and although Germany had an extra incentive to act, Russia and France had an extra incentive to be cautious and put off the conflict if they could. It seems in fact that Russian leaders understood the situation in these terms.[76] Why did the two effects not cancel each other out? If they did not neutralize each other, other factors must have intervened, in which case they, and not the "window" arguments, were the crucial factors as far as the war origins question is concerned. And certainly some of these factors were not military in nature—for example, the astonishing irrationality of the Russian leadership at the time, in the sense of its willingness to plunge into a venture that it knew was beyond Russia's strength.[77]

---

[74] This emphasis on the construction of strategic railroads thus reflects a basic understanding of the logic of the Schlieffen Plan by the French and Russian military leadership. The French were especially eager for the construction of these railroads, and made Russian cooperation in this area a condition for the issuance of new loans to Russia. This was thus not a subject that the military could keep to themselves; the civil authorities had to be brought in. Much of the story can be followed in *Documents diplomatiques français*, series 3, vols. 7–9; see also René Girault, *Emprunts russes et investissements français en Russie, 1887–1914* (Paris, 1973), pp. 561–68.

[75] For an exceptionally well informed discussion of this issue, see Norman Stone, *The Eastern Front 1914–1917* (New York, 1975), pp. 39–43.

[76] See, for example, I. V. Bestuzhev, "Russian Foreign Policy, February–June 1914," in Walter Laqueur and George Mosse, eds., *1914: The Coming of the First World War* (New York, 1966), p. 91, and also the testimony of General Yanushkevich, in 1914 the Chief of Staff, quoted in Albertini, *Origins*, vol. 2, p. 559.

[77] In 1909, Russia had given in during the Bosnian Crisis after General Roediger, the war minister, had stated that the army could not even wage a defensive war against Germany and Austria. But the war minister in 1914, Sukhomlinov, while admitting in private, as Albertini says, that "Russia was throwing herself unprepared into a venture beyond her strength," and even warning Sazonov through an intermediary that Russia was not fully prepared for war, was unwilling to come out openly and tell the Council of Ministers what the real situation was. The minister of the interior, Maklakov, when asked to sign the mobilization *ukaze*, spoke about how war would bring revolution; but "sitting at a table laden with ikons and religious lamps," crossed himself, saying "we cannot escape our fate," and

What difference then did the "cult of the offensive" make? If the military situation had been correctly understood, would matters have been all that different? One can scarcely argue that if the power of the defense had been understood correctly, the situation would have been more stable because instead of attacking, the armies would have simply "rushed for the trenches":[78] if the Russians had just entrenched themselves on their borders, they would have been writing off Serbia; but if they were willing to do that, what was the point of going to war in the first place? Moreover, if the Germans had opted for a more defensive strategy in the west and conducted their offensive operations mainly in the east, the effect would have been to strengthen the German position. France, in the event of such a war, might well have felt obliged to relieve pressure on her ally by throwing her armies against the German border. But this would have been a hopeless effort if the Germans had built modern fortifications in that area.[79] The political benefits to Germany of such a strategy—not having to invade Belgium, not appearing as the aggressor, an increased probability that Britain would remain neutral—were yet an additional source of strength. But the stronger Germany was, the more unyielding she could be in the dispute over southeastern Europe. Perhaps Russia, for opposite reasons, would in such a case have been more willing to sacrifice Serbia. But even if these two effects just canceled each other out, it is hard to see how an eastern strategy—that is, a strategy based on a better understanding of military realities—would have made war less likely in 1914.

To the extent that a belief in the power of the offense had in 1914 come to mean a belief that one's own side would prevail in war quickly and easily, the "cult" might well have been an important source of instability. It is clear that there is a certain psychological affinity between a strategy that stresses offensive action and a belief that such action would be successful. But the two ideas are not the same: a general judgment about how well the attacker will do on the battlefield is by no means equivalent to an assumption that one's own side is likely to win. Conquest cannot simultaneously be easy for both sides; in an offense-dominant world, one side will win relatively quickly, and the other side's defeat will be absolute. In such a world, the stronger side's greater hope of victory might be

---

then signed the document. Albertini, *Origins*, vol. 2, p. 546; Lieven, *Russia and the Origins of the First World War*, pp. 108–9, 115.

[78] As both Jervis and Van Evera argue: Jervis, "Security Dilemma," pp. 191, 214; Van Evera, "Cult of the Offensive," p. 105.

[79] The French border fortifications had convinced the Germans that frontal attack was no longer possible. Indeed, this realization was one of the great taproots of the Schlieffen strategy of outflanking the French forces by marching through Belgium. German fortifications on their side of the border would presumably have a similar effect. See Albertini, *Origins*, vol. 3, p. 243.

balanced—perhaps, in general, more than balanced—by the weaker side's greater fear of defeat. Even if the outcome of the war could objectively be rated a toss-up, the fear of total defeat might be expected for both sides to outweigh the hope of total victory; if so, the net impact would be to make the two sides more cautious than they would be if the risks were relatively limited. Indeed, one might argue—and Jervis at one point in fact does argue—that in a defense-dominant relationship where the risks *are* limited, statesmen might approach war in a much more cavalier way.[80] It is important to note in this connection, moreover, that political and military leaders in 1914 thought of a European war as a very serious undertaking. If a conflict broke out, the British foreign secretary, Sir Edward Grey, said, it would be "the most terrible war which Europe had ever seen"; "rivers of blood would flow," said the Russian foreign minister, Sazonov; and even Moltke spoke of the European states tearing "one another to pieces," and of a war which would "annihilate for decades to come the civilization of almost the whole of Europe."[81]

In short, the "cult of the offensive" theory, while highly suggestive and in some respects quite elegant analytically, does not really provide the key to the puzzle of how the First World War broke out. The world of 1914 was not a world whose natural equilibrium had been destroyed by an exaggerated belief in the importance of offensive action. The military plans themselves, while certainly highly offensive in terms of their basic orientation, did not generate the political conflict that had led to the war, nor did they preclude its peaceful resolution.

MOBILIZATION PLANS AND PREEMPTION

"World War I," says George Quester, "broke out as a spasm of pre-emptive mobilization schedules."[82] It was this system of interlocking mobilization plans, Paul Bracken writes, that "swamped the political process in 1914."[83] Statesmen tried to draw back on the eve of the war, according to Barbara Tuchman, "but the pull of military schedules dragged them

[80] Jervis, "Security Dilemma," p. 176. The relationship between Britain and Russia in the 19th century, a defense-dominant relationship if there ever was one, is an excellent example. See especially the extraordinary evidence on Disraeli's attitude toward war with Russia in 1877, presented in R. W. Seton-Watson, *Disraeli, Gladstone and the Eastern Question* (London, 1935), esp. pp. 217–18.
[81] Albertini, *Origins*, vol. 2, pp. 307, 410, 488. See also General Ludwig Beck, *Studien*, ed. Hans Speidel (Stuttgart, 1955), pp. 105–6, 150–51, and Snyder, *Ideology of the Offensive*, pp. 153–54.
[82] George Quester, *Deterrence Before Hiroshima* (New York, 1966), p. 17.
[83] Paul Bracken, *Command and Control*, p. 2.

forward."[84] A.J.P. Taylor agrees: in 1914, Schlieffen's "dead hand automatically pulled the trigger."[85] Arguments of this sort are extremely common and form the heart of the "inadvertent war" thesis. Given how important and how widespread they are, it is amazing how little critical analysis such arguments have received.[86] The goal of this section is to examine these claims in a more or less systematic way, and this examination will show, I think, just how weak this set of arguments is.

It is not that the conventional wisdom is wrong in assuming that there was a system of interlocking mobilization plans in 1914. A system of this sort certainly did exist, with the Schlieffen Plan as its linchpin. That strategy proposed to take advantage of the relative slowness of Russian mobilization: the idea was that Germany, by mobilizing rapidly and then attacking in the west with the great mass of her army, would be able to defeat France before having to face Russia. The Germans could not therefore allow a Russian general mobilization to run its course without ordering their own mobilization and in fact attacking France. Russian mobilization would lead to German mobilization, and under the German war plan mobilization meant war.

A mechanism of this sort clearly existed, but was it actually a *cause* of the war? It is important to think through what is implied by the claim that this mechanism of interlocking mobilization plans helped bring on the cataclysm. One can begin with a simple analogy. Suppose it takes me thirty minutes to get home when the traffic is light, but a full hour during the rush hour. I promise to be home by 6:00, but I choose to leave at 5:30 and arrive a half-hour late: "I'm sorry about the delay, but it's not my fault. It was because the traffic was so bad." The rush hour traffic, however, could hardly be said to be a *cause* of the delay, since I had chosen to leave at 5:30, knowing full well what the situation was. Knowledge of the situation had been factored into the original decision. On the other hand, if the heavy traffic had been caused by something that had not been anticipated—by an accident, for example—then it would make more sense to blame it for the delay.

Similarly, if in 1914 everyone understood the system and knew, for example, that a Russian general mobilization would lead to war, the existence of the system of interlocking mobilization plans could hardly be said in itself to have been a cause of war—assuming, that is, that the political authorities were free agents and that their hands had not been forced by military imperatives. Some people argue that the mobilization system was a "cause" of war because once it was set off the time for

[84] Tuchman, *Guns of August*, p. 72.
[85] A.J.P. Taylor, *Illustrated History of the First World War* (New York, 1964), p. 15.
[86] The best discussion is in Van Evera, "Cult of the Offensive," pp. 71–79.

negotiation was cut short. But if the working of the system was under-stood in advance, a decision for general mobilization was a decision for war; statesmen would in that case be opting for war with their eyes open. To argue that the system was a "cause" of the war would be like arguing that any military operation that marked the effective beginning of hostil-ities—the crossing of borders, for example, or an initial attack on enemy forces—was a real cause of an armed conflict, simply because it foreclosed the possibility of a negotiated settlement. Such operations are in no real sense a "cause" of war, because their implications are universally under-stood in advance. Similarly, assuming everyone understood how the sys-tem worked, the mobilization process could not be viewed as a cause of the war, but should instead be seen simply as its opening phase.

It follows, therefore, that for the inadvertent war theory to hold, it must be shown *either* that the implications of mobilization were not un-derstood, *or* that the political leadership was under such great pressure to act that it was not really free to hold back. The "inadvertent war" argu-ments in this area in fact fall into these two categories.

The first basic set of arguments focuses on the alleged failure of the political leaders to understand what the military plans actually meant. As a result, it is said, they made their moves and ordered their mobilizations light-heartedly, thinking that they were engaged in simple political ma-neuvering, seeking only to deter their adversaries. But once set loose, the forces they had unleashed could scarcely be controlled.[87] "The absence of all understanding of military matters on the part of the responsible states-men" is for Albertini a major cause of the war. "It was," he says, "the political leaders' ignorance of what mobilization implied and the dangers it involved which led them light-heartedly to take the step of mobilizing and thus unleash a European war."[88] The basic contention here is that the statesmen did not understand that general mobilization meant war. This claim will be examined in the next section. But it is also argued that the political leadership failed to understand that even a *partial* Russian mo-bilization, directed only against Austria, would have led to war "no less surely than general mobilization," and that this was also a major cause of the disaster.[89] So to test the claim that ignorance of crucial military reali-ties played an important role in bringing on the conflict, a second section will examine the argument that even a partial mobilization would have inevitably led to war.

[87] Taylor, *Illustrated History*, pp. 14–15; Howard, "Lest We Forget," p. 65; Lebow, *Nu-clear Crisis Management*, pp. 26, 109–12.

[88] Albertini, *Origins*, vol. 2, pp. 479–83, 579. L.C.F. Turner, in *Origins of the First World War* (New York, 1970), p. 99, follows Albertini on this point.

[89] Turner, *Origins*, pp. 92, 108; Albertini, *Origins*, vol. 2, pp. 392, 485n. (for the quote), 529–30, 541.

The other set of arguments focuses on the claim that the statesmen were not really free agents when the mobilization decisions were made. The basic argument here is that military considerations, and especially the pressure to move preemptively, came at the crucial moment to dominate policy. It is often taken for granted that the very existence of a military regime based on mass armies and mobilizations automatically created incentives for preemption. Writing of World War I, for example, Herman Kahn remarked: "This ability to increase one's force by a large factor and in a very short period of time gave a disastrous instability to the situation, because it promised to give the nation that mobilized first a crucial advantage."[90] The point is hardly self-evident, since mobilizations are difficult to conceal, and if detected quickly might lead to such rapid counter-mobilizations that there may be scarcely any advantage to going first.[91] Was it in fact the case, however, that the incentive to go first, to the extent that it really did exist, played a significant role in shaping at least some of the key decisions that were made on the eve of the war? Was it true that "general staffs, goaded by their relentless timetables, were pounding the table for the signal to move lest their opponents gain an hour's head start"?[92]

There is also the closely related issue of whether the military effectively took control of policy—at least in Germany and perhaps in Russia as well. According to Craig, for example, by the end of the crisis Moltke "had superseded the Chancellor in all but name"; the military technicians "had overborne the civilian authorities and brought war on in their own way"; in the end "the great decision of 1914 was made by the soldiers."[93] Albertini also has Bethmann "surrendering" to Moltke, "capitulating" to his "will to war," and says: "at the decisive moment the military took over the direction of affairs and imposed their law."[94] With regard to Russia, he remarks that after the Austrian declaration of war on Serbia, Sazonov lost "control of the situation" which, he says, "passed into the hands of the military."[95] If these claims are valid, it would make sense to hold the system in some measure responsible for the coming of the war.

The claim that policymakers were "stampeded" into war in 1914 thus needs to be tested.[96] This set of issues will therefore be examined in a third

[90] Herman Kahn, *On Thermonuclear War* (Princeton, 1960), p. 359.

[91] As far as I can tell, Van Evera is the only one to make this point. Van Evera, "Cult of the Offensive," p. 75.

[92] Tuchman, *Guns of August*, p. 72.

[93] Craig, *Politics*, pp. 291, 294, 295.

[94] Albertini, *Origins*, vol. 3, pp. 13, 27, 31, 190, 232, 248.

[95] Ibid., vol. 2, p. 540.

[96] See, for example, Lebow, *Nuclear Crisis Management*, pp. 34, 60.

section focusing on the most important phase of the crisis: the final hours before Russia ordered general mobilization on July 30.

The Meaning of Mobilization

On July 23 the Austrians issued their ultimatum to Serbia; the Serbs were given forty-eight hours to reply; on July 24 the Russian government considered and on July 25 decided to prepare a partial mobilization against Austria. The Russians also decided on the 25th to enforce "throughout the entire Empire the order for the period preparatory to war." Important pre-mobilization measures were to be put into effect secretly the next day.[97] The crisis had moved into its military phase.

With the decisions of July 25, Russia was moving closer to general mobilization. Did the Russian leaders understand what they were doing—that their full mobilization would lead to a German mobilization, and that for Germany mobilization meant war? It is an important element of the "inadvertent war" thesis that they did not, and Albertini returns to this point repeatedly. "Russia," he says, "had no knowledge of the fact that for Germany mobilization meant going to war," and Sazonov in particular did not understand that Germany could not afford delay, but would begin military operations almost immediately.[98] Many political scientists seem to have accepted these arguments, and have perhaps even taken them a step or two further. According to Lebow, for example, "Russian political leaders mobilized in 1914 in the belief that mobilization would be a deterrent to war"; "neither the czar nor Sazonov," he says, "believed that their action would directly trigger war."[99] It is quite clear, however, from the evidence that Albertini himself presents, that the Russian government understood very well what mobilization meant when it made its mobilization decisions at the end of July.

The Russian documents show, first of all, that support for general mobilization was rooted in a belief in the virtual inevitability of war. On July 30, the day the fateful decision was made, A. V. Krivoshein, the leading figure in the government, met with Sazonov before the latter was scheduled to see the Tsar. According to Baron Schilling, whose official diary is the single most important source on Russian policy during the crisis, their conversation "was almost exclusively concerned with the necessity for insisting upon a general mobilization at the earliest possible moment, in

[97] Albertini, *Origins*, vol. 2, pp. 290–94, 304–8; Geiss, *July 1914*, p. 207.

[98] Albertini, *Origins*, vol. 3, p. 245; vol. 2, pp. 579–81. See also Paul Kennedy's comments in Kennedy, *War Plans*, p. 16, and Stephen Van Evera, "Why Cooperation Failed in 1914," *World Politics*, vol. 38, no. 1 (October 1985), p. 104.

[99] Lebow, *Nuclear Crisis Management*, pp. 26, 111.

view of the inevitability of war with Germany, which every moment became clearer." When Sazonov saw the Tsar, he argued along similar lines:
"During the course of nearly an hour the Minister proceeded to show that
war was becoming inevitable, as it was clear to everybody that Germany
had decided to bring about a collision, as otherwise she would not have
rejected all the pacificatory proposals that had been made and could easily have brought her ally to reason. . . . Therefore it was necessary to put
away any fears that our warlike preparations would bring about a war
and to continue these preparations carefully, rather than by reason of
such fears to be taken unawares by war."

Sazonov here was virtually conceding that mobilization ("our warlike
preparations") would in all probability bring on war; his argument was
that since war was now unavoidable, this point could no longer carry
weight. The Tsar, however, resisted Sazonov's arguments, because he also
knew what mobilization meant: "The firm desire of the Tsar to avoid war
at all costs, the horrors of which filled him with repulsion, led His Maj-
esty, in his full realization of the heavy responsibility which he took upon
himself in this fateful hour, to explore every means for averting the approaching danger." As a result, the Tsar "refused during a long time to
agree to the adoption of measures which, however indispensable from a
military point of view"—again, an allusion to general mobilization—
"were calculated, as he clearly saw, to hasten a decision in an undesirable
sense," i.e., to precipitate the war. But finally he agreed that "it would be
very dangerous not to make timely preparations for what was apparently
an inevitable war, and therefore gave his decision in favour of an immediate general mobilization."[100]

The argument for holding back had thus been based on the idea that it
might still be possible to save the peace. This in turn reflected an assumption that a decision for mobilization would in itself make it for all practical purposes impossible to avoid war. It was taken for granted that there
was a trade-off between seizing the military advantages of the first mobilization and paying the price of precipitating the war; the argument for
making the move thus turned on the point that the price now was really
low, because war was virtually inevitable anyway. The notion that the
Russians ordered general mobilization in the belief that "mobilization
would be a deterrent to war" is without foundation. It was clearly understood that to order mobilization was to cross the Rubicon: there could be
no turning back.

Sazonov had certainly been told many times what the situation was. As

---

[100] Baron Schilling, *How the War Began in 1914* (London, 1925), pp. 62–66; Albertini,
Origins, vol. 2, pp. 565, 571–72. Note also the account of the meeting held the previous
day that had led to Russia's first decision for general mobilization, a decision later revoked
by the Tsar: Schilling, *How the War Began*, pp. 49–50; Albertini, *Origins*, vol. 2, p. 555.

early as July 25, for example—that is, before any irrevocable decision had been taken—the British ambassador had warned him that "if Russia mobilized, Germany would not be content with mere mobilization or give Russia time to carry out hers, but would probably declare war at once." Sazonov did not dispute the point. He simply pointed out that because the political stakes were so great, Russia, sure of French support, would "face all the risks of war."[101] The following day, Bethmann instructed Count Pourtalès, the German ambassador in Russia, to issue a warning: "Preparatory military measures on the part of Russia aimed in any way at us would compel us to take measures for our own protection which would have to consist in the mobilization of the army. Mobilization, however, would mean war."[102] The warning was issued the next day, but Sazonov did not show alarm, and Albertini infers from this that it failed to register on the foreign minister.[103]

The evidence that Albertini gives to support his argument about Sazonov not understanding what mobilization meant is extremely weak. Sazonov had admitted in his memoirs that Pourtalès had warned him that German mobilization would immediately lead to war. But according to Albertini, the foreign minister was mistaken about having been warned, and the proof, he says, comes from Pourtalès himself: "Sazonov put the question: 'Surely mobilization is not equivalent to war with you, either, is it?' I replied: 'Perhaps not in theory. But . . . once the button is pressed and the machinery of mobilization set in motion, there is no stopping it.' "[104] Pourtalès was thus clearly saying that for all practical purposes mobilization meant war, but Albertini insists on interpreting the remark in exactly the opposite sense: the ambassador's remark "seemed to imply that mobilization was not yet war."[105] Similarly, referring to Bethmann's important warning of the 29th that "further progress of Russian mobilization measures would compel us to mobilize and that then a European war could scarcely be prevented," Albertini emphasizes that Bethmann said " 'scarcely,' but not 'not at all' "—as though this had the slightest practical importance.[106]

Indeed, earlier that day Pourtalès and Sazonov had another meeting, the record of which shows that the foreign minister understood that for

[101] Buchanan to Grey, July 25, 1914, Great Britain, Foreign Office, *British Documents on the Origins of the War*, vol. 11 (London, 1926), no. 125; Albertini, *Origins*, vol. 2, p. 307.

[102] Bethmann to Pourtalès, July 26, 1914, *Outbreak of the World War*, doc. 219; Albertini, *Origins*, vol. 2, p. 428.

[103] Albertini, *Origins*, vol. 3, p. 43.

[104] Ibid., p. 42.

[105] Ibid., p. 43.

[106] Ibid. Note, similarly, the discussion in Lebow, *Nuclear Crisis Management*, pp. 112–13.

Germany mobilization meant war. Sazonov pointed out that "in Russia, *unlike western European states*, mobilization is far from being the same as war. The Russian army could, at need, stand at ease for weeks without crossing the border."[107] There is no question that by "western European states," Sazonov had Germany in mind, and Albertini in effect admits as much later in the book.[108] The Russians, of course, had an interest in arguing that their mobilization did not necessarily mean war, since if they could get Germany to tolerate a Russian mobilization, the military position of the Entente in the event of war would improve dramatically. This point was very widely understood in Europe; even Grey realized that asking Germany to acquiesce in a Russian mobilization of any sort, even one directed only against Austria, would be tantamount to asking her to "throw away the advantage of time."[109] For the same reason, however, the Germans had a great interest in explaining why they could not do this.[110] Thus, for example, Pourtalès pointed out to Sazonov on the 29th that "the danger of all military measures lies in the counter-measures of the other side. It is to be expected that the General Staffs of eventual enemies of Russia would not want to sacrifice the trump card of their great lead over Russia in mobilization and would press for counter-measures."[111] If Sazonov had not already understood this, one would again expect some expression of surprise or dismay. But in Pourtalès's account, there is no record of any such reaction. Sazonov once again took the point in stride.

In short, the Russian leadership certainly understood what mobilization meant. The evidence is quite overwhelming. Albertini himself admits in the end that Sazonov advised the Tsar to order general mobilization, although he was "well aware that this would bring Germany on the scene, and render war practically inevitable."[112] Even the Tsar, more removed from the situation than Sazonov, spoke about being "forced to take ex-

[107] Pourtalès to Foreign Office, July 29, 1914, quoted in Albertini, *Origins*, vol. 2, p. 549. Emphasis added.

[108] Ibid., p. 658.

[109] Quoted in ibid., p. 339. See also the extract from Grey's memoirs quoted in ibid., p. 392.

[110] Assuming, that is, that their goal was to avoid war by getting the Russians to back down. If, as the Fischer school argues, their aim was to provoke a war for which Russia would be blamed, a Russian mobilization would have been welcome, and the German government would not have attempted to deter Russia from ordering it by issuing this series of warnings.

[111] Albertini, *Origins*, vol. 2, p. 549.

[112] Ibid., p. 581. As for the French, note the analysis in ibid., vol. 3, pp. 105–8. Albertini argues, quite persuasively in this case, that President Poincaré and Prime Minister Viviani were disingenuous in declaring that "mobilization is not war," and that it was "the best means of assuring peace with honor."

treme measures which will lead to war"—an obvious reference to general mobilization.[113] At the crucial moment, moreover, when he was asked to sign the general mobilization decree, Nicholas clearly realized what was at stake. "Think of the responsibility you are advising me to assume," he said to Sazonov. "Consider that it means sending thousands and thousands of men to their deaths."[114]

It follows that a failure to understand what general mobilization meant was not the problem. For tactical reasons, certain statesmen might have pretended to believe that a Russian general mobilization need not lead to war, but such assertions can scarcely be taken at face value. The Russian political leadership certainly understood how risky this movement toward mobilization was, and, as Bethmann's warnings show, German statesmen were also fully aware of the situation.

The Russian Partial Mobilization

On July 28, Austria, finding the Serbian reply to her ultimatum unsatisfactory even though most of her demands had been accepted, declared war on Serbia. As a result, the Russian government decided later that day to order a partial mobilization against Austria. Neither of these moves was made for essentially military reasons. From the military point of view, the Austrian declaration of war came two weeks too early. Baron Conrad, the chief of the Austrian general staff, had told the foreign minister, Count Berchtold, that he wanted war declared only when he was capable of beginning military operations, "say on August 12." But the foreign minister wanted to act quickly in order to put an end to "various influences." "The diplomatic situation," he told Conrad, "will not hold so long."[115]

As for the Russian decision to mobilize against Austria, this too was taken for political and not military reasons.[116] "Its object," Schmitt writes, "was to indicate Russia's earnestness of purpose and to compel Austria-Hungary, under pressure of a 'military demonstration,' to consent to negotiate a pacific settlement of her quarrel with Serbia."[117] From

---

[113] This is from a telegram he sent to the Kaiser, dispatched at 1 a.m. on July 30, quoted in Albertini, *Origins*, vol. 2, p. 542.

[114] Schmitt, *Coming of the War*, vol. 2, p. 243. See also Albertini, *Origins*, vol. 2, p. 558.

[115] Baron Franz Conrad von Hötzendorf, *Aus meiner Dienstzeit 1906–1918*, 5 vols. (Vienna, 1921–25), vol. 4, pp. 131–32; quoted in Turner, *Origins*, p. 98.

[116] See Albertini, *Origins*, vol. 2, pp. 291–92, 529.

[117] Schmitt, *Coming of the War*, vol. 2, p. 94. Note also the discussion, based on important material from the Bark papers, in Lieven, *Russia and the Origins of the First World War*, pp. 142–44. The goal was to deter Germany, but the Russian leaders were acutely

a purely military point of view, moreover, it did not make much sense to mobilize against Austria alone at that point—or at least this is what Albertini and L.C.F. Turner both argue. Russia, they say, would have been better off waiting until Austria had concentrated her forces in the south and perhaps even became involved in military operations against Serbia. Then Austria would be more vulnerable in the north, and thus more susceptible to the pressure of a Russian partial mobilization.[118] Conrad himself thought that this was the most dangerous, and therefore the most likely, Russian strategy.[119] The original Russian plan had in fact been to wait until Austria actually invaded Serbia before ordering partial mobilization, but Sazonov impulsively jumped the gun and opted for this measure right after hearing about the Austrian declaration of war.[120]

The "inadvertent war" argument turns in this case not on causes but on consequences. The decisions had been made freely, not as the result of undue pressure from the military. But the statesmen, it is argued, had set off a process they simply could not control. "For the Austrian government," Howard writes, "a declaration of war was a political manoeuvre, for the Russian government a mobilisation order was a counter-manoeuvre; but such orders set in motion administrative processes which could be neither halted nor reversed, without causing a chaos which would place the nation at the mercy of its adversaries."[121]

The political leaders—not just Sazonov, but Grey and Jagow, who each in their way had consented to the Russian partial mobilization—certainly did not believe that it would lead inevitably to war. If they were wrong in this regard—if, in fact, irreversible "administrative processes" had been set off—then this would be an important point in favor of the argument that the political leaders' ignorance of military matters helped bring about the war, and in fact both Albertini and Turner argue along these lines. The claim is that a Russian partial mobilization against Austria would have led to an Austrian general mobilization, which "in turn would require Germany to mobilize." It was "ridiculous," Albertini says, to think that Germany could stand idly by and allow Russia, through even a partial mobilization, to deploy her forces more quickly in the event

---

conscious of the fact that this might not work; in such a case, they were prepared to go to war.

[118] See Turner, *Origins*, pp. 92–93; Albertini, *Origins*, vol. 2, p. 482.

[119] Stone, "Moltke and Conrad," in Kennedy, *War Plans*, p. 228.

[120] Albertini, *Origins*, vol. 2, pp. 305, 484, 532, 538. Albertini says that Sazonov acted precipitately "possibly in the belief that the invasion of Serbia would follow immediately" (p. 538). But the Austrians had told the British that if the Serbs did not accept their demands, they would not begin military operations immediately, and the British had passed this information on to the Russians. *British Documents*, vol. 11, nos. 104 and 105, and Schilling, *How the War Began*, pp. 35–36.

[121] Howard, "Lest We Forget," p. 65.

of a European war and thus make the success of the Schlieffen Plan more problematic. "It is quite clear," he argues, "that even if Russia had confined herself to ordering partial mobilization, the logic of the case as presented by Conrad and Moltke would have forced Germany to demand that it be cancelled, or, in case of a refusal, mobilize in her turn in order to go to the help of Austria. In short, partial mobilization would have led to war no less surely than general mobilization."[122]

Germany's alliance arrangements with Austria were, however, a good deal more ambiguous than Turner and Albertini imply. The important exchange of letters between Moltke and Conrad that had taken place in 1909 during the Bosnian Crisis was, as Schmitt says, the equivalent of a military convention. With the emperor's and the chancellor's approval, Moltke had promised that "at the moment that Russia mobilizes, Germany will also mobilize and will mobilize her entire army."[123] But it is by no means clear that this arrangement applied to the case of a partial mobilization against Austria. In view of Austria's well-known alliance with Germany, Moltke might well have calculated that mobilization against Austria alone made little military sense, that this contingency was thus unlikely to arise, and was therefore not worth worrying about.[124]

It is striking that neither Conrad nor Moltke nor the Russians took it for granted that mobilization by Austria and Russia against each other would in itself lead to war. Berchtold, on the 30th, did say that such a joint mobilization would lead to war, but Conrad replied "that if the Russians do not touch us, we need not touch them either."[125] The Russians, who of course had an interest in allowing their mobilization to proceed

---

[122] Albertini, *Origins*, vol. 2, pp. 340, 344, 392, 529–30, 541, and (for the final quotation) 485n.; Turner, *Origins*, pp. 92, 104. Fischer also accepts this conclusion: *War of Illusions*, p. 491. Albertini makes this argument even though he accepts the view of the Russian military leaders that a partial mobilization would have made a general mobilization more difficult, and thus would have placed Russia in a weaker position in the event that war broke out with Germany. Albertini, *Origins*, vol. 2, pp. 292–94, 541–43. If true, the Germans therefore should have had no military basis for objecting to partial mobilization, since it would have placed them in a stronger position if war came, all the more so since it would have put pressure on the Austrians to deploy their forces along their border with Russia instead of against Serbia, and this would have facilitated the implementation of the Schlieffen Plan.

[123] Quoted in Schmitt, *Coming of the War*, vol. 1, pp. 15, 17.

[124] The Entente, on the other hand, was more careful in this regard, and in their military understandings took such contingencies explicitly into account. Under the 1913 arrangement, any German mobilization or attack would automatically lead to French and Russian mobilization, but even a general Austrian mobilization would not have such an automatic effect; specific arrangements would have to be worked out at the time. "Procès-verbal des Entretiens du mois d'août 1913 entre les chefs d'état-major des armées française et russe," *Documents diplomatiques français*, series 3, vol. 8, doc. 79.

[125] Conrad, *Dienstzeit*, vol. 4, pp. 150–51; quoted in Albertini, *Origins*, vol. 2, p. 670.

for as long as possible before hostilities broke out, and who in any event had an interest in avoiding blame for the war, naturally made the same sort of argument, even about a general mobilization. "There was no fear," said Sazonov, "that the guns would go off by themselves."[126] It is much more significant that Moltke himself, after learning of the partial mobilization, told the Austrians in very direct language on the morning of the 30th that the Russian move gave the Germans "no reason" to mobilize. German mobilization, he said, would only begin after war broke out between Austria and Russia, and he advised the Austrians not to "declare war on Russia but wait for Russia to attack."[127] It is true that his attitude was to change that afternoon, but this apparently had more to do with early indications that the Russians were moving toward *general* mobilization than with his changing his mind about *partial* mobilization.[128]

Finally, there is the argument that Germany could not tolerate even a partial Russian mobilization directed only against Austria: after having encouraged the Austrians to move against Serbia, the Germans would find it impossible to stand by while Austria was subjected to this form of extreme Russian military pressure. The Germans therefore had to try to prevent the Russians from implementing the partial mobilization order. Bethmann, Albertini argues, therefore on July 29 "sent Pourtalès a telegram containing such threats that they powerfully contributed to persuading Sazonov that he must mobilize not only against Austria but also against Germany."[129] In this way the partial mobilization, he says, helped bring on the war.

It is wrong, however, to say that Russia's partial mobilization led to Bethmann's warning on the 29th, which in turn led to general mobilization and thus to war. This could not possibly have been the case, because, as Albertini's own evidence shows, the warning had been issued *before* the Germans even knew about the partial mobilization. Bethmann's telegram—"Kindly impress on M. Sazonov very seriously that further progress of Russian mobilization measures would compel us to mobilize and

---

[126] Quoted in Albertini, *Origins*, vol. 2, p. 682.

[127] Ibid., pp. 671–72, quoting a telegram and a letter from the Austrian liaison officer in Berlin, Captain Fleischmann, to Conrad, both of July 30, 1914. It is important to note that Moltke was now drawing back from the position he had taken earlier. On July 28, Moltke had drafted his well-known memorandum for Bethmann analyzing the situation. In it, he had argued that a Russian partial mobilization would lead Austria to order general mobilization, and that then "the collision between herself and Russia will become inevitable." Geiss, *July 1914*, p. 283.

[128] See Ulrich Trumpener, "War Premeditated? German Intelligence Operations in July 1914," *Central European History*, vol. 9, no. 1 (March 1976), p. 79.

[129] Albertini, *Origins*, vol. 2, p. 485.

that then European war could scarcely be prevented"[130]—left Berlin a little before 1 p.m. on the 29th. The Germans only learned of the partial
mobilization later that afternoon.[131] What the Germans seem to have
been reacting to when they issued their warning were the far-reaching
Russian pre-mobilization measures, many of which were directed against
them.[132] In any case, the Germans seemed to be demanding a standstill,
and not a revocation of measures already put into effect.

Instead of leading to war, the partial mobilization played a key role in
bringing about an important softening of German policy on the night of
July 29–30. Up to the 29th, Germany had been hoping for a localization
of the conflict. But now the partial mobilization order was demonstrating
quite dramatically that this probably would not be possible. It was one
thing to talk about backing Austria even at the risk of a European war at
the beginning of the crisis when that risk was judged to be low. But it was
an entirely different matter to take such a line at a time when the risk
appeared much greater. Bethmann's attitude, in fact, began to shift almost as soon as he learned of the Russian move. The reply he sent off at
11 p.m. on the 29th to the telegram from Pourtalès reporting the partial
mobilization "struck a different note," as Albertini says, "from his earlier
one of intimidation." "Russian mobilization on the Austrian frontier,"
Bethmann pointed out, "will, I assume, lead to corresponding Austrian
measures. How far it will still be possible to stop the avalanche then it is
hard to say."[133] The reference here to Austrian, and not German, countermeasures was particularly significant.

Indeed, Bethmann's general attitude on the night of July 29–30 under-
went a stunning shift. He comes across as a man desperately anxious to
avoid war. Up to then, he was scarcely interested in working out any kind
of peaceful settlement. He had effectively sabotaged all proposals that
might have prevented an Austrian attack on Serbia, including an important one that had come on the 28th from the Kaiser himself.[134] But on the

[130] Ibid., p. 553.

[131] Ibid., pp. 498, 553. Jagow, however, did threaten war as a response, which was quite
extraordinary, given that he himself, as his interlocutor, the Russian ambassador Sverbeev,
was quick to point out, was the one who had just given assurances that Germany would
tolerate such a move. Jagow added, however, that the views he expressed were purely personal, and that he would have to talk with Bethmann before giving a definite reply. Ibid., p.
499. Sazonov used the warning to defend his policy of moving toward general mobilization;
but this was evidently a debater's argument, since he had begun to push energetically for
general mobilization the previous day. Ibid., pp. 540, 556.

[132] See ibid., pp. 489, 592.

[133] Ibid., p. 562.

[134] The Kaiser had suggested that a settlement be based on the Serbian reply to the ultimatum; compliance would be guaranteed by the temporary occupation of Belgrade. Bethmann, in passing on a somewhat distorted version of the idea to Vienna, told the German

night of July 29–30, the chancellor sent off a series of increasingly tough telegrams demanding that the Austrians do what was necessary to head off a war. This effort culminated in a dispatch sent out at 3 a.m.: we "must decline to let ourselves to be dragged by Vienna, wantonly and without regard to our advice, into a world conflagration."[135]

Why this shift? Albertini contends that it was a threat from Grey, warning that Britain would intervene in a continental war, that had led Bethmann to alter his position so radically. The Chancellor, he says, had "based his whole policy on the assumption that, in case of war, England would remain neutral."[136] The Fischer school also argues that Grey's warning explains the series of telegrams Bethmann sent to Vienna in the early hours of July 30. The German leaders, Fischer says, had been willing to face war "with equanimity" because they believed that Britain would probably stay out. When they received Lichnowsky's telegram containing Grey's warning, they were "shattered" and "grew unsure of themselves." "The foundation of their policy during the crisis"—the belief that Britain would remain neutral if Germany handled events the right way—"had collapsed." Geiss thinks that Bethmann really shifted course and was now trying to avert the catastrophe; Fischer sees only momentary shock, followed by a return the next morning to the earlier policy.[137]

The problem with this interpretation, in any of these variants, is that it vastly overestimates the degree to which the Germans had been counting on British neutrality, ignores the degree to which the Germans had already been warned that Britain would intervene in a European war, and—most important of all in this context—plays down the significance of the one really great event, the announcement of Russian partial mobilization, that immediately preceded the change in Bethmann's policy. There is, first of all, little evidence to support the claim that Bethmann had been confidently counting on British neutrality. On the eve of the crisis (which according to Fischer the Germans had provoked with this calculation about Britain in mind), Bethmann was quite pessimistic about the chances that Britain would stay neutral in a continental war.[138] Dur-

---

ambassador there that in presenting it, he was "to avoid very carefully giving rise to the impression that we wish to hold Austria back." Geiss, *July 1914*, pp. 256–57, 259–60.

[135] Albertini, *Origins*, vol. 2, pp. 504, 522–25.

[136] Ibid., vol. 2, p. 520; vol. 3, pp. 3, 4.

[137] Fischer, *Germany's Aims*, pp. 78–80, and *War of Illusions*, pp. 495–96; Geiss, *July 1914*, p. 269.

[138] See, for example, all the evidence in Wolfgang J. Mommsen, "Domestic Factors in German Foreign Policy before 1914," *Central European History*, vol. 6, no. 1 (March 1973), p. 38n. Fischer's contrary argument on this point is laid out most extensively in his "The Miscalculation of English Neutrality" (see n. 25). But the evidence he presents here shows only that the Germans were hoping for British neutrality in a European war, not that they were counting on it. At one point, Fischer even quotes Bethmann, evidently without

ing the crisis itself, moreover, he was repeatedly warned by Lichnowsky that Britain would not stay out of any war in which France was involved.[139]

While the German government certainly would have been delighted if Britain remained neutral, and did what it could to maximize the probability that Britain would stay out of the war, it is going much too far to say that the hope of British neutrality was the basis of German political or military calculations. Grey's warning was of course a blow to Bethmann, but not quite as severe a blow as is often argued, since there had been many earlier indications that Britain would probably not stand by and allow France to be crushed.

It seems rather that it was the news from Russia about partial mobilization that played the key role in bringing about the shift in Bethmann's attitude. The evidence strongly suggests that the decisive change took place *before* the Chancellor learned of Grey's warning, but *after* he had found out about Russia's partial mobilization. The authorities in Berlin became aware of Russia's move at about 5 p.m. on the 29th; the telegram containing Grey's warning was received there at 9:12 p.m. The first of the telegrams reflecting Bethmann's newly found eagerness for a negotiated settlement was dispatched from Berlin at 10:18 p.m.[140] Given how long it generally took for a dispatch to be deciphered, delivered and read, for a new dispatch to be thought out, composed, sent over for coding, and then encoded and transmitted, it is very hard to believe that all this could have been done in barely more than an hour.[141] And yet this would have had to be the case for the telegram received at 9:12 to have led directly to the telegram sent out at 10:18—that is, for the news from London to have

realizing how this contradicts his basic argument, as writing to a friend in December 1912 that "Britain continues to uphold the policy of the balance of power and that it will therefore stand up for France if in a war the latter runs the risk of being destroyed by us" (p. 374). This has to be interpreted in the light of the fact that Bethmann at this point understood that the main goal of the Schlieffen Plan was indeed to crush France.

[139] Albertini, *Origins*, vol. 2, pp. 432, 442, 501. During the crisis, Bethmann and Jagow did occasionally predict—to the French ambassador, for example, and to the emperor—that Britain would remain neutral, at least at the start of the war, but the aim here was probably tactical in nature: to convince the French of German resolve, or to dissuade the emperor from calling a halt to the tough policy the government was pursuing. The Berlin authorities, moreover, may have viewed Lichnowsky as "soft," and thus might have discounted his opinions; but his reports of British thinking could not be dismissed out of hand, and Bethmann and Jagow were too experienced to think they could count confidently on British neutrality without hard evidence—and no really satisfactory indicators were forthcoming during the crisis. Indeed, the amount of attention the Germans gave to Britain and the important efforts they made to influence British policy show in themselves that British neutrality was not simply taken for granted.

[140] Ibid., pp. 498, 504, 520.

[141] For a brief discussion of these sorts of delays, see ibid., p. 525 n. 6.

brought about the dramatic shift in Bethmann's position. It is much more likely that the information about Russia's partial mobilization had led to this change in policy. Albertini himself recognizes the importance of the news from Russia in bringing about this shift on Bethmann's part, and he says explicitly that even before receiving the message containing Grey's warning, "the Chancellor was clutching at the idea"—the Kaiser's proposal for a peaceful settlement that Bethmann had tried to sabotage the previous day—"like a shipwrecked man at a lifebuoy."[142]

Thus, far from leading inevitably to German counter-measures which would have brought on a war, the Russian decision to order partial mobilization actually led to a *softening* of German policy, breaking the deadlock and at least in theory opening the way to a political settlement.

The Final Hours

So Bethmann now wanted to head off a European war. So did the Entente powers. Austria by herself could not have stood in their way. How then was war possible? Many assume there is only one answer to the riddle: the political process that should normally have brought about a negotiated settlement was overwhelmed in those momentous final hours of the crisis by forces welling up from within the military sphere, by generals "pounding the table for the signal to move lest their opponents gain an hour's head start."[143] The validity of the whole "inadvertent war" thesis, therefore, turns on a close analysis of the events of those fourteen fateful hours, the period from Bethmann's dramatic dispatch to Austria sent out at 3 a.m. on July 30, to the Russian order for general mobilization, issued at 5 p.m. that afternoon.

One can begin with the case of Germany, the most militaristic of the European powers, the state whose whole strategy was most strongly based on the idea of swift offensive action: if there is anything to the argument about the importance of preemption in 1914, surely here is where the evidence will be found. Yet as one studies the German case, one is struck by the unwillingness of that government to force the pace of the crisis in those final days, its preference for leaving the initiative in the hands of others. A basic goal, shared by the political and the military leadership, was that Germany not appear the aggressor. Germany would, of course, have to *react* quickly if Russia or France mobilized first; but the more rapidly Germany could respond, the less incentive there would be for her adversaries to make the first move.

[142] Ibid., pp. 500–502, 522.
[143] Tuchman, *Guns of August*, p. 72.

The Germans, in fact, were reluctant to take even the sort of pre-mobilization measures that they knew the Russians (and eventually even the
French and the British) were taking. On the 29th, but before the news of
Russia's partial mobilization had reached them, the top German leaders
met at Potsdam. General Erich von Falkenhayn, the war minister, called
for the pre-mobilization regime to be put into effect—for the proclamation of the "Kriegsgefahrzustand," the declaration of "threatening danger
of war"—but Moltke was opposed even to that and Falkenhayn deferred
to the chief of staff.[144] Later that evening, the new situation resulting from
the partial mobilization was discussed. "Against slight, very, very slight
opposition from Moltke," Bethmann ruled out German mobilization as a
response; this would have to wait until Russia actually unleashed a war,
"because otherwise we should not have public opinion with us either at
home or in England." As for Falkenhayn, he was by no means pressing
for preemptive action. There was no need, he thought, to be the first to
move, because "our mobilization, even if two or three days later than that
of Russia and Austria, would be more rapid than theirs."[145]

The following afternoon, Moltke began to call for a tougher policy,
probably because new information had been received about the seriousness of Russian military preparations.[146] He and Falkenhayn now asked
for the proclamation of the "Kriegsgefahrzustand." Bethmann refused to
agree to it then and there (even though this would by no means have made
mobilization, and therefore war, automatic), and simply promised that
the generals would get an answer by noon the next day.[147] By that point,
the news of Russia's general mobilization had reached Berlin, so the issue
had been overtaken by events. But some new evidence on Moltke's reaction to this information hardly supports the image of a general "pounding
the table for the signal to move." Moltke reacted to the first report of
general mobilization "with some skepticism" and wondered whether the
evidence had been misinterpreted. When he was told that the report had
been "very specific" and that "similar information had just arrived" from

[144] Albertini, *Origins*, vol. 2, pp. 495–97, 499–500 (for the chronology).
[145] Ibid., p. 502.
[146] Trumpener, "War Premeditated?" p. 79.
[147] Albertini, *Origins*, vol. 3, pp. 10, 18; on the issue of the "Kriegsgefahrzustand," see
ibid., vol. 2, pp. 491, 599. When defending his decision not to proclaim the "Kriegsgefahrzustand," Bethmann did claim that it meant mobilization and therefore war, but this can
scarcely be taken at face value. See ibid., vol. 3, p. 15. An Army document also strongly
suggests that war was not viewed as following automatically from the proclamation of the
Kriegsgefahrzustand. See the extract from the "Protokoll der Chefkonferenz in Frankfurt a.
M. am 21. Januar 1914," in W. Knoll and H. Rahne, "Bedeutung und Aufgaben der Kon-
ferenz der Generalstabschefs der Armeekorps in Frankfurt a. M. am 21. Januar 1914," *Mi-
litärgeschichte* vol. 25, no. 1 (1986), p. 58: "The Corps should not allow their hands to be
tied" by a proclamation of threatening danger of war, "for example, by buying horses."

two other intelligence posts, he "turned toward the window, took a deep breath, and said: 'It can't be helped then; we'll have to mobilize too.' "[148]

Nor did Bethmann, contrary to what both Craig and Albertini argue, "capitulate" to the generals during the crisis. It is amazing how common this notion is, given how little evidence there is to back it up. Moltke was not able to get Bethmann to agree even to the Kriegsgefahrzustand until after news of the Russian general mobilization reached Berlin. The chief of staff, to be sure, went behind Bethmann's back on the afternoon of the 30th and urged Austria to mobilize against Russia and reject mediation.[149] But this is hardly proof that Bethmann was capitulating to the military, or even that Moltke was overstepping his own authority, since the Kaiser may have authorized his messages to the Austrians.[150] In any case, the move could hardly be viewed as a cause of the war, since, as Gerhard Ritter, for example, once pointed out, Moltke's messages were submitted to the ministers in Vienna "only on the morning of July 31," after the Austrian decision for general mobilization had been made, and thus had no "practical effect."[151]

Finally, there is the episode late that evening of Telegram 200, which Albertini treats as decisive. In this dispatch, Bethmann called on Austria once again to accept mediation. His language was not as strong as it had been the previous night, but even so the instruction contained in the tele-

[148] Trumpener, "War Premeditated?" p. 82.

[149] Albertini, *Origins*, vol. 3, p. 11.

[150] Ibid., pp. 11–13; Schmitt, *Coming of the War*, vol. 2, p. 198. In *War of Illusions*, Fischer does not take a consistent line on this issue. In trying to prove that Germany was to blame for the war, he naturally has to argue that other powers were not responsible and that in particular Russia should not be blamed for ordering general mobilization, since the Germans would have started the war in early August even if the Russians had not made this move. This conclusion he reaches after making the following series of claims. First he says (pp. 493–94) that there was a sharp conflict between the German military, thinking "exclusively in terms of keeping strictly to the strategic time-table," and thus pushing for war as early as July 29, and the political leadership, which calculated that for political reasons Russia had to be the one to take the first crucial step by ordering a full mobilization before Germany did. Just two pages later, and without explanation, he takes the opposite line and argues that the military and the political leadership were "unanimous in their demand that Austria should in no circumstances appear as the aggressor but that it must be left to Russia to take the decisive step which would lead to war" (p. 496). Two pages after that he reverts to the original line and has Bethmann giving in to the military and agreeing that the Kriegsgefahrzustand would be proclaimed the next day, a step which he incorrectly claims would inevitably have led to mobilization and thus to war, and that, in so doing, "Berlin had fixed the beginning of the war for the first days of August even without the government being driven to this by Russia's general mobilization" (p. 498). In reality, all Bethmann had promised was that a decision would be made the next morning. See Albertini, *Origins*, vol. 2, pp. 491, 496, 502, and vol. 3, pp. 7, 10, 18, and also n. 147 above.

[151] Gerhard Ritter, *The Sword and the Scepter: The Problem of Militarism in Germany*, vol. 2 (Coral Gables, Fla., 1970), p. 258.

gram was suspended soon after it was dispatched. The telegram ordering the suspension referred to information from the General Staff about "the military preparations of our neighbors, especially in the east." Albertini interprets this suspension as a "capitulation" and says that the "Chief of Staff was no longer allowing the political leadership to waste time in attempts to save the peace and compose the conflict."[152] But again, this conclusion hardly follows from the evidence. The fact that Bethmann agreed with, or was convinced by, arguments and information coming from the military scarcely proves that he was surrendering to their will. In fact, Albertini himself suggests that information was being received in Berlin that evening indicating that the Russian general mobilization, which indeed had been decided upon at 5 p.m. that afternoon, might be imminent.[153] If that were the case, and war was about to break out, what was the point of irritating Germany's only ally with a démarche which would almost certainly do no good anyway? If this, as seems likely, was Bethmann's calculation, the cancellation of Telegram 200 can hardly be interpreted as a "capitulation," and in fact there is no real evidence supporting the argument that by this time the military had effectively taken over control of German policy.

The real problem was not that the civilians had lost control, but rather that Germany's political strategy and her military strategy were pulling in opposite directions. The demands of the Schlieffen Plan implied that Germany had to act quickly, but this meant that Germany would be the first to cross borders. Germany would have to invade Belgium and attack France, but one of Bethmann's basic goals was for Germany to avoid coming across as the aggressor and to make it appear that Russia was responsible for the war. "The fact is," says Albertini, "that Bethmann, who had made every effort to cast the blame on Russia, failed to see that his endeavours would be defeated by the very demands of the Schlieffen Plan."[154] On the other hand, important military measures had been delayed for political reasons, and given Germany's military strategy, even short delays might have had serious consequences. The two sides of their policy were working at cross purposes, but this particular difficulty did not actually help bring on the war. It should have had the opposite effect of pushing Germany toward a peaceful settlement. If the German leadership had faced up to the problem, which was to some extent rooted in an astonishing lack of coordination between the political and the military authorities,[155] they would have recognized that this was a major source

[152] Albertini, *Origins*, vol. 3, pp. 21–24.

[153] Ibid., pp. 24, 27.

[154] Ibid., p. 249. See also the discussion of this issue in ibid., pp. 186–87.

[155] Ibid., p. 250. Nor was there any serious coordination between the Army and Navy general staffs. Admiral Tirpitz claimed that he "was never even informed of the invasion of

of weakness, and, as Albertini argues, this should have made them move energetically to settle the dispute.[156] But instead events were allowed to take their course.

The most striking thing, in fact, about German policy on the 30th is that Bethmann did seem to resign himself to the situation and gave up trying to prevent war. On the night of July 29–30, he had begun to move energetically to head off a war, but by the following morning—that is, even before Moltke's shift that afternoon—the effort had ended. The pressure on Austria subsided, and Bethmann certainly did not do the one thing he would have had to do if he had really wanted to prevent war. His first priority, in that case, would have been to keep the Russians from ordering general mobilization, and to do this, he would have had to make it clear to them that war was not inevitable, that a political settlement was within reach, that Austria could be led to moderate her demands on Serbia, but that he needed a little time to bring her around. And to increase the pressure on Russia to hold back, he could have approached the' western powers, explaining why a political settlement was within sight, and asking them to do what they could to keep Russia from resorting to general mobilization and thus setting off the avalanche. But Bethmann made none of these moves. The Russians ordered general mobilization that afternoon, and the great war could no longer be prevented.

Had the war come because, as Bethmann himself said at the time, "control had been lost"? The "stone had started rolling," he declared; war was being unleashed "by elemental forces."[157] But there had been no "loss of control," only an abdication of control. Bethmann had chosen not to act. He had decided to let events take their course—and thus to take his "leap into the dark."[158] If war had to come—and if the Russians were not going to give way this time when they were relatively weak, a conflict with them was probably unavoidable in the long run—then maybe the generals were right, maybe it was better to have it now rather than later. His hands were clean—more or less. He had not set out to provoke a great war with this

---

Belgium." Alfred von Tirpitz, *My Memoirs* (New York, 1919), vol. 1, p. 346. Similarly, the lack of military coordination with Austria is astounding. Although some loose agreements covering this matter had been reached in 1909, more precise arrangements were not worked out during the crisis, and it was only at the last minute that Moltke asked Austria "to employ her main strength against Russia and not disperse it by a simultaneous offensive against Serbia." But this the Austrians refused to do. Albertini, *Origins*, vol. 3, pp. 45–46; N. Stone, "Moltke and Conrad." This hardly fits in with the picture of a German government carefully and systematically plotting a war of aggression. For a similar point based on a study of German intelligence operations during the crisis, see Trumpener, "War Premeditated?" pp. 83–85.

[156] Albertini, *Origins*, vol. 3, p. 249.

[157] Ibid., pp. 15–17.

[158] Erdmann, *Riezler*, entry for July 14, 1914, p. 185.

calculation in mind. He had even made a certain effort to get the Austrians to pull back. But war was almost bound to come eventually, so he would just stand aside and let it come now. The preventive war argument, which had not been powerful enough to dictate German policy at the beginning of the crisis, now proved decisive. It might have been difficult, if only for moral reasons, for the German leadership to set out deliberately to provoke a great war. It was much easier just to let the war come—to not "hide behind the fence," as Jagow put it.[159] Bethmann probably had something of this sort in mind when he later admitted that "in a certain sense, it was a preventive war."[160]

This, however, has nothing to do with preemption: there had been no "loss of control" resulting from the pressure to mobilize first. Indeed, as far as the German side is concerned, the argument about preemption carries surprisingly little weight. With the Russian mobilization the die had been cast: after that point, any specific incentive to move quickly that the Germans may have felt could do little more than affect the exact timing of the German attack: from that point on, it was extremely unlikely that war itself could be avoided.[161]

---

[159] Jagow to Lichnowsky, July 18, 1914, in Geiss, *July 1914*, p. 123.

[160] Quoted, for example, in Konrad Jarausch, "The Illusion of Limited War: Chancellor Bethmann Hollweg's Calculated Risk, July 1914," *Central European History*, vol. 2, no. 1 (March 1969), p. 48.

[161] The Germans' need to seize Liège quickly is often cited as a major source of such pressure for preemption. But while the German general staff was certainly concerned with the Liège situation at the end of July, there is little evidence that this factor contributed in any major way to the German decision for war. Ritter, for example, blamed the Liège problem for Germany's "unbelievable haste" in declaring war on Russia on August 1, and Churchill thought that if it were not for Liège, the armies might have mobilized without crossing frontiers while a peace settlement was worked out. Snyder, on the other hand, says that "Moltke's attitude was not decisively influenced by this incentive to preempt." There is much about the Liège issue that remains obscure. It is not clear exactly when German troops would have begun their attack and crossed the Belgian frontier if the earlier plan had not been altered in 1911 to include the Liège operation as one of its vital elements. Given the basic philosophy of the Schlieffen strategy, which even in its original form of a one-front war against France "depended," as Ritter says, "on the speed and surprise of the German advance through Belgium," Germany could not hold off for long after the Russian general mobilization had begun. If it were not for Liège, would Germany have postponed her declaration of war for a brief period after ordering mobilization? The answer is by no means obvious, but even if a certain delay was possible, the argument that the Liège factor played a key role in bringing on the war would turn on the claim that there was a real chance of saving the peace during those extra few days while Germany was still mobilizing, but before war absolutely had to be declared. There is, however, little basis for this assumption. It is not as though serious negotiations had been going on that might have led to a settlement if they had not been cut off by the declarations of war. Gerhard Ritter, "Der Anteil der Militärs an der Kriegskatastrophe von 1914," *Historische Zeitschrift*, vol. 193, no. 1 (August 1961), pp. 89–90; Ritter, *Schlieffen Plan*, p. 90; Winston Churchill, *The World Crisis: The*

It remains to be seen, however, whether preemption was a more compelling factor on the Entente side. To begin with France: the chief of staff and the war minister did urge Russia to move against Germany as soon as possible after war broke out, which of course was exactly what the prewar military arrangements had called for. Turner argues that this was pressure "calculated to drive the Russian General Staff into demanding general mobilization."[162] Perhaps so, but the evidence presented is hardly sufficient in itself to warrant this conclusion, and there is really no indication in the Russian sources of pressure from French military authorities making any important difference.

It is therefore on Russian policy that an analysis of the preemption question in 1914 must focus. In this case it does turn out to have some substance. It clearly mattered a great deal to the Russian authorities whether Germany or Russia was the first to mobilize. This is the only way to make sense of the constant allusions to the great risks of delaying a general mobilization that one finds in the records of the meetings where these mobilization decisions were made. On July 30, for example, the chief of staff "pleaded" with Sazonov to convince the Tsar "to consent to a general mobilization in view of the extreme danger that would result for us if we were not ready for war with Germany." Sazonov did precisely that. Since "war was becoming inevitable," he told the Tsar when he saw him that afternoon, "it was necessary to put away any fears that our warlike preparations would bring about a war and to continue these preparations carefully, rather than by reason of such fears to be taken unawares by war." The Tsar "agreed that in the existing circumstances it would be very dangerous not to make timely preparations for what was apparently an inevitable war, and therefore gave his decision in favour of a general mobilization."[163] The mobilization decision was thus based on a political assessment: there was a diplomatic deadlock, Austria was beginning to move against Serbia, the issue could no longer be avoided. It is important to note that the Russian mobilization was not precipitated by the fear that Germany was about to act. In the key meetings at which the mobilization decisions were made, the argument was that it was war itself, and not a German mobilization as such, that was imminent.

Did "pressure from the Russian generals" cause the political leadership

---

Eastern Front (London, 1931), p. 93, quoted in Turner, "Significance of the Schlieffen Plan," in Kennedy, *War Plans*, p. 213; Snyder, "Civil-Military Relations," p. 113.

[162] Turner, *Origins*, p. 104. See also his "The Role of the General Staffs in July 1914," pp. 320–21. The sort of attitude to which Turner refers was evidently not limited to French military circles: see, for example, Doumergue's comments quoted in Maurice Paléologue, *Au Quai d'Orsay à la veille de la tourmente. Journal 1913–1914* (Paris, 1947), p. 269.

[163] Schilling, *How the War Began*, pp. 64–66.

to "lose control" of the situation?[164] The generals' main argument was that "in resorting to partial mobilization, there was a big risk of upsetting plans for general mobilization."[165] Albertini, who blames pressure from the generals for helping push Europe into war, thinks that the generals were correct in this assessment: a partial mobilization, he says, would "have been a blunder," since if war came Russia would have to face both Austria and Germany.[166] But could the generals be blamed for exercising undue influence if they had simply given an accurate assessment of the situation? As long as they limited themselves to a purely military judgment, only one conclusion followed: partial mobilization was out of the question, so the choice had to be between "general mobilization and none at all."[167] Their preference for general mobilization was based on political considerations, and especially on the belief that it would be impossible to abandon Serbia, that the Central Powers were intent on crushing the Serbs, and that war could therefore not be avoided.[168] If the political leadership had held more moderate views, and especially if the generals rationalized their preference for general mobilization with spurious military arguments, there would be some basis for the argument that pressure from the generals was a major cause of the war. But the striking thing here is that Sazonov shared their assessment of the probability of war. It was not as though he tried to resist the generals' views and only reluctantly gave way. On July 28, he was, according to General Dobrorolski, "penetrated by the thought that a general war is unavoidable," and even went so far as to express his astonishment to the chief of staff that full mobilization had not been begun earlier.[169]

Had Sazonov, however, been trapped by his own ignorance and impulsiveness? The argument is that he had blindly ordered a partial mobilization without any real understanding of the problems it would cause; but having ordered it, he had no answer for the technical arguments the generals raised against it. He therefore had to choose between revoking the partial mobilization order or escalating to general mobilization. To cancel the partial mobilization order would be taken as a sign of weakness; Sazonov was therefore led, however reluctantly, to opt for a full mobilization.[170] But again this theory cannot withstand the simple test of chronology. Sazonov had accepted the generals' argument about the dangers

[164] Albertini, *Origins*, vol. 2, pp. 539–45.

[165] General Yuri Danilov, the Quartermaster-General, quoted in ibid., p. 542.

[166] Ibid., p. 543.

[167] Ibid.

[168] Ibid.

[169] Dobrorolski is commonly viewed as a reliable source; his account is quoted in ibid., p. 540.

[170] See, for example, Van Evera, "Why Cooperation Failed in 1914," p. 104.

of partial mobilization on July 28—that is, before the partial mobilization had actually begun, probably before the decision to order it had even been made, and certainly long before the Germans learned of the order.[171] The real puzzle here is that Sazonov opted for partial mobilization even though he had already been persuaded by the arguments against it. One possible answer is that he calculated that a partial mobilization would be a bridge to the general mobilization he had by that point come to view as necessary: once partial mobilization was ordered, the Tsar could more easily be brought to accept a full mobilization against both Germany and Austria. Sazonov had not been trapped by his own ignorance, nor had he been overwhelmed by pressure from the generals. He had made his choices with his eyes open; he had not been stampeded into them.

So to sum up: although preemption evidently was a factor in 1914, its importance is greatly exaggerated in much of the literature. It played a role on the Russian side in the final hours of the crisis, and even then only because the political judgment had been made that war was inevitable. Its role was quite marginal in comparison with all those factors that had given rise to this judgment in the first place. On the German side, its role was minimal. The Germans wanted Russia to be the first to order mobilization, and they would have been delighted if, after mobilization, France had been the first to attack.[172] Their strategy was not preemptive but reactive: for political reasons, they were conceding the first move to their adversaries. In contemporary terms, this was more like a "second strike" than a "first strike" strategy, and thus in this respect can hardly be considered "destabilizing."

CONCLUSION

The aim here was not to offer yet another interpretation of the coming of the First World War. This was instead meant mainly as an exercise in intellectual housekeeping. There are many claims about the origins of the war that have been accepted more or less uncritically, and the goal here was to test some of the more important ones against the evidence. What was at stake was not simply our historical understanding of this particular episode. It was really because so much of our thinking today about issues of strategy and foreign policy rests in such large measure on a specific interpretation of the July Crisis that an effort of this sort was worth undertaking.

[171] Albertini, *Origins*, vol. 2, pp. 540–45.

[172] "For about forty-eight hours after the issue of the respective mobilization orders the [French and German] armies stood face to face, each waiting and hoping that the other would be the first to open hostilities." Albertini, *Origins*, vol. 3, p. 204.

Did the war come because statesmen in 1914 were overwhelmed by forces they could not control, and, for the most part, scarcely even understood? Was Europe carried into war by the rigidity of its military plans, and by the premium they placed on preemption? Was the problem rooted in the fact that military planning had taken place in a political vacuum, that the soldiers were apolitical technicians, that the political leadership had been kept in the dark? During the crisis, were the political leaders stampeded into war by the generals and by the system the military had created? Did the political authorities surrender to the generals, who eventually took control of policy and made the crucial decisions that led to the war?

The answer in every case is essentially no. The military plans were not based on purely technical considerations; the generals had strong political views of their own, which were certainly reflected in the strategies they adopted. The political leaders were well aware of the basic thrust of the war plans, and they understood what they meant—not to the last detail of course, but they did understand the basic logic of the situation that these plans had created. There was, moreover, no "capitulation" to the generals; the military had in no real sense taken control of policy.

The First World War did not come about because statesmen had "lost control" of events; preemption was not nearly as important in 1914 as is commonly assumed. Instead of generals "pounding the table for the signal to move," one finds Falkenhayn saying on the 29th that it would not matter much if Germany mobilized two or three days after Russia, and Moltke that same day not even supporting the proclamation of the "Kriegsgefahrzustand." On the afternoon of the 30th, Moltke did begin to press for military measures, but this was very probably in reaction to what the Russians were doing in this area. As long as German policy was reactive, it can hardly be considered a source of "instability" in the contemporary sense of the term.

The Russian generals, on the other hand, did press for early mobilization. But this was only because they thought that war was unavoidable, a view that the civilian government also shared. A decision for general mobilization was a decision for war: it was not that Sazonov and the political leadership as a whole were trying desperately to preserve the peace, but were drawn into the abyss by the "pull of military schedules." It hardly makes sense, therefore, to see the Russian decision to seize the military advantages of the first mobilization as proof that "control had been lost" or that war had come "inadvertently." In 1941, the Japanese government attacked American forces at Pearl Harbor and in the Philippines after becoming convinced that war with the United States could not be avoided. Even if this judgment had been mistaken—even if one assumes that President Roosevelt could not have taken the country into war if the Japanese had avoided contact with American forces and limited their attack to the Dutch East Indies—no one would say that the fact that the Japanese chose to seize the first strike advantage by launching a surprise attack against vulnerable American forces means that the War in the Pacific was essentially an "inadvertent" conflict. The same point, however, applies to 1914.

The idea that the First World War came about because statesmen were overwhelmed by military imperatives and thus "lost control" of the situation came to be accepted for essentially political reasons, and not because it was the product of careful and disinterested historical analysis. It was hardly an accident that the first to propagate this idea were the statesmen whose policies in 1914 had led directly to the conflict—that is, the very people who had the greatest interest in avoiding responsibility for the catastrophe. On the very eve of the disaster—on July 31, 1914—Bethmann was already arguing along these lines.[173]

After the war, it became apparent that the Germans would never accept a peace settlement based on the notion that they had been responsible for the conflict. If a true peace of reconciliation was to take shape, it was important to move toward a new theory of the origins of the war, and the easiest thing was to assume that no one had really been responsible for it. The conflict could be readily blamed on great impersonal forces—on the alliance system, on the arms race and on the military system that had evolved before 1914. On their uncomplaining shoulders the burden of guilt could be safely placed. For many people, it thus became an article of faith that military factors, and especially the arms competition, had led directly to the catastrophe. "Great armaments," Grey, for example, wrote in his memoirs, "lead inevitably to war." This, he said, was the obvious moral to be drawn from a study of the pre-1914 period.[174]

---

[173] Ibid., pp. 15–17.

[174] Viscount Grey of Fallodon, *Twenty-Five Years* (New York, 1925), vol. 1, pp. 89–90. Arguments of this sort rarely take cognizance of even the basic figures on the defense burden, which in fact throw a very different light on this whole issue. In Germany, for example, defense spending as a proportion of national income had been somewhat higher at the end of the Bismarckian period in 1889 and 1890 than it was on the eve of the war. Indeed, for most of the immediate prewar period, defense spending as a percent of GNP had been in decline, going from 2.98 percent in 1901 down to 2.46 percent in 1912, before rising back to 3.02 percent in 1913. (The corresponding figure for 1890 had been 3.47 percent.) If this was a race, Germany obviously was not running very hard: these figures are of course quite low by contemporary standards. The percentages were computed from the national income figures in B. R. Mitchell, *European Historical Statistics 1750–1970*, abridged edition (New York, 1978), table J1, and from the figures for defense spending in W. G. Hoffmann, *Das Wachstum der deutschen Wirtschaft seit der Mitte des 19. Jahrhunderts* (Berlin, 1965), table 199, col. 6. Contemporary equivalents are conveniently summarized in the statistical tables in United States Arms Control and Disarmament Agency, *World Military Expenditures and*

With the resurgence of German power, and particularly during the period of Hitler's successes in the late 1930s, the great war itself came to be widely regarded in the West as a terrible mistake—as something which had been quite literally pointless—which could only be explained if it was assumed that the political leaders had stumbled into it blindly, pulled along by their military advisers, or trapped by military arrangements whose implications they had never really understood. The argument was sometimes carried to extremes. David Lloyd George, for example, the Chancellor of the Exchequer in July 1914 and Prime Minister from 1916 to 1922, in March 1936—the month of Hitler's coup in the Rhineland—blamed the prewar military plan worked out by the British and French general staffs for landing Britain in the war. "Had it not been," he said, "for the professional zeal and haste with which the military staffs set in motion the plans which had already been agreed between them the negotiations between the governments, which at that time had hardly begun, might well have continued, and war could, and probably would, have been averted." This claim, as Albertini says (and as Duff Cooper said at the time) is certainly false: it was not the eagerness of the British military authorities to implement their war plan that prevented a negotiated solution from being worked out; a peaceful settlement had been ruled out by events on the continent, culminating in the movement of German armies into Belgium on August 4.[175] But given prevailing beliefs about the role that the military system had played in bringing on the war, even such extreme claims were taken seriously.

By the 1950s and 1960s, these ideas had taken on a life of their own. During this period, American strategists developed a way of thinking about issues of war and peace that placed an extraordinary emphasis on military factors—especially on preemption and the "reciprocal fear of surprise attack." In such an environment, the notion that the First World War was a product of the military system in place in 1914 had an obvious appeal. This interpretation seemed to provide an important degree of empirical support for conclusions reached through an essentially abstract process of analysis.

In the 1970s and 1980s, the environment shifted once more, but the theory, which by now had been around long enough to become part of the conventional wisdom, was again able to find a new niche. In the aftermath of the Vietnam War, and even more with the fading of the Cold War in the 1980s, the "Munich analogy" was discredited as a basic paradigm for foreign policy. The "Sarajevo analogy" was drawn into the

---

Arms Transfers, an annual publication available from ACDA's Defense Program and Analysis Division.

[175] Note especially the Lloyd George-Duff Cooper exchange, summarized and commented on in Albertini, *Origins*, vol. 3, pp. 524–25.

vacuum. In an age which took the stability of great power political relations for granted, it was particularly important—the argument now ran—
to remember what had happened in 1914. Secretary of State Henry Kissinger, for example, pointed out in 1976 that the lesson of the July Crisis
was that one could have a war "without any conscious decision to over-
turn the international structure." War could come about because "a crisis
much like any other went out of control. Nation after nation slid into a
war whose causes they did not understand but from which they could not
extricate themselves."[176]

It was in fact commonly assumed that even in the nuclear age there was
a real danger that the world might slip into war in this way. Today, in a
world where all of the major powers obviously want very much to avoid
a new world war, the only real fear is that the great nations might somehow stumble into one more or less inadvertently. The "inadvertent war"
interpretation of the events of 1914 gives focus and substance to this fear
and thus appeals particularly to those in the defense and arms control
communities who have a professional interest in taking the risk of great
power war seriously.

During this whole process, this interpretation was accepted because it
was what people wanted to believe. It is important, however, that our
basic thinking about issues of war and peace not be allowed to rest on
what are in the final analysis simply myths about the past. The conventional wisdom does not have to be accepted on faith alone: claims about
the past can always be translated into historically testable propositions.
In this case, when one actually tests these propositions against the empirical evidence, which for the July Crisis is both abundant and accessible,
one is struck by how weak most of the arguments turn out to be. The
most remarkable thing about all these claims that support the conclusion
about events moving "out of control" in 1914 is how little basis in fact
they actually have.

[176] Speech of March 11, 1976, *New York Times*, March 12, 1976, p. 4.

CHAPTER THREE

A "Wasting Asset": American Strategy and the Shifting Nuclear Balance, 1949–1954

IN JANUARY 1946, General Leslie Groves, the wartime commander of the Manhattan Project, prepared a memorandum on the military implications of the atomic bomb. "If we were ruthlessly realistic," he wrote, "we would not permit any foreign power with which we are not firmly allied, and in which we do not have absolute confidence, to make or possess atomic weapons. If such a country started to make atomic weapons we would destroy its capacity to make them before it had progressed far enough to threaten us."[1]

In the late 1940s and well into the early 1950s, the basic idea that the United States should not just sit back and allow a hostile power like the Soviet Union to acquire a massive nuclear arsenal—that a much more "active" and "positive" policy had to be seriously considered—was surprisingly widespread. The American government, of course, never came close to implementing a preventive war strategy. As far as the public as a whole was concerned, the idea seems to have had only a limited appeal.[2]

An earlier version of this paper was presented at a conference held in May 1988 under the auspices of the American Academy of Arts and Sciences' Committee on History, the Social Sciences and National Security Affairs. It was subsequently published, in more or less its present form, in *International Security*, vol. 13, no. 3 (Winter 1988–89), and I am grateful to the editors of that journal for permission to republish it here.

[1] "Statement on the atomic bomb and its effect on the Army," appendix to JCS 1477/6, January 21, 1946, in CCS 471.6 (8-15-45) sec 2, Record Group [RG] 218, United States National Archives [USNA], Washington. There is a slightly different version, dated January 2, 1946, in U.S. Department of State, *Foreign Relations of the United States* [FRUS], 1946, vol. 1, pp. 1197–1203. Eisenhower, who thought Groves's views were "perhaps extreme in some respects," nevertheless had a high regard for the paper as a whole. See Louis Galambos, ed., *The Papers of Dwight David Eisenhower*, vol. 7, pp. 760–61, 641–42, n. 7. See also James Schnabel, *The History of the Joint Chiefs of Staff*, vol. 1 (1945–47) (Washington, 1979), pp. 281–82.

[2] Thus in September 1954 a Gallup poll asked: "Some people say we should go to war against Russia now while we still have the advantage in atomic and hydrogen weapons. Do you agree or disagree with this point of view?" Thirteen percent of the sample agreed, 76 percent disagreed, 11 percent had no opinion. Similarly in July 1950, right after the outbreak of the Korean War, 15 percent of a Gallup sample thought the United States "should declare war on Russia now." Hazel Gaudet Erskine, "The Polls: Atomic Weapons and Nuclear Energy," *Public Opinion Quarterly*, vol. 27 (1963), p. 177; George Gallup, *The Gallup Poll: Public Opinion 1935–1971* (New York, 1972), vol. 1, p. 930. For a brief survey

What ran deep, however, was a tremendous sense of foreboding. If the Soviets were allowed to develop nuclear forces of their own, there was no telling what might happen. If they were so hostile and aggressive even in the period of America's nuclear monopoly, what would they be like once this monopoly had been broken? There was no reason to assume that a nuclear world would be stable; wouldn't the Soviets some day try to destroy the one power that prevented them from achieving their goals by launching a nuclear attack on the United States? The clouds of danger were gathering on the horizon. Was the West, through its passivity, simply drifting toward disaster? Wasn't some sort of more "positive" policy worth considering?

The basic goal here is to study how people dealt with these problems—how they came to terms with the dramatic shifts in the military balance and the extraordinary changes in the overall military environment that were taking place in the first decade of the nuclear age. The nuclear revolution, the loss of the American atomic monopoly, and finally the coming of thermonuclear weapons in the early 1950s were all enormously important events. Moreover, it had been clear from the very beginning that America's nuclear monopoly, and even her nuclear superiority, was inevitably a "wasting asset."[3] But what did this imply in terms of foreign and military policy?

Most of the analysis here will focus on the purely historical problem of how this set of concerns worked its way through the political system. But two important points will emerge from this reexamination of the period. The first has to do with the role of trends in the military balance. Concerns about the way the balance was changing—about the expected opening and closing of "windows of vulnerability"—carried a good deal of political weight; indeed, they turned out to be far more important than I ever would have imagined.[4] The whole concept of "windows," it became clear, was not simply an abstract, academic construct, artificially imposed on historical reality. Although the term itself was not used at the time, one is struck by how real the concept was; the impact of this whole way of thinking on actual policy was both enormous and pervasive. In particular, concerns about anticipated shifts in the military balance played a critical role in shaping not only grand strategy, but policy on specific issues, especially during the Korean War. The reluctance to escalate during

---

of popular attitudes on nuclear questions, see Marc Trachtenberg, "American Thinking on Nuclear War," in C. G. Jacobsen et al., *Strategic Power: USA/USSR* (London, 1990).

[3] The term was quite common at the time. See, for example, Schnabel, *History of the Joint Chiefs of Staff*, vol. 1, pp. 258–59.

[4] For a discussion of some of the theoretical issues relating to this question, see especially Stephen Van Evera, "Causes of War," unpublished dissertation (Berkeley, 1984), chapter 3, and Jack Levy, "Declining Power and the Preventive Motivation for War," *World Politics*, vol. 40, no. 1 (October 1987), pp. 82–107.

the winter of 1950–51 was due to a sense among "insiders" familiar with the true state of the military balance that a "window of vulnerability" had opened up, and that the Soviets might be tempted to strike before the United States was able to close it. It followed that this was not the time to run risks. By 1953 the situation had altered dramatically as a result of the extraordinary buildup of American military power that had taken place during this period; this shift in the balance led to a greatly increased willingness to escalate in Korea if the war could not be ended on acceptable terms. America's window of vulnerability had been shut; and a "window of opportunity" opened. A key question during the early Eisenhower period, therefore, was whether this new situation should be exploited before it too disappeared.

The second major point to emerge from the study is that aggressive ideas were taken very seriously in the American government in the early 1950s, even at the highest levels of the administration. This aggressive mood was in part rooted in concerns about the shifting military balance. This is not to say that an aggressive policy was ever implemented. The real question is not whether such a policy was adopted, but what sort of political weight this kind of thinking carried.

This article, therefore, has the following structure. A brief survey of preventive war thinking in the first section simply sets the stage. It turns out that support for a highly aggressive strategy was much more widespread than has ever been recognized. But these explicit calls for a showdown with the Soviets "before it was too late" were just the tip of the iceberg, a surface manifestation of a pervasive but amorphous set of concerns about what the loss of America's nuclear advantage might lead to.

Was all of this just talk, or did these anxieties have a real impact on policy? The issue will be addressed in two parts. First, I want to examine the sort of thinking that took shape as high government officials grappled with these issues on a fairly abstract and general level. The analysis in the second section will therefore focus on statements of grand strategy, and especially on NSC 68. The test, however, of how seriously such documents are to be taken is whether the sort of thinking they reflected had any real impact on policy on specific issues. The third section, therefore, examines how concerns about the shifting balance affected actual policy, especially during the Korean War. The fourth section takes the story to its conclusion by looking at how preventive war arguments were finally confronted and laid to rest during the early Eisenhower period, in the Solarium exercise and its aftermath in 1953–54. I end by exploring some of the implications of the argument for understanding the overall course of American foreign and military policy in the early 1950s, in the Far East, Central Europe, and elsewhere around the globe.

"PREVENTIVE WAR" THINKING, 1945–53

The sort of argument that General Groves made in 1946 was quite common in the early atomic age. The idea that the United States had to take some sort of action before its nuclear edge was neutralized was by no means limited to the lunatic fringe. William L. Laurence, for example, the science correspondent for the *New York Times* and then America's leading writer on nuclear issues, in 1948 wanted to force the Soviets to accept nuclear disarmament, through an ultimatum if necessary. If they turned down this American demand, their atomic plants should be destroyed before bombs could be produced. If that meant war, he said, it would be one forced on America by Soviet "insistence on an atomic-armament race which must inevitably lead to war anyway. Under the circumstances, it would be to our advantage to have it while we are still the sole possessors of the atomic bomb."[5]

Those who wanted a more "positive" policy often argued that an unrestricted nuclear arms race would "inevitably" lead to war. Groves also assumed that "the world could not long survive" an "armament race in atomic weapons."[6] Senator Brien McMahon, the influential chairman of the Joint Committee on Atomic Energy, thought that "almost nothing could be worse than the current atomic armaments race and that victory in a future war, whatever its sequel in other respects, would at least assure effective international control over weapons of mass destruction."[7]

This argument for a more "positive" policy was also a favorite theme of a number of scientists and intellectuals. It is well known that Bertrand Russell had advocated a Laurence-style ultimatum in 1946.[8] By 1948, he was calling for preventive war pure and simple.[9] The famous physicist Leo Szilard had evidently made a preventive war argument at the very beginning of the atomic age: it was "from the lips of Leo Szilard," Ber-

[5] William L. Laurence, "How Soon Will Russia Have the A-Bomb?" *Saturday Evening Post*, November 6, 1948, p. 182.

[6] Groves, "Statement on the atomic bomb."

[7] McMahon to Truman, November 21, 1949, FRUS, 1949, vol. 1, p. 591. Note also McMahon's remarks in a top secret hearing held on January 20, 1950, Stenographic Transcript of Hearings before the Joint Committee on Atomic Energy, January 20, 1950, vol. 1, "Projected Development of Super Weapons," (TS), CD 471.6 A-Bomb, RG 330, USNA, quoted in Samuel Williamson (with Steven Rearden), "The View from Above: High-Level Decisions and the Soviet-American Strategic Arms Competition, 1945–50," p. 199 (unpublished manuscript, October 1975, available from Office of the Secretary of Defense, Freedom of Information Office), and also *The Journals of David E. Lilienthal*, vol. 2, pp. 584–85. For additional information on preventive war thinking in the Senate, see n. 62 below.

[8] See his statement in the *Bulletin of the Atomic Scientists*, October 1, 1946, pp. 19–21.

[9] See the report of his speech of November 20, 1948, at the New Commonwealth School, London, in the *New York Times*, November 21, 1948, p. 4.

nard Brodie wrote, that he had "heard, in October of 1945, the first out-right advocacy in my experience of preventive war." The noted mathematician John von Neumann, the founder of game theory, was a particularly strong supporter of the idea, and remarked in 1950: "If you say why not bomb them tomorrow, I say why not today? If you say today at 5 o'clock, I say why not one o'clock?"[10]

Preventive war was also a very live issue among the civilian strategists at the RAND Corporation well into the early 1950s, and there is some evidence that the Navy was interested in the question in 1948.[11] At the State Department, even moderates like Charles Bohlen and George Kennan were worried about what would happen if matters were allowed to drift and the Soviets began to build large nuclear forces of their own. Bohlen raised the issue in April 1949. "We were not now in the military phase of our relations with the Russians," he said at a State Department meeting, but America had to "look ahead" and think in long-range terms. Suppose that by 1953 Russia had recovered from the war and was "in possession of the atomic bomb." The United States might then wonder: "what should we have done in 1949?"[12] As for Kennan, he thought in 1950 that a war that the Soviet Union stumbled into at that point, before she had really built up an impressive nuclear force, might in the long run "be the best solution for us."[13]

[10] Brodie's recollection is in Brodie to Schelling, January 8, 1965, enclosure, Brodie Papers, Box 2, UCLA Library. See also the last paragraph of Szilard to Bush, January 14, 1944, in Gertrude Weiss Szilard and Spencer Weart, eds., *Leo Szilard: His Version of the Facts* (Cambridge, Mass., 1978), p. 163. Szilard's article, "Calling for a Crusade," *Bulletin of the Atomic Scientists*, April 1947, p. 103, while not of course an argument for preventive war, nonetheless betrays a certain attraction to the idea. Note finally the Fermi-Rabi statement of October 1949 opposing the development of the hydrogen bomb: the last sentence seemed to take it for granted that the U.S. could retaliate even against Soviet *production* of a "Super." FRUS, 1949, vol. 1, p. 573. On von Neumann: Steve J. Heims, *John von Neumann and Norbert Weiner: From Mathematics to the Technologies of Life and Death* (Cambridge, Mass., 1980), pp. 247, 484.

[11] The mathematician John Williams, then one of the leading figures at RAND, was the principal champion there of a preventive war strategy. He and Brodie had a very interesting memorandum debate on the issue in 1953 and 1954. See John Williams, "In Response to Paxson's Memo on the Probability of War," February 3, 1953, and his "Regarding the Preventive War Doctrine," July 27, 1953, unpublished RAND papers. The memoranda Brodie, Williams, and others exchanged on the question are in the folder "Strategic Objectives Committee," in James Digby's personal files at RAND; I am grateful to Mr. Digby for allowing me to consult them. On Navy interest in the idea, see the "Agenda for [Navy] General Board Serial 315. Study of Nature of Warfare within Next Ten Years and Navy Contributions in Support of National Security," March 30, 1948, CD 23-1-10, RG 330, 1947–50 series, USNA, especially question 119.

[12] Record of the Under Secretary's Meeting, April 15, 1949, FRUS, 1949, vol. 1, p. 284. Emphasis added.

[13] "Memorandum of National Security Council Consultants' Meeting," June 29, 1950,

Or take the case of Winston Churchill. In 1946, he predicted that there would be a war with Russia in perhaps seven or eight years. How, he was asked, could Britain take part in an atomic war? "We ought not to wait until Russia is ready," he replied. "I believe it will be eight years before she has these bombs."[14] He argued repeatedly in 1948 for a showdown with the Russians—for "bringing matters to a head" before the American nuclear monopoly was broken. If this led to a war, he told the House of Commons at the beginning of the year, having it then offered "the best chance of coming out of it alive."[15] If the Soviets were so aggressive now, he argued in October, when only America had the bomb, imagine what they would be like "when they get the atomic bomb and have accumulated a large store." Matters could not be allowed to drift; a more active policy was necessary; "no one in his senses can believe we have a limitless period of time before us."[16] Thus Churchill, even before the Berlin blockade, privately urged the American government to present the Soviets with an ultimatum: they must either withdraw from East Germany or see their cities destroyed by atomic attack.[17]

The real heart of preventive war thinking at this time, however, lay within the U.S. Air Force. The preventive war policy was, as Brodie

---

FRUS, 1950, vol. 1, p. 330. See also John Lewis Gaddis, *Strategies of Containment* (New York, 1982), p. 48n. Note also some information that came out during the John Paton Davies affair of November 1954: when Davies was dismissed as a security risk, he defended himself (among other ways) by presenting evidence that he had called in 1950 for a "preventive showdown with the Soviet Union." *The New York Times*, November 6, 1954, pp. 8, 9.

[14] This is an extract from Lord Moran's diary: *Winston Churchill: The Struggle for Survival, 1940–1965* (London, 1966), p. 315; note also pp. 505, 545.

[15] *Parliamentary Debates*, House of Commons, January 23, 1948, p. 561.

[16] Llandudno speech, October 9, 1948, *New York Times*, October 10, 1948, p. 4. These speeches made a big impression on the famous political scientist Hans Morgenthau, who also stressed the dangers of a policy of drift and agreed with Churchill that matters needed to be brought "to a head" with the Soviets. See his article in the *Bulletin of the Atomic Scientists*, January 1950, esp. pp. 23–26. Morgenthau complained that the American government ignored the tremendous significance of the breaking of the U.S. nuclear monopoly, but he was reacting simply to the blasé image that American officials were deliberately trying to project: see, for example, the instructions on how to react to the Soviet atomic test in the William Frye memo, September 23, 1949, P & O 091 Russia (sec 1), RG 319, USNA.

[17] Douglas to Lovett, April 17, 1948, FRUS, 1948, vol. 2, p. 895. 1948 was also the year that Churchill published *The Gathering Storm* (Boston, 1948), his account of the origins of the Second World War. This book can be viewed as the intellectual pivot linking the interwar period with the nuclear age. The political message of the book certainly has to be interpreted in the light of the other things Churchill was saying that year. Note especially the "theme of the volume": "how the English-speaking peoples through their unwisdom, carelessness, and good nature allowed the wicked to rearm." Or consider the extraordinary passage on pp. 346–48 (pp. 310–11 in the Bantam paperback edition), a powerful argument for acting before it was too late.

pointed out in 1953, "for several years certainly the prevailing philosophy at the Air War College."[18] General Orvil Anderson, the commanding officer at that institution, was dismissed in 1950 by President Truman for going public with the idea. Anderson's comments were by no means limited to vague support for the general principle of a preventive attack. He had in fact "been in the habit of giving students at the college a completely detailed exposition, often lasting three or four hours, on how a preventive war through strategic airpower could be carried out." "Give me the order to do it and I can break up Russia's five A-bomb nests in a week," he was quoted as saying. "And when I went up to Christ—I think I could explain to Him that I had saved civilization."[19]

General Anderson's views were evidently shared by other high-ranking Air Force officers, including General George Kenney, the first commander of the Strategic Air Command, and his successor, General Curtis LeMay.[20] General Nathan Twining, Air Force Chief of Staff and then Chairman of the Joint Chiefs of Staff [JCS] under Eisenhower, was also sympathetic to Anderson's point of view. In the mid-1960s, a good ten years after preventive war had essentially died out as an issue, he wrote that Anderson had been a "brilliant officer," and his difficulty "lay in his

---

[18] Bernard Brodie, "A Commentary on the Preventive-War Doctrine," RAND paper, June 11, 1953, p. 1. See also his Air War College talk of April 17, 1952, "Changing Capabilities and National Objectives, Brodie Papers, Box 12, UCLA, p. 23ff. Both papers have been published in Marc Trachtenberg, ed., *The Development of American Strategic Thought* (New York, 1988), vol. 3.

[19] *The New York Times*, September 2, 1950, p. 8.

[20] The point about Kenney is based on William Kaufmann's personal recollections; it came out in a conversation I had with him in 1986. Kaufmann knew Kenney quite well in the late 1940s. Kenney, however, was more discreet than Anderson in his public remarks, and did not go beyond an argument about the inevitability of war. See "White Star vs. Red," *Newsweek*, May 17, 1948, pp. 30–32. As for LeMay, he pointed out much later that there had been a time, before the Soviets had accumulated a stockpile of atomic bombs, when the U.S. could have destroyed the entire Soviet capability to wage war "without losing a man to their defenses." He denied that he had ever formally advocated a preventive war strategy, but he did admit that he might have said to some people at SAC, "We've got this capability. Maybe the Nation ought to do it" (in *Mission with LeMay* [Garden City, N.Y., 1965], pp. 481–82). Note also the discussion in the book by his successor as SAC commander, General Thomas S. Power. Power discussed the idea at some length and took a "balanced" approach to the subject: "the concept of 'preventive war,' " he said, "is too complex to justify conclusive opinions either for or against it." Thomas Power, *Design for Survival* (New York, 1965), pp. 79–84. And finally, see the transcript of a series of discussions held in Princeton in late 1953 and early 1954, pp. 1317–19, Acheson Papers, Box 76, Harry S Truman Library [HSTL]—hereafter cited as "Princeton Seminar." According to Nitze, there was a group, centering on elements in, or connected with, the Air Force, that was convinced in 1950 that general war was inevitable, and that this notion had implied something like a preventive war strategy. The group (as he recalled it) included Colonel Herschel Williams of the Air Force; apparently the prominent right-wing intellectual James Burnham (the name is garbled in the transcript) was the major figure in the group.

outspoken evaluation of the basic moral issue involved in our confrontation of the Communist conspiracy." For Anderson preventive war had simply been the lesser of two evils. But his views, Twining complained, "were never given a fair hearing by the State Department, or for that matter, by the military establishment."[21]

THE LOSS OF MONOPOLY: NSC 68 AND AMERICAN
STRATEGY, 1950–52

The most important government officials at the time were quite hostile to the "preventive war" thesis. But this is not to say that they were not concerned with the problems that would result from the ending of America's nuclear monopoly. The Soviet detonation of an atomic device in late 1949, in fact, led to a major rethinking of American strategy. NSC 68, the basic document here, was written mainly by Paul Nitze, Kennan's successor as head of the State Department's Policy Planning Staff. The document also reflected the views of Secretary of State Dean Acheson, its chief defender in high government circles; it can in fact be seen as a kind of fleshing out of the Acheson strategy of creating "situations of strength."[22]

The authors of NSC 68 believed that America's atomic monopoly was the one thing that had balanced Soviet superiority in ground forces; they were concerned, therefore, that with growing Soviet atomic capabilities, America's nuclear edge was being neutralized more rapidly than conventional forces could be created to fill the gap. Hence the sense of a danger zone. But they did not believe that once American ground forces had been built up and an overall balance had been restored, that would be the end of the problem: they did not believe that the threat of retaliation would be an adequate deterrent to nuclear attack. The Soviets, it was predicted, would be able to deliver a hundred atomic bombs on target by 1954. This did not mean the USSR could wipe out American industry as such, for this was still the early atomic age, but it could destroy America's "*superiority* in economic potential." The Soviets could thus prevent the United

[21] Nathan F. Twining, *Neither Liberty Nor Safety: A Hard Look at U.S. Military Policy and Strategy* (New York, 1966), pp. 18–19. See also pp. 49, 56, 60, 276. Note also the August 1953 Air Force study "The Coming National Crisis," discussed in David Rosenberg, "The Origins of Overkill: Nuclear Weapons and American Strategy, 1945–1960," *International Security*, vol. 7, no. 4 (Spring 1983), p. 33. This study, Rosenberg says, argued that "the time was approaching when the U.S. would find itself in a 'militarily unmanageable' position. Before that time arrived, the nation would have to choose whether to trust its future to 'the whims of a small group of proven barbarians' in the USSR, or 'be militarily prepared to support such decisions as might involve general war.' "

[22] See, for example, Dean Acheson's "total diplomacy" speech of February 16, 1950, *Department of State Bulletin*, March 20, 1950.

States from "developing a general military superiority in a war of long duration." Even if they had to absorb an American retaliatory attack, it was "hardly conceivable that, if war comes, the Soviet leaders would refrain from the use of atomic weapons unless they felt fully confident of attaining their objectives by other means."[23] In fact, as a Policy Planning Staff paper emphasized in mid-1952, NSC 68 did not hold that "the existence of two large atomic stockpiles" would result in a nuclear standoff, but instead had predicted that it might well "prove to be an incitement to war."[24]

Because of the advantages of getting in the first blow, there would be a constant danger of surprise attack: the incentive to preempt would be a permanent source of instability. The need, therefore, was not simply to cover a gap; the concern was not limited to the next four or so years. The real problem was more far-reaching, but what could be done about it?

NSC 68 explicitly ruled out a strategy of preventive war, in the sense of an unprovoked surprise attack on the Soviet Union.[25] But a number of the document's key points echoed the standard preventive war arguments: the developing situation was not stable, the country was moving into a period of enormous danger, and this situation could not last indefinitely. Nitze and Acheson took it for granted that America was dealing not with an ordinary adversary, but with a ruthless enemy intent on world domination, and ultimately on the destruction of the United States.[26]

It was widely assumed in official circles that it might not be possible to work out a satisfactory modus vivendi with the Soviets. One high official in the State Department went even further and "suggested that in the last

[23] NSC 68, April 7, 1950, FRUS, 1950, vol. 1, pp. 251, 266, 268. Emphasis added. See also a Policy Planning Staff paper written in mid-1952, FRUS, 1952–54, vol. 2, p. 62, para. 9.

[24] Enclosure in Nitze to Matthews, July 14, 1952, FRUS, 1952–54, vol. 2, p. 62. These were all very controversial issues within the government, especially in 1950. Nitze himself had earlier leaned toward the line that nuclear forces tended to neutralize each other [FRUS, 1950, vol. 1, p. 14], and it is not clear to what extent NSC 68 marked a genuine shift in opinion on his part, as opposed to an accommodation to those, especially in the military, who took the opposite line. For a fascinating inside account of these disputes, see Harvey to Armstrong, June 23, 1950, Records of the Policy Planning Staff, Box 7, folder "Atomic Energy—Armaments 1950," RG 59, USNA. For the views of the military, see JIC 502, January 20, 1950, CCS 471.6 USSR (11-8-49) ("Implications of Soviet Success in Achieving Atomic Capability"), sec. 1, USNA; this document was their contribution to the process that culminated in NSC 68. For a CIA contribution, see ORE 91–49, February 10, 1950, file CD 11-1-2, Box 61, RG 330 (1947–50 series), USNA.

[25] FRUS, 1950, vol. 1, pp. 281–82. According to General Twining, however, in the discussions leading to NSC 68, the preventive war option was "advocated with much more vigor" than two of the four alternatives considered in the report. Twining, *Neither Liberty nor Safety*, p. 49.

[26] FRUS, 1950, vol. 1, pp. 207–8, 145.

analysis we may find that we have to drive out the rulers of the Kremlin completely."[27] Acheson himself argued that we already were in a "real war" with them, although the American people still did not realize it.[28] And Robert Lovett, then a consultant to the NSC, developed the point: we should "start acting exactly as though we were under fire from an invading army. In the war in which we are presently engaged, we should fight with no holds barred. We should find every weak spot in the enemy's armor, both on the periphery and at the center, and hit him with anything that comes to hand. Anything we do short of an all-out effort is inexcusable."[29]

The most important point to be made about NSC 68 is that this was *not* a defensive-minded, status quo–oriented document.[30] For Acheson and Nitze, the fundamental aim of American policy was to bring about a "retraction" of Soviet power—to force the Soviets to "recede" by creating "situations of strength."[31] The policy of NSC 68 was, in its own terms, a "policy of calculated and gradual coercion"; the aim was "to check and to roll back the Kremlin's drive for world domination." To support such

[27] R. Gordon Arneson, Special Assistant to the Under Secretary of State for atomic energy policy, from the Record of the Meeting of the State-Defense Policy Review Group," February 27, 1950, in FRUS, 1950, vol. 1, p. 174.

[28] Ibid., p. 207; see also ibid., p. 293.

[29] Record of the Meeting of the State-Defense Policy Review Group, March 16, 1950, ibid., p. 198. Lovett had been Under Secretary of State until January 1949; he was appointed Deputy Secretary of Defense in September 1950, and the following year succeeded Marshall as Secretary of Defense. After the Korean War began, this sort of attitude became very common. See for example Gov. Thomas Dewey's remarks, *New York Times*, August 24, 1950, p. 6. On August 19, the Gallup Poll reported that 57 percent of its sample thought that the U.S. was "now actually in World War III," and only 28 percent felt the fighting in Korea would "stop short of another world war." *The Gallup Poll, 1939–1971*, vol. 1, p. 933.

[30] The large literature on the subject generally assumes that NSC 68 called for an essentially defensive policy. The early account by Paul Hammond, "NSC-68: Prologue to Rearmament," in Warner Schilling, Paul Hammond, and Glenn Snyder, *Strategy, Politics, and Defense Budgets* (New York, 1962), was written before the text of the document became available. The more recent literature is therefore more interesting in this connection. See in particular Samuel Wells, "Sounding the Tocsin: NSC 68 and the Soviet Threat," *International Security*, Fall 1979, and Steven Rearden, *The Evolution of American Strategic Doctrine: Paul Nitze and the Soviet Challenge* (Boulder, Colo., 1984), esp. pp. 22–26. The chapter on NSC 68 in John Lewis Gaddis, *Strategies of Containment* (New York, 1982), is as close to a standard account as we have. Gaddis here (p. 100) repeats his earlier judgment (in "NSC 68 and the Problem of Ends and Means," *International Security*, Spring 1980, p. 168) that the military buildup called for in the document was intended "to be defensive in nature."

[31] For Acheson: see Memorandum of Conversation, March 24, 1950, FRUS, 1950, vol. 1, p. 208. The term "retraction" appears in many documents from this period. See especially NSC 68, April 7, 1950, FRUS, 1950, vol. 1, pp. 252, 289. Note also a Nitze memorandum of July 14, 1952, in FRUS, 1952–54, vol. 2, pp. 58–59.

a policy, it was important to go beyond merely balancing Soviet power and build up "clearly superior overall power in its most inclusive sense."[32]

What was the point of such an ambitious strategy? The document itself presented two rationales, but neither is entirely satisfactory. First, it argued that a merely defensive policy was inadequate because the "absence of order among nations [was] becoming less and less tolerable." The enormous tensions of the Cold War, NSC 68 argued, could not continue for long and would eventually be replaced by "some kind of order," either on their terms or on ours.[33] But an argument of this sort seems much too abstract and academic to be the real taproot of thinking about basic policy.

The other argument was that a "process of accommodation, withdrawal and frustration" was needed in order to bring about "the necessary changes in the Soviet system." The Kremlin could be "a victim of its own dynamism": if its "forward thrusts" were frustrated, and the Soviets had to deal with a "superior counterpressure," "the seeds of decay within the Soviet system would begin to flourish and fructify."[34] All this, of course, is quite similar to the argument Kennan had made a few years earlier in the famous X-article, but there the claim was that an essentially defensive strategy would be sufficient to produce these results. Why did NSC 68 propose to go further? Why was a more aggressive American strategy more likely to bring about these changes in the Soviet system than the sort of strategy that Kennan, for example, had in mind? Despite its length, NSC 68 contained no answer to this basic question. One is therefore left with the suspicion that some unarticulated motive was the real basis for the aggressive strategy called for in the document.

It seems that concerns about the shifting balance played a major role in shaping the policy outlined in NSC 68. The report assumed that in time a Soviet surprise attack on the United States might well be militarily decisive. An American buildup "might put off for some time" the date when the Soviets would be able to launch such an attack. But when that time came—and the document seemed to assume that it would come eventually—the Soviets "might be tempted to strike swiftly and with stealth."[35] The assumption that the Soviets were intent on world domination and thus on the destruction of American power, and the belief that they were

---

[32] FRUS, 1950, vol. 1, pp. 253, 255, 284. Note also the reference to the H-bomb in ibid., p. 267: "If the U.S. develops a thermonuclear weapon ahead of the U.S.S.R., the U.S. should for the time being be able to bring increased pressure on the U.S.S.R."

[33] FRUS, 1950, vol. 1, pp. 241, 263. See also Paul Nitze, "Coalition Policy and the Concept of World Order," in Arnold Wolfers, ed., *Alliance Policy in the Cold War* (Baltimore, 1959).

[34] FRUS, 1950, vol. 1, pp. 248, 287.

[35] Ibid., pp. 266–67.

absolutely ruthless and that their policy was "guided only by considerations of expediency," implied that they would strike when they had developed this capability.[36] In that case, it did not make sense to opt for a
strategy of simply "buying time," in the hope that there might be a basic
transformation of the Soviet system in the next few years.[37] Taken to their
logical conclusion, these arguments pointed to a much more extreme policy than the one called for in NSC 68—perhaps to a strategy of "bringing
matters to a head" with the Russians before it was too late. But this was
not the strategy that people like Nitze and Acheson seem to have been
reaching for. One has the sense instead that the architects of NSC 68 could
scarcely bring themselves to accept the conclusions that followed from
their own arguments. It seems instead that they settled, as a kind of psychological compromise, for the lesser strategy of "rollback" and forcing
a "retraction of Soviet power," and for the buildup that might make these
possible.

This is not to argue that NSC 68 had a hidden agenda and that the real
goal of the aggressive strategy was to generate situations that might lead
to a war before America's nuclear advantage was lost forever. It is clear,
in fact, that neither Nitze nor Acheson actually wanted a war, above all,
not in 1950. What they wanted was to create such overwhelming power
that the United States could achieve its goals without actually having to
fight. But the military strategy they would have liked to pursue was extremely ambitious. As Nitze put it in mid-1952, it would take "clearly
preponderant power" to make progress by peaceful means, "probably
more power than to win military victory in the event of war."[38]

At the end of the Truman administration, Nitze would complain that
even the extraordinary buildup of military power that had taken place
during the Korean War had been inadequate. The defense budget may
have tripled, but the "situations of strength" that national policy had
called for had never been created. In January 1953, he worried that the
United States was becoming "a sort of hedge-hog, unattractive to attack,
but basically not very worrisome over a period of time beyond our immediate position"; Nitze was upset that the goals laid out in documents
like NSC 68 were not being taken "sufficiently seriously as to warrant
doing what is necessary to give us some chance of seeing these objectives
attained."[39]

A war itself was never desired, but it does seem clear that Nitze was

[36] The quotation is from Paul Nitze, "Recent Soviet Moves," February 8, 1950, ibid., p.
145.

[37] On "buying time," see a Policy Planning Staff document of December 9, 1950, FRUS,
1950, vol. 1, p. 464; also see NSC 68, ibid., p. 287.

[38] Nitze to Matthews, July 14, 1952, FRUS, 1952–54, vol. 2, p. 59.

[39] Nitze to Acheson, January 12, 1953, FRUS, 1952–54, vol. 2, p. 205.

willing to accept a real risk of a nuclear conflict, but only after the trends had been reversed and American power had been rebuilt. For the time being, he wrote in 1950, the United States was weak and needed above all "to build a platform from which we can subsequently go on to a successful outcome of this life-and-death struggle" with the Kremlin. "We must," he stressed, "avoid becoming involved in general hostilities with the USSR in our present position of military weakness if this is at all possible without sacrificing our self-respect and without endangering our survival."[40] But then? The clear implication is that when "our position of weakness" turns into a "position of strength," it would become less necessary to tread cautiously.[41]

In the meantime, however, the country was going to have to cross a kind of danger zone. With the outbreak of the Korean War and the rearmament decisions that were made in its wake, the argument was extended to take note of another danger: the risk that the Soviets might strike preemptively, in order to head off the shift in the balance of military power that American rearmament would bring about. The assumption was that a "window" favoring the Soviets had opened, and that the American attempt to close it might well lead to a war.

Such window thinking is a recurrent theme in the published *Foreign Relations* documents. NSC 73/4 of August 25, 1950, for example, argued that the Korean events might be "the first phase of a general Soviet plan for global war." In that case, the Soviets would avoid war until they had calculated that "the United States had reached the point of maximum diversion and attrition of its forces-in-being," or until the USSR had developed its nuclear forces "to the point which it deemed desirable for a general attack on the West." As long as American forces were being drawn increasingly into the fighting in Korea, "the Kremlin might not

---

[40] FRUS, 1950, vol. 1, p. 464. This sort of thinking was fairly common during the late Truman period.

[41] Nitze in fact made this point explicit in a paper he wrote for the Air Force's Project Control. The attack on South Korea, he said, had made it possible to implement much of the rearmament program called for in NSC 68. "At the time," he added, "it was hoped to accelerate the program to a target date of 1952 in order to lay the basis for taking increased risks of general war in achieving a satisfactory solution of our relations with the U.S.S.R. while her stockpile of atomic weapons was still small." Paul Nitze, "A Project for Further Analysis and Study of Certain Factors Affecting our Foreign Policy and our National Defense Policy," September 15, 1954, Project Control Papers, U.S. Air Force Historical Research Center, Maxwell Air Force Base, Alabama. See also n. 154 below. I am grateful to Tami Davis Biddle for providing me with a copy of this document. Note also in this general context Acheson's complaints in May and June 1953 about the "weakness" of the Eisenhower policy, and the new administration's failure to follow through on Truman's policy of "building strength." Acheson to Truman, May 28, 1953, Box 30, folder 391, and Acheson Memorandum of Conversation, June 23, 1953, Box 68, folder 172, both in the Dean Acheson Papers, Sterling Library, Yale University, New Haven, Connecticut.

hasten the outbreak of general hostilities since the USSR would be increasing its own capabilities as those of the U.S. diminished." But this could change, the document warned, "at the point where the Kremlin estimated that our maximum weakness had been reached, and that further passage of time leading to the material strengthening of the relative position and military posture of the United States would not work to Soviet advantage."[42]

A CIA memorandum a few weeks later was more specific about dates: "In the belief that their object cannot be fully attained without a general war with the Western Powers, the Soviet rulers may deliberately provoke such a war at the time when, in their opinion, the relative strength of the USSR is at its maximum. It is estimated that such a period will exist from now through 1954, with the peak of Soviet strength relative to the Western Powers being reached about 1952."[43] Window arguments of this sort were very common, especially in 1951.[44]

The sense that a great window of vulnerability had opened up helps explain why the U.S. government as a whole, and especially those officials who really understood military matters, were so afraid of general war in late 1950 and 1951. For the time being, the military balance favored the Soviets, who might therefore soon choose to precipitate a war with the West at this time. For the same reason, the West had to move with great caution during this period. Indeed, these assumptions had begun to take shape in early 1950, even before the outbreak of the Korean War. It had been predicted that the shift in the balance resulting from the ending of the American nuclear monopoly would embolden the Soviets and lead to an increase in Communist aggressiveness.[45] The events in Korea seemed to confirm this prophecy, and thus to vindicate this whole way of viewing things; in fact, a good part of the reason why the Korean War had such an extraordinary impact on American policy in this period is that the ground had been prepared in this way. Indeed, what the Korean War showed was that the situation was even more serious than NSC 68 had

[42] FRUS, 1950, vol. 1, p. 378. See also FRUS, 1950, vol. 7, p. 523.

[43] NIE-3 of November 15, 1950, FRUS, 1950, vol. 1, p. 415. Even more specific is the estimate of the "Moscow-Peiping Time-Table for War," written by the Director of the State Department's Office of Chinese Affairs (Clubb), December 18, 1950, ibid., p. 478ff. See also CIA Director Bedell Smith's memo of December 11, 1950, FRUS, 1951, vol. 1, p. 3.

[44] See FRUS, 1951, vol. 1, pp. 40, 111, 126, 131, 153, 198–99 for various documents with similar "window" themes. Note also an interesting variation in an NSC staff document of August 12, 1952, FRUS, 1952–1954, vol. 2, p. 74, para. 3: this was a "bringing matters to a head" argument in reverse.

[45] For a typical example of such a prediction prior to the outbreak of the Korean War, see the Policy Planning Staff paper, "The Current Position in the Cold War," April 14, 1950, FRUS, 1950, vol. 3, esp. pp. 858–59; note also Nitze's comments in FRUS, 1950, vol. 1, p. 143.

assumed. The fact that the Soviets had been willing to accept the risk of war with America—first, in approving the North Korean attack, and then in supporting China's intervention in the war—showed how strong they thought their position now was, and thus how far they might now be prepared to go, not just in the Far East, but in Europe as well.[46]

It followed that the central goal of diplomacy, as Bohlen put it in 1951, was to steer the country through this danger zone: "It is axiomatic that when one group of powers seeks to close a dangerous disparity in its armed strength in relation to another group of powers, a period of danger by that factor alone is to be anticipated. The diplomatic arm of the United States should be utilized in this period in such a fashion as to minimize rather than intensify the danger of a general war resulting from a Soviet response to what they might regard as an increasing threat to their existence."[47]

It was, therefore, important to be discreet about America's real long-term goals. There was a great danger, according to a 1952 Policy Planning Staff paper, that if the Soviets thought war was unavoidable, they might initiate a war that would push the United States "back to the Western hemisphere" and allow them to take over the vast resources of Eurasia. To achieve this goal, which would put them in a commanding position for the final phases of the world struggle, they might even be willing to absorb "whatever damage we can inflict" through atomic bombardment. It was thus important at present to avoid giving them the impression that war was inevitable. Talk of rollback was therefore ill-advised at a time when a period of stability was needed to enable the West to develop its power, and in particular to build up its forces in Europe. It followed that

[46] See especially Acheson's remarks in the special NSC meeting held on November 28, 1950, especially the passage summarized on p. 15 of Elsey's notes of this meeting, Elsey Papers, Box 72, "Korea. National Security Council Meeting, 3:00 p.m., November 28, 1950," HSTL: "Time is shorter than we thought, Mr. Acheson said. We used to think we could take our time up to 1952, but if we were right in that, the Russians wouldn't be taking such terrible risks as they are now." (There is a less revealing record of this meeting in FRUS, 1950, vol. 7, pp. 1242ff.) Note also NIE-15, "Probable Soviet Moves to Exploit the Present Situation," December 11, 1950, President's Secretary's Files [PSF], Box 253, HSTL, especially the first paragraph in this document. Finally, see Acheson's later discussion of all this in the Princeton Seminar, p. 906. None of this, of course, should be taken as implying that there was no hard evidence that fed into these assessments. There were in fact important indications from intelligence sources of a general increase in Soviet aggressiveness and preparations for war. See in this regard Kennan's comments in the Princeton Seminar, pp. 1189–90, and the memorandum of an intelligence briefing requested by the Secretary of Defense on "Soviet Activity in Europe During the Past Year Which Points Toward Offensive Military Operations," October 26, 1950, CD 350.09, RG 330 (July–December 1950 series), USNA.

[47] Bohlen memorandum, September 21, 1951, FRUS, 1951, vol. 1, p. 172. The last phrase hints at a sense of the "security dilemma" aspect of the situation; the first sentence echoes Tirpitz's pre-World War I arguments about a "danger zone."

public pronouncements for the time being had to be strictly defensive in tone. "It seems dangerous," the paper argued, "to adopt the political posture that we must roll back the Iron Curtain" when the West was not yet able to defend even the present line of demarcation.[48]

POLICY IN PRACTICE: KOREA AND ELSEWHERE

In this section, I want to show first how the sort of thinking described in the previous section was related, (a) to the decision not to escalate in Korea during the terrible winter of 1950–51; and (b) to the extraordinary rearmament decisions made in late 1950. I then want to examine how the dramatic buildup of American military power that eventually did take place, and the shift in the strategic balance that this brought about, affected the course of American strategy, especially in Korea, but elsewhere as well.

The first point to make about the Korean War is that the United States never really opted for a "limited war" strategy in that conflict. American policy was *not* shaped by a belief that as a matter of principle any escalation of the fighting was to be avoided. Rosemary Foot's conclusion about the "thinness of the dividing line between a limited and an expanded conflict" is correct.[49] It was taken for granted that a serious Soviet intervention in the war would lead to World War III, and not just to a local U.S.-Soviet war in the Far East.[50] As for a Chinese intervention,

[48] Policy Planning Staff paper, n.d., FRUS, 1952–1954, vol. 2, pp. 67–68. Once again, the parallels with pre-World War I Germany are striking. Paul Kennedy gives some amazing examples of German frankness (among themselves) about the importance of concealing their ultimate goals from the outside world while German naval power was being built up. For example, when Prince Henry of Prussia visited Britain in 1903, he "informed Tirpitz that 'the cat is out of the bag,' and regretfully added that 'we would have been much further than we are now, had we understood the art of keeping quiet.' " Paul Kennedy, *The Rise of the Anglo-German Antagonism, 1860–1914* (London, 1980), pp. 257–58. Note also the examples of the German recognition of the need for discretion in his "Strategic Aspects of the Anglo-German Naval Race," in his *Strategy and Diplomacy* (London, 1984), pp. 132, 159–60. Note similarly the evidence on German foreign minister Rathenau's basic policy in 1922 in Marc Trachtenberg, *Reparation in World Politics* (New York, 1980), p. 218.

[49] Rosemary Foot, *The Wrong War: American Policy and the Dimensions of the Korean Conflict, 1950–1953* (Ithaca, 1985), p. 37. Later on, however, she implies that there was a more or less definitive decision to fight a limited war. A "crucial turning point" was reached in early 1951: unless the administration soon opted for "expanded operations against China," she says, the Americans would be settling "for a limited conflict" (p. 120).

[50] This was a very common assumption in the documents. For the JCS views, see the Bradley memoranda of July 10, 1950 (circulated as NSC 76) and November 9, 1950, FRUS, 1950, vol. 7, pp. 346 and 1121. The more guarded official State Department view is reflected in NSC 76/1 of July 25, 1950, ibid., pp. 475–77. Formal policy was reflected in NSC 73/4 of August 25, 1950, FRUS, 1950, vol. 1, p. 375ff; see esp. p. 386. The less formal documents

there was originally no intention to fight a war limited to the Korean peninsula; the initial impulse was to respond to a Chinese attack by a certain widening of the conflict.[51] In fact, American officials at this point even considered the possibility that the U.S. should respond to a Chinese intervention with an attack on the Soviet Union itself.[52]

This extreme idea was quickly ruled out. But reading the documents, one does detect a certain undercurrent of emotion—an impulse to escalate, held in check only by considerations of expediency. As CIA Director Walter Bedell Smith put it at an NSC meeting in November 1950, the Chinese intervention had raised "the question as to what point the U.S. will be driven to, to attack the problem at its heart, namely Moscow, instead of handling it on the periphery as at present."[53] The implication was that this point was not that far off, that the United States could only be pushed so far and was rapidly reaching that limit. The same kind of thinking is reflected in a JCS paper of January 3, 1951, which argued that it was "militarily foolhardy" to get involved in a land war against China while the "heart of aggressive COMMIE power remained untouched."[54]

President Truman himself was also attracted, at least on a visceral level, to the idea of bringing matters to a head with the Russians. He warned publicly in July 1950 that new acts of aggression "might well strain to the breaking point the fabric of world peace."[55] On September 1 (that is, two months before the Chinese intervened), he issued another warning that fighting in Korea might "expand into a general war" if "Communist im-

---

are more revealing: see esp. the "Summary of United States-United Kingdom Discussions," July 20–24, 1950, FRUS, 1950, vol. 7, p. 463, para. 8, and Memorandum of Conversation, August 25, 1950, ibid., p. 647. For the views of important officials, see the record of U.S.-Canadian discussions, May 25 and June 14, 1951, FRUS, 1951, vol. 1, pp. 841, 850 (Nitze and Acheson); and the minutes of a meeting between high State and Defense Department officials, August 6, 1951, ibid., p. 878 (Lovett). The one piece of evidence I saw that points in the opposite direction is the record of a high-level meeting held in late June. When General Vandenberg pointed out that American air power would only be effective against North Korean armor if Soviet jets did not intervene, Truman asked about America's ability to knock out Soviet bases in the area, and then ordered the Air Force to "prepare plans to wipe out all Soviet air bases in the Far East." Memorandum of Conversation, June 25, 1950, FRUS, 1950, vol 7, pp. 157–61.

[51] Foot, *Wrong War*, pp. 82–84.

[52] "Summary of United States-United Kingdom Discussions," July 20–24, 1950, FRUS, 1950, vol. 7, p. 463, para. 9; see also p. 465.

[53] Minutes of the 71st Meeting of the National Security Council (November 9, 1950). Available on microfilm: "Minutes of Meetings of the National Security Council," University Publications of America, reel 1. Henceforth cited as: MNSC.

[54] JCS 1776/180, January 3, 1951, "Records of the Joint Chiefs of Staff," University Publications of America microfilm publication (1979), Part II (1946–53), Section C (Far East), reel 9, frame 832. Henceforth cited in the form: RJCS/II/C/9/832. Emphasis in original.

[55] *Public Papers of the Presidents of the United States: Harry S Truman*, 1950, pp. 527–37; cited in FRUS, 1951, vol. 1, p. 837.

perialism" drew new armies and governments into the Korean conflict. The warning was given despite the fact that Truman had just approved the important document NSC 73/4, which pointed in exactly the opposite direction.[56] Perhaps the President's warning was essentially a bluff, or maybe it is to be understood in domestic political terms, as a response to Republican pressure, since leading Republican politicians had been loudly calling for threats of this sort.[57] But it seems that something visceral was expressing itself, something that also comes out in Truman's famous diary reflections written a year and a half later, where he played with the idea of issuing a nuclear ultimatum to the Soviets as a way of ending the war.[58]

The late summer of 1950 saw a flurry of articles in the public press dealing with preventive war. The secretary of the navy, Francis Matthews, gave a speech on August 25 calling for the United States to initiate a "war of aggression." Americans, he said, should become the world's first "aggressors for peace."[59] This was followed by a report by the *Times*'s well-informed military correspondent, Hanson Baldwin, that Matthews was launching a trial balloon, and that his speech reflected the thinking of Secretary of Defense Louis Johnson, "who has been selling the same doctrine of the preventive war in private conversations around Washington."[60] A day later, the same day that Truman's warning about

[56] *New York Times*, September 2, 1950, p. 4. NSC 73/4 would limit the American response to a Chinese intervention to "appropriate air and naval action" against China. A widening of the war to include, in such a case, an attack on the Soviet Union itself was not even considered in the document, which generally took the line that in dealing with Communist moves "over the next two or three months" conflicts were to be localized. FRUS, 1950, vol. 1, p. 375ff, esp. pp. 385–88.

[57] *New York Times*, August 16, 1950, pp. 1:7, 17:1.

[58] The passages are quoted and commented on in Foot, *Wrong War*, p. 176, and in two articles by Barton Bernstein: "Truman's Secret Thoughts on Ending the Korean War," *Foreign Service Journal*, November 1980, and "New Light on the Korean War," *International History Review*, April 1981. Note also General Douglas MacArthur's "Memorandum on Ending the Korean War" in his *Reminiscences* (New York, 1964), pp. 410–12, and Bob Considine's related interview with MacArthur, published immediately after his death, *New York Times*, April 9, 1964, p. 16.

[59] *New York Times*, August 25, 1950, p. 1:6.

[60] Ibid., September 1, 1950, p. 4:2, and republished in part in the *Bulletin of the Atomic Scientists*, October 1950, p. 318; a similar report had appeared in Marquis Childs' column in the *Washington Post* on August 31. Note also Truman's objection to the last paragraph in the DoD's proposed directive to MacArthur in an NSC meeting held on June 28, 1950, which, he said, seemed to imply that "we were planning to go to war with Russia." Memorandum for the President, June 30, 1950, MNSC, reel 1. On this, see also Harry Truman, *Memoirs*, vol. 2, *Years of Trial and Hope* (Garden City, 1956), p. 341. Given his general approach, it is astonishing that Johnson as late as July 1949 had been unwilling to increase the budget for analyzing the intelligence on Soviet nuclear capabilities that had been gathered—an increase that had been strongly recommended to him by a committee that had

a "world conflict" was printed, the *Times* published the story about General Orvil Anderson and preventive war.[61] Even before the Korean War, the preventive war idea had some support in the Congress, and now Senator John McClellan went public and gave a speech endorsing this policy.[62]

The Matthews and McClellan speeches appear to be the most extreme outcroppings of a somewhat inchoate but very widespread wave of feeling: that the aggressive thrust of Soviet policy reflected in the North Korean attack was something the United States could not live with forever, and that perhaps the time was coming when it would have to be dealt with directly, before matters got completely out of hand. What kept this in check was not an abstract commitment to the philosophy of limited war, but rather a sense for America's current military weakness. Major rearmament decisions were made in late 1950, but it would be a long time before the actual military balance could be reversed. The period from 1950 through 1954 would therefore, it was assumed, be a time when "the strength of the Soviet Union vis-à-vis the Western Powers is at a maxi-

---

looked into this issue. Memorandum of July 8, 1949, CD 11-1-2, Box 61, RG 330 (1947–50 series), USNA.

[61] Anderson was fired for going public with his views. It is sometimes implied (e.g., by Dean Acheson, in *Present at the Creation* [New York, 1969], p. 478) or claimed (e.g., by Barton Bernstein, in "Truman's Secret Thoughts," p. 31) that Matthews was also removed from his position for taking this line. But in fact when he offered to resign Truman simply told him to "forget about it," and in spite of his general incompetence was allowed to continue in office for another year. George Elsey, "Memorandum for File," October 2, 1950, Elsey Papers, Box 72, HSTL.

[62] McFall memorandum, January 26, 1950, FRUS, 1950, vol. 1, pp. 140–41; and *Newsweek*, February 13, 1950, p. 20 (where Congressman Henry Jackson was linked to the "preventive war" idea). McClellan's remarks are quoted in "Both Parties Back Truman Arms Call," *New York Times*, September 3, 1950, p. 11:1. Another Senator (Millikin) is identified as a supporter of preventive war in Williamson, "The View from Above," p. 195. On the mood in the country at the time, note the discussion between Secretary Acheson and a group of Senators and Congressmen on August 10, 1950, in FRUS, 1950, vol. 3, pp. 197–204. Here Senator Kefauver insisted that "sentiment throughout the country was building up" in the direction of preventive war (pp. 199, 204). See in this context Demaree Bess, "How Close is War with Russia?" *Saturday Evening Post*, November 24, 1951, esp. p. 107, and also Senator Paul Douglas's view, reported in *Time Magazine*, December 18, 1950, pp. 20–21, that in the event of new Communist aggression, the U.S. should "unleash such power as we have directly upon Russia itself." The fact that Douglas was one of the most liberal members of Congress shows just how far this sort of thinking extended at the time. The leading newspapers generally reacted negatively to the Matthews speech, but some important journalists supported the navy secretary. See, for example, David Lawrence, "Matthews Speech is Realistic if Not in Line with Policy," *Washington Star*, August 28, 1950. Note finally a short article in *Time Magazine*, September 18, 1950, p. 30: "Background for War: War Now? Or When? or Never?" This article called for a buildup followed by a "showdown" with the Russians by 1953.

mum."[63] It was therefore the Soviets who might deliberately provoke a war during this period; for the United States to plunge into a general war, or take actions which ran a serious risk of it, might actually play into Russian hands. A general war that broke out in 1950 or 1951 might well be a disaster for the West. As General Omar N. Bradley, Chairman of the Joint Chiefs of Staff, pointed out at an NSC meeting in November 1950, just after the Chinese intervention, if a global war broke out, "we might be in danger of losing."[64]

To understand this fear, it is necessary to probe a bit more deeply into how global warfare was understood at this time. This was still not a period when it was taken for granted that all-out war meant the destruction of whole societies. The Harmon and Hull reports of 1949 and 1950 had made it clear that the initial "atomic blitz" could not be counted on to destroy the war-making power of the Soviet Union.[65] By the same token, a Soviet atomic attack in the early 1950s would have only a limited effect on the American war economy: it could not prevent the United States from mounting a major military effort.[66] The reason was that unlike the high-yield weapons being developed in the early 1950s, the early fission bombs were weapons of relatively limited power. As Edward Teller pointed out in 1947, even if a large number of such bombs—"say a thousand or ten thousand"—were launched against America, "many millions" would die, but, if certain elementary precautions were taken, the country as a whole "could survive heavy atomic bombardment" and go on to win the war. This would not be the case with the new weapons already on the horizon.[67]

It was thus taken for granted in the early 1950s that a third world war would be long.[68] In the first few weeks of the war, the United States would be swept off the continent of Europe, at least up to the Pyrenees. America would then begin to mobilize its resources and mount a sustained bomb-

[63] CIA memorandum, October 12, 1950, FRUS, 1950, vol. 7, pp. 937–38.

[64] Minutes of the 71st Meeting of the National Security Council, November 9, 1950, MNSC, reel 1.

[65] Harmon Report: JCS 1953/1, May 12, 1949, CCS 373 (10-23-48), RG 218, USNA, analyzed in David Rosenberg, "American Atomic Strategy and the Hydrogen Bomb Decision," Journal of American History, June 1979. Hull Report: JCS 1952/11, 10 February 1950, same file, discussed in Richard Rowe, "American Nuclear Strategy and the Korean War," M.A. thesis, University of Pennsylvania, 1984, p. 26ff. See also the second paragraph in section C of NSC 68, FRUS, 1950, vol. 1, p. 281.

[66] See the report of the Special Evaluation Subcommittee of the National Security Council (Edwards Committee), NSC 140/1, May 18, 1953, FRUS, 1952–54, vol. 2, p. 343.

[67] Edward Teller, "How Dangerous Are Atomic Weapons?" Bulletin of the Atomic Scientists, February 1947, pp. 35–36.

[68] The JCS mobilization guidance, for example, assumed that it would last at least five years. "National Stockpiling Program," prepared by the Defense Department and the Office of Defense Mobilization, October 12, 1951, FRUS, 1951, vol. 1, p. 211.

ing campaign with atomic bombs and aircraft produced after the outbreak of the war. The Soviets, who now had the great resources of Western Europe to draw on, would at the same time be conducting their own
air offensive against the United States and its bases and allies overseas.
This would be a war of endurance, and the intensity with which this air
war was conducted would be an important determinant of its outcome.
The ability therefore to base forces overseas (so that a much more intense
bombing campaign could be conducted with medium bombers) was
therefore still very important. It was for this reason that the bulk of the
bomber fleet was composed of medium bombers, B-29s and B-50s; the B-
36 intercontinental bomber, which became operational in 1947, and
which like the B-29 could carry just one fission bomb, made up only a
small fraction of the bomber force. At the end of 1950, for example, there
were only thirty-eight B-36s in the Air Force, in contrast to 477 medium
bombers. Such a small force could scarcely operate effectively by itself.[69]

America was therefore highly dependent on the use of bases in Britain,
and the implications of this point were well understood by many American officials in this period.[70] But this dependence on Britain was a source

[69] For the figures, see Walter Poole, *History of the Joint Chiefs of Staff*, vol. 4 (1950–52),
p. 168. The conclusion about the limited effectiveness of air warfare with such a small force
is based on the following considerations. Soviet air defenses would be proportionately more
effective against a B-36 attack; a more massive strike that used both medium and heavy
bombers would be better able to saturate the air defense network. Attrition of the B-36 force
might therefore be significantly higher, and the Air Force might be forced to adopt tactics—
night bombing, for example—that reduced attrition, but sacrificed a degree of accuracy. But
since the goal was to destroy war-sustaining industrial installations which as a rule were
located on the outskirts of cities, a loss of accuracy could seriously affect the ability of the
air offensive to achieve its goals. Because the shock wave from the bomb spreads over three
dimensions, the blast effect falls off roughly in proportion to the cube of the distance from
the center of the explosion—i.e., a doubling of the average error, for instance, would mean
that overpressure would be cut on the average by a factor of eight. Given the limited power
of the early fission bombs, what all this meant was that an air offensive with B-36s in late
1950 might have had only a very limited impact on Soviet war potential. Even the admittedly less powerful bombs dropped on a completely unprepared and undefended Hiroshima
had left the bulk of the city's industrial plant intact. According to the U.S. Strategic Bombing
Survey, factories "responsible for nearly three-fourths of Hiroshima's industrial product
could have resumed normal operation within thirty days of the attack, had the war continued." USSBS, *The Effects of Atomic Bombs on Hiroshima and Nagasaki* (Washington,
1946), reprinted in David MacIsaac, ed., *The United States Strategic Bombing Survey* (New
York, 1976), vol. 7. This analysis had a major impact on thinking about strategic air warfare
in the early atomic age.

[70] Thus when Truman in December 1950 alluded (correctly, as we now know) to the fact
that nuclear weapons were being considered for use in Korea, Prime Minister Attlee quickly
came over to Washington to try to make sure that nothing of that sort would happen. Acheson commented in this connection that British views could not be ignored "since we can
bring U.S. power into play only with the cooperation of the British." Memorandum for the
President, December 12, 1950, MNSC, reel 1.

of weakness for both military and political reasons. The bases that the Strategic Air Command (SAC) planned to use in Britain, first of all, were considered "exceedingly vulnerable to air attack." In early 1950, none of them even had any "organized ground defenses."[71] Beyond such technical considerations, there was a persistent and pervasive fear that the Soviet ability to bring the British isles under air attack might well lead to a "neutralization" of the United Kingdom, and thus to the loss of these bases, even if Britain itself could not actually be conquered.[72]

In a long war, there were many uncertainties, and no one could be sure what the outcome would be. To those familiar with America's military problems, it was also clear that the outbreak of the Korean War had exacerbated an already dangerous situation. As the JCS's Joint Strategic Plans Committee (JSPC) pointed out on July 14, 1950, the allocation of forces to Korea had "drastically reduced" America's "capability to implement our plans for global war." It followed from that, the JSPC argued, that top priority had to be placed on the "regaining of our ability to implement our plans for a global war." This point would be stressed in many important documents from the period.[73]

Concerns about current weakness lay at the heart of the Nitze strategy. Nitze's analysis, and especially the assumptions about a danger zone that the country would have to cross, had (as noted above) led him in early 1950 to expect an increase in Soviet aggressiveness.[74] The North Korean

[71] This was the judgment of the Hull Report, paragraph 79 (see n. 65).

[72] Even before the Soviets had tested their first atomic bomb, this fear of a "neutralization" of Britain through air attack was very real. In BROILER, the Joint Outline War Plan for 1949, it was noted that the plan "depends critically on the use of the U.K. as an operational base," and it had been assumed in the plan that this would be possible. But the Joint Intelligence Group, the document pointed out, had noted that "neutralization of the U.K. by air and guided missile attacks and partial air and submarine blockade would probably be a Soviet capability in 1948" (Enclosure to JSPG 496/4, March 8, 1948, p. 3). BROILER is available on microfilm in RJCS/II/A/4/353ff. With the Soviet atomic bomb, these fears became much more intense: see for example JIC 435/36 of October 5, 1949, RJCS/II/A/3/257ff., and JIC 435/52, February 7, 1951, "Estimate of the Scale and Nature of a Soviet Attack on the United Kingdom between now and mid-1952," RJCS/II/A/6/849ff.

[73] JCS 1924/20, July 14, 1950, RJCS/II/C/9/135, 138, 159. For another example, note a letter that Vannevar Bush, at this time one of the most important American scientists involved with military issues, wrote General Bradley in April 1950: "If war should break out tomorrow, it would be a long desperate war, in which we would suffer major initial disasters, and in which we could hope to prevail only after a period of years by the ultimate weight of our industrial potential, and after irreparable damage." Bush to Bradley, April 13, 1950, Hoyt Vandenberg Papers, Box 83, Miscellaneous File, Library of Congress; see also Air Force General Landon's memorandum on this for General Vandenberg, same file, generally agreeing with the picture Bush had painted. There are copies of both letters in the Kaplan Files, file 30, National Security Archive, Washington.

[74] Paul Nitze, "Recent Soviet Moves," February 8, 1950, FRUS, 1950, vol. 1, p. 147. Korea was in fact mentioned as one of the places where Soviet moves might be made.

attack, and then the Chinese intervention, seemed to support the idea that the Soviets at the very least were willing to accept an increased risk of war during this period of America's relative weakness. But by the same token it was important that America avoid a war with Russia at this time. The United States therefore had to avoid action that might increase the risk of such a war—such as crossing the 38th Parallel, or (after the Chinese intervention) expanding the war into Manchuria. It was for this reason that Nitze took a relatively dovish line on issues relating to the escalation of the war. In this he was joined by officers like General Bradley who, while obviously extremely frustrated by the situation, were nevertheless convinced that this was not the time to take risks.[75]

The turnabout of John M. Allison, director of the State Department's Office of Northeast Asian Affairs, provides a good example of the link between this sense of weakness and the reluctance to escalate in Korea. On July 24, 1950, Allison had attacked Nitze's line as "a policy of appeasement," "a timid half-hearted policy designed not to provoke the Soviets to war." He argued instead for the conquest of North Korea. "That this may mean war on a global scale is true," he said, but "when all legal and moral right is on our side why should we hesitate?" "The free world," he concluded, "cannot any longer live under constant fear."[76]

But by mid-August he had changed his mind. He now recognized the need to avoid a global war as a limiting factor, and it is clear that a new sense for America's current military weakness played the key role in bringing about this shift in position. The argument in the memorandum where Allison registered his new opinion turned on a key passage from NSC 73/1: "The United States is not now capable of conducting immediately a general military offensive against the USSR because our forces are either not appropriately positioned or are so inadequate as to be incapable of effective action."[77]

The Allison example illustrates in a particularly striking way the important distinction between the views of "outsiders" and "insiders" on these issues. 1950 may have marked the high tide of "preventive war" agitation, but those who called for such highly aggressive strategies were as a rule simply ignorant of military realities. The "insiders" were acutely conscious of American weakness at that point. Indeed, what they were

---

[75] Policy Planning Staff memo, July 22, 1950, FRUS, 1950, vol. 7, pp. 449–54; "Chinese Communist Intervention in Korea," NIE-2, November 8, 1950, ibid., p. 1102; JCS memo, November 9, 1950, ibid., p. 1121; Memo of DoS-DoD meetings, December 1 and 3, 1950, ibid., p. 1279 (for Bradley's caution) and p. 1330 (for his frustration); Minutes of Truman-Attlee talks, December 7, 1950, ibid., p. 1457 (for Secretary Marshall's frustration). See also Foot, *Wrong War*, p. 117.

[76] Allison memorandum, July 24, 1950, FRUS, 1950, vol. 7, pp. 460–61.

[77] Allison memo, August 12, 1950, FRUS, 1950, vol. 7, pp. 571–72.

afraid of was that the Soviets would take advantage of the opportunity that had opened up for them and deliberately pursue aggressive policies that might well lead to war with the United States. The Soviets might even choose to initiate a war before the balance began to turn against them.

For the "insiders," both civilian and military, it was therefore clear by the end of the year that a major escalation which ran the risk of Soviet involvement, and thus of global war, had to be ruled out, even though the military situation in Korea was extremely bleak. The one partial exception among top military officers was General Hoyt Vandenberg, the Air Force Chief of Staff. In a discussion with high Defense Department officials in December 1950, he pinpointed August 1951 as the "point of greatest danger," the point at which the Soviets were most likely to "initiate an early war." If this was correct, he said, the next eight months "would not work in our favor since we would not improve our ground potential significantly but would in that period have given the Soviets a chance to produce additional atomic bombs." "He did not say so specifically," according to the record of the meeting made by Assistant Secretary of State Dean Rusk, "but the implication was that it would be better for us to precipitate hostilities at an early date in order to prevent further USSR atomic buildup."[78]

It is striking that the most forceful air power advocates were the ones who took the most aggressive line at this time. Stuart Symington, for example, secretary of the Air Force from September 1947 to April 1950 and then chairman of the National Security Resources Board, was a great champion of air power. Although in two memoranda written during this bleak period of the war he denied that he wanted to expand the Korean conflict into a general war with Russia, these documents sounded the standard themes of the "preventive war" thesis. The United States was already at war with the Soviets, he said, and the country was currently losing this life-or-death struggle, because it had opted for the purely defensive policy of containment; it had sought always to "localize" aggres-

---

[78] Dean Rusk, Memorandum of Conversation, December 19, 1950, FRUS, 1950, vol. 7, pp. 1572–73. In general, the Air Force's access to inside information was more than balanced by what can only be called its nonrational attachment to air power, which led it to overestimate the effectiveness both of a Soviet air strike on the U.S. and of a U.S. air attack on the USSR—the two arguments together greatly strengthening in the Air Force's own mind the case for a "positive" policy. The nonrationality of Air Force thinking on this issue—what the Army liked to refer to as the Air Force's "subjectivity"—comes out very clearly in the documents recording the extraordinary debate on basic strategy that took place at the JCS level from 1948 to 1950. See, in RG 218 at the National Archives the portion of the file CCS 373 (10-23-48) covering this period; and in RG 319, the file P & O 373 TS for 1949 and P & O Hot Files for 1950–51, Box 11. On Air Force subjectivity: Gen. Ray Maddocks, Memoranda for the Army Chief of Staff, February 8, and especially March 16, 1949, P & O 373 TS, RG 319, USNA.

sion, and had drawn back from dealing with the problem at its heart. A "clear and positive" policy had to replace the policy of drift, because, with the development of Soviet nuclear capabilities, time was "running out far more rapidly" than most Americans realized. Symington argued for a strategy of withdrawal from Korea, and the replacement of the ground war by an air and naval war against China; if this led to Soviet involvement, the result (announced in advance) would be "the atomic bombardment of Soviet Russia itself."[79]

The general response to Symington's arguments was quite hostile, and shows that the more extreme "air power" position had very limited appeal at this point.[80] President Truman's personal reaction was quite negative. He characterized a long series of Symington's points as "bunk" or "drivel"; and he drafted (but evidently did not send) a short note to Symington: "My dear Stu, this is [as] big a lot of Top Secret malarky as I've ever read. Your time is wasted on such bunk as this. H.S.T."[81]

The mainstream position, shared by the Joint Chiefs and the State Department, was that the United States could not run the risk of escalation *at that point*. It was currently too weak to take on a global war. The top priority was therefore to build up American power first. As Admiral Forrest Sherman, the Chief of Naval Operations, put it in a memorandum which was to become the basis of the official JCS position, the crucial thing was to "*delay* a general war with Russia until we have achieved the necessary degree of military and industrial mobilization."[82] General J. Lawton Collins, the Army Chief of Staff, was more precise as to when escalation might be possible: "Since the United States is not now prepared to engage in global war, and will not be ready before 1 July 1952, we should take all honorable means to avoid any action that is likely to bring Russia into open conflict with the United States prior to that date."[83]

---

[79] NSC 100, January 11, 1951, and Symington memo, n.d., FRUS, 1951, vol. 1, pp. 7–18, 21–33. See also Foot, *Wrong War*, pp. 115–16. According to Harriman in the Princeton Seminar, Symington took the position that there was going to be a war with Russia, and that total mobilization was therefore necessary, "under [Bernard] Baruch's influence." It was taken for granted in the discussion that followed that these arguments were closely related to the preventive war idea. Princeton Seminar, p. 1317ff. Harriman's account is substantiated by the file of correspondence with Symington in Box 95 of the Baruch Papers at the Mudd Library in Princeton. See for example Baruch to Symington, November 21, 1950, Symington to Baruch, November 24, 1950, and especially Baruch to Symington, December 5, 1950.

[80] See Foot, *Wrong War*, pp. 115–16.

[81] FRUS, 1951, vol. 1, pp. 21–33. The Truman note is on p. 33.

[82] Sherman memo on "Courses of Action Relative to Communist China and Korea," JCS 2118/5, January 3, 1951, JCS Records, II/C/2/677. Emphasis added. The final document, recording the JCS position (JCS 2118/10 of January 12, 1951) was revised to take account of General Collins's memo, cited below. The text was circulated as NSC 101, FRUS, 1951, vol. 7, p. 71.

[83] JCS 2118/9, January 12, 1951, RJCS/II/C/2/688. The July 1, 1952 date in fact corre-

Once the general thinking about trends in the global military balance is understood, many of the documents relating to Korean War strategy take on new meaning. Phrases that one might otherwise overlook, or dismiss as merely pro forma, are suddenly seen in a new light—for example, General Bradley's comment on December 1, 1950, that if Chinese air came in, the United States might have to "defer" striking back, or the military view in February 1951 that "retaliatory action against China," because it might lead to Soviet intervention, "would involve excessive risks *at this time*."[84]

General Bradley's famous comment, in particular, that a war with China would be "the wrong war, at the wrong place, at the wrong time, and with the wrong enemy," takes on a whole new dimension of meaning when seen in this context. This remark has come to be taken as a symbol of the "limited war" policy—of America's desire to avoid an expansion of the conflict. But viewed in this general light, what Bradley was implying was that if the United States was forced to fight the Communists, the *right war* was a war against Russia itself, and that the *right place* to fight it was not at the periphery, but at the heart of Soviet power. Most important in this context, it implied that if it had to be fought at all—and Bradley of course hoped it could be avoided—there was a *right time* for fighting it, namely, after American power had been built up. Indeed, after he made this remark (in the MacArthur hearings) he went on to point out that the United States was "not in the best military position to seek a showdown," and that he would not support any policy that would "rush us headlong into a showdown before we are ready."[85] Similar themes were reflected in many documents of the period—for example, in Acheson's comment in December 1950 that the "great trouble is that we are fighting the wrong nation. We are fighting the second team, whereas the real enemy is the Soviet Union."[86]

---

sponded to official policy. As a result of the new crisis created by the Chinese intervention in the Korean War, the target date for completing the military buildup needed to support the goals laid out in NSC 68 was advanced from mid-1954 to June 30, 1952. The new date was set in NSC 68/4 of December 14, 1950. See FRUS, 1950, vol. 1, pp. 467ff. for that document; for related documents, see ibid., pp. 466–67, 474–75, and FRUS, 1951, vol. 1, pp. 131–32.

[84] Memorandum of Conversation, December 1, 1950, FRUS, 1950, vol. 7, p. 1279; Record of DoS-JCS meeting, February 13, 1951, FRUS, 1951, vol. 7, p. 177. Emphasis added.

[85] 82d Congress, First Session. Senate Committees on Armed Services and Foreign Relations. *Military Situation in the Far East* (Washington, 1951), pp. 1917–20.

[86] Memorandum of Conversation, December 3, 1950, FRUS, 1950, vol. 7, p. 1326. Such views persisted well into the early Eisenhower period. Thus in late 1954, at the beginning of the first Taiwan Straits Crisis, Eisenhower told the NSC that "if we are to have general war, he would prefer to have it with Russia, not China. Russia can help China fight us without getting involved itself, and he would 'want to go to the head of the snake.' " He returned to the point in another NSC meeting two months later, and his remarks seem to reflect a certain interest in taking the initiative in escalating to the level of all-out war with

State Department views were not far removed from those of the military. It was taken for granted that the United States should avoid an extension of the Korean conflict and prevent "the development of general war, particularly during the period in which the United States and its allies are in the process of achieving the requisite degree of military and industrial mobilization."[87] A month later, Acheson reiterated the point: a general advance north of the 38th Parallel, he wrote Secretary of Defense Marshall, was to be avoided because of the "risk of extending the Korean conflict to other areas and even into general war at a time when we are not ready to risk general war."[88]

It was absolutely crucial, therefore, to build up America's general military power, and one of the most important themes stressed in these documents was the vital importance of such a buildup.[89] In fact, the rate of American military spending was to triple during this period, and only a small fraction of this was due to the Korean campaign as such.[90]

The result was an extraordinary buildup of military strength, which acted like an acid, gradually eating away at all those constraints that had kept the United States from escalating at the end of 1950 and in early 1951. The key to the history of the Korean War, in fact, is America's increasing willingness to escalate the conflict. This shift took place in two phases. First, in 1951, it gradually became clear that the government's worst fears had been exaggerated: East Germany did not invade the Federal Republic, there was no new Berlin Crisis, Yugoslavia was not attacked, Soviet forces did not move into Iran.[91] As the sense of a great risk

---

the Soviet Union. When Dulles pointed out that the crisis might escalate to the level of a general Sino-American war, Eisenhower "observed that when we talk of general war with Communist China, what we mean is general war with the USSR also. Once this is made clear, the next question is, where does the U.S. want to launch an attack upon such an enemy coalition? The President said he was not sure, but almost certainly not in the area of the offshore islands." Minutes of NSC meetings, September 12 and November 2, 1954, FRUS, 1952–54, vol. 14, pp. 617, 831.

[87] "U.S. Action to Counter Communist Chinese Aggression," January 17, 1951, FRUS, 1951, vol. 7, pp. 1515–16.

[88] Acheson to Marshall, February 23, 1951, enclosure, FRUS, 1951, vol. 7, p. 193. Emphasis added. Note also Truman to MacArthur, January 13, 1951: "*pending the build-up of our national strength*, we must act with great prudence in so far as extending the area of hostilities is concerned." Published in Truman, *Years of Trial and Hope*, pp. 435–36, and reprinted in James F. Schnabel and Robert J. Watson, *History of the Joint Chiefs of Staff*, vol. 3, *The Korean War* (Wilmington, Del., 1979), p. 420. Emphasis added.

[89] For example: JCS memo, July 13, 1951, Schnabel and Watson, *History of the* JCS, p. 667; Position Paper for Washington Foreign Ministers' Meeting and British talks, September 8, 1951, ibid., p. 889.

[90] The ending of the Korean War, it was assumed in 1953, would result in a $2 billion saving in a projected $41 billion defense budget. FRUS, 1952–54, vol. 2, pp. 279, 284, 311.

[91] These fears are reflected in many documents from the early Korean War period. See, for example, "Meeting of the NSC in the Cabinet Room of the White House," June 28, 1950,

of war with the Soviets began to fade, the American government felt somewhat freer to act in the Far East.

The second and more dramatic phase began with the resurgence of American military power in late 1952 and 1953. This led to a much greater willingness to escalate, if that was needed to bring the Korean conflict to an acceptable conclusion. The decisions of the Eisenhower period, with regard both to the war in Korea and to global strategy as a whole, have to be understood as the climax of a process begun years before in the Truman administration.

The relatively small issue of the bombing of Rashin, a port near North Korea's border with the Soviet Union, provides one early indicator of this shift. In 1950, the State Department was able to block plans for the bombing of Rashin; it feared that such action "might entail the gravest consequences." As one official put it, "both the Defense Establishment and the State Department feel very strongly that we do not want active Soviet participation in the Korean war or the commencement of worldwide hostilities *this year*. We believed that if the Soviet authorities are undecided or are hesitating as to whether to move on a wider basis now, the bombing of Rashin or similar moves might well prove an important deciding factor."[92] But the decision was reversed as early as August 1951.[93]

There was a striking evolution of American policy more generally on the extension of the air war. JCS 2118/4 of January 12, 1951, had provided for air strikes against China only if the Chinese Communists attacked American forces "outside of Korea."[94] But in April 1951, General Ridgway, the U.S. Commander in the Far East, was authorized to attack enemy air bases in Manchuria and the Shantung peninsula "in the event of a major enemy air attack from outside Korea."[95] In November and December the terms were extended a bit further. The JCS wanted American planes to be able to attack air bases in China "whenever the scale of enemy air activity is such as seriously to jeopardize the security of United States forces in the Korean area."[96] What this meant was that *preemptive* action would be authorized if the Chinese built up their bomber force to

---

Acheson Papers, Box 65, "Memoranda of Conversation, May–June 1950," HSTL, and especially NIE-15, "Probable Soviet Moves to Exploit the Present Situation," December 11, 1950, PSF, Box 253, HSTL. Note also Acheson's and Nitze's later comment in the Princeton Seminar, pp. 906, 908.

[92] Matthews memo, August 14, 1950, FRUS, 1950, vol. 7, p. 574. Emphasis added.

[93] See Foot, *Wrong War*, pp. 76, 149–50.

[94] Schnabel and Watson, *History of the* JCS, p. 419.

[95] JCS to Ridgway, April 28, 1951, FRUS, 1951, vol. 7, p. 386.

[96] JCS memo, November 3, 1951, FRUS, 1951, vol. 7, p. 1108.

a level that might jeopardize the security of American forces.[97] The proposal was approved, but with the provisos that such action would have to be "specifically authorized by the President," and that if there was time, the key allies would be informed of the decision in advance.[98] These conditions somewhat limited the effect of the decision, but it is nonetheless clear that the Truman administration was becoming increasingly willing to escalate the war.

These early shifts, however, were minor compared with what would come later when the mobilization effort finally made itself felt in terms of increasing military end-products. For example, General Vandenberg pointed out in September 1951 that the production curve for fighters would begin to go up in the spring, but "we won't really get rolling until next fall."[99] Overall output did increase dramatically in 1952. "U.S. monthly production of military end items," one document reported in August of that year, "is five or six times as large as it was in June 1950. Between July 1951 and May 1952 the monthly deliveries of military end items have risen from an annual rate of $6.4 billion to $17.8 billion, and the trend is sharply upward."[100]

The American military buildup was particularly dramatic in the nuclear weapons area. Since 1950, there had been a great expansion in the production of fissionable material, and there had been very important

[97] Johnson memo, November 7, 1951, FRUS, 1951, vol. 7, p. 1094. Similarly, during the first Taiwan Straits Crisis, JCS Chairman Radford endorsed a preemptive strategy—"the minute we knew that the Chinese Communists were about to launch an air attack on Quemoy, we should go after the airfields in China from which they would launch an attack"—but this President Eisenhower was unwilling to do without prior congressional authorization. Minutes of NSC meeting, September 12, 1954, FRUS, 1952–54, vol. 14, p. 618.

[98] Ibid., pp. 1261, 1383. For some indication of the seriousness with which this matter was taken at the highest political level, see Churchill to Acheson, February 18, 1952 (with enclosure), and Acheson to Churchill, February 19, 1952, Acheson Papers, Box 63, folder "Churchill, Winston S.," HSTL. Note also Admiral Blandy's reference (in this context) to "anticipatory retaliation" on the "Longines-Wittnauer Chronoscope," June 11, 1951, videotape T76: 0145, Museum of Broadcasting, New York. Blandy, who had recently retired from the Navy, had long been close to nuclear weapons matters. He had, for example, been the commander at the Crossroads tests in 1946.

[99] Notes of DoS-JCS meeting, September 25, 1951, FRUS, 1951, vol. 7, p. 943.

[100] NSC 135/1, Annex, August 22, 1952, FRUS, 1952–54, vol. 2, p. 106. Some of the reasons why mobilization was taking so long are discussed in NSC 114/1, August 8, 1951, enclosure, FRUS, 1951, vol. 1, p. 137 and in NSC 114/3, enclosure 1, May 10, 1952, FRUS, 1952–54, vol. 2, pp. 29–30. For a detailed description of the mobilization program, see Annex 1 to NSC 114, July 27, 1951, in Documents of the National Security Council (University Publications of America microfilm publication) Supplement 1, reel 1. [Henceforth: DNSC] There are frequent references in the documents to the depressingly slow pace of industrial mobilization. See, for example, the summaries of discussion at the 103d and 105th meetings of the NSC, September 27 and October 18, 1951, PSF, Box 220, HSTL. Note also the discussion at the Princeton Seminar, p. 1314.

qualitative changes as well, especially with regard to tactical nuclear weapons.[101] By early 1952, the Atomic Energy Commission had developed atomic bombs small and light enough to be used by "such fighter aircraft as the F-84 and some Navy carrier planes." As a result, "between May 1951 and July 1953 the Air Force moved rapidly to build a tactical atomic force."[102] By 1952, "techniques and procedures" for the use of atomic weapons on the battlefield had been worked out.[103] At about the same time, the stockpile of bombs had become so large that, from the JCS point of view, scarcity no longer carried any weight as an argument against the use of nuclear weapons in Korea.[104]

The result of this buildup was an increasing willingness in 1952 and early 1953 to escalate the war in Korea if no armistice agreement could be reached. By early 1953, it was clear that the use of nuclear weapons had become an integral part of a policy of escalation.[105] Expansion of the war would involve, at the very minimum, an attack on air bases in Manchuria; nuclear weapons would provide a very effective way of destroying those targets.[106] It should be noted that this shift was not due solely to the

[101] See Rosenberg, "Origins of Overkill," esp. pp. 23–24, and the sources cited there. Note also C. Savage, "Increase in Production of Fissionable Material," September 26, 1950, Records of the Policy Planning Staff, Box 6, folder "Atomic Energy—Armaments, 1950," RG 59, USNA: "This program to increase the production of fissionable material calls for an expansion of production at a rate as rapid as the limiting factor of ore permits, without resorting to extreme measures of diminishing returns. The rate of production under it probably could not be appreciably increased even if we were *sure* that war was inevitable." Emphasis in original.

[102] George F. Lemmer, "The Air Force and Strategic Deterrence, 1951–1960," pp. 14–15. A sanitized, declassified version is available at the Office of Air Force History, Bolling Air Force Base, Washington. For some indication of the increasing size of nuclear forces deployed to Europe in support of NATO in this period, see JCS 2220/4, January 31, 1952, "Information for General Eisenhower on Availability of Atomic Weapons," RJCS/II/G/3/ 1077, and JCS 2220/19, May 6, 1953, "Revision of Information for General Ridgway on Availability of Atomic Weapons," RJCS/II/G/4/54ff.

[103] Rowe, "American Atomic Strategy," pp. 61–64. The tactics and operational techniques were developed partly through tests conducted in Korea in October and November 1951 involving "actual atomic bombs, less nuclear components." Ibid., p. 62.

[104] Ibid., p. 64. Note also Nitze's comments in a memo to Acheson of January 12, 1952, FRUS, 1952–54, vol. 2, p. 204.

[105] Joint Strategic Plans Committee, "Future Courses of Action in Connection with the Situation in Korea (Estimate)," JSPC 853/145, January 26, 1953, RJCS/ II/C/11/1041ff., esp. frames 1051, 1052; JCS memo of March 28, 1953 on "Future Courses of Action in Connection with the Situation in Korea," White House Office Papers, NSC Series, Policy Papers sub-series, Box 2, Eisenhower Library, Abilene, discussed in Rowe, "American Atomic Strategy," pp. 66–68; JCS memo, May 19, 1953, FRUS, 1952–54, vol. 15, pp. 1059–64, and esp. the minutes of the May 20, 1953, NSC meeting, ibid., 1064–68.

[106] JCS memo, May 19, 1953, FRUS 1952–54, vol. 15, p. 1061; memorandum of DoS-JCS meeting, March 27, 1953, ibid., p. 818 (Vandenberg's remarks). Note also Gen. Hull's comment in the May 13, 1953, NSC meeting, ibid., p. 1014, General Clark's June 1952 request

change of administration. It was the same JCS that had been so cautious at the end of 1950 and in early 1951 that now advocated a nuclear escalation: the thinking in JCS circles in this regard had obviously begun to shift before the new Eisenhower administration took over.[107]

By the beginning of 1953, it was clear that the overall balance had shifted dramatically in America's favor. The United States, said Secretary of State John Foster Dulles in early 1953, could now get better armistice terms in Korea than had earlier been possible "in view of our much greater power and the Soviet Union's much greater weakness currently."[108]

The shift in the military balance between 1950 and 1953 had a major impact on American policy not just in Korea but elsewhere around the globe as well. There was a striking shift in U.S. policy on Berlin in this period. In the policy documents on Berlin from the end of the blockade in 1949 through early 1951, caution had been the keynote: if the blockade were reimposed, there should be no "probe"; the JCS thought the Western Powers were too weak to undertake a ground action of this sort. In February 1951, the JCS was reluctant to recommend any major military action, even if Soviet forces attacked West Berlin: "only the Berlin garrison, augmented by the West Berlin police, should be used to resist the attack, pending further consideration at the highest governmental level." The United States had, of course, undertaken to defend West Berlin; the problem was, as the Joint Strategic Plans Committee bluntly pointed out, that the country neither had, nor would soon have, "the military capability to carry out completely our commitments in this regard."[109]

By the spring of 1952, however, high officials had already begun to rethink American policy on the use of force in a new Berlin crisis: "we were opposed to it before," General Bradley said on May 14, "but it

---

for nuclear-capable F-84's for the counterair mission, and General Collins's favorable answer, anticipating they would be sent by November, in RJCS/II/C/10/1102, 1106.

[107] Eisenhower was sworn in as President on January 20, 1953. JSPC 853/145, the document on which the JCS based its recommendations, was circulated just six days later, and it in turn was based on a report by the Joint Strategic Plans Group, JSPC 853/142, the work for which had been done considerably earlier.

[108] Notes of NSC meeting, April 8, 1953, FRUS, 1952–54, vol. 15, p. 894.

[109] See especially NSC 24/3, "Possible U.S. Courses of Action in the Event the USSR Reimposes the Berlin Blockade," June 14, 1949, DNSC, reel 1; Marshall to Lay, October 18, 1950, in NSC 89, FRUS, 1950, vol. 4, pp. 893–94; JCS 1907/62, January 24, 1951, RJCS/II/G/5/418ff. This last document was the basis for the official JCS memorandum to Secretary of Defense Marshall, February 7, 1951, FRUS, 1951, vol. 3, pp. 1892ff. During the blockade itself, the American attitude was surprisingly weak: Truman was unwilling even to shoot down a barrage balloon if that had proved necessary to maintain access to Berlin, because that might have led to a war for which "the U.S. did not have enough soldiers." Williamson, "The View from Above," p. 104.

should be reconsidered now."[110] And in fact, by mid-1952, the U.S. line on Berlin had completely swung around to a much tougher position: in NSC 132/1 of June 12, 1952, a military probe was accepted, and it was now taken for granted that an attack on Berlin would almost certainly lead to general war. The American position on Berlin became even tougher during the early Eisenhower period; and the JCS documents make it clear that it was, at least from their point of view, the improved military situation that had made possible this dramatic shift of policy on this issue.[111]

There was a parallel shift in American policy on Indochina during this period. In 1950, the military felt that the United States was too weak to risk escalation of the conflict even if the Chinese intervened in force in the area; by 1952, the American strategy for the defense of Indochina was based on the idea that if the Chinese moved in, the Western Powers would have to widen the war and attack China itself.[112]

All this is important because of the light it sheds on the way nuclear forces influence political behavior. It was the overall strategic balance that was crucial, not specific, isolated gestures like particular deployments of nuclear-capable bombers at various points in time. What counted was the actual thrust of policy—the actual willingness to escalate—rather than

[110] FRUS, 1952–54, vol. 7, p. 1241.

[111] The basic document on Berlin for the late Truman period was NSC 132/1, June 12, 1952 (FRUS, 1952–54, vol. 7, p. 1261ff.), much of which was evidently carried over into NSC 5404/2, the key Berlin policy document for the early Eisenhower period. This latter document has not been declassified, but one can learn a good deal about it from the Operations Coordinating Board Progress Reports on it of January 7, 1955 and May 17, 1956, DNSC, Supplement 2, reel 1, and Supplement 4, reel 1, respectively. For the military view that the shift in the balance had made all this possible, see the Joint Strategic Survey Committee (JSSC) report on NSC 173, JCS 1907/101 of December 5, 1953, in RJCS/II/G/5/909ff. Note especially the JSSC's contrast with the earlier period "when the military posture of the Allies was too weak to permit of forceful measures in the assertion of the Allied right of surface entry into Berlin." This text was carried over into the JCS Memorandum of January 19, 1954 on NSC 5404, which pressed for a toughening of the document with the argument that there was "no question, all factors considered, but that the Western Powers are now in a stronger military position relative to the Soviet Bloc than they were in 1949." Declassified Documents Collection, 1984/ 828. Comparing this document, for example, with, say, the corresponding JCS documents from the beginning of 1951, one cannot help but be struck by an extraordinary difference in tone: the virtual defeatism of early 1951 was replaced by an attack on "temporizing measures" and an insistence that the West not hesitate to take "positive action" as soon as its position in Berlin was challenged.

[112] See "The History of the Joint Chiefs of Staff. The Joint Chiefs of Staff and the War in Vietnam. History of the Indochina Incident, 1940–1954," JCS Historical Division, 1971, Military Records Branch, USNA, pp. 190, 194–98, 225, 241–58, 294–95, 388, 453–54. A number of the documents summarized here have been published in FRUS and in the Pentagon Papers, but some of the most important ones are still classified.

overt threats or ultimata, which the Eisenhower administration was in fact anxious to avoid.[113]

A TIME FOR DECISION: "PREVENTIVE WAR" UNDER EISENHOWER

In May 1953, when the Eisenhower administration was making its final decisions about the Korean War, Vice President Richard Nixon argued at an NSC meeting that these choices should be made "only in the context of the longer-term problem which would confront us when the Soviet Union had amassed a sufficient stockpile of atomic weapons to deal us a critical blow and to rob us of the initiative in the area of foreign policy." The President "agreed with the views of the Vice President, and explained that Project Solarium was being initiated with this precise problem in mind."[114]

The result of the Korean War buildup had been to transform America's "window of vulnerability" into a "window of opportunity." Would the United States take advantage of it, or would it allow its strategic edge simply to waste away as the Soviets built up their nuclear forces? The aim of this section is to show how this issue was handled during the early Eisenhower period. What is striking here is, first, how seriously this problem was taken: the most aggressive strategies were never simply dismissed out of hand, but instead had broad appeal, even at the highest political level. But it is also important to note that the impulse to pursue a "dynamic" and "positive" policy was contained; a more or less final decision to rule out such a policy was reached at the end of 1954.

It was during the Solarium exercise of 1953 and its aftermath in 1954 that the Eisenhower administration confronted the issues raised by the shifting nuclear balance. But it was not just the balance in the sense of asymmetries in military capabilities that was important; the military environment as a whole was changing dramatically at this time. In the early

---

[113] As early as November 1950, Bedell Smith, then CIA Director, argued against laying down an ultimatum, and spoke instead of "quiet exploration with implied threats." Memorandum for the President, November 10, 1950, MNSC, reel 1. Smith, one of Eisenhower's closest associates from World War II, became Under Secretary of State in 1953. He soon took a hand in a diplomatic initiative aimed at getting the Soviets to help bring about a Korean armistice. Once again, there is the theme of avoiding the appearance of "a threat or ultimatum" and just setting forth a "simple statement of facts" as to what was likely to happen if an arrangement was not worked out. FRUS, 1952–54, vol. 15, p. 915; see also pp. 1081, 1096, 1103, 1110–11. This is in fact one of the basic techniques of coercive diplomacy: the pose of an impartial observer objectively pointing out—even regretfully—how matters were likely to evolve. Another related technique is the ruling out of alternative possibilities—that is, pointing out what the U.S. was *not* going to do.

[114] Minutes of NSC meeting, May 13, 1953, FRUS, 1952–54, vol. 15, p. 1016.

atomic age, a full-scale nuclear war was still actually fightable. If war had broken out in 1953, for example, the American estimates implied that a surprise Soviet nuclear attack might have caused something on the order of 3 million deaths; the casualty estimates could perhaps be cut in half if the United States took some rudimentary civil defense measures.[115] An attack that resulted in even a million deaths would of course have been an appalling catastrophe; but the level of devastation that such a figure represents was quite modest compared with what was to come a few years later.[116] And these estimates assumed a Soviet surprise attack; if the United States struck first, the Soviet retaliatory attack, if one could in fact have been mounted, might have had a very limited impact. What this meant was that even as late as 1953 or 1954, one could actually imagine fighting and, in some meaningful sense, winning an air-atomic war. It would probably be a long war, and the devastation would be terrible, but the country would survive as a functioning society.

The extraordinary advances in nuclear weapons technology taking place in the early 1950s were to shatter this image of what a general atomic war would be like. The coming of high-yield weapons, and especially of thermonuclear weapons, was to be of fundamental importance. As Edward Teller had predicted as early as 1947, a single weapon could now devastate "three or four hundred square miles," instead of just three or four square miles, and the radiological effect might be even more important than the increased yield.[117] It was clear, even from the open sources, that, depending on how the bomb case was designed, these new weapons could generate vast amounts of lethal fallout.[118] The combina-

[115] In mid-1953, the best American estimate was that the Soviets then had about 120 bombs of 80 kiloton yield. In late 1951, it had been estimated that a midday surprise attack on major urban areas could cause casualties on the order of 175,000 per bomb. With the improved yields available in mid-1953, the casualty rate would be somewhat higher. It was also assumed that only half the bombs would be dropped on urban targets, and that, because of the Soviet lack of air combat experience and various technical problems, about 40 percent of the bombers launched in the attack would not be able to complete their missions. An additional 7 percent of the attacking planes, it was estimated, would be shot down by American air defense "under the most probable conditions of attack"—which was to say a nighttime attack, and delivered bombs would cause fewer casualties at night than during the day. As a rough estimate, all this implied a casualty rate of about 6 million or, using the standard 50 percent rule of thumb, about 3 million fatalities. For the sources, see FRUS, 1951, vol. 1, pp. 187, 225, and FRUS, 1952–54, vol. 2, pp. 334–35, 337, 344–45.

[116] See the chart in FRUS, 1952–54, vol. 2, p. 651.

[117] Teller, "How Dangerous Are Atomic Weapons?" p. 36.

[118] Hans Bethe, "The Hydrogen Bomb," *Bulletin of the Atomic Scientists*, April 1950, pp. 99–104, 125. The passage referred to is on p. 101, and is immediately followed by a reference to the Teller article cited above, which, Bethe said, had already described this threat. Because Bethe here seemed to hint at the way the H-bomb was actually being designed, this article "caused a memorable storm" in the AEC. On the AEC reaction, see the editorial note

tion of increased yields and fallout meant that the new hydrogen bomb was truly an area weapon. The United States could scarcely survive an attack with even a relatively small number of these bombs.

For some people in the government, the increased potential for devastation simply underscored the importance of not allowing the enemy to strike first. This emphasis on getting in the first blow was not new: from the beginning of the atomic age, preemption had been considered very important, especially in military circles.[119] By 1952, the basic point had worked its way up to the Presidential level: "startled" by a briefing on U.S. vulnerability he had received in September of that year, Truman concluded that "there wasn't much of a defense in prospect except a vigorous offense."[120] Under Eisenhower, this point became absolutely central to American strategy. As David Rosenberg says, massive retaliation really meant massive preemption—certainly at the level of military operations, but also, in a more ambiguous way, at the level of general strategy.[121]

It was understood that the question of how dangerous this new world was going to be turned on the issue of the vulnerability of strategic forces, or more precisely on the tractability of the vulnerability problem, which

by Eugene Rabinowitch, *Bulletin of the Atomic Scientists*, December 1952, p. 298. A basic description of the link between fallout and bomb design was laid out in J. Rotblat, "The Hydrogen-Uranium Bomb," *Bulletin of the Atomic Scientists*, May 1955, pp. 171–72, 177.

[119] The "principle of pre-emptive attack," characterized by the author of the official JCS history as a "strange, new strategic concept for U.S. military planners," had emerged in late 1945. See Schnabel, *History of the Joint Chiefs of Staff*, 1, 278, summarizing JCS 1477/1, October 30, 1945, a study of the military implications of the atomic bomb, and p. 148, summarizing JCS 1518 of October 9, 1945, the basic JCS "strategic concept and plan"; see ibid., p. 305, for the effect of this line of thinking on JCS basing policy. See also ibid., pp. 58, 311. Note finally the Compton Board's argument for a strategy of preemption, and thus for the need to "redefine" what constituted an "aggressive act"—an idea that General LeMay quickly picked up on. "The Evaluation of the Atomic Bomb as a Military Weapon. The Final Report of the Joint Chiefs of Staff Evaluation Board for Operation Crossroads," June 30, 1947, President's Secretary's Files, Box 220, Subject File—NSC—Atomic—Atomic Test—Crossroads," HSTL. For LeMay's thinking, see Lemmer, "Air Force and Strategic Deterrence," p. 35.

[120] Minutes of NSC meeting, September 3, 1952, FRUS, 1952–54, vol. 2, p. 121.

[121] A strategy of preemption is implied in a large number of documents from the Eisenhower period. See, for example, A. J. Goodpaster, Memorandum of Conference with the President, December 22, 1954, pp. 1, 3, Ann Whitman File (AWF), Ann Whitman Diary (AWD), Box 3, ACW Diary, December 1954 (2), Dwight D. Eisenhower Library (DDEL). Note also Eisenhower's remarks at an NSC meeting on July 29, 1954, especially the allusion to Clausewitz's principle of "diminishing as much as possible the first blow of an enemy attack," and his comment at another NSC meeting in early 1957 that since a massive Soviet nuclear attack would cause casualties "on the order of 50,000,000 people," "the only sensible thing for us to do was to put all our resources into our SAC capability and into hydrogen bombs." It is obvious that the only way this additional capability could make a difference was if the U.S. struck first. Discussion at 208th and 312th meetings of the National Security Council, AWF, NSC series, boxes 5 and 8, DDEL.

ultimately would determine how much of an incentive there would be to preempt. As an NSC study pointed out in 1952, "the controlling relationship in the atomic equation appears not to be that of stockpiles to each other, but rather the relationship of one stockpile, plus its deliverability, to the number of key enemy targets, including retaliatory facilities, which must be destroyed in order to warrant an attack."[122] The Soviets might therefore launch an attack even though they had far fewer weapons than the United States. In 1951, the Air Force believed that the Soviets had already achieved the capability "critically to hamper" America's ability to strike back after an attack.[123] The Policy Planning Staff therefore wondered whether it was possible to build forces that could survive a surprise attack and go on to launch a heavy retaliatory strike. If this turned out to be impossible, a fundamental "reconsideration of national strategy" would be required.[124]

The "reappraisal" of strategy thus turned in large part on issues related to what would now be called the stability of deterrence. One State Department official outlined some of the basic questions in May 1952: "Does currently approved U.S. national strategy remain valid in the light of apparently rapidly growing atomic, and possibly thermonuclear, capacity of the USSR? In other words, is time of the essence? Can we really hope to 'contain' the Soviet Union even if we maintain a high-level military strength indefinitely? Or must we adopt a more 'aggressive' policy?"[125] The argument for a new and more aggressive strategy was based on the assumption that there was no way, short of striking first, of preventing the Soviets from developing forces able essentially to destroy America's retaliatory capability in a surprise attack.

But this was only part of the problem. The extraordinary changes in the nature of general nuclear warfare that were taking place in the early 1950s were raising a whole series of fundamental questions about national policy. Should the nation simply accept this new world of thermonuclear weapons and nuclear plenty? Should it resign itself to an almost inevitable loss of strategic superiority, and to living in a world where an absolutely devastating surprise attack might be a very real risk? Gordon Dean, the recently retired Chairman of the Atomic Energy Commission, did not mince words on this issue: "Can we as a nation and can the

[122] "NSC Staff Study on Reappraisal of United States Objectives and Strategy for National Security," August 22, 1952, FRUS, 1952–54, vol. 2, p. 111.

[123] Memorandum by the Policy Planning Staff to the Secretary of State, FRUS, 1951, vol. 1, pp. 224–25, 227. See also Nitze to Acheson, January 12, 1953, FRUS, 1952–54, vol. 2, p. 203: "I do not think that there is, even now, a general understanding in the U.S. government that vulnerability to Soviet attack may prevent SAC from ever leaving the ground."

[124] October 16, 1951 memo, FRUS, 1951, vol. 1, p. 227.

[125] Schwartz to Bohlen, May 12, 1952, FRUS, 1952–54, vol. 2, p. 14.

nations of the now free world permit the Soviet Union to reach the position where, if it chooses, it can completely annihilate this country?"[126] The implication was that the United States might have to do something about this developing situation before it was too late, while it still had enough of a strategic edge to take some sort of "decisive action."

Project Solarium was the key device the new administration used to bring such basic policy issues into focus. The idea for this unusual exercise in the making of grand strategy came from Secretary of State Dulles, and Eisenhower himself took it very seriously.[127] Three task forces were set up. Each was to elaborate and defend a different line of strategy. Even the most cautious strategy, Alternative A, called for the United States "to assume the strategic offensive in its conflict with Soviet Communism." Rollback was to be a basic goal.[128] Alternative B, which called for drawing a line and threatening massive retaliation if the Soviets should cross it, was more a strategy than a policy—a means of supporting the goal of containment, rather than an alternative to it.

Alternative C was by far the most extreme position: "The U.S. cannot continue to live with the Soviet threat. So long as the Soviet Union exists, it will not fall apart, but must and can be shaken apart."[129] This task force concluded that "time has been working against us. This trend will continue unless it is arrested, and reversed by positive action."[130] The idea was to take American *war* objectives—ending Soviet domination outside Russia, "curtailing Soviet power for aggressive war," reducing the strength of "Bolshevik elements left in Soviet Russia"—and consider them as the "*true* objectives of the United States," to be achieved through cold war, "although admittedly running greater risk of general war." There is no doubt that this line of policy proposed to rely not just on the

[126] Quoted in a lead article in *Time*, October 5, 1953, p. 24. For a fuller text, see Dean's "Tasks for the Statesmen," *Bulletin of the Atomic Scientists*, January 1954. Note also his memorandum of September 30, 1949, outlining a plan for preventing the USSR from building a stockpile of atomic bombs: Roger Anders, ed., *Forging the Atomic Shield: Excerpts from the Office Diary of Gordon E. Dean* (Chapel Hill, 1987), pp. 40–41.

[127] See Robert Cutler, *No Time For Rest* (Boston, 1966), pp. 307ff.

[128] FRUS, 1952–54, vol. 2, pp. 400–401, 406.

[129] "Summary of Points Made in Discussion Following Presentation by Task Forces July 16, 1953," FRUS, 1952–54, vol. 2, p. 434. The full Solarium reports were declassified in 1987 (with portions exempted), and are available in Office of the Special Assistant for National Security Affairs [OSANSA], NSC series, Subject subseries, Box 9, DDEL, and also in the NSC files at the USNA.

[130] The rest of this section is deleted from the published version of the document, probably indicating it is even more extreme than what was left in. That the censors sometimes sanitize out the more extreme passages of this sort is clear from a comparison of a reference to a report by Arthur Flemming, Director of Defense Mobilization, during an NSC meeting in November 1954, and the "sanitized" text of the report. FRUS, 1952–54, vol. 2, pp. 782–83, 791.

usual instruments of cold war strategy—covert operations, propaganda, economic measures—but on military power as well. One of its basic principles was to "exploit to the fullest, use of military forces as instruments of national policy to achieve political, propaganda and prestige objectives by both military and diplomatic means." The one limitation was that the country should not *initiate* a general war, but it should be perfectly willing to risk one. To support this strategy, a massive expansion in the military budget was called for.[131]

In setting its timetable for action, Task Force C's "basic problem was to correlate the timing of actions by the United States against the time when the Soviet Union will be capable of dealing a destructive blow to the United States (five years)." Its fundamental assumption "was that under current policies, or under those of A and B, time will be working against us to the point where the Soviet threat will soon become unbearable and the survival of the United States problematical."[132] The short-term goals were thus those that this group hoped to achieve by exploiting American nuclear superiority, and included such things as the "withdrawal of Soviet forces from East Germany and Austria." During this period, there would be a war with China, perhaps growing out of a new war in Korea: by 1958, the United States would have dealt "a severe blow to Chinese prestige through the administration of a sound military defeat and the destruction of some of her industrial centers," presumably through atomic bombardment.[133] The two basic long-term goals, to be achieved after 1965, were the "overthrow of the Communist regime in China" and "the reduction of Soviet power and militancy and the elimination of the Communist conspiracy."[134]

It was against the backdrop of the Solarium discussions that Eisenhower and Dulles came to grips with the basic dilemma of the New Look: the sense that nuclear weapons had become a fact of life, and that policy had to be built on a nuclear basis, but on the other hand, that the nuclearization of global politics might generate a fear of nuclear war that could shatter the Western alliance. It was clear, especially to Eisenhower, that primary reliance would have to be placed on nuclear forces, and especially on the Strategic Air Command. It was not that the president viewed nuclear weapons as a godsend, in that only they allowed the West to neu-

[131] "Summaries Prepared by the NSC Staff of Project Solarium Presentations and Written Reports," transmitted July 22, 1953, FRUS, 1952–54, vol. 2, pp. 417–18, 422.

[132] Ibid., p. 416; "Project SOLARIUM. Summary of Basic Concepts of Task Forces," July 30, 1953, NSC Meeting Files, No. 157 Tab D, NSC Records, USNA.

[133] This was obviously closely related to the debate which had just come to a head on an expansion of the war in Korea. The discussion can be followed in FRUS, 1952–54, vol. 15, part 1.

[134] FRUS, 1952–54, vol. 2, pp. 423, 430–31.

tralize the massive military manpower of the Soviet bloc. He in fact thought it was unfortunate that nuclear weapons even existed, since in any nonnuclear war, "he was certain that with its great resources the United States would surely be able to whip the Soviet Union."[135] But the clock could not be turned back, and there was no way that any agreement could be worked out that would assure with certainty that these weapons could be abolished.

The basic realities of this new world had to be faced without sentimentality. Eisenhower was never able to accept the argument about a nuclear stalemate and the possibility that a general war might be fought with only conventional weapons.[136] Nuclear weapons dominated all lesser forms of weaponry, and it was obvious to him that in a major conflict they would in the final analysis be used. His thinking was right out of the first few pages of Clausewitz: war has an innate tendency to become absolute. It followed also that no restrictions or limitations could be placed on the way nuclear forces would be used in a general war with the Soviet bloc. Winning was the only thing that mattered. "In such a war," he said, "the United States would be applying a force so terrible that one simply could not be meticulous as to the methods by which the force was brought to bear."[137] Thus for Eisenhower, the fundamental role of nuclear weapons was something permanent and ultimately inescapable.

It was, however, also simply a fact of international life that the nuclearization of great power politics was generating fears that might well lead to a neutralization of front-line allies in Europe and the Far East.[138] The

[135] Notes of NSC meeting, June 23, 1954, ibid., p. 1469. He repeated the point the next day: "He would gladly go back to the kind of warfare which was waged in 1941 if in 1945 the A-bomb had proved impossible to make." Notes of NSC meeting, June 24, 1954, ibid., p. 688.

[136] General Ridgway, at an NSC meeting in December, had argued that if the U.S. did not resort to nuclear attack, the Russians might not use nuclear weapons either. But Eisenhower "said he did not believe any such thing." Notes of NSC meeting, December 3, 1954, ibid., p. 804. This sort of argument, he said in another meeting, was "completely erroneous." Notes of NSC meeting, June 24, 1954, ibid., p. 689. Eisenhower held to this view throughout his administration. For example, in a conversation with Robert Bowie in August 1960, Eisenhower "said that he agreed that we are not going to have a tactical nuclear war in Western Europe. In fact, he said he cannot see any chance of keeping any war in Europe from becoming a general war. For this reason he thought we must be ready to throw the book at the Russians should they jump us. He did not see how there could be such a thing as a limited war in Europe, and thought we would be fooling ourselves and our European friends if we said we could fight such a war without recourse to nuclear weapons. If massive land war operations such as the Ludendorff offensive in early 1918 in World War I were to occur, he was sure that nations would use every weapon available to them." A. J. Goodpaster, "Memorandum of Conference with the President," August 19, 1960, Declassified Documents Collection, 1987/1139.

[137] Notes of NSC meeting, March 25, 1954, FRUS, 1952–54, vol. 2, pp. 639–41.

[138] The fear of a nuclear-generated neutralization of Europe and the Far East was a minor

United States, however, could not go it alone in the world. Secretary Dulles hammered away at this theme again and again. "No single country," he said, "not even the United States, could, out of its own resources, adequately match the strength of a powerful totalitarian state. We were in no position to extract from our people what tyrannical rulers could extract from their people. The attempt to do so would 'bust us.' Accordingly, the only way the free world could hope to maintain sufficient strength so that each of its members did not 'go broke,' was the pooling of resources." Isolation, he warned, "would cost the United States dearly in the long run."[139]

Dulles laid out the basic problem in an important memorandum of September 6, 1953. On the one hand, the United States was going to shift its military policy in the direction of increased emphasis on nuclear capabilities and the withdrawal of ground forces from Europe. But with the growth of Soviet nuclear forces, he wrote, "the NATO concept [was] losing its grip" in Europe. SAC bases overseas were coming to be seen more as "lightning rods" than as "umbrellas." America was becoming so vulnerable to Soviet retaliatory attack that the Europeans were beginning to believe "that we might stay out if Europe were attacked first. And if the U.S. were attacked first, Europe might prefer to stay out." The American strategy of redeployment and a buildup of continental defense would, moreover, be interpreted "as final proof of an isolationist trend and the adoption of the 'Fortress America' concept." Dulles doubted "that any eloquence or reasoning on our part would prevent disintegration and deterioration of our position, with our growing isolation through the reaction of our present allies. The resources of the free world would then no longer be in a common fund to be drawn on for community security, and the balance of world power, military and economic, would doubtless shift rapidly to our great disadvantage." A basic conclusion followed: "we cannot avoid a major reconsideration of collective security concepts." For Dulles, there was only one answer to the dilemma: détente with the Soviet Union, "a spectacular effort to relax world tensions on a global basis."[140]

But for Eisenhower détente was not the only solution. He reacted to

---

theme in the *Foreign Relations* documents as early as 1950; see, for example, a passing reference to this prospect in NSC 68, FRUS, 1950, vol. 1, p. 265. By 1953, it had become considerably more important: see Nitze's comments, FRUS, 1952–54, vol. 2, p. 203 (where he called this "a subject of utmost delicacy"); the National Intelligence Estimate of October 23 1953, para. 4(a), ibid., p. 552; State Department Paper, November 15, 1954, ibid., p. 773; Allen Dulles paper, November 18, 1954, ibid., p. 777.

[139] Notes of NSC meeting, August 27, 1954, ibid., p. 452.

[140] Dulles memorandum, September 6, 1953, ibid., pp. 457–60. According to Dulles, the "line of thinking" initiated here ended in Eisenhower's "Atoms for Peace" speech of December 1953. Dulles, Memorandum for the President, May 12, 1954, Dulles Papers, White House Memoranda Series, Box 1, "White House Correspondence, 1954 (1)," DDEL.

Dulles's argument by briefly considering the idea of preventive war. He and his secretary of state discussed the issue at length on September 7, and on September 8 he summed up his views in a memorandum to the Secretary of State. If there was to be a "real revision in policies—some of which may temporarily, or even for a very extended time, involve us in vastly increased expenditures," he said, we would have to start educating the American people now. Given the power of nuclear weapons, and the fact that the Soviets blocked international control, the only reasonable assumption was that they were "contemplating aggressive use." America's policy therefore "could no longer be geared" toward simply avoiding "disaster during the early 'surprise' stages of a war." The United States would instead "have to be constantly ready, on an instantaneous basis, to inflict greater loss upon the enemy than he could reasonably hope to inflict upon us." This, he said, "would be a deterrent—but if the contest to maintain this relative position should have to continue indefinitely, the cost would either drive us to war—or into some form of dictatorial government." "In such circumstances," he concluded, "we would be forced to consider whether or not our duty to future generations did not require us to *initiate* war at the most propitious moment that we could designate."[141]

This was not the only instance of Eisenhower's interest in preventive war at the time. Lord Moran, for example, recalled in his diary an encounter between Churchill and Eisenhower at the Bermuda conference in December 1953: " 'Of course,' said the P.M. pacing up and down the room, 'anyone could say the Russians are evil minded and mean to destroy the free countries. Well, if we really feel like that, perhaps we ought to take action before they get as many atomic bombs as America has. I made that point to Ike, who said, perhaps logically, that it ought to be considered.' "[142] And when Dulles, in an NSC meeting in June 1954, pointed out that most of America's allies would not support a tough policy, Eisenhower said "that if this were indeed the situation, we should perhaps come back to the very grave question: Should the United States now get ready to fight the Soviet Union? The President pointed out that he had brought up this question more than once at prior Council meetings, and that he had never done so facetiously."[143]

Why then was a preventive war strategy, in any of its variants, never

[141] Eisenhower to Dulles, September 8, 1953, FRUS, 1952–54, vol. 2, p. 461. Emphasis in original. Note also Dulles, "Memorandum for Mr. Bowie," September 8, 1953, Dulles Papers, White House Memoranda series, Box 1, "White House Correspondence 1953 (2)," DDEL. The reference to "vastly increased expenditures" suggests a link to Alternative C from the Solarium Study, which had recently been discussed at the NSC level.
[142] *Winston Churchill: The Struggle for Survival*, p. 505.
[143] Notes of NSC meeting, June 24, 1954, FRUS, 1952–54, vol. 2, p. 696.

adopted as policy? It was not that Eisenhower was shocked or appalled by this way of thinking.[144] But with a decision of this magnitude, many considerations had to be taken into account, and one in particular was always decisive: even if a general war was won in some meaningful sense, the problems that would have to be faced in the postwar period would be staggering. There was one point, Eisenhower said, that he, as President, had to live with all the time, "namely, what do you do with the world after you have won victory in such a catastrophic nuclear war?"[145] "The colossal job," he said, "of occupying the territories of the defeated enemy would be far beyond the resources of the United States at the end of such a war."[146] He in fact doubted "whether any nations as we now know them would continue to exist at the conclusion of this war."[147] At one point he even made the startling comment that "the only thing worse than losing a global war was winning one."[148]

In terms of formal policy, Alternative C was already in decline when NSC 162/2, the Eisenhower administration's first basic national security policy document, was adopted on October 29, 1953. The sense of a need to act before America's nuclear lead had been lost was reduced to a fairly anodyne sentence in paragraph 45 of that basic document: "In the face of the developing Soviet threat, the broad aim of U.S. security policies must be to create, prior to the achievement of mutual atomic plenty, conditions under which the United States and the free world coalition are prepared to meet the Soviet-Communist threat with resolution and to negotiate for its alleviation under proper safeguards."[149]

By 1954, what was left was simply a strong feeling that perhaps the United States ought to take advantage of her fading nuclear superiority before she lost it completely. Those, especially in the military, who argued along these lines predicted that the loss of America's nuclear edge would lead to a dangerous upsurge in Soviet aggressiveness. In such a case, the only alternative to appeasement would be an enormously destructive war, one that the nation could scarcely hope to win in any meaningful sense.

---

[144] See, for example, his reaction to the Solarium presentations, FRUS, 1952–54, vol. 2, pp. 397–98, 438. What the President wanted was a blending of all three alternatives, which (to his annoyance) those who had worked on the project rejected as impossible. Note also his reaction to the "preventive war" briefing by the JCS's Advanced Study Group, 200th Meeting of the NSC, June 4, 1954, AWF, NSC series, Box 5. For more on this briefing, which had earlier been presented to Eisenhower, see Rosenberg, "Origins of Overkill," p. 34.

[145] Notes of NSC meeting, December 3, 1954, FRUS, 1952–54, vol. 2, p. 804. See also his comments to some military officers in June 1954, in R. H. Ferrell, ed., *The Diary of James Hagerty* (Bloomington, Ill., 1983), p. 69.

[146] Notes of NSC meeting, March 4, 1954, FRUS, 1952–54, vol. 2, p. 636.

[147] Notes of NSC meeting, March 25, 1954, ibid., p. 642.

[148] FRUS, 1952–54, vol. 2, p. 397.

[149] Ibid., p. 595.

But they did not argue that the United States should therefore try to provoke a war before this situation came to pass. Instead, they called simply for a more "active," "dynamic," or "positive" policy, without spelling out precisely what they had in mind.

As in Solarium, the interest in a more "aggressive" strategy was clearly linked to concerns about the shifting nuclear balance. This is illustrated by two memoranda presented by the new Joint Chiefs of Staff in 1954.[150] The first was a JCS attack, dated June 23, 1954, on the whole idea of negotiation with the Soviet bloc. The enemy was unrelenting, it argued, and would settle for nothing less than total victory. From the U.S. standpoint, things were already bad, and, with the development of Soviet nuclear capabilities, could only get worse: "The engulfment of a large segment of the world and its people by the Soviets has been accomplished during the period in which the United States first held a monopoly and then a significant superiority in atomic weapons and in the means for their delivery. It may properly be assumed that, unless the Soviet attitude is altered by outside influences, the aggressive and irresponsible tactics pursued with success by the Soviets thus far will be only a prelude to the proportions which such tactics will attain once the present atomic superiority of the United States has been neutralized." The United States, the Chiefs argued, had to exploit its present nuclear superiority by taking "positive actions": the Soviets had to be made to see that failure on their part to make concessions would "involve grave risks to the maintenance of their regime."[151]

The JCS contribution to the annual review of basic national security policy, dated November 22, 1954, similarly argued that the world conflict was now in a "critical" stage, and within a few years would "probably reach a decisive state."[152] It too pointed out that the allies were drifting away: the fear of atomic war was driving them toward neutralism. (One thinks of the Kaiser on the eve of World War I complaining about how his allies were falling away "like rotten pears.") And then the call for action:

> The non-Communist world, if it takes positive and timely *dynamic* countermeasures, presently has ample resources to meet this situation, and with high chance of maintaining world peace without sacrifice of either vital security interests or fundamental moral principles, or in the event of war being forced

[150] For the context, see Robert J. Watson, *History of the Joint Chiefs of Staff*, vol. 5 (1953–54) (Washington, 1986), chap. 2, esp. pp. 45–46, 48–52.

[151] JCS to Wilson, June 23, 1954, FRUS, 1952–54, vol. 2, pp. 680–86.

[152] Taken literally, what this implied was that matters were coming to a head, and the struggle would be *decided* one way or the other. Admiral Radford, in an NSC meeting at which these issues were discussed, said specifically that unless Communist action was forestalled, we could not "hope for anything but a showdown with Soviet Communists by 1959 or 1960." Notes of NSC meeting, November 24, 1954, ibid., p. 792.

upon it, of winning that war beyond any reasonable doubt. On the other hand, failure on the part of the free world and particularly of the United States to take such timely and dynamic action could, within a relatively short span of years, result in the United States finding itself isolated from the rest of the free world and thus placed in such jeopardy as to reduce its freedom of action to two alternatives—that of accommodation to Soviet designs or contesting such designs under conditions not favorable to our success.

Complaining that the government has not acted with the proper sense of urgency, and that policy has been too passive and reactive, the JCS called for a policy "of unmistakably positive quality." The nation should not be "required to defer" to the most cautious allies. The United States, they argued, had to be ready "to undertake certain risks inherent in the adoption of dynamic and positive security measures."[153]

How is all this to be understood? What sort of "timely and dynamic action" could possibly solve the problems resulting from the growth of Soviet nuclear power? Perhaps the JCS had some sort of hidden agenda that they did not dare to set out explicitly; perhaps they were forced to speak in "code language" because the preventive war option had been ruled out in 1953. There is some evidence that the Chiefs, and especially JCS Chairman Radford, were indeed thinking in these terms.[154] But the

---

[153] Wilson to Lay, November 22, 1954, ibid., 785–87. Emphasis in original.

[154] Radford, it is now clear, was in favor of a highly aggressive strategy that would have forced the Soviets both to disarm and to abandon their empire in Eastern Europe; a rejection of these demands would have led to a discriminate counterforce attack and perhaps ultimately to full-scale war. This was the basic strategy called for in the Air Force's Project Control, a major study conducted out of the Air War College in 1953–54; when Radford was briefed on the project in August 1954, these ideas received his enthusiastic support. "If the U.S. did not adopt and successfully follow through on a course of action similar to Project Control," it was his belief "that in the period mid 1957–1960 there would be either an all-out atomic war or the U.S. would be forced into an agreement which would mean victory for the U.S.S.R." Radford commented that this strategy would face political obstacles: the idea would, he thought, be resisted by both the State Department and the allies. In fact, when Project Control was briefed to the State Department, Robert Bowie, the head of the Policy Planning Staff, opposed it as "simply another version of preventive war." This is based on Tami Davis Biddle, "Handling the Soviet Threat: Arguments for Preventive War and Compellence in the Early Cold War Period," unpublished manuscript, pp. 44–55 (the Project Control strategy), pp. 61–62 and n. 148 (Radford and Bowie). Note also her discussion of the official Air Force reaction, pp. 55–57, and an excerpt from a 1953 book by Air Force General Dale Smith, quoted in George Lowe, *The Age of Deterrence* (Boston, 1964), p. 54. As for the other Chiefs, note some rather suggestive passages in a speech given by the Chief of Naval Operations, Admiral Carney, in May 1954. In dealing with the Communists, Carney argued, the United States should not simply "rush around plugging the dike" with localized military actions, but should have the "guts" to take the "rougher road" that at least gave some hope of a decent outcome. The choice had to be made quickly; "we're traveling at high speed and I don't believe much time will be vouchsafed us." According to Lowe (p. 56), Carney was "widely thought to be suggesting a preventive war." The text of the speech is in the *New York Times*, May 28, 1954, p. 2. Air Force Chief of Staff Twining's

evidence is by no means conclusive, and it is certainly possible that top military leaders at the time had never really worked this issue through in their own minds: they knew what they did not like, namely, the growth of Soviet nuclear capabilities, and felt very strongly that a policy of drift might lead to catastrophe, but were not quite sure what could be done about it.

In any case, the JCS soon got a hearing: the issue of a more "positive policy" came to a climax in the NSC at the end of 1954. In these discussions it was Dulles, a hawk during the discussions about ending the Korean War, the man who had called during the presidential campaign for a "policy of boldness," who now took the lead in arguing for a relatively mild policy.[155] What, he asked, was the point of the aggressive strategy that the Chiefs had recommended? The problem was not simply that the Allies would not follow us; this was an important consideration, but if the policy was right, Dulles said, he would go along with it anyway.[156] The real problem was that it did not make any strategic sense. There was only one respect in which the United States was facing a deterioration in its global position, "namely, the forthcoming achievement of atomic plenty and a nuclear balance of power between the U.S. and the USSR." "But how," Dulles asked in a key NSC meeting in November 1954, "were we to prevent the Soviet Union from achieving such a nuclear balance of power without going to war with the USSR? Certainly no actions on the periphery of the Soviet Union would stop the growth of the atomic capabilities of the Soviet Union."[157] Eisenhower himself had long had doubts about "how much we should poke the animal through the bars of the cage."[158]

Dulles now appeared comfortable with present American policies, which he described in surprisingly Kennanesque terms: "Our alliance sys-

sympathy for this sort of thinking is suggested by the passages quoted above from his book: if Twining took this line in public even in the mid-1960s, one imagines that the line he took in private around 1954 must have been considerably stronger, especially given the kind of thinking common in Air Force circles at the time. Even General Ridgway, Army Chief of Staff and by far the strongest advocate of the "limited war" philosophy in the JCS, had by 1954 evidently moved very far toward the idea of hitting the enemy at his heart: if the U.S. were to intervene militarily in the Indochina conflict, it should avoid getting bogged down in a local war and should instead initiate mobilization and "neutralize the sources of Viet Minh strength" by taking military action against China. JCS Historical Division, "History of the Indochina Incident," p. 388.

[155] On Dulles's line at the start of the Eisenhower administration, see especially his handwritten notes of his comments at a high-level meeting on December 11, 1952, Dulles Papers, Subject File, Box 8, "S. S. Helena Notes," DDEL.

[156] Notes of NSC meeting, June 24, 1954, FRUS, 1952–54, vol. 2, pp. 694–95.

[157] Notes of NSC meeting, November 24, 1954, ibid., 789–90. The kind of minor aggressions that had been proposed were "such projects as the detachment of Albania or an assault on Hainan Island." Notes of NSC meeting, October 29, 1953, ibid., p. 569.

[158] Cutler to Dulles, September 3, 1953, ibid., p. 457.

tem has staked out the vital areas of the world which we propose to hold even at the risk of general war. These vital areas include currently all the areas of immediate strategic value to us or which possess significant war potential. The NATO area is by all odds the greatest single U.S. asset."[159] Dulles stressed his personal sympathy for the JCS position. He reminded the chiefs that he himself had called for a more dynamic policy during the 1952 presidential campaign. Even after taking office, he had supported a policy of bringing about "the disintegration of Soviet power."[160] But, he noted in the December 1954 NSC meeting, his views had changed. Experience had shown that beyond a certain point, the "dynamic" policy could not be translated into specific courses of action.[161]

The general mood at this NSC meeting was in harmony with Dulles's more relaxed views. Treasury Secretary Humphrey and Defense Secretary Wilson were essentially willing to accept coexistence (although the latter did not particularly like the word). As for Eisenhower, he was not opposed to the idea of negotiations with the Soviets. Even the old idea that all outposts had to be held, which Dulles had supported at the beginning of the Eisenhower period, was now abandoned: Indochina, Dulles said, was not terribly significant to us, and Eisenhower had already pointed out at an earlier meeting that if people did not want to be free, and would not fight for their freedom, there was not very much the United States could do about it.[162]

The December 24, 1954, NSC meeting marks, in a sense, the end of an era. The period had begun with the Soviet atomic test in late 1949. The tensions generated by that event had played an important role in the American policy debates of the early 1950s. But by the end of 1954, these tensions had essentially worked themselves out. This is not to argue that "preventive war" thinking disappeared without a trace: even as late as 1959, Eisenhower was still wondering whether America "should start fighting now" instead of "waiting to go quietly down the drain."[163] And in 1960, fed up with "Khrushchev and his threats," the President "strongly intimated that he wished there was no moral restriction that prevented him from one night pushing the proper button and sending all of our atomic bombs in the direction of the Communist bloc."[164]

[159] Notes of NSC meeting, December 21, 1954, ibid., pp. 833–34.

[160] Notes of NSC meeting, March 31, 1953, ibid., p. 267.

[161] Ibid., p. 833.

[162] Ibid., p. 837 (for Humphrey), p. 840 (for Wilson), p. 843 (Eisenhower on negotiations); p. 266 (for Dulles's domino argument in early 1953); p. 835 (for his later, milder views on the subject); p. 709 (for Eisenhower on people not willing to fight for their freedom).

[163] Bryce Harlow, Memorandum for the Record, March 26, 1959, Ann Whitman File, DDE Diaries, Staff Notes, March 1–15, 1959 (1); also Declassified Documents Collection, 1978/118C.

[164] Notes for Files, September 25, 1960, AWF, AWD, Box 11, DDEL.

But these were now merely isolated expressions of frustration. It was too late for anything like this to be seriously considered as a real policy option. Dulles's reaction in 1958 to an argument that the United States should consider taking some action before it lost its strategic edge over the Soviet Union probably comes much closer to capturing the heart of Eisenhower administration thinking on this issue in the late 1950s. The question of preventive war, of course, had been around for a long time: Dulles recalled how in June 1946 he and Senator Vandenberg had "speculated" on whether force would be justified if the Soviets refused to accept international control of nuclear weapons. But this was no longer an open question: "no man," Dulles felt, "should arrogate to himself the power to decide that the future of mankind would benefit by an action entailing the killing of tens of millions of people."[165]

CONCLUSION

The nuclear revolution was like a great earthquake, setting off a series of shock waves that gradually worked their way through the world political system. The basic aim here was to study one part of this process, the way people dealt with the problem of the shifting strategic balance, and especially the loss of the American nuclear monopoly, in the period from 1949 to 1954. This story is of interest because of the light it sheds on the problem of how the world came to terms with nuclear weapons—how they were absorbed into the international system, and how people accommodated to the basic realities of the nuclear age.

[165] Dulles's interlocutor was Robert Sprague, in 1954, consultant to the NSC on continental defense, in 1957, chief architect of the Gaither Report. In his 1958 conversation with the secretary of state, Sprague argued that for the next two and a half years, "the U.S. position vis-à-vis the Soviet Union will be at its strongest," and that "during this period we can knock out the Soviet Union's military capability without taking a similar blow from the Soviet Union." He had therefore asked the President to appoint a study group to consider "what the U.S. should do during the few years in which we will retain a margin of advantage." Memorandum of Conversation, January 3, 1958, Dulles Papers, General Correspondence and Memoranda Series, Box 1, "Memoranda of Conversation—General—S(1)," DDEL. A few years earlier, Sprague, in briefing the NSC on continental defense, had evidently referred to preventive war as an option open to the U.S.; in another NSC meeting a few weeks later, he argued that the U.S. could not afford "to leave in Soviet hands the question of whether they should or should not attack us" in the near future. "Discussion at the 208th Meeting of the National Security Council, Thursday, July 1, 1954" (allusion by Dulles, p. 19), and "Discussion at the 208th Meeting of the National Security Council, Thursday, July 29, 1954," p. 4, both in AWF, NSC series, Box 5, DDEL. Incidentally, in November 1957, three members of the Gaither Committee urged reconsideration of the whole idea of preventive war. David Rosenberg, "Toward Armageddon: The Foundations of United States Nuclear Strategy, 1945–1961," unpub. diss., University of Chicago, 1983, p. 236.

What surprised me the most as I went through these sources was that so much attention was given to the extraordinary *shifts* then taking place, both in the military balance and in the military environment as a whole. It was a surprise that such window thinking loomed as large as it did; it was perhaps not quite so surprising that the global balance, as such, played an important role in shaping policy. But once this became clear, all kinds of other things began to fall into place.

In this concluding section, I want to explore some of the implications of the argument here in three areas, specifically: (*a*) American military policy, (*b*) American foreign policy, and (*c*) global politics as a whole. The sort of thinking discussed above was obviously not *directly* translated into policy, but this set of concerns did enter into the matrix out of which policy developed, and the *indirect* effects were of considerable importance.

MILITARY POLICY. The sort of thinking that was emerging in response to concerns about the shifting nuclear balance was clearly one of the major elements factored into the Eisenhower strategy. The New Look took it for granted that if the Soviets turned out to be totally impossible to live with, that if they insisted on pursuing highly aggressive policies and sought relentlessly to force a retreat of American power especially from Europe and the Far East, then the United States would have to go to war with them. In such a war, the goal would be to destroy Soviet power totally, once and for all. If the Soviets were in fact this bad, and if as a result a war of this sort had to be fought, it might be dangerous to try too hard to avoid a showdown. Given the way the military balance was bound to shift, the United States would be well-advised to make its stand sooner rather than later. Moreover, if general war was a real possibility, then it was obviously important that the United States be able to strike quickly, so that any Soviet counterattack could be blunted.

This thinking helps explain the emphasis that American military policy in the 1950s placed on preemption, as well as the targeting philosophy based on destroying the "heart of Soviet power." All of these ideas were cut from the same cloth, and tended, at least in a psychological sense, to be mutually reinforcing. They all added up to a way of looking at the world that carried a certain political weight—influencing, for example, how broadly the conditions for preemption were defined.[166] This body of evidence thus helps support the conclusion that the Eisenhower strategy has to be taken seriously, that it was not at bottom (as some people argue) simply a gigantic bluff. Ideas of this sort, in their pure form, were never

---

[166] The term "preemption" was not used in the NSC documents; they generally referred instead to the conditions under which the United States would have to assume that general war was imminent.

able to dictate policy, but they certainly affected the way the policy balance was struck.

FOREIGN POLICY. How did these concerns about trends in the military balance relate to American foreign policy as a whole in this period? The strategy of building up American and allied power, especially the dramatic shift in late 1950 on the German question—that is, the opting for the rearmament of West Germany—clearly has to be understood in this context.

In the Far East, concerns about the balance played an important direct role in foreign policy. In the winter of 1950–51, they acted as a force for restraint. But after the balance had shifted in late 1952, the tenor of high-level American policy discussions became noticeably more hawkish.[167] The evidence is spotty, but one suspects that the increasing pressure for a more aggressive American policy in East Asia was linked to the sort of thinking reflected in documents like the Solarium Task Force C report. From the point of view of people like Admiral Radford, the China area must have seemed like the best place in the world to try to implement a "dynamic" and "positive" policy.[168] Indeed, for some military officers, a general war with China was attractive precisely because it might have led to an all-out war with the Soviet Union as well, before it was too late. General K. D. Nichols, who for years had been one of the most important army officers concerned with nuclear matters, argued at the end of 1952 for the deliberate use of nuclear weapons in the war against China. One goal, he said, was to "precipitate a major war," evidently against the USSR, "at a time when we have greatest potential for winning it with minimum damage to the U.S.A."[169]

By the end of 1954, however, American policy as a whole was drawing back from what was referred to even in internal documents as an "aggressive" strategy against China; from that point on, the United States sought in practice simply to support the status quo in the Far East.[170] This

---

[167] This can be followed in some detail in FRUS, 1952–54, vol. 14; there is also some relevant material in vol. 12.

[168] Even in 1952 (when he was U.S. commander in the Pacific), he was pressing for a more aggressive U.S. policy in the China area. See the report by General Merrill to the Policy Planning Staff, April 17, 1952, Records of the Policy Planning Staff, Box 32, "Policy Planning Staff Meetings (1950)," RG 59, USNA. Radford was thinking in terms of the seizure of Hainan Island by the Chinese Nationalists (with U.S. support), and maybe even a "lodgment" in "one of the coastal provinces."

[169] Memorandum quoted in K. D. Nichols, *The Road to Trinity* (New York, 1987), p. 12; see also p. 291. Nitze referred to Nichols in 1950 as "probably the principal Pentagon authority on the bomb." Nitze to Acheson, July 17, 1950, Records of the Policy Planning Staff, Box 7, folder "Atomic Energy—Armaments. 1950," RG 59, USNA.

[170] The JCS were informed on September 28, 1954, that the president had "suspended" the policy of supporting Chinese Nationalist raids on the mainland. JCS Memorandum for

was probably linked to what was going on at the level of general policy-making at exactly this time—the defeat of the JCS in the NSC also in late 1954, and the opting for a policy of coexistence with the Soviets.

GLOBAL POLITICS, 1949–54. Finally, the shifting balance seems to have had an important bearing on the course of global politics as a whole in the period up to 1954. The Soviets were deeply concerned with what was going on in the United States in this period. The harsh anti-Communist rhetoric coming out of Washington was bad enough; but now, on top of this, the West had taken a series of extraordinary moves to build up its military power. In this context, certain signals were especially important. Remarks that seemed to indicate that influential elements in the U.S. government thought the emerging military situation was intolerable and that a more "positive" strategy might be necessary, were bound to alarm the Soviets. Thus, for example, Senator William Knowland's call in late 1954 for a basic change in U.S. policy before time ran out and the Communists were able to resume their advance under cover of an "atomic stalemate" was just one of many pronouncements that might have been taken as indications of the way official thinking was moving in the United States. Knowland was the Republican leader in the Senate; although the administration publicly distanced itself from his views, the Soviets might well have wondered whether this was because Knowland was more radical than Eisenhower and Dulles, or simply less discreet.[171]

Statements coming from more authoritative sources were worrisome enough. In August of 1954, General Twining had made the somewhat

the Secretary of Defense, October 1, 1954, File for NSC Meeting No. 216 Tab C, NSC Records, USNA. Another important development a little later was the conclusion of the Mutual Defense Treaty with the government on Taiwan. This had been considered earlier, but the U.S. had preferred in 1954 not to negotiate such a pact "primarily because a defensive pact might have the effect of tying the hands of the GRC." NSC Operations Coordinating Board, Progress Report on United States Objectives and Courses of Action with Respect to Formosa and the Chinese National Government, July 16, 1954, p. 5, NSC 146 File, NSC Records, USNA.

[171] "Knowland Warns of Policy Danger; Calls for Review," *New York Times*, November 16, 1954, p. 1. The text of the statement is on p. 18. There are many indications of Soviet interest in and concern with the shifting strategic balance; indeed, when I was doing the research for this article, some of my best leads came from Soviet denunciations at the time of preventive war thinking in the West. For a discussion of some of the evidence on the Soviet side, see Jack Snyder, "Russia's Nuclear Window of Vulnerability, 1948–1955: Soviet Perceptions and Debates," unpublished paper, April 1988. Note also an unpublished paper by Col. Prof. L. S. Semieko, "Military-Political Aspects of Soviet-American Relations in the Years of 1950–1955," presented to a meeting of American and Soviet historians, October 1988. The United States, says Semeiko, called its policy "massive retaliation," but the Soviets in the early 1950s could not believe that America would only use its forces for purely retaliatory purposes: "U.S. readiness for launching a preventive war was obvious in many purely military indications"—a remark that should be interpreted in the light of the fact that Semeiko worked for Soviet military intelligence at the time.

ambiguous point that the proof of America's peaceful intentions was that "there is already sufficient reason for war, if we are seeking war."[172] Eisenhower himself, in his first State of the Union address in early 1953, also made a comment that was susceptible to more than one interpretation: he warned that the "free world cannot indefinitely remain in a posture of paralyzed tension." It is unlikely that remarks of this sort passed unnoticed in the USSR. Indeed, as Eisenhower himself put it, the Russians must have been "scared as hell" at this time.[173]

It seems quite clear that the USSR accommodated to the new thrust of American policy. The most important shift was on Soviet policy on the German question. There were three great steps along the road to a full resurgence of German power: the creation of the Federal Republic, the rearmament of West Germany, and the nuclearization of the Bundeswehr. The first and third led to crises. The decisions taken at the London Conference in 1948 made it clear that a West German state would soon be brought into being, and the Soviets reacted by blockading West Berlin in 1948–49. In the late 1950s, it seemed that West German armed forces were well on their way toward acquiring nuclear forces of their own, and this also led to a very serious Berlin Crisis.[174] But the second phase in this process, the rearmament of West Germany, did not lead to anything comparable, in spite of the fact that a very sharp Soviet reaction was widely expected at the time.[175]

[172] Quoted in the *New York Times*, August 21, 1954, p. 5.

[173] *Public Papers of the Presidents: Eisenhower*, 1953, p. 13; notes of NSC meeting, June 4, 1953, FRUS, 1952–54, vol. 2, p. 369.

[174] See chapter five below.

[175] The key decisions on the American side were made in late 1950 after the outbreak of the Korean War. Even before Korea, the Soviet reaction to German rearmament was a source of great anxiety, not just in Western Europe but even in the United States. "The rearmament of Germany," U.S. High Commissioner John McCloy wrote in early June 1950, "would undoubtedly speed up any Soviet schedule for any possible future action in Germany and would, no doubt, be regarded by them as sufficiently provocative to warrant extreme countermeasures." McCloy to Acheson, June 13, 1950, President's Secretary's Files, Box 178, "Germany. Folder 2," HSTL. After the war in Korea broke out, these fears became more intense, although they were counterbalanced by fears about what would happen if the West did nothing while its nuclear advantage gradually disappeared. The CIA, for example, in early 1951, thought there was a better than fifty-fifty chance that West German rearmament would lead to war with the Soviets. Memorandum for the President, January 25, 1951, p. 4, MNSC, reel 1. See also the CIA study, "Probable Soviet Reactions to a Remilitarization of Western Germany," NIE-17, December 27, 1950, PSF, Box 253, HSTL, esp. paragraphs 7 and 9. In 1952, when the agreements creating a framework for German rearmament were finally signed, there was again a great fear that the Soviets would react by provoking a new Berlin Crisis. But again, the American government, somewhat to its surprise, was struck by the fact that no aggressive moves were taken around Berlin: the situation on the access routes remained normal in 1952–53. FRUS, 1952–54, vol. 7, pp. 1236, 1239, 1272, 1294, 1373.

This, in other words, was a Berlin crisis that did not happen. Instead of responding aggressively to what was going on, the Soviets opted for a conciliatory policy. The series of moves culminating in the famous Soviet note on Germany of March 10, 1952, certainly has to be understood in the context of these Soviet fears and anxieties.[176] The Soviets, in other words, had accommodated to the shift in the balance that had taken place in the early 1950s.

This, in any case, was the view the Soviet leaders themselves came to have of this period. Nikita Khrushchev, for example, later referred with apparent distaste, and evidently to the period around 1952 to 1954, as a time when the West really did have the upper hand strategically. "It is high time," Khrushchev said in his speech of November 10, 1958, "to realize that the times when the imperialists could act from 'positions of strength' with impunity have gone never to return, and try as they may, the imperialists will not be able to change the balance of forces in their favor."[177] These shifts on the Soviet side, especially the turn toward con-

---

[176] There was, and to a certain extent still is, a tendency in the West to dismiss these offers as being purely tactical in their purpose, the aim supposedly having been to derail the process leading to the military integration of West Germany into the NATO bloc. The best scholarship, however, demonstrates that this was not the case. A superb dissertation by Paul Willging provides a very effective analysis of this issue: Paul R. Willging, "Soviet Foreign Policy in the German Question: 1950–1955," unpublished dissertation, Columbia University, 1973. This work can now be supplemented by important documents from British, French, and American archival sources, which show that many Western statesmen believed at the time that these Soviet moves were more than a simple maneuver, but reflected a real shift in policy on the German question. There was a parallel shift in the tone of official East German utterances in this period. In late 1950, East German Prime Minister Grotewohl quite clearly threatened that what had happened in Korea might well be repeated in Germany, and party leader Ulbricht said the regime had decided against building a new seaport "since soon 'democratic Germany' would have Hamburg and Lubeck." Cited in Thomas Schwartz, "From Occupation to Alliance: John J. McCloy and the Allied High Commission in the Federal Republic of Germany, 1949–1952," unpub. diss., Harvard University, 1985, p. 303; see also p. 354, n. 14. By early 1952, however, the East Germans increasingly emphasized defense. The parallel with Korea, still a theme in Grotewohl's remarks, was now much more ambiguous. It was no longer an East German invasion of the West that was threatened; instead, Grotewohl spoke simply of the "great danger" of a "fratricidal war of Germans against Germans." Quoted in McCloy to State Department, May 16, 1952, FRUS, 1952–54, vol. 7, p. 341.

[177] This speech marked the beginning of the great Berlin Crisis of 1958–62. For the text, see U.S. Senate Committee on Foreign Relations, *Documents on Germany, 1944–1961* (Washington, 1961), p. 339. There is an even more striking admission in Khrushchev's August 11, 1961, speech. "There was a time," he said, "when American Secretary of State Dulles brandished thermonuclear bombs and followed a position of strength policy with regard to the socialist countries. . . . That was barefaced atomic blackmail, but it had to be reckoned with at the time because we did not possess sufficient means of retaliation, and if we did, they were not as many and not of the same power as those of our opponents." Ibid., pp. 718–19. A series of other retrospective comments by East German and Soviet leaders

ciliation during the late Stalin and early post-Stalin periods, in turn had a major impact on the policy of the Western powers, and all this was part of a much broader process whereby the fate of Germany, and with it the structure of power in Europe, was worked out.

We as a society suffer today from what can only be called an extraordinary case of collective nuclear amnesia. A picture of the past has taken shape that has very little to do with what our nuclear past was really like.[178] It is now often taken for granted that even in the 1950s nuclear war was simply "unthinkable" as an instrument of policy; that nuclear forces were never "usable" and served only to "deter their use by others"; and that the threat of "massive retaliation" was at bottom just pure bluff, because the United States would never be the first to launch a nuclear strike. This picture has taken shape because it serves important political purposes for both the left and the right, but one cannot immerse oneself in the sources for this period without coming to the conclusion that something very basic has been forgotten. The historical documents themselves certainly give a very different picture.

It is important to see the past as it really was, to understand that thirty-five years ago people lived in a different world, a much more frightening world than anything we know today. Out of that world a stable peace eventually took shape. How this happened is obviously a problem of more than just historical interest. The one thing that is now clear is that this is an extremely interesting problem to explore, and one where historical scholarship has barely begun to scratch the surface.

---

are quoted in the Willging dissertation cited above. Note finally, for what it is worth, Khrushchev's comment in his memoirs that Stalin "lived in terror of an enemy attack." *Khrushchev Remembers*, ed. and trans. by Strobe Talbott (Boston, 1970), p. 393.

[178] For a couple of interesting examples, see Paul Nitze, "Assuring Strategic Stability in an Era of Detente," *Foreign Affairs*, vol. 54, no. 2 (January 1976), p. 211, and Henry Kissinger, "A New Era for NATO," *Newsweek*, October 12, 1987, p. 60. Kissinger said here that he had "argued for 30 years that the threshold at which nuclear weapons have to be used should be raised much higher." But exactly thirty years previously he had published *Nuclear Weapons and Foreign Policy*, the book that established his reputation, in which he argued for a limited war strategy based on tactical nuclear weapons. These, he wrote, needed to be employed more freely than was possible in a strategy based on massive retaliation. The Eisenhower strategy had locked us into a posture that was much too defensive; strategy instead needed to be oriented toward such "positive goals" as the reunification of Germany and the liberation of Eastern Europe. Needless to say, all this is forgotten today. See Henry Kissinger, *Nuclear Weapons and Foreign Policy* (New York, 1957).

CHAPTER FOUR

The Nuclearization of NATO and U.S.–West European Relations

IN THE EARLY 1950s NATO went nuclear. It is often assumed that in opting for a strategy that placed such great emphasis on nuclear weapons, the Atlantic Alliance made the wrong decision: the nuclear-based strategy, it is argued, never really made sense even in purely military terms. The better strategy, the argument runs, was to build up conventional forces to the point where they alone would be able to defend Western Europe against a Soviet attack. But this turned out to be beyond reach for political and budgetary reasons. Nuclearization therefore supposedly emerged as a panacea—as the only way of bringing defense requirements into line with political realities. Budgetary constraints are thus seen as driving the whole process; the assumption is that from an essentially military point of view, the nuclear strategy was misguided from the start.

But in reality, the nuclear-oriented strategy did make military sense in the early 1950s. It is not that budgetary constraints were irrelevant. Fiscal considerations certainly played an important role in the policy process on both sides of the Atlantic, but their ultimate effect was to force a clarification of strategy. The policy that emerged was not out of line with the best military thinking at the time.

To understand what happened, one must go back to the great debate in the late 1940s and early 1950s over what American strategy in Europe should be. The argument was not really between "internationalists" and "isolationists." The real debate was between those who wanted to defend Europe as far to the east as possible—the supporters of "forward defense"—and the advocates of a "peripheral strategy," which contemplated withdrawing from the continent and relied primarily on air and naval power.

Within the military establishment, the Army naturally championed the idea of forward defense, while the Air Force leaned strongly toward the peripheral strategy. The Navy generally sided with the Army, at least during the crucial 1949–1950 period, and indeed often took the lead in op-

This paper is based on a talk given at a conference held at the Truman Library in late 1989 to commemorate the fortieth anniversary of the founding of NATO. It is also being published in a volume based on the papers presented at that conference: John Gillingham and Francis Heller, eds., *NATO, The Integration of Europe and the Atlantic Alliance* (London, 1991).

posing the Air Force position. In 1949, the Navy was in fact embroiled in a very bitter and very public dispute with the Air Force: this was the period of the famous "revolt of the admirals," touched off by the cancellation of an aircraft carrier whose keel had just been laid. This controversy was marked by a sharp attack by the Navy on strategic bombing in general, and on the B-36 bomber in particular.

It was precisely during this period that the dispute over basic war-fighting strategy came to a head at the level of the Joint Chiefs of Staff. Secretary of Defense James Forrestal had asked the Chiefs in October 1948 for an evaluation of current plans for a strategic air offensive against the Soviet Union: could the United States successfully bring off such an attack, and if so, what effect would it have on the Soviet war effort?[1] The crisis over Berlin might possibly lead to war; it was important that this question be answered honestly and rapidly.

On December 21, General Hoyt Vandenberg, the Air Force Chief of Staff, proposed that the Chiefs tell the Secretary simply that the attack could be carried out as planned. His memorandum set out the basic Air Force position. "Major Soviet urban industrial concentrations" would be the "highest priority target system" for atomic attack. "Destruction of this target system," he wrote, "should so cripple the Soviet industrial and control centers as to reduce drastically the offensive and defensive power of their armed forces. This could well lead to Soviet capitulation and in any event should destroy their over-all capability for major offensive operations."[2]

Admiral Denfeld, the Chief of Naval Operations, strongly objected to these claims. The opinions expressed in Vandenberg's memorandum, he said, were "predicated on assumptions not supported by known facts."[3] The Director of Army Intelligence also thought that the inadequacy of "existing industrial intelligence on the USSR does not warrant an attack of the scale and magnitude envisaged" by the current Air Force strategy. "In view of the doubt that exists concerning target analysis and the underestimation of Soviet air defenses," he felt that Vandenberg's conclusions were "overly optimistic."[4]

A great deal was at stake in this argument between the Air Force on the

[1] McNeil to Gruenther, October 3, 1948, and Forrestal to Joint Chiefs of Staff, October 23 and 25, 1948, CCS 373 (10-23-48) sec 1, RG 218 (Records of the Joint Chiefs of Staff), United States National Archives (USNA), Washington. See also David Rosenberg, "American Atomic Strategy and the Hydrogen Bomb Decision," *Journal of American History*, vol. 66 (June 1979), pp. 73–75.

[2] JCS 1952/1, December 21, 1948, CCS 373 (10-23-48) sec 1, RG 218, USNA.

[3] JCS 1952/2, January 11, 1949, CCS 373 (10-23-48) sec 1, RG 218, USNA.

[4] Appendix A to JIC 439/5, February 26, 1949, CCS 373 (10-23-48) sec 1, RG 218, USNA; see also Enclosure A to JIC 439/3, February 15, 1949, same file, giving the views of Army Intelligence on the subject in greater detail.

one hand, and the Army and Navy on the other. This was a formative period for American nuclear strategy. What was decided now would determine fundamental military policy for years to come. The dispute over basic strategy was, moreover, closely related to parallel arguments about the control of the weaponry—both the bombs themselves and the forces that would deliver them—and control of the target intelligence process. This last issue was quite important: these other conflicts among the military services turned in large measure on who controlled the target intelligence system. At the time, all of these issues were the object of fierce and prolonged dispute within the JCS.[5]

With so much at stake, Vandenberg responded very defensively to the criticism of his Army and Navy colleagues. Strategic bombing, he said, was the business of the Air Force. He was clearly angry that Admiral Denfeld would question "the ability of the United States Air Force to judge the feasibility, technical or otherwise, of conducting strategic air operations."[6] Wasn't this its main area of expertise?

But this was just so much hand-waving. Vandenberg simply did not want to engage in serious debate with the other services over what was clearly the most basic issue of national strategy. The Army and the Navy, however, refused to defer to the Air Force. The Army's analysis in particular was very detailed and closely reasoned. Vandenberg's conclusions were based on certain optimistic assumptions about the ineffectiveness of Soviet air defense; the Army intelligence division pointed out that the Air Force's own intelligence reports contained information that directly refuted some of the claims Vandenberg had made.[7] The Army was able to prove, in its internal documents, that the Air Force was not being honest or objective on this matter.[8]

[5] For example: Sullivan to Symington, August 9, 1948, and Symington to Forrestal, October 6, 1948, CD 16-1-8, Records of the Office of the Secretary of Defense, RG 330, 1947–50 series, USNA; Maddocks to Army Chief of Staff, February 8, 1949, on "Final Report to the Joint Chiefs of Staff Evaluation Board for Operation 'CROSSROADS,' " P & O 000.99 RD/TS (25 Jan 49), RG 319, P & O Army—Operations, Hot Files, Box 10, 1949 Hot File.

[6] JCS 1952/3, January 21, 1949, CCS 373 (10-23-48) sec 1, RG 218, USNA.

[7] Enclosure A to JIC 439/3, February 15, 1949, CCS 373 (10-23-48) sec 1, RG 218, USNA.

[8] Vandenberg had claimed in his reply to Denfeld—JCS 1952/3, cited above—that the Air Force had consulted with the JCS's Joint Intelligence Committee (JIC) "in arriving at the Intelligence estimates" contained in his original memorandum. But General Ray Maddocks, Director of Army Plans and Operations, noted that according to the JIC secretariat, the original Vandenberg document had *not* been referred to that body for comment. Maddocks also complained repeatedly about the Air Force's "lack of objectivity" in its use of intelligence. When it was arguing for support of its guided missile program or for the development of certain forms of aircraft, it strongly emphasized Soviet air defense capabilities. But when demonstrating its ability to deliver "the air offensive as planned, Russian anti-aircraft interceptor capabilities and other factors are greatly de-emphasized." Maddocks to Army Chief of Staff, February 8, 1949, P & O 323 TS, RG 319, USNA; Maddocks to Army Chief of

The general issue was referred to the JCS's Joint Intelligence Committee for further analysis. The JIC report, concurred in by the Director of Air Intelligence, supported the Army-Navy point of view.[9] Eventually, the whole problem was turned over to two groups from outside the JCS system. An ad hoc committee under Air Force General H. R. Harmon would evaluate the effect of the bombing offensive on the Soviet war effort. The Weapons System Evaluation Group, then headed by Army General John Hull, would consider whether the attack could be carried out as planned. The Harmon Committee reported in May 1949 that the attack, even if successful, would have a much more limited effect than Vandenberg had claimed, and that in particular it would not be able to knock the Soviets out of the war. The Hull Report of February 1950 cast grave doubts on the ability of the Air Force to execute the attack successfully in the first place. These reports were based on quite thorough analysis, and the leaders of these groups were highly respected throughout the military establishment. The effect of this review was therefore to pose a very serious challenge to the Air Force position.[10]

It is important to note, moreover, that an alternative strategy was available at this time. The Army throughout the 1949–54 period had a clear conception of how a general war should be fought. It was not opposed to strategic bombing as such, and it certainly was not against the use of atomic weapons in a global conflict. But given the small numbers and limited power of the atomic bombs available in the first part of this period, the Army insisted repeatedly that targets had to be chosen with great care. It objected strongly to the Air Force strategy of urban-industrial targeting because even the successful destruction of much of the enemy's industrial infrastructure would not have a timely effect on the outcome of the land battle in Europe. Strategic bombing there would be, but only certain crucial targets—especially the enemy liquid fuels industry—would be hit. As the World War II experience had shown, this sort of attack could have a dramatic and almost immediate impact on the ground war.[11]

Staff, March 16, 1949, and especially the enclosure ("Typical Examples of the Subjective Use of Intelligence by USAF"), P & O 373 TS series 1a, RG 319, USNA.

[9] Maddocks to Army Chief of Staff, March 16, 1949, P & O 373 TS series 1a, RG 319, USNA. The JIC report to the JCS, JCS 1952/4, is summarized here; the original has evidently not been declassified, since the text is missing from the appropriate section of CCS 373 in RG 218.

[10] Harmon Report: JCS 1953/1, May 12, 1949, CCS 373 (10-23-48) Bulky Package, RG 218, discussed in Rosenberg, "American Atomic Strategy," p. 16. Hull Report: JCS 1952/11, February 10, 1950, same file in RG 218, discussed in Richard Rowe, "American Nuclear Strategy and the Korean War," M.A. thesis, University of Pennsylvania, 1984.

[11] This account of the Army strategy is based on two types of sources from the 1949–50 period. Of prime importance are the speeches given by top Army leaders to military audiences at the time, especially General Omar Bradley's address at the National War College,

In the theater itself, the Army view was that the Red Army's supply system was its "Achilles heel"; Soviet lines of communication were "long and vulnerable."[12] The West might have to retreat during the initial phase of the war, but through "properly executed delaying tactics and demolitions" during this period, "the Soviet advances can be channelized into a few corridors." To conduct major offensive operations in Western Europe, the Soviets would have to "stockpile supplies at the end of long and very meager lines of communication." Both their concentrated forces and especially these stockpiles would be vulnerable to atomic attack.[13] If such a strategy were implemented, and appropriate weapons and delivery systems developed, even a numerically inferior land force might well be able to hold the line during the early part of the war against a full-scale attack from the east.

The Army strategy, moreover, corresponded to the political need for forward defense. The idea that the alliance with Western Europe implied a forward defense was constantly stressed by Army leaders at this time. General Omar Bradley, the Army Chief of Staff, made the point quite effectively in April 1949:

> It must be perfectly apparent to the people of the United States that we cannot count on friends in Western Europe if our strategy in the event of war dictates that we shall first abandon them to the enemy with a promise of later liberation. Yet that is the only strategy that can prevail if the military balance of power in Europe is to be carried on the wings of our bombers and deposited in reserves this side of the ocean. It is a strategy that would produce nothing better than impotent and disillusioned Allies in the event of a war.
>
> Unless plans for common defense of the existing free world provide for the security of Western Europe, these people cannot be expected to stake their

---

May 24, 1949, P & O Decimal File, 1949–February 1950, 350.001 sec 1, RG 319, USNA, and General J. Lawton Collins address to the Command and General Staff College, May 5, 1950, same file, sec 2. This was supplemented by various documents from the JCS papers and the P & O (Army Plans and Operations) files. For a representative sample: Briefing Sheet for JCS Chairman for December 1, 1949 meeting on JCS 2056/3, a JIC evaluation of JCS 2056, "Target System for Implementation of Joint Outline Emergency War Plan," CCS 373.11 (12-14-48), RG 218; Schuyler to Lindsay, Ingersoll, and Smith, March 8, 1950, on "Employment of the Strategic Air Command in Support of CINCEUR and CINCFE," P & O Hot Files, Box 11, 1950–51 Hot File, RG 319; Bolté to Army Chief of Staff, August 14, 1950, on "Target Selections for the Strategic Air Offensive"—note especially the reference here to the "long-standing Army concept of the Strategic Air Offensive"—OPS 416 RD/TS (12 Aug 50), same box; and draft enclosure in Schuyler to Lindsay, Ingersoll, and Smith, October 4, 1950, on "Target Selection for Strategic Air Offensive," same box.

[12] Collins speech (see n. 11), p. 13.

[13] "Employment of Atomic Weapons against Military Targets," study prepared by Joint War Plans Branch, Assistant Chief of Staff, G-3, General Staff, U.S. Army, pp. 49, 51, OPS 416 RD/TS (30 June 50), Army G-3 (1950–51) Hot File, 471.94 Box 11, RG 319, USNA.

lives on the common cause. As long as the helplessness of Western Europe would invite military aggression, its increasing prosperity shall grow more tempting to the armies from the east. Not until we share our strength on a common defensive front, can we hope to replace this temptation with a real deterrent to war.[14]

It was, finally, militarily vital that the United States not lose at least a foothold on the continent of Europe: in the nuclear age, a repeat of the Normandy invasion would be practically impossible.

Thus the Army had come out with a strategy in the 1949–50 period that made a good deal of sense, given the military realities of the early atomic age. My own view is that if the debate on strategy had been decided on intellectual merit alone, the basic Army approach would certainly have prevailed. But strategy is not decided by judges in a debating society, and what really proved decisive in this case was operational control. The Air Force controlled the bombers, the Strategic Air Command effectively controlled targeting, and the older services did not have enough clout to force a radical change in bombing strategy.[15] As for the

[14] Bradley remarks of April 5, 1949, quoted in draft aide-memoire attached to Ives memo, June 24, 1949, CD 6-4-18, RG 330, 1947–50 series, USNA.

[15] This is one of the basic themes in David Rosenberg's work. See especially his "The Origins of Overkill: Nuclear Weapons and American Strategy, 1945–1960," *International Security*, vol. 7, no. 4 (Spring 1983). It is also reflected in many documents in the JCS files. For example, in April 1949, President Truman, after expressing some concern that the Air Force was relying too heavily on strategy bombing, was given a briefing by the Air Force on its plans for strategic bombing operations in the event of war. When he heard about this, Army General Glover wrote to General Gruenther as follows: "If the Air Force have plans for strategic bombing operations authentic enough to present to the President, it would appear to me that they should have been reviewed first by the Joint Chiefs of Staff. I know that you are familiar with the fact that the Joint Chiefs of Staff have not yet received plans from the Commander in Chief Strategic Air Command and that this is the only major command that has not submitted plans in support of our current emergency war plan." On the origins of the original briefing: Landry to Truman, April 16, 1949, CD 12-2-8, RG 330, 1947–50 series, USNA. For Truman's allusion to the briefing and Glover's comment: Truman to Secretary of Defense, April 21, 1949, and Glover to Gruenther, April 27, 1949, both in CCS 373 (10-23-48) sec 2, RG 218, USNA. This problem of control of targeting persisted throughout this period. See, for example, the memorandum the Army Chief of Staff wrote for the JCS on target intelligence in April 1955: "I am concerned that the operations of the 'Joint Arrangement' established by JCS 2056/47, dated 27 May 1953, have not resulted in the production of studies meeting the needs of the Joint Chiefs of Staff. The seriousness of this situation is evidenced by the fact that a firm intelligence basis for control by the Joint Chiefs of Staff of the use of nuclear weapons is not yet available. Participation under the 'Joint Arrangement' by Service representatives, in the production of studies of joint interest, has been under the control of the Directorate of Intelligence, U.S. Air Force. Unilateral control of the production of these studies largely accounts for their not being responsive to the needs of the Joint Chiefs of Staff. It is doubtful that the needs of the Joint Chiefs of Staff could be satisfied by target studies unilaterally produced by ANY single service." Enclosure to JCS 2056/71 of April 12, 1955, CCS 373.11 (12-14-48) sec 23, RG 218, USNA.

political authorities, it is not clear whether they were interested in this debate, or, even if they were, whether they were ever tempted to intervene. But by late 1950 President Truman and Secretary of State Acheson were in any event probably too weak politically to bring about a radical change in the situation.

The upshot of all this was that for the time being—that is, for the period from 1949 through about 1952—forward defense meant effectively conventional defense. The situation only changed when the nuclear stockpile became so large as a result of the Korean War buildup and the technological breakthroughs taking place in this period that a significant number of weapons could be assigned to the sorts of targets called for in the Army strategy. This, in fact, was the most important reason why NATO planning during the late Truman period emphasized conventional defense and a conventional buildup. It should not be taken for granted, therefore, that from a purely strategic point of view the conventional strategy was clearly the "best" strategy, and that later departures from it did not make sense in strategic terms.

All these developments, however, paved the way for the nuclearization of NATO. There are three points to be made in this connection. First, there was an effort made to implement the strategy of the massive conventional buildup, symbolized by the Lisbon force goals, and this effort clearly failed. For political and budgetary reasons, it was simply beyond reach. In effect—although it is not at all clear that this was the original intent—the United States was telling its European allies: "You want forward defense? Then come up with the troops. But if you can't, then don't complain if we end up relying on nuclear weapons."

The second point is that the American military authorities most interested in the ground defense of Europe—namely, the Army leadership—were from a very early point strongly attracted to a strategy in which nuclear forces played a central role. The move toward such a strategy cannot therefore be attributed essentially to political or budgetary considerations. The conceptual basis for the nuclear defense of Western Europe had been laid long before the formal strategy was worked out in the New Approach studies of 1954.

And finally, the third point is that the strength of the Air Force position, even after the signing of the NATO treaty in 1949, tended to confirm widespread fears in Western Europe that the "peripheral strategy" was not dead. This greatly increased their willingness to accept any American strategy—and in particular a nuclear-based strategy—that held out the prospect of an effective forward defense. Even as late as 1954 the French military authorities, for example, strongly recommended that the important "capabilities plan" worked out by the Supreme Allied Commander in Europe (SACEUR), General Alfred Gruenther, be accepted. They agreed with Gruenther that the one and only way that Western Europe could be defended was through the massive and indeed immediate use of nuclear weapons, both strategically and in the theater. This policy, they stressed, was the only alternative to the peripheral strategy.[16]

NATO GOES NUCLEAR: THE EMERGENCE OF A FORMAL STRATEGY

This was the general context within which NATO strategy began to take shape in the early 1950s. At the end of 1950, Eisenhower was made the first NATO commander, and in January 1951 he outlined his strategic concept for the defense of Western Europe. His basic idea was to exploit the advantages of the defender: a numerically inferior force, well-entrenched and supported by massive air and naval power, might well be able to hold the line against a full-scale Soviet offensive:

> Europe appears to him to be shaped like a long bottleneck. The wide part of the bottle is Russia, the neck is Western Europe, stretching down to the end of the bottle, Spain. On either side of this neck are bodies of water that we control, with land on the far side of the water which is good for air bases. The North Sea with England behind it, is on one side and the Mediterranean with the Near East and North Africa is on the other. We must apply great air and sea power on both these sides and we must rely on land forces in the center. "I want to build a great combination of sea and air strength in the North Sea," Eisenhower said. "I'd make Denmark and Holland a great 'hedgehog' and I'd put 500 or 600 fighters behind them and heavy naval support in the North Sea. I'd do the same sort of thing in the Mediterranean, I'd put a great fleet of air and sea power in the Mediterranean and I'd give arms to Turkey and the 'Jugs.' " "Then," Eisenhower went on, "if the Russians tried to move ahead in the center, I'd hit them awfully hard from both flanks. I think if we built up the kind of force I want, the center will hold and they'll have to pull back."[17]

He wanted a 50–60 division force in Europe. Some people thought such a force would threaten Russia and thus might provoke a Soviet attack. This, he said, was "nonsense," and his reasoning again reflects his understanding of the great advantages of defense over offense in ground warfare:

[16] "Examen du 'Plan des Possibilités' établi par le commandement suprême des forces alliées en Europe," folder "Comité de Défense Nationale du 10 Septembre 1954," Box 2, Blanc Papers (1K145), French War Ministry Archives, Vincennes. See also Annex to JP (54)76(Final), September 2, 1954, and Annex to JP (54)77, August 19, 1954, DEFE 6/26, Public Record Office, Kew (Great Britain).

[17] Notes on a Meeting at the White House, January 31, 1951, U.S. Department of State, *Foreign Relations of the United States* (FRUS), 1951 series, vol. 3, part 1 (Washington, 1981), p. 454; see also p. 427.

A 50 division force on the Rhine posed no threat to Russia at all and Russia knew it. Fifty divisions couldn't possibly attack Russia. Fifty divisions on the Rhine is a lot different from 50 divisions on the Vistula. When an army moves forward, it has to leave all kinds of troops on its flanks, and in the zone of the interior. A 50 division army would be too feeble, by the time it got to the borders of Russia, to do anything at all. On the other hand, he thought that a 50 or 60 division force was quite capable of *defending* Western Europe under the general strategic concept he had outlined above. He thinks that the Russians would believe the same thing.[18]

Eisenhower was thus taking a middle position. Not only did he reject the more extreme "air power" notion that strategic bombing could win the war on its own, but he was also taking his distance from the more traditional Army view. "Do not let anyone tell you that the essential nature of war has in any way changed," General J. Lawton Collins, Army Chief of Staff, told the students at the National War College in May 1950. "A final decision must always be reached on the ground."[19] Eisenhower would never have taken this sort of line at the time.

Given his basic approach, Eisenhower was relatively relaxed about the balance of forces in Europe, even during the great war scare of the winter of 1950–51. The situation, he for example thought at the time, was not so desperate that the West needed to pay whatever price was necessary in order to get the Germans to provide troops for the defense of Western Europe. Eisenhower wanted German troops under his command, but only if "they came in without conditions and without strings attached."[20]

The Eisenhower strategy for the defense of Europe was the centerpiece of American military policy during the final part of the Truman administration. This in itself points to a certain continuity in basic strategy from the Truman to the Eisenhower administration. This was a point that Eisenhower himself, as president, stressed repeatedly during the early days of the New Look. The basic strategy his administration adopted, he said in August 1953, was a "reaffirmation and clarification" of the earlier strategy and should "never be presented as a 'new concept.' "[21]

The New Look can in fact be understood as Eisenhower's 1951 NATO strategy writ large. All of the key elements were in place prior to 1953. A meaningful ground defense of the continent, the crucial role that air and naval power would play in support of that defensive effort, the relaxed acceptance of a certain inferiority on the ground,[22] and the desire even-

---

[18] Notes on a Meeting at the White House, January 31, 1951, FRUS, 1951, vol. 3, p. 455; see also p. 734.

[19] The reference for the Collins speech is given in n. 11 above.

[20] "Notes on a Meeting at the White House, January 31, 1951," FRUS, 1951, p. 453.

[21] Cutler to Dulles, September 3, 1953, FRUS, 1952–54, vol. 2, p. 456.

[22] Indeed, Secretary of State Dulles accepted the principle of ground force inferiority as a

tually to withdraw American troops after the Europeans had built up defensive forces of their own—all of these elements may have been brought into sharper focus in 1953–54, but the basic strategy had taken shape long before the new administration took over.

The heart of the Eisenhower strategy as it developed in the 1953-54 period was the idea that Europe could be defended, even with numerically inferior forces, provided a massive air attack was launched at the outset of the war. This was also the basic idea behind the fundamental NATO strategy adopted at the end of 1954, and summed up in the important NATO document MC-48.[23] The fundamental strategy was outlined by President Eisenhower in a meeting with the military leadership on December 22, 1954: "The President stressed that he does not contemplate allowing Europe to be overrun. The Soviets will, however, have great trouble maintaining an offensive. He indicated his firm intention to launch a strategic air force immediately in case of alert of actual attack. He stressed that a major war will be an atomic war."[24]

Note especially the reference in this document to the force being launched on "*alert* of actual attack." As America's nuclear forces grew, and as her ability to launch a rapid and massive attack developed, her strategy became increasingly "front-loaded." The first priority, Eisenhower said in the December 1954 meeting with the military leaders, was "to blunt the enemy's initial threat—by massive retaliatory power and ability to deliver it; and by a continental defense system of major capability." The "blunting" of the initial attack meant, in the idiom of the day, the destruction of the enemy's strategic forces, and this would only be possible if the United States struck first. Preemption, in fact, played a major role in the NATO strategy outlined in MC-48; in the case of a surprise attack on NATO, authority to order a nuclear strike was evidently predelegated to SACEUR.[25] This emphasis on preemption was based on the notion that "our only chance of victory" would be, in Eisenhower's words, "to paralyze the enemy at the outset of the war."[26]

basis for a European arms control formula in a conversation with his Soviet counterpart Molotov in February 1954. FRUS, 1952–54, vol. 7, p. 987.

[23] There is some material on this subject in FRUS, 1952–54, vol. 5, p. 482ff. The long French document cited in n. 16 above is also quite revealing. My understanding of these matters, however, is based primarily on a series of papers by Robert Wampler, one of which is also being published in this volume.

[24] Goodpaster Memorandum of Conference, December 22, 1954, Ann Whitman File, Ann Whitman Diary, Box 3, file "ACW Diary December 1954 (2)," Dwight Eisenhower Library, Abilene, Kansas.

[25] See the French document cited in n. 16, pp. 10, 22.

[26] Notes of NSC Meeting, December 3, 1954, FRUS, 1952–54, vol. 2, p. 805. Eisenhower went on to say, however, that such a war could not be provoked by the United States, and that "if war comes, the other fellow must have started it." Note also Eisenhower's comment in 1957 that the Strategic Air Command had to realize that "we must not allow the enemy

The Europeans accepted this strategy. In so doing, they were transferring to the American president, and in some cases even to American military commanders, the power to start a war—a power which in extreme cases might have to be exercised without even consulting them. This was of course an extraordinary concession for them to make. It was natural that in exchange they would want to have some control over American policy during a crisis, or even before a crisis developed.[27] The Americans, for their part, understood that there was a fear in Europe that the United States might be too "trigger-happy"; the Europeans were particularly concerned about American policy in the Far East.[28]

My guess is that the U.S. government sensed that for the arrangement to work in the military area—for the MC-48 strategy to be accepted for any period of time—the United States would have to draw in its horns and pursue a strictly defensive strategy. It is probably no accident that the proponents of a more aggressive American policy were defeated in the National Security Council at the end of 1954 at about the same time that MC-48 was adopted; arguments about the effect on the alliance played a major role in the defeat of that policy.[29]

The other great event that took place at the end of 1954 was the final settlement between the Western Powers and West Germany. This settlement had taken years to work out and had involved very complicated negotiations. The relationship between the nuclearization of NATO and the settlement with the Federal Republic is not totally clear, but I suspect that there was an important link: nuclearization meant that the Americans, who controlled the most important forces and who in effect operated the strategy, would have to stay in Europe for a very considerable period of time, and as long as the Americans were in, the French and many of the other allies could be relatively relaxed about a buildup of German power. Any possible German threat would be contained in a structure dominated by American power.

The problem here, however, was that the Americans did not want to stay in Europe indefinitely. Their presence in Europe, as Eisenhower said

---

to strike the first blow." Quoted in Rosenberg, "Origins of Overkill," p. 47; see also the Eisenhower quotation on p. 42.

[27] Note in this connection the views of French prime minister Pierre Mendès France, FRUS, 1952–54, vol. 5, p. 535.

[28] See, for example, a State Department memorandum of January 5, 1951, FRUS, 1951, vol. 3, p. 398: "There is also a belief [in Europe] that the United States is more prone to adopt an aggressive attitude toward the Soviet Union than is wise." Note also Bevin to Attlee, January 12, 1951, in PREM 8/1439, Public Record Office, Kew. Prime Minister Attlee had evidently argued that the American arms buildup might "force the United States into aggressive action because they will not be able to reconvert to civilian production without economic chaos."

[29] See chapter 3 above, pp. 144–45 and the references cited there; note also the references to U.S. China policy in late 1954 on p. 148.

over and over again, was supposed to be temporary, "a stop-gap operation to bring confidence and security to our friends overseas."[30] The ultimate goal for Eisenhower was to transform Europe into a "third great power bloc"; after such a "solid power mass" emerged, America, he said, could "sit back and relax somewhat."[31]

American support for European political and military integration was thus not rooted in an essentially idealistic preference for transnational political structures as a kind of end in itself. America wanted Europe to pull together because she herself wanted eventually to pull out. Thus the more "isolationist" the United States was, the more ardently she supported the goal of European integration.

In the military sphere, the building up of European power came to mean the eventual nuclearization of the European armed forces. If the Europeans were armed only with conventional weapons, they would be no match for the Red Army. It was immediately understood that the nuclearization of NATO implied the nuclearization of the major European armies, and even of the West German army. But the prospect of the Federal Republic acquiring nuclear forces under its own control was to be a source of very serious trouble in the late 1950s.[32]

How then is the nuclearization of NATO to be understood? The reliance on nuclear forces was by no means a strategic absurdity. It made sense, given the military situation at the time. It was an artifact of the early atomic age, when explosive yields were low and weapons relatively scarce. During this period, an atomic war was actually fightable: the destruction would be immense, but the nations involved would survive as functioning societies. The nuclear strategy perhaps even made sense in military terms in the early thermonuclear era, because Soviet nuclear forces throughout the 1950s were quite vulnerable to attack. The strategy is particularly defensible if one believes, as Eisenhower did, that general wars are inherently uncontrollable. But in the 1950s environment, a strategy for the nuclear defense of Europe was bound to depend increasingly on rapid, and indeed on preemptive attack.

[30] Cutler to Dulles, September 3, 1953, quoting a text that Eisenhower dictated "as he walked up and down the room"; FRUS, 1952–54, vol. 2, p. 456. There are many other references. See, for example, Eisenhower's remarks in an NSC meeting, October 7, 1953, FRUS, 1952–54, vol. 2, p. 527: "The President went on to point out that properly speaking the stationing of U.S. divisions in Europe had been at the outset an emergency measure not intended to last indefinitely. Unhappily, however, the European nations have been slow in building up their own military forces and had now come to expect our forces to remain in Europe indefinitely." Of course, one reason why they were slow was their reluctance to build up conventional forces—the only kind they were then capable of creating—which were viewed as obsolescent in the new military environment.

[31] Notes of NSC meeting, November 21, 1955, p. 10, Ann Whitman File, NSC series, Box 7, Eisenhower Library.

[32] See chapter 5 below.

How did these developments affect the stability of the international system? Nuclearization tended to lock all the powers into essentially defensive policies. The counterpart to MC-48, with its emphasis on preemption and predelegation, was a drawing in of America's horns, the final abandonment of the aggressive options that were quite seriously considered in the early 1950s—although these options themselves, one should add, had only emerged in the first place as a by-product of the nuclear revolution.[33]

The existence of nuclear forces, moreover, was one major reason why Eisenhower felt so comfortable about accepting Soviet superiority on the ground. The Army, in 1954, opposed cuts in ground forces with the argument that it would "lose any offensive capability, or ability to exploit the effects of air operations during the early phase" of the war.[34] But Eisenhower was not interested in offensive capabilities of that sort, which in any case would have required much higher force levels than were needed for an essentially defensive strategy.

Nuclearization, furthermore, helped transform the American presence in Europe from temporary expedient to permanent fact of life. It is easier to imagine an American withdrawal in a non-nuclear environment than in a nuclear one. For one thing, in a nuclear regime, a permanent American presence solved a whole series of problems, relating to such things as control of nuclear escalation and West Germany's acquisition of nuclear forces, that would have been much harder to resolve if the United States had withdrawn its troops from Europe.

The transformation of the American commitment to Europe in the course of the 1950s was undoubtedly an important element in the stabilization of great power politics.[35] For over a generation, American power balanced Soviet power so completely that neither the USSR nor the United States nor any of the European powers had any room to maneuver for fundamental change in the status quo.

THE POLITICS OF THE ALLIANCE

The transformation of the American presence from stopgap arrangement to permanent feature of the system also had a dramatic effect on U.S.-West European relations. During the period when the Europeans were afraid that America would fall back to a "peripheral strategy," they went

---

[33] This argument is developed at some length in chapter 3 above.

[34] The views of General Ridgway, Army Chief of Staff, are summarized in the Goodpaster Memorandum of Conversation, December 22, 1954 cited in n. 24 above.

[35] For an exceptionally elegant analysis of this issue, see Pierre Hassner, "The American World Power and the Western European Powers," in Karl Kaiser and Hans Peter Schwarz, eds., *America and Western Europe* (Lexington, Mass., 1977), pp. 335–36.

to great lengths to accommodate American views, and were ready to support any strategy that would provide for an effective forward defense.

As the American presence became permanent, however, the whole structure of power within the alliance was bound to shift. These shifts were related to other changes taking place at the time, especially the growth of Soviet nuclear capabilities, something which tended to make the implementation of formal NATO strategy increasingly problematic, and the growth also of European economic power. But the transformation of the American commitment was of fundamental importance: as the Europeans came to take the American presence for granted, they felt freer to take a much more independent line.

Eisenhower and Dulles certainly understood what was going on. They understood the iron law of alliance politics: the more absolute our commitment, the less leverage we have over our allies.[36] Throughout his administration, Eisenhower had sought to withdraw American troops eventually from Europe, but these efforts had all been frustrated. The result, he said in 1961, was that "because we have had our troops there, the Europeans had not done their share. They won't make the sacrifices to provide the soldiers for their own defense."[37]

There is no question that these developments led to a certain resentment against the Europeans, especially during the period when de Gaulle was viewed as making trouble for the United States. President Kennedy, for example, understood that de Gaulle's attitude was not really based on the fear that the United States would abandon Europe. Quite the contrary: it was the American presence in Germany that shielded France and this gave de Gaulle the freedom to pursue an anti-American policy: "In analyzing de Gaulle's present actions, the President said de Gaulle did not question our support of Europe. The proof that he does not fear we would desert him is the deployment of only a small number of French troops opposite the Russians in Germany. He relies on our power to protect him while he launches his policies based solely on the self-interest of France." And then, turning to economic issues, he called for a very tough

---

[36] On Eisenhower, see, for example, n. 39 below. As for Dulles, note this extract from the minutes of a meeting with top military leaders held on January 28, 1953. Dulles asked whether, if the European Defense Community negotiations failed, one might have to give up on continental defense, and instead "think of a defense based on Spain, Turkey, and various islands." When General Bradley replied that that alternative was not very good, Dulles pointed out that "from the negotiations standpoint, it is useful to have alternatives. If the French and Germans should come to see that the military position would be tolerable for us if we could hold Turkey, Spain, etc., that would create pressures on them which would not exist if they think we are so committed that we must carry the entire load in the area." FRUS, 1952–54, vol. 5, pp. 712–13.

[37] Allen Dulles, Memorandum for the President, August 22, 1961, National Security Files, Box 82, John F. Kennedy Library, Boston.

line toward Europe in the forthcoming trade negotiations: "We have been very generous to Europe and it is now time for us to look out for ourselves, knowing full well that the Europeans will not do anything for us simply because we have in the past helped them."[38]

The amazing thing, however, is not that such attitudes were expressed from time to time, but rather that they carried so little political weight. The whole ideological thrust of U.S. Cold War policy had given America's allies the idea that they were doing America a favor by allowing her to defend them—which incidentally was one of the reasons why Eisenhower personally disliked taking a "strong anti-Communist line."[39] But the resentments generated in the United States by the allied policies that the gradual transformation of the American commitment had made possible were always kept within bounds. One can choose practically any year from 1949 to the present and find some book or article with a title referring to disarray within NATO. But it is an extraordinary fact that the politics of the alliance never really became a politics of mutual resentment.

And finally, one last point to make about this story is how inappropriate it is to talk about the Atlantic alliance in terms of American "imperialism," or to refer to the western bloc as an American "empire," even an "empire by invitation."[40] During the crucial formative period in the early 1950s, everyone wanted a permanent American presence in Europe—everyone, that is, except the Americans themselves. It is hard to understand why the intensity and persistence of America's desire to pull out as soon as she reasonably could has never been recognized, either in the public discussion or in the scholarly literature, because it comes through with unmistakable clarity in the *Foreign Relations* documents.[41]

The real criticism to be leveled against American policy was not that the United States was "imperialistic" and sought to impose its presence and its control on its allies. It was that it failed to understand why its continued presence was a vital element in a stable international system, and thus failed to pursue a policy based on that premise.

To an American, in fact, the disgraceful thing about the policy of with-

[38] "Remarks of President Kennedy to the National Security Council Meeting of January 22, 1963," National Security Files, Box 314, folder "NSC Meetings, 1963: No. 508," Kennedy Library.

[39] The United States, he said in 1956, was taking "in many areas such a strong anti-Communist line that our allies are able to make demands on us, and claim that they are fighting our fight for us." Goodpaster Memorandum of Conference with the President, March 13, 1956, Staff Secretary Collection, Subject Series, Department of Defense Subseries, Box 4, file "Joint Chiefs of Staff (2) [January–April 1956]," Eisenhower Library.

[40] This is a reference to Geir Lundestad, "Empire by Invitation? The United States and Western Europe, 1945–52," *Journal of Peace Research*, vol. 23 (September 1986).

[41] Especially in FRUS, 1952–54, vols. 2 and 5, where the references to an eventual American withdrawal are quite common.

drawal (or "redeployment," as it was euphemistically called) was that it was a policy based on deceit: if the Europeans knew that the Americans intended to pull out, they would not agree to measures, relating especially to the rearmament of West Germany, that would make an American "redeployment" a real possibility. So the real American goal had to be concealed from them, and they had to be given false assurances about America's intention to stay in Europe. Dulles, for example, complained in an NSC meeting in December 1953 that the word was leaking out that the United States wanted eventually to pull out of Europe. Every time statements of this sort were made by U.S. officials, he immediately had to issue denials. But "the more often such denials had to be issued, the more solidly frozen was the United States position on this issue." Eisenhower agreed: "he wanted everybody to keep still." The goal, he said, was to get the European Defense Community agreements ratified, and get "German contingents in place. Until these objectives have been achieved, let us all keep quiet on redeployment."[42]

The whole story of U.S.-West European relations in the 1950s is thus full of cross-currents that scholars have barely begun to examine. The story, in fact, is not easy to sort out. But in these days when people should be thinking about the problem of how to create a stable political system in Europe in the aftermath of the Cold War, it is important to look back and try to understand how the Cold War system itself took shape. The way people interpret the past certainly affects the way they think about the future. There are always lessons to be learned. But even more important than that, there are always false lessons to be unlearned.

[42] Notes of NSC meeting, December 10, 1953, FRUS, 1952–54, vol. 2, p. 450; see also Eisenhower's comment on p. 451. For one of the promises Dulles alluded to, see ibid., p. 447.

_____ CHAPTER FIVE _____

The Berlin Crisis

IN NOVEMBER 1958, the Soviet government announced that it intended to sign a peace treaty with Communist East Germany. The rights of the Western Powers with regard to Berlin, which the USSR had recognized in an agreement signed in 1944, were declared to be "null and void." The Soviets proposed that West Berlin be transformed into a "free city," and gave the West six months to negotiate a settlement of the Berlin issue along these lines. If no agreement was reached during this period, the treaty with East Germany would be signed and the rights of the Western Powers terminated. The East Germans would then control access to West Berlin. If America and her friends refused to accept this and tried to maintain their rights by using force against East Germany, the Soviets would "rise in defence" of their Warsaw Pact ally.[1] The USSR was thus in effect threatening war if the Western Powers did not accept her demands. The result was a serious crisis that lasted with varying degrees of intensity for four years.

The Berlin Crisis was in fact one of the most important episodes in the history of great power politics in the nuclear age. Given its importance, it is surprising how little scholarly attention it has received. Only a handful of serious studies exist, and they were all written before the archival evidence began to open up.[2] The result is that major issues relating to the crisis have been treated at best in a rather speculative fashion.

A version of this paper was originally presented at a conference held at West Point in 1988, and I am grateful to the history department there for helping to fund the research on which this work is based. This article is also being published in the volume based on the papers presented at that conference: Charles Brower, ed., *The Theory and Practice of American National Security.*

[1] Address by Premier Khrushchev on Germany and Berlin, November 10, 1958 [extract], and Note from the Soviet Foreign Ministry to the U.S. ambassador in Moscow, November 27, 1958, U.S. Senate, Committee on Foreign Relations, *Documents on Germany, 1944–1961* (New York, 1968), pp. 339–43, 348–63. Henceforth this source will be cited as "DG." (A key to the abbreviations used in this chapter can be found at the end of the book.)

[2] The best general introduction is still Jack Schick's *The Berlin Crisis, 1958–1962* (Philadelphia, 1971), a book based entirely on press accounts, memoirs, and similar sources. See also Robert Slusser, "The Berlin Crises of 1958–59 and 1961," in Barry Blechman et al., *Force Without War* (Washington, 1978), and Walther Stützle, *Kennedy und Adenauer in der Berlin-Krise, 1961–1962* (Bonn-Bad Godesberg, 1973).

The goal here is to explore some of these issues in the light of the remarkable body of evidence, mainly from American archives, that has become available over the past ten years. How, in general, is the Berlin Crisis to be interpreted? What led up to the crisis, what were the Soviets trying to accomplish, and how exactly does it fit into the broader history of the postwar period as a whole?

The argument here is that the crisis was not the result of a Soviet decision to try to drive the Western Powers out of Berlin itself, but rather has to be seen in the context of Soviet fears about Germany as a whole—fears that were brought to life when it became clear to the Soviets in the late 1950s that West Germany was well on the way to acquiring nuclear forces under her own control. The general point that the Berlin Crisis was rooted in Soviet anxieties about a nuclear-armed West German state has of course been made many times before, most notably by such scholars as Adam Ulam and Jack Schick. But the depth and seriousness of the German nuclear weapons question in the late 1950s have never really been recognized in the scholarly literature.

As for the crisis itself, perhaps the most striking results relate to American policy. Soviet provocations were not met by American intransigence. President Eisenhower, in fact, was even willing to consider the Soviet "free city" proposal: "the time was coming and perhaps soon when we would simply have to get our forces out." No arrangement of this sort was, of course, reached. But the Berlin Crisis did help bring about a remarkable shift in American policy, especially on the German question as a whole: by the end of 1961 the U.S. government, in fact if not in words, had come to accept the division of Germany.

WHAT WAS THE CRISIS ABOUT?

In raising the Berlin issue, the Soviets were putting pressure on the West at its most vulnerable point. One look at the map and one could see what the problem was. West Berlin was a land island in the middle of East Germany, locally indefensible, completely surrounded by massive Soviet military power. West Berlin was not part of West Germany, although it was linked to the Federal Republic by many ties. From a legal point of view, it was still under allied occupation. American, British, and French forces stationed in the city were the guarantors of its rather unusual status. Threatening Berlin was therefore a means of exerting pressure on the West as a whole.

What, however, was the point of this effort? It is quite clear that the Soviets were concerned mainly with Germany in general, and not with Berlin itself. The Soviet pronouncements that led to the crisis stressed the

German question, and not the problem of Berlin; and in meetings with western diplomats Soviet representatives were much more interested in talking about the German question than about the status of the city.[3] The Soviet leader, Nikita Khrushchev, emphasized this point when he met with President Eisenhower at Camp David in September 1959: "He wanted to make it clear that the Soviets had not raised the issue of Berlin as such, but rather the question of the conclusion of a peace treaty in order to terminate the state of war with Germany."[4] Berlin itself was basically a lever. Khrushchev was quite blunt about this. The "Berlin question," he told U.S. ambassador Llewellyn Thompson, "was one of geography that he intended [to] make use of."[5]

In fact, if the Soviet goal had simply been to take over West Berlin, it would have been more logical and less risky to try to undermine the economic life of the city by gradually cutting off commercial traffic between Berlin and West Germany. This was an area where the East German authorities already exercised control, and where (as the U.S. government recognized) the Western Powers' legal rights had been "weakened by Allied inaction" in the face of East German harassment in the 1950s.[6] President Eisenhower himself assumed in 1959 that the East Germans could "stop all economic connection with West Berlin. They could make West Berlin a dead weight on us." This, he had earlier remarked, was a "nagging fact" that had to be kept in mind whenever the Berlin problem was considered.[7]

[3] See, for example, the two documents cited in n. 1, and also the (then secret) Soviet aide-mémoire presented by Soviet Deputy Premier Mikoyan to Secretary of State John Foster Dulles on January 5, 1959, SS/I/6/Berlin—Vol. I (2)/DDEL. See also *Foreign Ministers Meeting, May-August 1959, Geneva*, U.S. Department of State, International Organization and Conference Series, No. 8 (Washington, 1959) [henceforth: FMM]. Note finally East German Prime Minister Grotewohl's comments on November 12, 1958, to the effect that Germany was the real issue, and that Berlin was not the "main problem," quoted in the *New York Times*, November 13, 1958, p. 1.

[4] Memorandum of Conversation, September 15, 1959, p. 9, POF/126/Vienna Background Documents (C)/JFKL.

[5] Thompson to Herter, January 1, 1960, DDC 1985/336. This is not a direct quotation, but is rather Thompson's rough paraphrase of a point Khrushchev made in their conversation.

[6] Martin Hillenbrand to Foy Kohler, November 22, 1958, 762A.00/11-2258/DSCF/USNA; Foy Kohler, "The Problem of Berlin Surface Access," July 25, 1961, POF/117/Germany. Security. 7/61/JFKL. Note also the following quotation from a letter that Averell Harriman wrote, but decided not to send, to President Kennedy, dated September 1, 1961: "At present, although of course we do not admit it, the right of civilian access to Berlin is not legally beyond question." (Arthur Schlesinger sent it over anyway.) NSF/82/Germany. Berlin. General. 8/29/61–8/31/61/JFKL.

[7] A. J. Goodpaster, Memorandum of Conference with the President [henceforth: MCP], October 22, 1959, DDC 1982/2219; Goodpaster, MCP, June 25, 1959, SS/S/DoS/3/State Department—1959 (May–September) (3)/DDEL. Note similarly Thompson to Dulles, March

The point, moreover, that the Soviets were basically concerned with Germany as a whole—that they were not simply trying to drive the Western Powers out of Berlin—was from the outset taken for granted by American and other western statesmen. Ambassador Thompson's initial reaction reflected a rough consensus among allied officials: the Soviet goal, he thought, was to force "our recognition in some form of the East German regime."[8] It was widely assumed that one of Khrushchev's major objectives was to create what he himself called an "enduring juridical order" in central Europe based on mutual acceptance of the status quo.[9]

Getting the West to give some sort of recognition to the East German regime, however, would only solve part of the problem. The Soviets, as Thompson later wrote, were "also deeply concerned with German military potential and fear West Germany will eventually take action which will face them with [a] choice between world war or retreat from East Germany."[10]

The heart of the Soviet argument during the Berlin Crisis, both in private discussions with western diplomats and, in much more tendentious form, in public pronouncements, was that their real goals were basically defensive in nature. Thus at the Geneva Foreign Ministers Meeting in May 1959, the French Foreign Minister, Couve de Murville, argued that

---

9, 1959, SS/I/Berlin—vol. II(1)/DDEL: "I believe we should very much keep in mind fact that West German access to Berlin is already in East German hands. Even if our troops remain in Berlin we may eventually be faced with East German attempt to strangle city and there would be considerable advantage to us if West German access could receive clear legal basis and international guarantees."

[8] Thompson to Dulles, November 11, 1958. 762.00/11-1158/DSCF/USNA. See also Lyon to Dulles, November 12, 1958, 762.00/11-1258/DSCF (for the French foreign ministry reaction); Hillenbrand to Kohler, November 22, 1958, 762A.00/11-2258/DSCF; State Department analysis of the USSR's November 27 note, November 29, 1958, used as the basis for Assistant Secretary Merchant's briefing of the President on November 30, 762.00/11-2958/DSCF; Prime Minister Macmillan to Dulles, January 8, 1959 (for the British view) DP/WHM/7/White House Correspondence—General—1959/DDEL.

[9] Quoted in FMM, p. 186.

[10] Thompson to Rusk, February 4, 1961, DDC 1977/74B. Views of this sort were quite common within the U.S. government during the crisis. For example, a 1961 study done for the U.S. Defense Department's Weapons Systems Evaluation Group argued that "the crux of the explosive 'German problem' is not the continued presence of U.S. forces, per se, in West Germany, or even the presence of Western forces in Berlin. It is the growing military power of West Germany (whose development these forces are making possible), and the potential implications of German military power for the unsettled situation in Eastern Europe." The report then quoted a reply Khrushchev had made to a question from Walter Lippmann about why he was in such a hurry to settle the German question: "I have to be in a hurry. I must have the German frontiers fixed before Hitler's generals get nuclear weapons." WSEG Staff Study No. 83, "U.S. Strategic Objectives and Military Deployments in NATO, as Related to the Problem of Arms Control," August 30, 1961, para. 94, CCS 3050 Disarmament (25 August 1961)/JCS 1961/USNA.

there was no need for peace treaties with the two German states because a stable de facto peace already existed: "We find ourselves in a situation in which there are two Germanys"; "today on both sides there is a state of peace"; "I do not think it is in anyone's interest to disturb the balance of power which exists at present, has existed for fifteen years now, and has been shown by experience to ensure, after a fashion, the stability of the continent."[11] Foreign Minister Gromyko's response reflected the basic Soviet position: there was no stable balance in Europe. In fact, according to Gromyko, a real threat to the peace was taking shape: "I have in mind above all measures for the remilitarization of Western Germany, for the equipment of the Bundeswehr with atomic and rocket weapons and the establishment of a network of rocket-launching sites on West German soil."[12]

During the crisis, over and over again, Soviet public statements stressed this theme: West Germany was going nuclear, and this was bound to create an extraordinarily dangerous situation. But was this all just propaganda, or did these pronouncements reflect genuine Soviet concerns? Wasn't Couve essentially correct in implying that the Western Powers, in fact if not in words, had accepted the division of Germany and the political system that had been based on it, and that the Soviets therefore had nothing to fear? To answer these questions, it is necessary to step back a bit and discuss Allied policy on Germany, especially how it had evolved in the course of the 1950s and where matters stood toward the end of the decade.

THE GERMAN QUESTION, 1949–1959

In the 1950s, and especially in the early part of the decade, American policymakers still took the goal of German reunification seriously. Opinion within high official circles was never unanimous, but the most important people in the Truman State Department—people like Secretary of State Dean Acheson and his close associate Paul Nitze—did not believe that a stable system could be based on the division of Germany.[13] Even someone as sophisticated as George Kennan thought that Europe could not permanently be divided between America and Russia. The partition of Germany, in particular, he saw as leading to trouble. With the revival of West German strength, he said in 1952, a German civil war was inev-

[11] FMM, pp. 160–63.

[12] Ibid., pp. 169–70.

[13] For evidence of this lack of unanimity, see for example the notes of a State Department meeting, April 2, 1952, FRUS, 1952–54, vol. 7, p. 195.

itable, and if the Federal Republic came into NATO there was a great danger that the United States might be drawn in.[14]

Under Eisenhower as well, the German question remained an open issue. American policy throughout the 1950s was drawn toward two conflicting goals. On the one hand, there was a real desire to bring about the reunification of Germany. Didn't history show that Germany could not be kept down forever? The interwar period, it was said over and over again, proved that Germany had to be given the same rights as any other great power. Wasn't this the lesson of Versailles? Hadn't Hitler come to power essentially because the Germans felt they had been singled out "as some sort of moral and political inferior," and that they had been treated as a "second-class power"?[15] It followed that Germany should be reunified with a government based on free elections, with borders and an international status that that government would freely negotiate with Germany's former enemies. In particular, the new German state should be treated like a great power and should be free to make whatever alliances it wished. There was throughout this period a pervasive, although not universal, assumption (again, in Ambassador Thompson's words) that a people "as strong and virile" as the Germans would not accept a long-term division of their country, "particularly when they are well-armed"—and a basic thrust of American policy in the 1950s was to make sure that the Federal Republic was indeed well-armed.[16]

The United States therefore took the goal of German reunification seriously throughout the Eisenhower period. A partition of Europe was simply not an acceptable basis for the peace.[17] In the early part of the decade, especially around 1952 and 1953, the American government hoped that a buildup of western power would force the Soviets to agree to a reunification of Germany on American terms—that is, a settlement

[14] Notes of Policy Planning Staff meeting, October 18, 1949, PPS/32/Policy Planning Staff Minutes of Meetings, 1949/USNA; Ferguson to Nitze, September 26, 1952, FRUS, 1952–54, vol. 7, p. 362.

[15] For the quotations: notes of three-power meeting in Bermuda, December 7, 1953, FRUS 1952–54, vol. 5, p. 1833. See also FRUS, 1952–54, vol. 5, p. 1020, and vol. 7, p. 986; FMM, pp. 98, 124, 133, 297.

[16] Thompson to Dulles, March 9, 1959, SS/I/6/Berlin—Vol. I (4)/DDEL. This was a reply to an earlier telegram from Ambassador David Bruce in Bonn. Bruce had wondered somewhat heretically whether the "generally accepted theory that [the] division of Germany constitutes [an] immediate threat [to the] peace of [the] world is sound." Bruce to Dulles, March 2, 1959, SS/I/6/Berlin—Vol. II (1).

[17] Thus Secretary of State Dulles was annoyed in 1954 that the British tended "to regard as acceptable some division of the world which would concede to the Soviet rulers control over the present captive states" in Europe. Dulles, "Specific Problems with the U.K.," May 16, 1954 (identified from withdrawal sheet for file, together with Dulles to Bowie, May 14, 1954), DP/WHM/8/General Foreign Policy Matters/DDEL.

which would allow the new German state to join NATO if it wished.[18] This, as Kennan pointed out in 1952, was tantamount to asking the Soviets "for unconditional surrender because we did not seem to be ready to pay any price."[19]

By the mid-1950s, however, Secretary of State Dulles had begun to think increasingly in terms of a negotiated settlement. As early as September 1953, he had argued that the Soviets had to be offered something in exchange for "giving up East Germany." But he was not willing at this point to go beyond promises that would "cater to" Soviet fears about a new German attack. As the Versailles Treaty had shown, he argued, "qualitative limitations" on German armaments were "totally unenforceable."[20] But by 1955 he had come to the conclusion that the Soviets had to be given something real if Germany was ever to be reunified. "We would never succeed in our objective of a united Germany," he told the National Security Council, if we ruled out any arrangement with the Soviets on arms levels in central Europe: "the unification of Germany would be impossible unless it was achieved under some sort of international control in which the Soviet Union would have a voice. The Soviets would never simply throw East Germany into the pot to be added to West Ger-

[18] Dean Acheson, Truman's Secretary of State, had outlined the strategy of building "situations of strength" at the beginning of 1950. This was paralleled in West Germany by Chancellor Adenauer's "policy of strength"; indeed, the connection here was not lost on contemporary observers. François-Poncet, the French High Commissioner in Germany, sent Foreign Minister Bidault an account of a meeting between Adenauer and the High Commission held in early 1953. Adenauer intimated that a reunification of Germany would take place as a "sort of Anschluss of the eastern zone into the Federal Republic, as the result of political and military pressure, designed to force the Soviets to accept, without compensation, a German solution based on free elections, something which would have led to their loss of East Germany." Adenauer had thus openly accepted "the 'rollback' thesis," François-Poncet added, perhaps with an eye toward pleasing "certain American circles." François-Poncet to Bidault, April 30, 1953, Europe 1949–55/Allemagne/11. French Foreign Ministry archives, Paris. Note also a similar argument in another François-Poncet dispatch to Bidault, June 30, 1953, same volume.

For a document that reflected President Eisenhower's belief in this sort of strategy, see especially Eisenhower to Montgomery, July 14, 1953, AWF/DDED/3/DDE Diary, 12/52–7/53 (1)/DDEL. If the Federal Republic was successfully integrated into the Western bloc, the President argued, we would "see a steady social, political, military, and economic advance in Western Germany." This would "greatly increase the pressures inside Eastern Germany to join up with other parts of their former Empire." The Communists might find it impossible even "to hold the place by force." The President admitted that "out of this situation there might develop conditions that could be *almost* provocative of general war," but if so, this would be because of the "cruelty" of Russia's own policy. (Emphasis in original.) It is not clear whether this letter was ever actually sent. Montgomery's original letter to Eisenhower is in PREM 11/370, Public Record Office [PRO], Kew.

[19] FRUS, 1952–54, vol. 7, p. 362.

[20] Notes of State Department meeting, September 26, 1953, FRUS 1952–54, vol. 7, pp. 635–37.

many and the united Germany to be further rearmed against the Soviet Union itself." And "with some heat" he warned "that if we say flatly 'no' to any European regional security arrangements we might just as well give up all hope of unifying Germany."[21]

As for President Eisenhower himself, he also never resigned himself to the idea of a permanently divided Germany. In 1958, for example, he was appalled that Walter Lippmann was ready to "acquiesce" to the status quo in Germany, and in Europe generally.[22] And in April 1959, he and Secretary of State Herter complained that the German government was dragging its feet on reunification: "Mr. Herter said it was obvious that what Adenauer and the Christian Democrats were scared of was that in a reunified free election the opposition Socialist party in West Germany would form a coalition with certain East German parties and throw the Christian Democrats out of office. The President said if they get a true free reunification, then they have to take their chances on politics."[23]

On the other hand, this interest in German reunification was balanced—indeed more than balanced—by the great importance attached to keeping at least the West Germans in the western bloc. The goal here, as Eisenhower put it in December 1953, was "to integrate them in a federation from which they could not break loose."[24] This turned out to be the dominant objective. If the choice was between a divided Germany, with the Federal Republic part of the West, and German reunification under some sort of neutralist formula, there was no question what the U.S. government would choose. As Dulles said in February 1959, it would "be a grave mistake to jeopardize" West Germany's military and economic ties with the West "in order to buy reunification."[25]

[21] Notes of NSC meeting of July 7, 1955, AWF/NSC/7/DDEL.

[22] Telephone Calls, April 1, 1958, AWF/DDED/31/Telephone Calls, April 1958/DDEL.

[23] Herter, Memorandum of Telephone Conversation with the President, April 4, 1959, HP/10/President's Telephone Calls 1959 (2)/DDEL. Note also Herter's comment, in a meeting with the President on August 21, that Adenauer "does not want a reunified Germany even though he continues to call for reunification publicly, as he must" because of the "large Socialist vote in East Germany." Goodpaster, MCP, August 24, 1959, AWF/DDED/43/Staff Notes. August 1959 (1). Note finally Ambassador Thompson's remark in March that "our allies, including West Germany, are lukewarm" about German reunification. Thompson to Dulles, March 9, 1959, SS/I/6/Berlin—Vol. I (4).

[24] Notes of three-power meeting in Bermuda, December 5, 1953, FRUS, 1952–54, vol. 5, p. 1783. Note also British prime minister Harold Macmillan's comment to the French ambassador in London in early 1959: "France and England had suffered a great deal in the past from the Germans cutting loose, and his own feeling was that one of the great advantages of NATO and other European institutions was that they mixed the Germans up very thoroughly with the West and made it difficult for them to escape." Record of a Meeting at 10 Downing Street, February 5, 1959, FO 371/145858, PRO.

[25] J. F. Dulles, "Memorandum of Conversation with Couve de Murville," February 7, 1959, DDC 1983/904.

But this in turn created a problem. For the German people, the reunification of their country was a matter of very great importance; if the Germans came to blame the West for the continued division of their country, the repercussions could be enormous. Hence the great nervousness that American, French, and British leaders felt whenever it seemed that the Soviets might actually accept German reunification on the basis of free elections: for while the Soviets might accept the de-Sovietization of East Germany and maybe even some sort of rearmed Germany as part of a general settlement, the one thing they would never agree to was that this new German state would be part of NATO. The West German Chancellor, Konrad Adenauer, the great champion of a pro-Western policy within Germany, felt these anxieties even more acutely.[26]

From Adenauer's point of view, there was no alternative to integrating Germany into the western alliance. Any sort of "neutralist" solution would leave Germany vulnerable to pressure from the east; it was therefore better "to renounce for a time the thought of a reunited Germany" than to negotiate a settlement with the Soviets that would involve a breaking of the Federal Republic's miltiary ties to the West.[27] But how long would the German people accept this sort of policy? American and other allied leaders were afraid that the Germans would some day conclude that the western alliance sealed the division of their country and would be tempted to reach some accommodation with the Soviet Union on their own. If it was at all possible, West German policy had to be prevented from moving in this direction.

For the time being, what this meant in practice was that the Adenauer government had to be supported. A great deal of attention was paid to the Chancellor's domestic political needs. In the early years, Adenauer was viewed by western statesmen, especially by those who remembered Weimar, as almost too good to be true, as much more committed to the West than they logically had any right to expect from a German states-

[26] On these matters in general, see FRUS, 1951, vol. 3, pp. 1763–64, 1785–91, 1796–97; FRUS, 1952–54, vol. 5, pp. 390, 1625–27, and vol. 7, pp. 227, 542–43, 742. On Adenauer's unease: notes of NSC meeting of November 21, 1955, p. 5, AWF/NSC/7/DDEL. The material in the French diplomatic archives at the Quai d'Orsay is particularly rich in this area. On the question of the seriousness of the famous Soviet offer on Germany of March 1952, see especially the Noblet despatches of March 14 and 21, 1952, series "Europe 1949–55," subseries "Allemagne," volumes 819 and 301 respectively, Foreign Ministry Archives, Paris. Note also Daridan's report from Washington, June 28, 1952, of a conversation with a low-level Soviet diplomat there on this issue, same series and sub-series, vol. 302. On the British attitude, see foreign secretary Eden to the Foreign Office, March 21, 1952, and Eden's handwritten marginal comments on Roberts to Strang, March 14, 1952, and on Roberts to Strang and Eden, March 15, 1952, FO 371/97878 and 97879, PRO.

[27] McCloy Memorandum of Conversation, December 16, 1950, FRUS, 1950, vol. 4, p. 674.

man.[28] The allies could not turn their backs on him without discrediting the whole pro-Western policy that he had come to symbolize. If the United States, for example, took too independent a line in negotiations with the Soviets, Adenauer's political position within West Germany might be undermined. This in effect gave the West German Chancellor considerable leverage, amounting almost to veto power, over the policy the Western Powers could pursue on the German question.

In the long run, however, even a policy of total support for Adenauer might not prevent the sort of drift in German policy that American officials most feared. The Chancellor was an old man. When he died or left office, the Germans might stray from the fold. As Ambassador Thompson wrote, we could not count upon a "man of Adenauer's wisdom always being in power in Germany."[29] And what would happen if the Federal Republic came to be led by a much more nationalist government?

This problem was complicated by the fact that the U.S. did not see eye-to-eye on the German problem with its two major allies in Western Europe. Dulles complained, for example, in 1956 that the allies were not clearly dedicated "to the policy of bringing about the unity of one of the most important members of NATO, i.e., Germany. Its continued division carries a threat to the wholehearted and lasting identification of Western Germany with the fortunes of the West."[30] To the U.S., it was important that the partition of Germany and the legitimacy of the East German regime—the "so-called German Democratic Republic"—not be accepted. The West Germans went even further, and refused to have diplomatic relations with any state, except the Soviet Union itself, that recognized the GDR. But the British especially were much more inclined to "accept realities." This position reflected the basic fact that the goal of German reunification was "not a cause which inspires any substantial measure of public enthusiasm in the United Kingdom."[31]

The French attitude was rather different. In the late 1940s, the French had taken the line that Germany should be reunified, albeit on a highly decentralized basis. But then, beginning in late 1951, and more strikingly in 1952 and 1953, the Soviets moved toward a position which made it seem that a reunification of Germany on the basis of free elections might

---

[28] See, for example, François-Poncet to Schuman, November 6, 1949, Europe 1949–55/Allemagne/vol. 254, French Foreign Ministry Archives, Paris.

[29] Thompson To Dulles, March 9, 1959, SS/I/6/Berlin—Vol. I (4)/DDEL.

[30] Dulles NATO "Think Piece," May 24, 1956, pp. 6–7, DP/S/5/NATO "Think Piece," 1956 (Drafts) (1).

[31] Shullaw to State Department, March 24, 1958, 762.00/3-2458/DSCF/USNA. This is an excellent analysis of British opinion on the German question. See also William Tyler's analysis of Anglo-German relations, February 7, 1958, 641.62A/2-758/DSCF, and, for the early crisis period, Whitney to Dulles, April 13, 1959, 641.62A/4-1359/DSCF.

actually be possible. The French government became quite alarmed; French officials worried that they might become the "dupes" of their own policy. They recognized, at least among themselves, that what they really wanted was to perpetuate the status quo in central Europe. "The only solution compatible with peaceful coexistence between the two systems," one high official at the Quai d'Orsay argued, "is the maintenance of the present division of Germany."[32] France thus became the first great power to reach this important conclusion.

As for the Soviets, they also suspected that Adenauer's prowestern policy was somewhat anomalous and recognized that he might be succeeded by more nationalistic leaders.[33] The Soviets knew, moreover, that the British and French were cool to German reunification. They themselves had evidently come to the conclusion around 1955—that is, three years after the French—that partition was probably the best solution for Germany.[34] In private conversations Khrushchev was quite blunt about this: in April 1956, for example, he told British leaders that "the Germans are beginning to get 'uppish' again, and it was probably a good thing for everybody that Germany was divided."[35] And in June 1959, in what was perhaps his most extraordinary meeting with a visiting American, he told Averell Harriman that "no one wants a united Germany. De Gaulle told us so; the British have told us so; and Adenauer himself when he was here said

[32] Sauvagnargues memo, April 22, 1953, Europe 1949–55/Allemagne/823, Foreign Ministry Archives, Paris (for the quote); Schuman to Washington Embassy, June 16, 1952, ibid., vol. 822 (for the reference to "dupes"). For a somewhat different interpretation, see Georges-Henri Soutou, "La France et les notes soviétiques de 1952 sur l'Allemagne," *Revue d'Allemagne*, vol. 20, no. 3 (July–September 1988), pp. 261–73.

[33] Note this extract from a February 1954 meeting between Anthony Eden and Soviet Foreign Minister Molotov. Molotov said the "USSR had good cause to be suspicious of Germany. Eden countered by saying Adenauer was a wise man who would not lead Germany back on path of militarism. Molotov nodded reflectively but said Adenauer was old and would not live long." FRUS, 1952–54, vol 7, p. 937. As for Khrushchev, he once told Eisenhower (probably at Camp David in September 1959) that Adenauer's support of German reunification "was nothing but a show; in Khrushchev's opinion, it was merely a ruse on Adenauer's part to stay in power." Dwight Eisenhower, *Waging Peace: 1956–1961* (Garden City, N.Y., 1965), p. 351n. Note also Khrushchev's warning to Harriman in June 1959 that "the day may come when Germany will turn against the West." "Of course, Adenauer could not," he added, "but maybe Strauss or some other German would." Owen to State Department, June 26, 1959, p. 7, POF/126/USSR. Vienna Meeting. Background Documents (D)/JFKL.

[34] The basic study here is a dissertation by Paul Willging, "Soviet Foreign Policy in the German Question: 1950–1955," Columbia University, 1973. For some comments by Soviet diplomats on the subject, see also FRUS, 1952–54, vol. 7, pp. 752–53, 961–62, and Bohlen memo of conversation, July 19, 1955, SS/I/ITM/1/Geneva Conference, Chronology (1)/DDEL.

[35] J. F. Dulles, "Memorandum of Conversation with Sir Roger Makins," April 30, 1956, DP/GCM/1/Memoranda of Conversation—General—L through M (2)/DDEL.

he was not interested in unification. Why then do you insist on talking about it?"[36]

Was there, however, any real danger for the Soviets in this situation? It was perhaps true that the Eisenhower administration, even in 1959, took the goal of German reunification seriously. But given that the U.S. government probably never felt that the reunification of Germany was worth a war, how could this American position be viewed by the Soviets as in any way threatening? The answer is that attitudes are bound to influence behavior. For who knew what the United States would really do if the situation in East Germany became explosive, if large-scale rioting broke out, if security forces began to fire into the population, if West German forces felt compelled to intervene? This prospect would be bound to cause the Soviets deep concern, especially since the likelihood of each step in the scenario would depend on how much power would be thrown into the balance at every point, and this in turn depended on the depth and intensity of basic feelings regarding German national rights.

And it would depend above all on how strong West Germany itself was. As long as the Federal Republic was utterly dependent on her allies, in the sense of being militarily incapable of taking too independent or nationalistic a line, there was little basis for fear. But if the West Germans gained some real political leverage by acquiring a strong, independent military force, then the situation could become dramatically different. For such a force to carry this sort of political weight, it would obviously have to be armed with nuclear weapons. It was for this reason that the nuclearization of the Bundeswehr was a matter of such great importance to the Soviet Union.

During the Berlin Crisis, both in public and in private, the Soviets complained repeatedly about West Germany getting nuclear weapons. The West replied that this was a misapprehension; that it was merely a question of West Germany acquiring nuclear-capable weapons—that is, just the delivery systems; and that this should be no cause for concern since the warheads themselves would remain under American control. The real story is not quite that simple.

NUCLEAR SHARING AND THE GERMAN NUCLEAR WEAPONS ISSUE

Should West Germany ever be allowed to possess nuclear weapons of her own? Throughout the 1950s, and especially in the latter part of the decade, this was one of the most basic issues of international politics. The

---

[36] Owen to State Department, June 26, 1959, pp. 6–7, POF/126/USSR. Vienna Meeting. Background Documents (D)/JFKL.

problem first emerged in the late Truman period. In the early 1950s, the Adenauer government insisted that the Federal Republic could be integrated into the western bloc only on the basis of full equality. There should be no restriction on West Germany that did not apply to everyone else, no special provisions that discriminated against her alone. To the Germans, nondiscrimination meant that the Federal Republic was not simply being exploited by the West, but was being accepted as a full partner; hence the tremendous importance that German opinion attached to this issue at the time. John McCloy, for example, then the U.S. High Commissioner in Germany, referred in February 1952 to the "almost hysterical attitude" of the Germans "on the discrimination issue."[37] The Western Powers, and especially the United States, agreed that relations with the Federal Republic had to be based on a principle of equality, but certain circumstances also had to be taken into account: the fear, particularly on the part of other Europeans, of too rapid a resurgence of German power, the sense that democracy was still not firmly entrenched in the Federal Republic, and anxieties about an eventual "defection" of West Germany from the western bloc. Adenauer accepted the legitimacy of these concerns and was willing to work around them. So without abandoning the principle of equal rights, he was quite flexible in working out how it would be applied in practice. And indeed the great settlement between the Western Powers and the Federal Republic, which was finally reached at the London and Paris conferences at the end of 1954, embodied what was in fact a large dose of discrimination, something for which Adenauer was bitterly attacked by his political opponents within Germany.

In particular, in the nuclear area, the Germans had argued during the long and complex negotiations that ultimately led to the settlement for at least a degree of equality. If West Germany "were to have no right to build aircraft or to manufacture heavy weapons or to engage in atomic research," Adenauer told the High Commissioners in September 1951, "this implied discrimination and lack of trust."[38] But in the end West Germany accepted a special status in this regard. The Federal Republic promised not to manufacture atomic weapons on her own territory, and agreed to allied supervision to ensure that this undertaking was observed.[39]

At the same time, however, as this political settlement was being reached, events were taking place in the military sphere which would push West Germany toward nuclearization. The NATO New Approach

---

[37] McCloy to State Department, February 1, 1952, FRUS, 1952–54, vol. 5, p. 15.

[38] FRUS, 1951, vol. 3, p. 1525.

[39] FRUS, 1952–54, vol. 5, p. 1447; note also the related Article 20 in Protocol IV to the Brussels Treaty, ibid., p. 1455.

studies had led by the end of 1954 to the adoption of MC 48: Europe would be defended with nuclear forces, both tactical and strategic.[40]

The adoption of this strategy had two very important consequences. On the one hand, it tended to discredit the idea of a conventional buildup. Dulles, in 1956, spoke for example of the "widespread inclination among our NATO allies to downgrade in importance the role of the NATO ground forces" because of their belief that any future war would be dominated by the strategic atomic offensive. They therefore believed that "there was not much point in developing and maintaining large ground forces." Since the Soviets were building up their nuclear forces, and since "our NATO allies do not have nuclear armament of their own, this fact contributed to the general feeling of discouragement."[41]

The other side of this coin was that the Europeans now had a strong incentive to develop the sort of forces that could fight a nuclear war. It was in fact understood very early on that something of this sort was implicit in NATO's New Approach.[42] In Germany in particular, the effect was to undermine Adenauer's general approach to military policy. He felt in August 1956 that he was, in Dulles's words, "risking his political life on a program for German and conventional rearmament, while many of his political opponents, and indeed many within his own party, seem to feel that this is outmoded and that this is shown by United States policy."[43] That same month, an American diplomat in London reported that the German ambassador there "has been saying to whomever will listen that Adenauer will be placed in 'impossible' position if twelve German conventional divisions are demanded by allies while at same time these 'conventional' forces are judged by leading British and American military opinion as of little or no value from a strictly military viewpoint. In the long run, he says, if only armies equipped with atomic weapons are valu-

[40] My understanding of these matters is based mostly on the as yet unpublished work of Robert Wampler.

[41] Notes of NSC Meeting of May 10, 1956, p. 5, AWF/NSC/7/DDEL.

[42] Goodpaster memorandum for Eisenhower, November 16, 1954, FRUS, 1952–54, vol. 5, pp. 534–35; notes of an Anglo-American meeting, December 11, 1956, FRUS, 1955–57, vol. 4, p. 125: "Mr. Selwyn Lloyd said that the strategic concept contemplated that everyone should have an atomic capability. Secretary Dulles responded that this was the implication of MC 48—that we should plan on the assumption that atomic weapons would be used." Dulles had just pointed out that "the Germans were forbidden from making atomic weapons but were not forbidden by the Treaty from buying them from the US." These implications of MC 48 are also apparent in the "Examen du 'Plan des Possibilités' établi par le commandement suprême des forces alliées en Europe," September 7, 1954, Blanc Papers, fonds 1K145, Box 2, folder "Comité de Défense Nationale du 10 Septembre 1954," War Ministry Archives, Vincennes. This is perhaps the most revealing document on the New Approach to have been made available so far.

[43] Dulles to Eisenhower, August 10, 1956, DP/WHM/5/Meetings with the President. August–December 1956 (8)/DDEL.

able then [Federal Republic] army too must be so equipped."[44] Many Germans had long argued that qualitative superiority, based on "modern" weapons, was needed to balance Soviet numerical superiority; it was clearly unacceptable in the long run that West Germany should be asked to fight a strong nuclear power armed only with conventional weapons.[45]

Within West Germany's ruling coalition, the issue evidently came to a head in September 1956. The conversion to a strategy based on nuclear weapons, which a reluctant Adenauer was more or less forced by his own party to accept, was symbolized by the appointment of Franz-Josef Strauss as defense minister.[46] According to information received by U.S. representatives in Germany, Strauss at this time was taking an "almost nationalistic" line, and "advocated a stream-lined German Army with the most modern weapons, including atomic weapons."[47] In 1961, a secret CIA report on Strauss pointed out that as defense minister, he "has consistently aimed at the creation of effective German military forces with the best possible equipment. He has taken it for granted that Bonn must have a nuclear weapons capability, and has attacked any 'discrimination' against the German forces. Shortly after becoming defense minister, he criticized what he called the 'two categories of NATO members, first class and tenth class.' In one of the impetuous statements he often finds it necessary to deny having made, he reportedly remarked that the German and other European armies would be equipped with atomic weapons, 'whether the Americans like it or not,' and that he had no intention of providing German 'foot-sloggers for the American atomic cavalry.' "[48] Indeed, Strauss made no secret of his ambitions: shortly after taking office as defense minister, he told a reporter that while "renunciation of atomic weapon production remains valid," this had "nothing to do" with the question of whether "atomic weapons should be made available to the Federal Republic."[49]

It was thus clear in 1957 and early 1958 which way the wind was blowing. West Germany was considering arming the Bundeswehr with "atomic weapons." (It was this term, and not "nuclear-capable weapons," that was most commonly used throughout this debate.) The official

[44] Barbour to Dulles, August 4, 1956, 762A.5/8-456/DSCF/USNA.

[45] For example: FRUS, 1951, vol. 3, p. 775; Trimble to Dulles, December 1, 1957, 762A.5/12-157/ DSCF/USNA.

[46] Catherine Kelleher, Germany and the Politics of Nuclear Weapons (New York, 1975), pp. 43–49, esp. p. 48.

[47] American Consul General in Munich to State Department, November 22, 1957, 762.00/11-2257/DSCF/USNA.

[48] Current Intelligence Weekly Summary, report on Strauss, July 6, 1961, POF/117/Germany. Security. July 1961/JFKL.

[49] Conant to Dulles, October 20, 1956, 762A.5/10-1956/DSCF/USNA. The quotation is Conant's paraphrase of Strauss's remarks.

line was that unless a general disarmament agreement was reached, the Federal Republic might have to go down this road.[50] The Military Annex to NSC 5727, the basic NSC paper on Germany, summed up the situation as the U.S. government saw it at the end of 1957:

> Defense Minister Strauss has reoriented defense planning toward smaller, combat ready forces equipped with the "most modern weapons." Both he and the Chancellor have made their position clear that, short of an over-all agreement on disarmament which included a political settlement for Germany, West German forces must in due course have tactical nuclear weapons. Meanwhile, West German military plans are for forces which can be readily adapted to such weapons.[51]

The American government tried to meet the situation by proposing a plan for a NATO nuclear stockpile at the North Atlantic Council meeting in December 1957. The allies would control the delivery systems, but the warheads themselves would normally be in American custody.[52] Would this be enough to satisfy the Europeans? Ambassador David Bruce in Bonn took it for granted that in the long run the Germans would, in all probability, want to have nuclear forces of their own; but for the moment, "such desire as may exist" to move in this direction was limited to a "handful of men headed by Strauss."[53]

---

[50] As Dulles pointed out to Eisenhower: "The Chancellor has taken the position that the German Federal Government is not seeking atomic weapons, but he has refused to foreclose the possibility of eventual German possession of tactical nuclear weapons if an agreement on disarmament is not reached in the next several years." Memorandum for the President, May 24, 1957, AWF/I/14/Adenauer, 1957–58 (5)/DDEL. It should be noted, incidentally, that the German government did not view general disarmament as a realistic goal. As one official in the German foreign office told the Americans explicitly in April 1958, the emphasis on disarmament was purely tactical—an effective response to Soviet demands for a regional arms limitation agreement. Tyler to State Department, April 29, 1958, 762A.00/4-2958/ DSCF/USNA.

[51] "U.S. Policy toward Germany," NSC 5727, December 13, 1957, Military Annex, p. 4, DDC 1982/2117.

[52] For a draft of the President's speech outlining the plan, December 10, 1957, see DDC 1987/556.

[53] Bruce also thought that Adenauer might not be completely aware of what Strauss was up to, and might be susceptible to American pressure designed to keep West Germany from developing its own nuclear weapons program. In any case, he warned, there was the danger that "our continued silence in this matter might be taken for consent." He was also "troubled by secrecy and obscurity surrounding FIG agreement and German plans in this field." Bruce to Dulles, February 28, 1958, 762A.5611/2-2858/DSCF/USNA. The FIG agreement was a French-Italian-German agreement for the joint development and production of weapons; the defense ministers of these three countries had secretly agreed in late 1957 to extend cooperation to nuclear weapons development, but this part of the arrangement was jettisoned after de Gaulle came to power in 1958. Current Intelligence Weekly Summary, July 6, 1961, POF/117/Germany. Security 7/61/JFKL. For the best recent account, see Georges

Was the United States willing to go any further than the stockpile scheme? The State Department was by this time hostile to the idea of the European allies controlling nuclear forces of their own, while the Joint Chiefs of Staff were more sympathetic.[54] Dulles in particular had his doubts about Strauss, who, it was widely believed, might eventually become Chancellor. Was Strauss "interested in ultimately influencing NATO to follow policies favorable to German interests," Dulles wondered, or would he "favor allowing it to wither as soon as he feels Germany is militarily capable of pursuing a more independent course?"[55]

Eisenhower's personal attitude was of great importance in this whole affair. He never felt that American troops had been sent to Europe on a permanent basis. Over and over again he pointed out (correctly in fact) that the deployment of U.S. forces to Europe in 1951 was supposed to be temporary, to protect the Europeans while they built up forces of their own. Looking back in 1961, he talked about how his goal of eventually withdrawing American troops from Europe had been frustrated: "every time he had tried to do something about bringing our troops back, Secretaries Dulles and Herter had pled with him with tears in their eyes not to talk about any withdrawal of American forces from Europe." The problem was that "because we have had our troops there, the Europeans had not done their share. They won't make the sacrifices to provide the soldiers for their own defense."[56]

Soutou, "Les Problèmes de securité dans les rapports franco-allemands de 1956 à 1963," *Relations internationales*, no. 58 (Summer 1989), pp. 228–31.

[54] On the JCS: Briefing sheet for JCS Chairman on "Department of Defense Position on Nuclear Sharing with Allies," for October 7, 1960 meeting, CCS 4610 (23 August 1960) sec 2/JCS 1960/USNA. On State: Gordon Gray, Memorandum of Meeting with the President, February 10, 1960, OSANSA/SA/P/4/1960—Meetings with the President—vol. 1 (7)/DDEL; see also Goodpaster, MCP, August 8, 1960, DDC 1978/451D. This, incidentally, marked a shift from the early Eisenhower period, when these positions were reversed. See FRUS, 1952–54, 5, pp. 1205ff., esp. 1207 and 1248.

[55] Dulles to U.S. Embassy in Bonn, July 25, 1958, 762A.00/6-558/DSCF/USNA.

[56] Allen Dulles, Memorandum for the President, August 22, 1961, NSF/82/JFKL. See also: Goodpaster, MCP, January 20, 1960 (of November 18, 1959, meeting), SS/S/DoD/4/Joint Chiefs of Staff/DDEL; Dulles, Memorandum of Conversation with the President, December 12, 1958, DDC 1985/1704. See also Goodpaster's record of the same meeting, MCP, December 15, 1958, SS/S/DoS/3/State Department—September 1958–January 1959 (4)/DDEL. For documents bearing on the original decision to send troops to Europe on a temporary basis: FRUS, 1951, 3, pp. 455–56, 802, 806, 816. For other documents reflecting Eisenhower's belief that our presence in Europe was supposed to be temporary: FRUS, 1952–54, 2, p. 456; Goodpaster, MCP, October 2, 1956, SS/ITM/3/NATO File No. 2 (2); Gordon Gray, Memorandum of Meeting with the President, July 29, 1959, OSANSA/SA/P/4/Meetings with the President, June–December 1959 (4). In fact it was partly because the President very much wanted eventually to withdraw the U.S. troops from Europe that the administration was attracted to disengagement plans, especially regional arms reduction and inspection schemes. See

Eisenhower's basic interest in withdrawing American forces, which (to his annoyance) was by no means kept completely secret, generated pressure on the Europeans to develop their own nuclear forces. A troop withdrawal would dilute the political value of the U.S. guarantee: if Europe could not in the long run rely on American nuclear power, perhaps European nuclear forces would have to be built. Soviet pressure, backed up by the USSR's nuclear might, could obviously not be offset by conventional military power alone. This prospect by no means appalled Eisenhower. He quite clearly wanted to see "a solid power mass" emerge in western Europe. After such a "third great power bloc" took shape, America, he said, could "sit back and relax somewhat."[57]

There are two points to be made about this policy. First, it tended increasingly to pivot on a buildup of German power. Britain no longer had the strength or what was seen as the political courage to take a firm stand.[58] As for the French, in the 1950s they had their hands full overseas, first in Indochina and then in North Africa; the military effort they could make in Europe was bound to seem inadequate. In the early part of the decade, the French had blocked too rapid a resurgence of West German power. But by 1958 Eisenhower had become more interested in building up German forces than in worrying about French sensibilities: when it was pointed out at this time that a big increase in German force levels would frighten the French, he "retorted that he would be glad to scare them; maybe that would have an effect on French pretentions at being a world power."[59]

The other point is that the nuclearization of the European armies was by no means an unintended by-product of the Eisenhower strategy. The President, it must be stressed, looked with favor on the development of European nuclear forces. In the 1955 NSC meeting where he spoke about creating a "third great power bloc" in western Europe, he argued for sharing nuclear weapons with the NATO allies:

Goodpaster, MCP, August 25, 1959, AWF/DDED/43/Staff Notes August 1959 (1), recording a discussion between the President and General Norstad.

[57] Notes of NSC Meeting of November 21, 1955, p. 10, AWF/NSC/7/DDEL.

[58] In late 1958, the JCS had done a study of British military capabilities; both the Chiefs and the Secretary of Defense "were surprised at how far down hill the British strength had gone." Goodpaster, MCP, September 15, 1958, SS/S/DoD/1/Department of Defense, vol. III (2) [Sept. 1958]/DDEL. Note also Admiral Arleigh Burke's reference a year later to British capabilities for amphibious lift: "The British capability is nothing short of pitiful when one considers that this is a type of force they particularly need." Burke was Chief of Naval Operations at the time. Goodpaster, MCP, January 20, 1960 (for meeting held November 18, 1959), SS/S/DoD/4/Joint Chiefs of Staff.

[59] Goodpaster, MCP, December 15, 1958, pp. 3–4, SS/S/DoS/3/State Department—September 1958–January 1959 (4)/DDEL.

Turning next to NATO specifically, the President exclaimed "For God's sake let us not be stingy with an ally." We should, for instance, give our NATO allies the chance to use some of our modern weapons. NIKE, for instance, should be made available, although, said the President laughingly, NIKE was obsolete—but he didn't wish to be quoted thereon. In point of fact, however, instead of being generous, we treat many of our NATO allies like stepchildren, and then expect them to turn around and commit themselves to fight with us. By such actions we cut our own throats. Our allies certainly ought to know more about our new weapons. Our policy was in great contrast to the generosity which the British had shown in sharing with us their discoveries about radar at the beginning of the second World War.[60]

From his point of view, there was in fact something absurd about denying to allies weapons that the Soviets were already deploying against them, weapons which they were bound to want and able to build, but with resources which might otherwise go toward building up the overall strength of the alliance. It was because there could be "no monopoly" on the possession of nuclear weapons within NATO that the President (as he said in February 1960) had "always favored the sharing of our weapons."[61] And it was for this reason that he was dissatisfied with his own government's—and by that he really meant the State Department's—attitude on this issue: "The U.S. Government seems to be taking the attitude that we will call the tune, and that they have inferior status in the alliance." He certainly did not want a whole series of unconnected national programs; the nuclear forces were to be worked into an overall NATO program based on a common strategic concept. But this he evidently saw as the product of voluntary collaboration that the NATO nuclear powers would freely enter into.[62]

Given the President's attitude, it is not surprising that high American officials from time to time encouraged the Europeans in general, and the Germans in particular, to go down the nuclear road. Secretary of Defense McElroy, for example, noted at the end of 1957 that the U.S., in deploying IRBMs in Europe, might give the allies control not just of the delivery

[60] Notes of NSC meeting, November 21, 1955, p. 11, AWF/NSC/7/DDEL.

[61] Goodpaster, MCP, February 12, 1960, DDC 1985/529.

[62] Goodpaster, MCP, August 8, 1960, pp. 2–3, DDC 1978/451D. On State Department obstruction, see esp. Gordon Gray, Memorandum of Meeting with the President, February 10, 1960, OSANSA/SA/P/4/1960—Meetings with the President, vol. I (7)/DDEL. Note also Goodpaster, MCP, July 15, 1959, SS/S/DoD/1/Department of Defense, vol. III (7), recording Admiral Radford's complaints on a related issue: the State Department, and especially Assistant Secretary Gerard Smith, were pushing the idea that it was possible to "fight a sizeable war without using atomic weapons."

systems but also of the warheads themselves.[63] "So long as the overall situation does not change," the NATO commander, General Lauris Norstad, told an interviewer on German television in February 1958, "defensive atomic weapons are absolutely indispensable for the strengthening of the defensive power of the Bundeswehr." In July 1960, Secretary of the Army Brucker said in a press conference in Bonn: "We know that Herr Strauss is interested in acquiring medium range ballistic missiles. We have no objection at all to their acquiring weapons with a strategic range."[64] And President Eisenhower himself, at a press conference on February 3, 1960, supported the general idea of nuclear sharing with the allies, and indeed implied that he wanted to change the law in order to make this possible.[65]

The nuclear sharing schemes of the late Eisenhower period thus had a rather ambiguous meaning. On the one hand, a fundamental goal was to head off the demand for national, and especially German, nuclear forces.[66] But they could also function as a bridge to the acquisition by the Europeans of nuclear capabilities under their own control, and the possibility that the situation could develop along these lines was by no means ruled out by the Eisenhower administration. Indeed, in June 1959, for example, "the President noted that we are willing to give, to all intents and purposes, control of the weapons. We retain titular possession

[63] *New York Times*, November 16, 1957, p. 1, cited in Schick, *The Berlin Crisis*, p. 8.

[64] Quoted in Kelleher, p. 94 (for Norstad), p. 106 (for Brucker).

[65] *Public Papers of the Presidents: Eisenhower*, 1960–61, p. 148. See also ibid., p. 193, for his comment later in the month that it was "natural" for countries like Britain and France to want nuclear forces of their own.

[66] See for example Goodpaster, MCP, August 19, 1960, SS/S/DoS/4/State Department—1960 (Aug.–Sept.) (1)/DDEL. Note also the discussion in Stikker to Acheson, March 20, 1961, esp. p. 6, AP/85/State Department and White House Advisor 1961—March/HSTL. It is interesting to note that Adenauer himself supported one of these plans, the Norstad proposal for a NATO MRBM force, for this reason: Stikker to Acheson, December 19, 1960, AP/85/State Department and White House Advisor, 1960—November–December/HSTL. The proof that Adenauer's interest was essentially political was his unwillingness to deal with the basic problem with all these schemes—namely, the way they either evaded the central issue of the control of nuclear forces, or effected no change in the fundamental reality that this power ultimately rested in American hands. When NATO Secretary General Spaak at this meeting raised the "question of 'who in NATO' would control these transferred weapons," Adenauer became "impatient with him." NATO, General Norstad then pointed out, had made a good deal of progress "without answering unanswerable question of exactly how alliance goes to war" and he thought "still further progress could be achieved without doing so." In other words, since the basic function was political rather than strategic, there was no point in trying to deal with these basic intractable problems that the alliance had been evading for years. Houghton to Herter, September 10, 1960, SS/ITM/5/NATO (4) [1959–1960]/DDEL.

only."[67] It is well known, in fact, that the custody arrangements were quite weak.[68]

Furthermore, it is important to note that the formal proposal for a NATO MRBM force that was considered in late 1960 was conceived of not as a final solution, but as something that might lay the basis for further, more radical change in the nuclear status quo. One of the three goals of the program for a NATO MRBM forced based on Polaris submarines, Under Secretary of State Livingstone Merchant said in an important White House meeting on the issue in October, was "to provide a framework within which we might eventually consider the question of nuclear sharing."[69] In other words, in the future, the U.S. might go much further.

And even at this point, the administration, while vacillating a bit, seemed ready to consider arrangements that would in effect enable foreign governments to control the weapons. One of the main issues that was considered at the October meeting was a dispute between the State and Defense Departments on the question of multinational crews. The State Department, basing its proposals on a plan worked out by Robert Bowie, wanted the submarines to be manned by mixed crews drawn from a number of countries. This was opposed by the Defense Department; the JCS, and especially the Army, felt that "multinational manning and common ownership" was "manifestly impractical from a military standpoint."[70] Eisenhower at this meeting supported the Defense Department's position that placing these submarines under NATO control would be suf-

[67] John Eisenhower, MCP, June 9, 1959, p. 2, SS/ITM/5/NATO (2) [1959–1960]/DDEL. This comment referred specifically to French demands for nuclear weapons, but it seems from context that the President had the NATO allies as a whole in mind.

[68] See Peter Stein and Peter Feaver, *Assuring Control of Nuclear Weapons: The Evolution of Permissive Action Links* (Cambridge, Mass., 1987), esp. p. 30. General Truman H. Landon, in 1961 the U.S. air commander in Europe, later discussed the issue in an oral history interview. He noted that allied aircraft on alert were equipped with American nuclear weapons, and the interviewer was surprised: "The French and the British would have hung American nuclear weapons on their aircraft?" "And the Germans and the Canadians," Landon replied. "Theoretically, they were in our hands. We had the nukes themselves. But we trained them completely. We didn't hide anything. I am sure that we violated rules 1 through 13, or maybe even more. But to us, it seemed necessary that they be trained and they appreciated the fact that they got it." U.S. Air Force Oral History Interview, General Truman H. Landon, Office of Air Force History, Bolling Air Force Base, Washington, D.C., 1977, p. 481.

[69] Memorandum of Conversation, October 3, 1960, SS/ITM/5/NATO (6) [1959–1960]/ DDEL.

[70] Ibid., and also "Briefing Sheet for the Chairman, JCS, on a Report by the J-5, for the JCS Meeting Friday, 7 October 1960, Agenda Item No. 5," and memo by Army Chief of Staff on "Department of Defense Position on Nuclear Sharing with Allies (JCS 2305/239)," October 10, 1960, both in CCS 4610 (23 August 1960) sec 2/JCS 1960/USNA. The Navy, however, dissented from the judgment about the impracticality of multinational manning.

ficient, "so that while they operated under common command one unit, for example, would be Dutch, another German, etc." By the next morning, however, he had evidently changed his mind: a NATO "Foreign Legion," he said in a meeting with NATO Secretary General Spaak, was the only solution.[71]

What all this meant was that the situation at the end of the Eisenhower period was very much in flux. The original NATO nuclear stockpile plan, which provided for American control of the warheads, would never solve Europe's basic strategic problem of total nuclear dependence on the United States. If the problem was to be dealt with in a meaningful way, the Europeans would have to be given something real, and the possibility was left open that the sharing arrangements could serve as a bridge to some form of European nuclear force. Eisenhower's hope was that this would be an integrated, international force, perhaps under a European NATO commander; but the integration was to be based on consent, rather than on some tight institutional arrangement that could guarantee against defection.

Could an arrangement of this sort have provided a lasting basis for the defense of Europe? Perhaps; but it seems more likely that the nuclear sharing plans if put into effect would have led eventually to a system of national nuclear forces in Europe. A pooling of military power implied a common foreign policy; but in the long run the gap between German national aspirations and what West Germany's partners would risk going to war over was probably too great for such arrangements to really work for an indefinite period. It was one thing to accept American leadership in exchange for an American presence in Europe that was a very effective guarantee of German security; it was quite another matter to allow the British, the French, and the other Western European allies to set limits to German policy.

In any case, the question of whether a multinational European system could be made to work would depend ultimately on whether the problem of the political control of nuclear forces could be satisfactorily resolved. How would the decision to use them be made? By whom, and in what way? How much predelegation could there be, or, given military realities, would there have to be? Could this include the authority to strike preemptively? And what would it take for such orders to be binding on the different national forces? These were all extremely difficult problems. As long as the United States was fully involved in Europe, there was a tacit solution to most of these problems: the key decisions would rest in the hands of the American president. American predominance was so obvi-

[71] Memorandum of Conversation, October 4, 1960, SS/ITM/5/NATO (6) [1959–1960]/ DDEL.

ous that the Europeans could accept or at least resign themselves to a solution of this sort. But if the Europeans had to manage this on their own, the problem could not be resolved, or perhaps evaded, so easily. The control issue was bound to exert a corrosive influence on any collective Western European military system, especially if the international political situation was tense, and the different nations felt that their lives were quite literally on the line. And if, as a result of the control problem, a multinational system broke down, an independent West German nuclear capability would by no means be an unlikely result.

All of which is a very long and roundabout way of saying that yes, there was a real basis in fact for Soviet concerns about West Germany eventually acquiring nuclear forces of her own.

THE CRISIS RUNS ITS COURSE, 1958–1960

By late 1958 the German nuclear weapons issue was coming to a head. In March of that year, Adenauer had decided on his own "to ask the Bundestag to approve the equipment of the Bundeswehr with atomic weapons."[72] General Norstad, also in 1958, made arrangements with German military authorities to train a German fighter-bomber unit so that "it might have a nuclear capability" and to construct a nearby storage facility; "this project, known as 'Wagon Train,' was successfully completed" in late 1958, about the same time as the Soviets provoked the Berlin Crisis.[73]

It was clear which way things were moving. The Soviets had completely failed in their earlier attempts to set up a nuclear-free zone in Central Europe. From their standpoint, events could not be allowed to drift any longer. It was important to do something about the German problem, and Berlin was the most convenient lever. Certainly this was Ambassador Thompson's impression at the time. "Khrushchev," he cabled Washington on November 18, "is a man in a hurry and considers that time is against him on this issue particularly in relation to atomic arming of West Germany. Therefore believe Western Powers should prepare for major showdown within coming months."[74]

As they moved toward confrontation with the West, did the Soviets feel they held all the cards? In military terms, the fact that West Berlin was an enclave in an area totally dominated by Soviet military power gave them certain obvious advantages. They could control the level of confrontation by varying the degree of harassment. They could engage in what were

[72] Tyler to State Department, June 2, 1958, 762A.5611/6-258/DSCF/USNA.
[73] Houghton to Dulles, December 20, 1958, AWF/DH/8/Dulles, December 1958/DDEL.
[74] Thompson to Dulles, November 18, 1958, 762.00/11-1858/DSCF/USNA.

called "salami tactics," gradually chipping away at Western rights by taking a series of moves none of which would provoke a war, but which together would undermine the position of the Western Powers in the city.[75] There was something ludicrous about going to war over whether the East Germans would be permitted to stamp documents that the Soviets were already stamping or whether the Communist authorities would be allowed to "peep" inside military trucks.[76]

The Soviets enjoyed other tactical advantages as well. A blockade would force their adversaries to be the first ones to use force, a threshold they might be extremely reluctant to cross. Moreover, the Soviets were aware that the Western Powers were divided among themselves on the German question, and also on issues relating to the use of force. Finally, there was the important fact that Soviet concerns were widely recognized by the USSR's former partners in the war against Germany as having a certain legitimacy. There was a reluctance, in spite of Khrushchev's crude tactics, to think of the Soviets as simple aggressors; there was from the beginning a sense that their basic motivation might be essentially defensive in nature. "One might take the view," Acting Secretary of State Robert Murphy, for example, wrote in April 1959, "—and the Soviets possibly do so—that the recent Soviet moves in Germany have been an attempt to maintain the status quo in the face of Western attempts to change it."[77]

On the other hand, there were also striking weaknesses in the Soviet position. First and most important, the strategic balance heavily favored the United States. Even though the Soviets had demonstrated in 1957 that they could build intercontinental ballistic missiles, throughout the Berlin Crisis their ICBM force remained quite small. The question of the strategic balance—both what the numbers were and what meaning they had—was of course quite controversial throughout this period. But it did seem to some of the most knowledgeable people at the time that for a variety of reasons Soviet strategic forces as a whole were quite vulnerable to an

---

[75] American officials were fully aware of these risks. See, for example, Norstad to Twining, November 23, 1958, CCS 381 (8-20-43) sec 41/JCS 1958/USNA, for a typical reference about the need to "draw the line now" lest we "begin a humiliating process of yielding step by step to the GDR." See also some notes on the Berlin question evidently used by Eisenhower as a basis for briefing President-elect Kennedy in December 1960, DDC 1978/119A and 1983/1335.

[76] This refers to an incident at one of the checkpoints on November 14, 1958. Two American covered trucks and a jeep with a covered trailer were detained by the Soviet officer in charge, who refused to release the vehicles—even to allow them to return to Berlin—unless his lieutenant was allowed "at least to peep under [the] covers." Although this was considered a very serious probe, it was "difficult to explain" (as one American official in Berlin commented) "why we make such an issue over a 'peep under the canvas.'" CGUSCOB Berlin to Washington, November 15, 1958, CCS 381 (8-20-43) sec 41/JCS 1958/USNA; Burns to Dulles, November 16, 1958, 762.00/11-1658/DSCF/USNA.

[77] Murphy to McElroy, April 17, 1959, 762A.00/4-1759, DSCF/USNA.

American first strike. "If we were to release our nuclear stockpile on the Soviet Union," Eisenhower, for example, told Lyndon Johnson in 1959, "the main danger would arise not from retaliation but from fallout in the earth's atmosphere."[78]

What this implied, especially given the emphasis that American military strategy placed on preemption, was that the Soviets would not want to come close to provoking war over Berlin. With regard to tactics, this meant that they would have to face the problem of how far to go in order to keep the pot boiling in political terms, while at the same time making sure that the crisis would not escalate to anything that approached the level of a military confrontation. This was linked to the problem of how to generate pressure without appearing to present an ultimatum. It certainly was not to their interest to come across as irresponsible and brutal, incurably addicted to the politics of intimidation; nor would it do their reputation much good if they repeatedly set deadlines and then suspended them. On the other hand, without a deadline of some sort, how could pressure be brought to bear? This issue was never satisfactorily resolved, and as a result Soviet policy swung back and forth, sometimes conciliatory, sometimes overbearing.

In any event, the purpose of the deadlines was obviously not to bring matters to the point of armed conflict. If the Soviets had really wanted to force a military showdown, why would they help their adversaries prepare for their moment of truth by twice giving them six months' advance notice? The deadlines were in both cases allowed to lapse; and practically from the outset the Soviets insisted that they were not trying to present the West with anything like an ultimatum. As Secretary of State Herter pointed out in June 1959, "the Soviets keep stressing that the specific time set is not a matter of importance or principle, but is intended to keep the present situation from dragging on indefinitely."[79] In fact, as early as December 3, 1958, Khrushchev (in a meeting with Senator Hubert Humphrey) was practically begging for negotiations: "Give us a counter proposal," he said; and later he again asked "What are your counter proposals, what do your Secretary of State and your President suggest?" It was quite typical of Soviet diplomacy under Khrushchev that this conversation was also full of blatant threats and complaints, especially about Berlin, "this thorn," this "bone in my throat."[80]

Finally, there was a series of minor problems that made it hard to take

[78] Eisenhower, *Waging Peace*, pp. 347–48.

[79] Goodpaster, MCP, June 25, 1959, SS/S/DoS/3/State Department—1959 (May–September) (3)/DDEL. Note also Dulles to Adenauer, January 28, 1959, DDC 1981/518A, reporting on the talks held earlier that month with Mikoyan. The Soviet Deputy Premier had stressed that their "demands were not intended as an ultimatum."

[80] Thompson to Dulles, December 3, 1958, POF/126/ Vienna Background Documents (D)/ JFKL.

Soviet arguments at face value, and thus to engage in a meaningful and possibly productive dialogue with them. Khrushchev spoke about creating an "enduring juridical order," but he proceeded by threatening to tear up the allies' legal rights. He talked about "accepting realities" like the East German state, but wasn't the odd status of West Berlin also one of those "realities" that had to be accepted? The situation in West Berlin was characterized as anomalous, but was the Soviet "free city" solution any less anomalous? The term itself was bound to evoke memories of Danzig and the beginning of World War II. As for Soviet rhetoric about peace and coexistence, how was this to be reconciled with Soviet threats to liquidate the regime in Berlin? "Who gives them this authority?" Dulles exclaimed. "How are you going to coexist with people who act in this way?"[81]

Given all this, what kind of reaction was to be expected from the United States? Would the American government simply dig in its heels and refuse to "be pushed around" in this way?[82] Eisenhower's own "instinct" at first "was to make a very simple statement to the effect that if the Russians want war over the Berlin issue, they can have it."[83] The military also wanted to take a tough line on the general issue of refusing to accept East German control and using force "to support this position if necessary."[84]

The first test of American policy came on November 14. The Soviets stopped a U.S. military convoy and refused to release it unless a Soviet officer was allowed "to peep under [the] covers" of the trucks. General Norstad and the JCS thought that force should be used in such situations. Dulles, however, insisted on the need for "careful consideration and adequate consultation with the allies." Norstad and the JCS then drew back. Their "rather extreme views," Dulles said, had been "moderated by better understanding of the facts and recognition that we needed to have a better understanding with the British, the French, and the Germans before we took a position that might lead to shooting."[85]

[81] Telephone Call to Mr. Merchant, December 12, 1958, DP/TC/9/Memoranda of Telephone Conversations—General—11/2/58 to 12/27/58 (1)/DDEL.

[82] The phrase is from Dulles to U.S. embassy, Paris, November 25, 1958, 762.00/11-2558/DSCF/USNA.

[83] Herter, Memorandum of Telephone Conversation with the President, November 22, 1958, DDC 1984/227.

[84] Norstad to Twining, November 23, 1958, CCS 381 (8-20-43) sec 41/JCS 1958/USNA. The Chiefs shared Norstad's views: JCS to Norstad, November 23, 1958, same file.

[85] On this incident, see n. 76 above. For official reaction: Norstad to Twining and McElroy, November 15, 1958, CCS 381 (8-20-43) sec 41/JCS 1958/USNA; Burns to Dulles, November 16, 1958, 762.00/11-1658/DSCF/USNA; Lyon to Dulles, November 16, 1958, 762.00/11-1758/DSCF; Burns to Dulles, November 17, 1958, 762.00/11-1758/DSCF; JCS SM-918-58, November 19, 1958, enclosing draft instructions for General Norstad, CCS 381

As for Eisenhower himself, he also on reflection came to take a moderate line. When, later in the crisis, some of the chiefs began to recommend actions which even the JCS Chairman, General Twining, considered provocative, Eisenhower set out his basic position. It was, he thought, necessary "to avoid over-reacting." He did not want a military buildup in Europe, which he said would in any case be "useless" in the event of war. The JCS would have to defer to his views. Twining was instructed to "caution the Joint Chiefs that the military in this country is a tool and not a policy-making body; the Joint Chiefs are not responsible for high-level political decisions."[86]

In general, instead of moving toward a confrontation, the administration preferred to engage the Soviets in negotiations. Maybe a conference would be a good idea. The point of this policy, according to Dulles, was to help the Soviets climb out of the hole they had dug for themselves. Indeed, the Soviet position had softened in January, possibly as a result of American firmness.[87] Soviet Deputy Premier Mikoyan took a conciliatory line when he visited America that month. This meant that a conference would not be seen as caving in to Soviet threats. Instead, as Dulles wrote Adenauer on January 28, such a meeting "would provide the Soviets with a certain protective coloration under which they might withdraw from the dangerous position Khrushchev has taken on West Berlin." It was "unlikely," he said, that the Soviets would postpone their plans "unless provided with some such face-saving camouflage."[88] A lengthy Foreign Ministers' conference was in fact held in Geneva that spring. Nothing much came of it, except that the Soviet six-month deadline for a resolution of the issue was allowed to lapse.[89]

What sort of arrangement did the American government have in mind? If it were up to them, both Eisenhower and Dulles would have been willing to work out an arrangement which allowed the allies to deal with East German officials as "agents" of the USSR, which incidentally was by no

---

(8-20-43) sec 41, JCS 1958. The call for "careful consideration": Dulles to Paris Embassy, November 17, 1958, 762.00/11-1758. The reference to "extreme views": Dulles, Memorandum of Conversation with the President, November 18, 1958, DDC 1985/2544.

[86] Goodpaster, MCP, March 9, 1959, AWF/DDED/39/Staff notes March 1-15, 1959 (1)/DDEL. For the memo that the JCS soon produced: JCSM-93-59, March 16, 1959, 762A.00/3-165/DSCF/USNA. The JCS memo was based on an earlier memo from the CNO, Admiral Arleigh Burke, JCS 1907/174, March 7, 1959, DDC 1982/1548.

[87] The American note of December 31, 1958, drafted by Dulles personally, was particularly striking in this connection. DG, pp. 378–81.

[88] Dulles to Adenauer, January 28, 1959, DDC 1981/518A.

[89] For the best account, see Selwyn Lloyd, "Foreign Ministers' Conference," June 15, 1959, C(59)102, CAB 129/98, PRO.

means a new idea.[90] On November 24 they discussed the issue in a phone conversation. Dulles said that "everyone is stirred up—the JCS want to do something fast and quick and Norstad wants us to fight our way through." The President agreed that action was necessary if they tried to stop convoys, but "if they want to do normal checking and searching for contrabands," that was another story. If the Russians abandoned their responsibilities, he thought that "in this kind of low level business we would have to go along if we were going to keep things straightened out"; if the East Germans took over from the Russians and behaved peacefully, the U.S. really had no basis for reacting violently.[91]

This in fact was a very common attitude in the West, even in Germany.[92] As NATO Secretary General Spaak put it, one could hardly risk war in order "to force the Russians to remain in Berlin."[93] On November 26, Dulles raised the possibility at a press conference that we might deal with the East Germans "as agents of the Soviet Union." He went even further on January 13: conducting free elections, he noted in public, was not the only way that Germany might be reunified. What this suggested was that it might also come about through negotiations between the two German states, which again implied a kind of de facto recognition of the East German regime.[94]

This certainly reflected the President's views about how Germany would be reunified. "Anything we can do," he said in April, "that opens up a real avenue between these two sides of Germany sets up a tremendous attraction; they are all the same people and they don't want to be apart; we should do everything we can to let nature take its course."[95] And in June, Christian Herter, by now Dulles's successor as Secretary of

[90] See for example the "Report to NATO on Berlin Contingency Planning," April 1, 1959, p. 1, DDC 1987/1056.

[91] Telephone Call to the President in Augusta, November 24, 1958, DP/TC/13/Memoranda of Telephone Conversations—White House, August 1, 1958 to December 5, 1958 (1)/DDEL.

[92] The Socialist leader Ollenhauer, for example, was reported as having said "privately that if to assure access to Berlin, the alternative to use of force is dealing with the GDR, surely some formula could be found, perhaps by treating the GDR officials as agents of the USSR." Bruce to Dulles, November 24, 1958, p. 2, 762A.00/11-2453/DSCF/USNA. A German foreign office official (Dr. Herbst, the American Desk Officer) took a similar line in a talk with an American diplomat a few months later. Tyler to State Department, April 6, 1959, 762A.00/4-659/DSCF. On opposition to Adenauer's "rigid" line within his own party, see the report from the U.S. embassy in Bonn on "main trends in 1958 and the German scene at the turn of the year," February 2, 1959, 762A.00/2-259/DSCF.

[93] Quoted in Nolting to Dulles, January 24, 1959, p. 3, 762A.00/1-2459, DSCF/USNA.

[94] DG, pp. 344-45, 406.

[95] Herter, Memorandum of Telephone Conversation with the President, April 4, 1959, HP/10/President's Telephone Calls 1959 (2)/DDEL.

State, made a comment that reflected what was by then the conventional wisdom within the U.S. government: sooner or later, "the Germans themselves will have to find the answer to their own reunification."[96]

But all of this was absolutely anathema to Adenauer. As soon as he heard about Dulles's new line on reunification, he sent for Ambassador Bruce and exploded. The "repercussions in Germany would be momentous," he said. His political opponents, "those naive people" who thought that talks with East Germany were possible, had been encouraged by Dulles's remarks. Adenauer's own position that "reunification could only be achieved through free elections" was being undermined. The very idea of conversations with the East Germans "was for him inadmissible," and the notion of a "confederation in any form," something which a policy of direct talks might eventually lead to, was "totally unacceptable." Ambassador Bruce characterized his and Foreign Minister Brentano's expressions "as being little short of violent."[97]

In the face of this opposition the American government retreated. On January 29, certain basic conclusions were reached at a White House meeting: "We do not acquiesce in the substitution of GDR for Soviet officials as regards the Western occupying powers' movements to and from West Berlin. Mere identification of the vehicles as those of one of the Western occupying powers will be provided to GDR officials on demand, and will not be construed as acquiescence in substitution. However, no stamping of papers or inspection will be acquiesced in."[98] (Under existing procedures, Soviet officials did stamp documents on the access routes.[99])

Eisenhower, however, was not happy with this policy on stamping. On March 17, he referred to "flaws in the U.S. position" on this issue. "If a final peace treaty" between the two parts of Germany—and it is striking that this was even being considered at this point—"specifies that: (1) there will be no interference with authorized traffic to and from Berlin, and (2) that stamping identification papers will merely verify this identification, then it is difficult for us to argue with them." Herter "agreed that the real issue is whether the Communists actually restrict our traffic." But, as the President pointed out, the real problem lay in Bonn. Even if the East Germans "were to pledge themselves to carry out the responsibilities heretofore exercised by the Soviets, we could not, even though tempted

[96] Goodpaster, MCP, June 25, 1959, SS/S/DoS/3/State Department—1959 (May–September) (3)/DDEL.

[97] Bruce to Dulles, January 14, 1959, 611.62A/1-1459/DSCF/USNA.

[98] Dulles, Memorandum of Conclusions of White House Conference re Berlin, January 29, 1959, DDC 1986/3476.

[99] See, for example, Dean Acheson, "The Problem of the Breaking Point on Access," July 1961, POF/117/Germany. Security. 7/61/JFKL.

to accept, give it consideration, because it would be death to Adenauer."[100]

It was Adenauer's "rigidity," his "inflexibility," that was rapidly emerging as the central problem. The West German Chancellor, of course, did not have any desire to push the confrontation to its bitter conclusion and face the prospect of war with the Soviets. When Dulles came over to discuss the Berlin problem with European leaders in early 1959, he met with Adenauer and the two men talked about what would happen if war did break out over this issue. Nuclear weapons, Dulles said, would of course have to be used. Adenauer exclaimed: "For God's sake, not for Berlin!"[101]

What then was the West supposed to do if the crisis moved to the point of a sharp and dramatic confrontation? This was a question that Adenauer was never really willing to confront.[102] But it is hard to imagine that American representatives let him off the hook on this issue, or that his evasiveness was anything other than a source of irritation to the Americans.

The U.S. government was not terribly happy with its other allies either. In spite of the well-known difficulties with de Gaulle, the French were ready to act, even without prior mobilization, and indeed took a tougher line in the crisis than the Americans. Dulles, however, was a bit cynical about the French position. "Perhaps their zeal," he wrote Eisenhower, "is due to the fact that it is we rather than they who would have to make most of the military effort as, I understand, they have very little military potential left in Germany."[103]

The British attitude posed a much more serious problem. From very early on, the British position struck the Americans as excessively weak. (In 1954, for example, the UK had proposed that "surrender instructions

[100] John Eisenhower, MCP, March 17, 1959, p. 2, SS/I/6/ Berlin—vol. II (1)/DDEL.

[101] This is according to David Klein, the Foreign Service Officer who served as interpreter at this meeting. Note also Bruce to Dulles, March 2, 1959, SS/I/Berlin—vol. II(1)/DDEL: Ambassador Bruce argued here that America had to be willing, "if necessary, to resort to nuclear war" to defend West Berlin, and that this was a position the United States might "only be able to sustain by unilateral action." "Even so stout a friend" as Chancellor Adenauer, he noted, "has revealed decided hesitation over awful prospect of recourse to total war." There is other evidence, dating from 1961 and to be discussed below, that also points to Adenauer's unwillingness in the final analysis to resort to nuclear weapons.

[102] See for example Thompson's comment in 1961: "I note [West German Foreign Minister] von Brentano in discussion with President evaded being pinned down on facing consequences of separate treaty as Adenauer has always done." Thompson to Rusk, March 16, 1961, DDC 1977/46D.

[103] Dulles to Eisenhower, February 8, 1959, DDC 1982/923. For an excellent account of French policy during the crisis, see Cyril Buffet, "La Politique nucléaire de la France et la Seconde Crise de Berlin (1958–1962)," *Relations internationales*, no. 59 (Fall 1989).

be provided Allied Commandants in Berlin."[104]) During the crisis itself, the British government came across as desperately anxious to avoid war, too prone to take a mild line when, in the face of Soviet threats, a measure of toughness was required.[105] Prime Minister Macmillan's trip to Moscow in February 1959, taken against American advice, reminded people of Neville Chamberlain flying to Germany to plead for peace with Hitler in 1938. The fact that Macmillan was (in his own phrase) "humiliated" by Khrushchev while in Russia simply confirmed the American government in its belief that the sort of policy that the British stood for would only make matters worse.[106]

In March Macmillan came to America. In 1957 he had resisted the popular call for a summit conference with the Soviets: "All this is pure Chamberlainism. It is raining umbrellas."[107] By early 1958, however, he had reversed his position, and during the crisis in 1959 the call for a summit meeting became a key element in British policy. Setting a date, he wrote in his diary shortly before he left England, "would force the allies to concentrate their minds on the real problem—an acceptable compromise on Germany and Berlin."[108] On March 20, he met Dulles in the hospital. Dulles asked: "What is the use of our spending $40 billion a year or more to create deterrent power if whenever the Soviets threaten us and want to take something from our present positions we feel that we have to buy peace by compromise"?[109] When the British Prime Minister met with Eisenhower that evening, the discussion became heated. The President would not deal with the Soviets under duress. "While others could talk about going to a Summit Meeting under threat of attack by the Soviets, he for one would not attend and they could hold their Summit Meeting without him." When Macmillan argued that World War I came "because of the failure of the leaders at that time to meet at the summit," Eisenhower countered by evoking the memory of Munich: "prior to

---

[104] The relevant documents, giving the British proposal and the American reaction, are in CCS 381 (8-20-43) sec 34, JCS 1954-56/USNA.

[105] The evidence on these points is abundant. See, for example, Telephone Call from the President, January 13, 1959, 12:06 p.m., DP/TC/13/Memoranda of Telephone Conversations—White House—Jan. 4, 1959 to April 15, 1959/DDEL; note also Dulles's Memorandum of Private Conversation with Prime Minister Macmillan, February 5, 1959, DP/GCM/1/Memoranda of Conversation—General—L through M (2)/DDEL. The basic point also comes through in both Eisenhower's and Macmillan's memoirs.

[106] Harold Macmillan, *Riding the Storm* (London, 1971), pp. 605, 611, 616–18.

[107] From Macmillan's diary, quoted in Alastair Horne, *Harold Macmillan*, vol. 2 (New York, 1989), p. 116.

[108] Ibid., p. 636.

[109] Dulles, Memorandum of Conversation, March 20, 1959, SS/ITM/6/Macmillan Talks, Friday March 20, 1959/DDEL.

World War II Neville Chamberlain went to such a meeting and it is not the kind of meeting with which he intends to be associated."[110]

The British goal, in fact, was to try to work out some accommodation with the Soviets on the basis of the status quo—that is, a divided Germany, with the Western Powers' right of access to West Berlin guaranteed. As far as the British were concerned, the East German government could control access to the city as long as western rights were respected. This solution was broached to the Soviets at the Moscow meeting in February and, in slightly different form, at the Geneva Foreign Ministers' Conference in the spring.[111] When the British cabinet first considered the problem at the beginning of the crisis, there was no thought that force might eventually have to be used to maintain western rights in the city; a new airlift was the most extreme measure contemplated. An "arrangement with the East German government" to permit transport to continue was seen as "the most realistic" option.[112] In March Macmillan laid out the basic policy for his cabinet colleagues: "we should recognize the Soviet determination to regularise the division of Germany, with some consequential adjustment in the status of Berlin, and should seek to extract the maximum advantage from the willingness of the Soviet leaders to negotiate that adjustment."[113]

This appeared to the allies as a policy of negotiation virtually à l'outrance. The British were disturbed by the American willingness to contemplate the eventual use of force; they opposed the Americans in early 1959 on the issue of military contingency planning; they were still attached to plans for some sort of "security zone" in central Europe, plans that seemed to look forward to some sort of great power "disengagement" from the area. For the West German government especially, anything that smacked of "disengagement," or even of a special military status for Germany, was anathema. Adenauer in particular was worried that Britain was willing to sell Germany "down the river" and make a deal with the Soviets at German expense.[114]

[110] Eisenhower, *Waging Peace*, p. 354; Goodpaster, MCP, March 23, 1959, memo of March 20 meeting, 7 p.m., SS/ITM/6/Macmillan Talks (1)/DDEL. Note also Herter's remark, in a despatch from Geneva in June, that British Foreign Secretary Selwyn Lloyd was willing "to grasp at any excuse to move on to the summit." Herter to Eisenhower, June 9, 1959, SS/S/DoS/5/Geneva Conference (3)/DDEL.
[111] Selwyn Lloyd note, February 28, 1959, PREM 11/2690, and Lloyd memo, June 13, 1959, C(59)102, CAB 129/98, PRO.
[112] Cabinet Conclusions, November 18, 1958, C.C. 81(2), CAB 128/32, PRO.
[113] Cabinet Conclusions, March 4, 1959, C.C. (59)14(1), CAB 128/33, PRO.
[114] Ibid.; Steel to Foreign Office, March 31, 1959, FO 371/145774. On the "security zone" idea, see folder WG 1075/238 in FO 371/145849; note also the six files from 1958 (all but two still closed, in spite of Britain's general adherence to a thirty-year rule for the opening of public records) left by the Foreign Office "working committee on military dis-

Macmillan tried to reassure Adenauer, and wrote to him in late March that British policy had been misunderstood. The British government, he said, was not considering measures that would discriminate against German forces. This particular assurance, on the "question of atomic discrimination," was in fact the only one that Adenauer was evidently interested in.[115] But all this was to little or no avail. Adenauer remained deeply suspicious of the British. Macmillan's trip to Moscow had come as a shock to him, and he obviously interpreted it as an "electoral maneuver" (and indeed a general election in Britain had been scheduled for later that year).[116] He had in fact a whole series of grievances about the British. Eisenhower, after meeting with him in late May, remarked that he seemed "to have developed almost a psychopathic fear of what he considers to be 'British weakness.'"[117] The British for their part had a number of complaints about Adenauer, especially his failure to support Britain on the issue of a free trade agreement between the European Economic Community and the other European countries.[118] The upshot was that relations between the U.K. and West Germany in 1959 were very bad. Eisenhower even wondered in March whether the British were "willing to break with Adenauer."[119]

One has the sense, reading the American documents, that the President was becoming increasingly fed up with the allies. He had tried to take a middle line—that the West should be firm but not truculent—but had to deal both with Adenauer's rigidity and with a British policy that verged on appeasement. It was, he said, like "walking a rickety fence": there were "difficulties in backing both Adenauer and the British, whose views appear to be diametrically opposed."[120]

The result was an increasing willingness on his part to move toward bilateral talks with the Soviets. The British Prime Minister had, after all, set the precedent with his trip to Russia. In March Eisenhower began to

---

engagement in Central Europe," FO 371/135627-632. On Germany being "sold down the river," see Steel to Foreign Office, March 25, 1959, PREM 11/2684, and on Anglo-German relations in this period in general, see FO 371/145773-774, all in the PRO. For an early but still useful account of Anglo-German relations in the 1950s, see D. C. Watt, *Britain Looks to Germany: British Opinion and Policy Towards Germany Since 1945* (London, 1965).

[115] Macmillan to Adenauer, March 24, 1959, and Steel to Foreign Office, March 25, 1959, PREM 11/2684.

[116] Steel to Foreign Office, February 3, 1959, FO 371/145773, PRO.

[117] Eisenhower, Conversation with Chancellor Adenauer, May 27, 1959, AWF/DDED/39/ Diary May 1959/DDEL.

[118] This was a very important theme in the British documents. See Cabinet Conclusions, November 18, 1958, C.C. (58)81(2), CAB 128/32; PREM 11/2714; Minutes of Macmillan-Adenauer meeting, November 19, 1959, FO 371/145780; Minutes of Cabinet Defence Committee, November 20, 1959, D(59)11(2), CAB 131/21, all in PRO.

[119] John Eisenhower, MCP, March 19, 1959, SS/I/6/Berlin—vol. II (1)/DDEL.

[120] John Eisenhower, MCP, March 17, 1959, p. 3, SS/I/6/Berlin—vol. II (1)/DDEL.

play with the idea: "We might startle Macmillan a little bit by saying now that he has seen Khrushchev, [the] President is thinking of asking Khrushchev to come over here."[121] Two weeks later, he told two congressional leaders that an invitation for Khrushchev to visit America was a "possible 'ace in the hole' " for "dealing with the Berlin crisis."[122] In July, after the failure of the Geneva Foreign Ministers' meeting, he thought a Khrushchev visit might be needed "to break the log jam."[123] It did not bother him that Khrushchev, in a very long meeting with Averell Harriman on June 23, had made some of the most appalling threats ever made in the nuclear age.[124] In fact, the President said, a meeting with the Soviet leader would be quite useful in this context: "If Khrushchev were to threaten war or use of force, he would immediately call his bluff and ask him to agree on a day to start."[125]

A meeting with Khrushchev was eventually scheduled to take place at Camp David in September. In what areas, Eisenhower wondered, might it be possible to work out some arrangement with the Russians? On June 15, the President said he "had racked his head to think of such things—that would not appear to be concessions—and was at his 'wits end.' He could not see anything as a possibility except some auxiliary activity. He did recall that Khrushchev has raised the question of IRBMs located in nearby countries. If we were to have a break-through in more advanced missiles, it might be possible to give up these IRBM plans."[126]

The immediate issue was the deployment of IRBMs to Greece. Eisenhower had never really liked the IRBMs.[127] On June 3 he had posed a series

[121] Telephone Conversation with the President, March 13, 1959, HP/10/Presidential Telephone Calls 1959 (2)/DDEL. Macmillan was in fact angered by the news that Eisenhower was going to meet with Khrushchev directly. See his *Pointing the Way* (New York, 1972), pp. 78–79.

[122] Bryce Harlow, Memorandum for the Record, March 26, 1959, p. 2, DDC 1978/118C.

[123] Memorandum of Telephone Conversation with the President, July 8, 1959, HP/10/Presidential Telephone Calls 1959 (2)/DDEL.

[124] A twelve-page report is in Owen to State Department, June 26, 1959, POF/126/USSR. Vienna Meeting. Background Documents (D)/JFKL. It should be noted that a good deal of alcohol was consumed in the course of this meeting, and that Khrushchev was "most genial throughout the evening," "smiling incessantly," and "constantly flattering" Harriman.

[125] Goodpaster, MCP, July 13, 1959 (of July 10 meeting), SS/S/DoS/3/State Department—1959 (May–September) (4)/DDEL.

[126] Goodpaster, MCP, June 17, 1959 (of July 15 meeting), SS/S/DoS/3/State Department—1959 (May–September) (3)/DDEL.

[127] See especially his remarks in the NSC, April 24, 1958, DDC 1980/384B. He was so critical of the Defense Department IRBM proposal that his National Security Advisor, Robert Cutler, assumed he had decided against it, and had to be corrected. Eisenhower's basic line about the IRBM was that "the weapon is one of tremendous psychological importance, although he was inclined still to discount its military significance." Goodpaster, MCP, March 23, 1957, p. 3, SS/S/A/16/IRBM for UK/DDEL. The basic military view was reflected, for example, in a WSEG report on European air defense, which concluded that nothing could be

of questions about this proposal. The Secretary of Defense replied on June 12. For example, the President had asked: "What particular advantage do we expect to gain from putting these weapons into Greece in view of the fact that this country is both small and exposed?" The Defense Department answered in part as follows: "Greece will provide IRBM coverage of many targets which cannot be reached by the U.K. THOR force. Further, it will provide another portion of the missile system with which we hope to ring the Soviet Bloc."[128]

These answers clearly had not satisfied him. On June 16 he met with Douglas Dillon from the State Department. After discussing the question of a direct meeting with Khrushchev, Eisenhower raised the Greek IRBM issue. His comments are in fact of considerable interest in the light of later events:

> The President said one thing is bothering him a great deal in the present situation, and that is the plan to put IRBMs in Greece. If Mexico or Cuba had been penetrated by the Communists, and then began getting arms and missiles from them, we would be bound to look on such developments with the gravest concern and in fact he thought it would be imperative for us to take positive action, even offensive military action. He could see the reason for Redstone, Corporal or Honest John missiles, which are short-range, but not IRBMs. He wondered if we were not simply being provocative, since Eastern Europe is an area of dispute in a political sense.
>
> The point of this, the President indicated, is that perhaps we can say to Khrushchev that we will not put the IRBMs there, and see what he is willing to do on his side to improve the situation.[129]

The next day, in a meeting with Dillon and Secretary of Defense McElroy, he again raised the issue:

> He said he could see reason for putting IRBMs into such areas as Britain, Germany and France. However, when it comes to the "flank" or advanced areas such as Greece, the matter seems very questionable. He reverted to his analogy—if Cuba or Mexico were to become Communist inclined, and the Soviets were to send arms and equipment, what would we feel we had to do then. He thought we would feel that we would have to intervene, militarily if necessary.

---

done to assure the survivability of fixed-site weapons like the early IRBMs. JCS 2073/1487, summarized in JCS 2073/1501, January 7, 1958, in CCS 092 Western Europe (3-12-48) sec 95, JCS 1958.

[128] McElroy Memorandum for the President, June 12, 1959, AWF/DDED/42/Staff Notes June 1–15, 1959 (1)/DDEL.

[129] Goodpaster, MCP, June 19, 1959, SS/S/DoS/3/State Department—1959 (May–September) (3)/DDEL.

But Dillon and McElroy both objected to what the President had in mind: the United States could not be seen as backing down on this after the Soviet threats; there would be major problems, Dillon added, if Greece and Turkey were treated differently from the other NATO allies. Eisenhower concluded by opting for what was essentially a half-measure: the deployment would be delayed, but these delays "should not be related to Khrushchev's threats."[130] The immediate result was that the IRBMs would not become a bargaining chip at Camp David.

Berlin itself was left as the one issue where Eisenhower thought that something might be worked out. The President had never been happy about the idea of American troops in Berlin. In his view, it had been a terrible mistake at the end of the war to create Berlin as a western island in the Soviet zone. He had warned against this at the time, he said, but when he had pointed out the dangers Roosevelt and Churchill had replied, "Oh, we can get along with Uncle Joe."[131] The time was coming, however, when the West would have to bite the bullet. "The Western world," he remarked a month after Camp David, "made a mistake in 1944 and 1945 and must now find a way to pay for it."[132]

As early as November 27, 1958, he was willing to consider making Berlin a "free city" under U.N. auspices, with "an avenue to it also under the jurisdiction of the U.N."[133] Dulles, however, did not like the idea: "paper agreements" were "no good," and the only thing that kept West Berlin free was the presence of American troops.[134] After Dulles's death, however, the President began to play with the notion again. On July 1, 1959, after meeting with Soviet Deputy Premier Kozlov, he told his secretary that the Russians say that our position on Berlin is illogical. "We admit it is illogical, but we will not abandon our rights and responsibilities—unless there is a way made for us to do so."[135]

At Camp David, he told Khrushchev that America had no intention of staying in Berlin forever. "Clearly," he said, "we did not contemplate 50 years in occupation there."[136] And on October 1, he told his national security advisor Gordon Gray

[130] Goodpaster, MCP, June 17, 1959, SS/S/DoD/1/Department of Defense, vol. III (6)/ DDEL.

[131] Telephone Calls, November 27, 1958, AWF/DDED/37/Telephone Calls—November 1958/DDEL. For a very interesting account of how the Berlin arrangements were worked out during and after the war, see William Franklin, "Zonal Boundaries and Access to Berlin," *World Politics*, vol. 16 (October 1963).

[132] Goodpaster, MCP, October 22, 1959, DDC 1982/2219.

[133] See the record of the telephone conversation with Dulles cited in n. 122.

[134] Telephone Call from the President, January 13, 1959, 9:18 a.m., DP/TC/13/Memoranda of Telephone Conversations—White House, Jan. 4, 1959 to April 15, 1959/DDEL.

[135] Entry for July 1, 1959, AWF/ACWD/10/July 1959 (2); also DDC 1983/633.

[136] Memorandum of Conversation, President's Report of his Private Session with Khrushchev, September 27, 1959, POF/126/USSR. Vienna Meeting. Background Documents (C)/

we must remember that Berlin is an abnormal situation; that we had found it necessary to live with it, and that it had come about through some mistakes of our leaders—Churchill and Roosevelt. However, he felt that there must be some way to develop some kind of a free city which might be somehow a part of West Germany, which might require that the U.N. would become a party to guaranteeing the freedom, safety and security of the city which would have an unarmed status except for police forces. He reiterated that the time was coming and perhaps soon when we would simply have to get our forces out.[137]

What came of all this? The State Department was willing to go along with it. Secretary Herter thought on October 22 that "we could work out some kind of a status for a 'guaranteed city' for West Berlin." But what would the allies, and especially Adenauer, accept? The Germans simply wanted to maintain the status quo with U.S. support; they were "showing themselves more and more rigid, with Adenauer less and less accessible." If that was the case, the President wondered what point there was to negotiation with the Russians. But he seemed unwilling to put pressure on the Germans: "he thought that he could strike a bargain on his own with Khrushchev if he were to try to do so, but he knew our allies would not accept his acting unilaterally."[138] Even as late as March 1960, he took Adenauer's veto as binding: "The President said that he felt that as long as Chancellor Adenauer's position is as inflexible as it seems to be there seemed to be little profit in discussing unification alternatives or alternatives with respect to Berlin."[139]

Although it is impossible to tell at this point what sorts of pressures were brought on Adenauer, and what effect, if any, they had, the basic impression one has about the period between the Camp David meeting in September 1959 and the May 1960 summit was that things were dead in the water. At Camp David, for example, Khrushchev seemed to hint at the possibility of a deal involving both Germany and China. On Germany itself, he took a very moderate line, and called simply for accepting things as they were:

> It would be desirable if we could work out common language, recognizing the fact of the existence of two German states, and confirming that neither side would try to bring about either a Socialist or a Capitalist solution by

---

JFKL. See also the minutes of the Eisenhower-Khrushchev meeting, 11:45 a.m., same date, same file. Secretary Herter had earlier urged Eisenhower to take this line: Goodpaster, MCP, August 24, 1959, p. 2, AWF/DDED/43/Staff Notes August 1959 (1)/DDEL.

[137] Gordon Gray, Memorandum of Meeting with the President, October 1, 1959, p. 3, DDC 1986/1107.

[138] Goodpaster, MCP, October 22, 1959, p. 3, DDC 1982/2219.

[139] Gordon Gray, Memorandum of Meeting with the President, April 5, 1960 (for March 29 meeting), OSANSA/SA/P/4/1960—Meetings with the President—vol. I (4)/DDEL.

force. If we could make that point clear, then we would remove the danger from the situation. If we were to speak of our sympathies, then we both knew where the sympathies of each other lie. American sympathies lie with West Germany and the system existing there. Soviet sympathies are with East Germany and the system prevailing on that side. It would be well to recognize the facts. That doesn't mean that the United States would accord juridical recognition to the GDR, but would accept the state of fact as it exists.[140]

A German settlement, he said, would solve the Berlin problem as well. But then, in a later meeting, he brought up the question of China, and stressed that American policy was inconsistent. The President, Khrushchev pointed out, had said "that if the two German states remained, they would be an indefinite hot bed of conflict. If this statement was true with respect to Germany, then it was true with respect to China too."[141]

Is it wrong to see in this a hint that Khrushchev wanted to work out an arrangement whereby the U.S. would accept the status quo in Germany, and the Soviets for their part would not support Chinese Communist attempts to conquer Taiwan?[142] If Dulles had been in office, he might have picked up on these suggestions. He was always more sophisticated than Eisenhower on the China issue, and was aware very early on in the Berlin Crisis that the Chinese and German questions were analogous: on December 2, 1958, he told an associate "to look up the parallel and see if the positions the Russians are now taking would not have [a] disastrous effect on them in the Pacific," Taiwan, presumably, being as much a "reality" as East Germany. But Eisenhower at Camp David merely replied to Khrushchev that while "it was possible to make such a comparison," human affairs get "very badly tangled at times," and the U.S. sought "peaceful settlements in both instances." A whole area for negotiation was again simply blocked off; and in the Berlin documents that have been released, it is amazing how few references there are to China or to Sino-Soviet relations.[143]

---

[140] Memorandum of Conversation, September 15, 1959, p. 9, POF/126/Vienna Background Documents (C)/JFKL.

[141] Notes of September 27 meeting, p. 5, ibid.

[142] It is worth noting in this context that, according to the Chinese, Khrushchev, after returning from Camp David, "tried to sell China the U.S. plot of the 'two Chinas.' " Quoted in Adam Ulam, *Expansion and Coexistence: The History of Soviet Foreign Policy, 1917–1967* (New York, 1968), pp. 627–28.

[143] In Dulles's mind, at least from 1954 on, China was ultimately to play the role of a counterweight to the Soviet Union—a view he shared with General Ridgway, but which Eisenhower himself found incomprehensible. For the time being, however, he preferred to take a tough position on China, in order to generate tensions between the Chinese and their Soviet ally. For a variety of reasons, having to do with both domestic and foreign policy, there was no point in being too open about his ultimate goals. See especially FRUS, 1952–54, 12, pp. 722–23 (for Ridgway's views), and 14, pp. 531–34 (for Dulles's support and

There was in fact very little that the Americans were willing to negotiate about. Some American officials—Ambassador Thompson in Moscow and Ambassador Bruce in Bonn—had understood all along that the question of German military power, and especially German nuclear forces, was of fundamental importance to the Soviets.[144] But it does not seem that the U.S. was ready to offer anything of substance in this area. This issue in fact evidently did not receive much attention at the highest levels of the government; it was never treated by Eisenhower and Dulles—or for that matter by Kennedy and his associates—as the most central issue, the real heart of the problem.

One result was that the Berlin Crisis evidently had little effect on the Eisenhower administration's nuclear sharing policy. As for the closely related issue of a security zone in central Europe—a zone where armaments would be limited, an idea on which Macmillan "had staked his political fate"—although Eisenhower and Norstad were interested in working out such an arrangement, Adenauer would not hear of it. Again Adenauer, as General Norstad said, was "the problem."[145]

If the German nuclear weapons issue was in fact the key question, why was it neglected by the administration? Part of the reason is that the Soviets, in diplomatic contacts, did not stress the issue nearly as much as one might have expected.[146] It was not that this issue was ignored completely in these discussions; it simply was not played up as the heart of the problem.

In any event, for one reason or another, every conceivable area of ne-

Eisenhower's rejection of them); FRUS, 1952–54, 5, p. 1809 (for the argument about maximum pressure straining relations between Russia and China). My understanding of these aspects of Dulles's thinking owes a good deal to talks with Robert Bowie. On the parallel between Berlin and China: Telephone Call to Gov. Herter, December 2, 1958, DP/TC/9/ Memoranda of Telephone Conversations—General—Nov. 2, 1958–Dec. 27, 1958 (1)/ DDEL. For Eisenhower's answer to Khrushchev at Camp David: Memorandum of Conversation, Sept. 27, 1959, p. 6, POF/126/Vienna Background Documents (C)/JFKL. For one of the few documents to deal direclty with the relation between Berlin and China: unsigned memo on "The Sino-Soviet Dispute and the Berlin Situation," March 27, 1961, DDC 1978/ 67C; also in NSF/81/JFKL.
[144] See, in addition to the sources already cited, Bruce to Dulles, February 16, 1959, 611.61/2-1659/DSCF/USNA (where Bruce suggests that a negotiation of this issue be considered), and Hillenbrand, Memorandum of Conversation, February 21, 1959, 611.61/2-2159/DSCF/USNA (for German objections to Thompson's interest in negotiation with the Soviets on this and other issues).
[145] Goodpaster, MCP, March 15, 1960, AWF/A/28/Norstad (1)/DDEL. The comment about Macmillan was expressed by Deputy Secretary of Defense Quarles, John Eisenhower, MCP, March 26, 1959, p. 5, OSANSA/SA/P/4/Meetings with the President—1959 (4)/DDEL.
[146] See, for example, the long accounts of Khrushchev's meetings with Harriman and Thompson, June 26, 1959, 611.61/6-2659, and with Nixon and Thompson, July 27, 1959, 611.61/7-2759 (where the issue came up in passing, section 6, p. 4), both DSCF/USNA.

gotiation had been blocked off. It therefore did not seem in early 1960 that a real settlement with the Soviets was possible in the near future. Indeed the common assumption was that the Paris summit was unlikely to accomplish much of any substance. Since a failure of the summit might lead to the signing of a peace treaty with East Germany, which might in turn set off a chain of events that could lead to general war, this prospect was viewed with some alarm.[147]

From the point of view of the U.S. government, there was now an urgent need for up-to-date target intelligence. In fact, it was probably because the chances for a successful summit had been written off that Eisenhower reversed his position and authorized the resumption of U-2 overflights of the Soviet Union. His earlier veto of the overflights had been based on an assumption that the summit might actually be productive: he had been concerned that "if one of these aircraft were lost when we are engaged in apparently sincere deliberations, it could be put on display in Moscow and ruin the President's effectiveness." This again was an amazing comment, given what was to happen less than three months later: the downing of a U-2 (the wreckage was in fact put on display in Moscow) led in May to the scuttling of the Paris Summit.[148]

Although in the final analysis Eisenhower had felt his hands were tied, one still has the sense that American policy in this period was moving toward the idea of an accommodation with the Soviet Union—toward the acceptance of some sort of "free city" solution for Berlin, toward some kind of de facto recognition of the East German regime, and toward a solution of the German question based not on free elections, but on negotiations between the two German states. How exactly is this evolution of policy to be explained?

In the 1950s and beyond, it was commonly argued by people like Henry Kissinger that under Eisenhower strategy had become dangerously rigid, too dependent on a threat of general war that no one would ever

---

[147] See especially the "Briefing Sheet for the Chairman, Joint Chiefs of Staff, for the Operations Deputies Meeting, Tuesday, 10 May 1960, Agenda Item No. 7," on JCS 1907/266, Berlin Contingency Planning, May 9, 1960, and especially the summary there of a Secretary of Defense memo of March 28, 1960, CCS 9172 Berlin/9105 (28 March 1960)/JCS 1960/ USNA.

[148] Goodpaster, Memorandum for the Record, February 8, 1960, SS/S/A/15/Intelligence Matters (13) [Aug. 1959–Feb. 1960]/DDEL. A year earlier, when the issue was discussed, it was clear that the need for the most up-to-date intelligence was a factor in the decision on the overflights. Eisenhower, for example, was against the overflights as long as there was any hope that a summit might succeed; he implied that if this hope vanished, and a real crisis seemed unavoidable, then the overflights might have to be resumed. Secretary Dulles also noted "that if the current negotiations fail, we must at once get the most accurate information possible." Goodpaster, MCP, April 11, 1959, SS/S/A/15/Intelligence Matters (1) [April 1959]/DDEL.

want to execute. America, it was claimed, had been forced to retreat in the 1950s because it lacked meaningful alternatives to strategic nuclear power: an effective foreign policy could only be supported by a more flexible military strategy. Was the Berlin Crisis, therefore, the decisive proof of this thesis? Was it because he wanted to avoid having to choose "between holocaust and surrender" that Eisenhower had moved toward acceptance of the Soviet position on Berlin, and, to a certain extent, on Germany as a whole?

The answer here is quite clearly no. In the first place, Eisenhower had by no means come so close to ruling out general war as an option that the risk of matters escalating to this level had ceased to carry political weight. The President, although obviously appalled by the devastation that a general thermonuclear war would cause, was by no means unwilling to launch a massive attack in certain extreme cases. He spoke during the crisis about the need for the U.S. to be ready to "push its whole stack of chips into the pot" when this became necessary; the question was whether we had the "nerve" to do this—whether, during an "acute crisis period," we would be willing "to engage in general war to protect our rights." If we were, then war could probably be avoided, although he recognized that this "firm position" might conceivably lead to general war through miscalculation. But the alternative was appeasement, which he was sure would lead to total defeat.[149]

In another document, he hinted that the U.S. might have to strike preemptively if the crisis began to get out of hand. One of the questions he wanted the NSC to consider, he wrote on February 27, was how we could "be sure of the necessary support from Congress even though we might suddenly face a critical emergency and would be under a compulsion to act quickly so as to avoid any unnecessary damage to ourselves."[150]

American nuclear power had not been neutralized, in terms of its political significance, by the threat of Soviet retaliation. But "massive retaliation" was not, in any event, America's only military option during the Berlin Crisis. It was clearly understood that a great deal could be done before the crucial decision about a nuclear strike had to be made.

The basic shift in planning for a possible Berlin crisis had taken place at the end of the Truman period. As late as 1951, the military felt that the U.S. was too weak to take strong action if the Soviets threatened Berlin.[151] But by mid-1952, with the revival of American military power, they, and

[149] See the two memoranda of his meetings with congressional leaders, March 6, 1959, DDC 1981/597B, 598A.

[150] Eisenhower, Memorandum for the Files, February 27, 1959, AWF/A/7/Berlin Paper/DDEL.

[151] See for example JCS 1907/66, February 7, 1951, FRUS, 1951, 3, pp. 1892–94.

with them the American government as a whole, were willing to take a much tougher line.[152] The change of administration in 1953 led to only a minor sharpening of policy. The key point is that Eisenhower, like Truman, was willing to take military measures, and indeed ultimately risk general war, if that became necessary to save the city. The fundamental Berlin policy paper for the mid-1950s, NSC 5404/1, is still classified, but an NSC Progress Report summarizes the key paragraph in this document as follows:

> If access to Berlin is seriously harassed or a blockade imposed, the U.S. should consult with its Allies and be prepared to protest at the local level and in Moscow; hold the USSR responsible; make use at an accelerated rate of any means of access still open; initiate mobilization; use in agreement with the Allies limited military force to determine Soviet intentions; solidify world opinion in our favor; evacuate dependents; use limited military force to re-open access.[153]

And another document from the period when NSC 5404/1 was taking shape reveals the basic thinking of the administration on how to deal with a threat to Berlin:

> *a.* The use of force should be limited to a small number of troops whose deployment would not risk SACEUR's primary mission.
> *b.* When it becomes evident that Soviet harassing measures were in effect intended to blockade access to Berlin the Allies would start mobilizing for a showdown.
> *c.* Time purchased by the Berlin stockpile would be used for such mobilization.
> *d.* The use of force to lift the Berlin blockade would be resorted to only when the Allies were mentally prepared to accept general war if the use of force failed.[154]

In the Berlin planning documents for the entire Eisenhower period, mobilization prior to the outbreak of hostilities played a central role.[155] This implied that the U.S. would be able to build up her forces while the crisis was developing. This was an obvious source of "flexibility" in both a political and a military sense.

[152] The basic document here was NSC 132/1, approved by the President on June 12, 1952. FRUS, 1952–54, 7, p. 1261ff.

[153] Progress Report on NSC 5404/1, April 30, 1954, p. 10, CCS 381 (8-20-43) sec 34/JCS 1951-53/USNA.

[154] Gerhart to JCS, on "Timing of Allied Use of Force to Determine Soviet Intentions Relative to a Possible Blockade of Berlin," December 8, 1953, CCS 381 (8-20-43) sec 32/JCS 1951-53/USNA. Gen. Gerhart was Special Assistant to the JCS for NSC Affairs.

[155] See, for example, Norstad to JCS, January 31, 1959, para. 4, CCS 9172 Berlin/9105 (12 Jan 1959)/JCS 1959/USNA.

It is also important to note the related point that the documents generally referred to the use of "limited military force" after mobilization, and implied that this was something different from, and presumably more massive than, the "testing of intentions" operations that would come before mobilization. It is unclear, however, and may even have been unclear at the time, what "limited military force" actually meant. Was it anticipated, for example, that in such an operation nuclear weapons would inevitably be used, or was this issue left open? And then there was the basic issue of how big these limited operations would have to be before they triggered a general war. There is still not enough evidence available to answer these questions with any confidence. Perhaps the most that can be said is that it seems that they were never really fully resolved in the Eisenhower period, although there was at least in the earlier part of this administration a tendency to move toward general war fairly rapidly.[156]

By early 1959, the government began to plan for the crisis that might come in May if the Soviets tried to liquidate the Western Powers' occupation rights in Berlin by signing a treaty with East Germany. The most important evidence on this subject is still classified, but there are some documents which throw a certain light on this issue. Eisenhower's aim, according to one document, was to gradually increase pressure through such measures as the "withdrawal of Ambassadors, breaking of relations, issuing of an ultimatum, etc., before major military action is resorted

[156] On the rapid escalation posture in the early years: see the JCS comments on NSC 173 (a draft of the basic Berlin paper, essentially a slight revision of NSC 132/1), enclosure to JCS 1907/101, Dec. 5, 1953 (and approved by the Chiefs on Dec. 9), CCS 381 (8-20-43) sec 32/ JCS 1951-53/USNA. These JCS views were accepted and incorporated in the revised Berlin paper, NSC 5404: JCS Memorandum for the Secretary of Defense, January 19, 1954, para. 9, OSANSA/NSC/PP/8/NSC 5404 (2)/DDEL.

In 1955, the JCS had been asked to define what "limited military force" actually meant. The answer they gave was that this would depend on conditions at the time. In other words, far from opting for a posture of instant massive retaliation as soon as U.S. rights were threatened, the JCS preferred to keep its options open—or at least was so divided on this issue that it had no choice but to take this line. JCS to Norstad, May 23, 1955, CCS 381 (8-20-43) sec 37/JCS 1954-56/USNA. That this dispute was never resolved during the Eisenhower period is suggested by a document from 1960, which gave Air Force comments on one of the Berlin operations plans. Vogt memo, March 14, 1960, CCS 3145 (1 Feb 1960) sec 2/JCS 1960/ USNA.

All this, of course, was clearly linked to the more general debate on what America needed in the way of a limited war fighting capability. Dulles and others often complained, especially toward the end of the decade, about excessive reliance on strategic nuclear power, but the Defense Department insisted that this point of view was based on a misunderstanding. Secretary McElroy argued in this connection that we had "a very sizeable limited warfare capability which is not really well understood," and he and the Chiefs wanted to sit down with Dulles and the others who had expressed these concerns and explain the situation to them. Herter, Memorandum of Telephone Conversation with Secretary McElroy, May 29, 1958, HP/4/Chronological File, May 1958 (1).

to."[157] Again, the term "major military action" implies something more than a probe designed to test intentions, but something less than an all-out nuclear strike. Even before hostilities, important political leverage could be derived from taking certain military preparations; in late February 1959, the JCS noted that U.S. commanders in Europe had "taken certain military actions pointed largely towards Berlin"; these, the Chiefs noted, would be "visible to Soviet intelligence," but would "not cause public alarm."[158]

None of the measures taken were very dramatic. In late March, for example, surveillance of Soviet submarine departures from Albania and Egypt was begun, U.S. submarines in the Pacific were stationed to monitor Soviet and Chinese submarines leaving bases at Petropavlovsk, Vladivostok, and Shanghai; U.S. forces in the Atlantic were to be ready to establish an antisubmarine barrier between Greenland, Iceland, and the British isles, and "to position nuclear subs in North Cape-Murmansk area to obtain early warning of Soviet submarine deployments." On April 22, with the foreign ministers meeting in Geneva, the situation seemed less tense, and these measures were suspended.[159] This was in fact typical of the way military pressure was turned on and off like a faucet as the level of political tension varied during the crisis.

Eisenhower felt that such relatively undramatic measures would suffice. Anything more at this point, he believed, would be counterproductive. He resisted calls, especially from the more hawkish elements in the Democratic Party, for a buildup of U.S. ground forces in Europe. This he thought would be an over-reaction. The Soviets intended "only to upset the United States." We have to see this problem in terms, he said, "not of six months, but of forty years." During that time, the Soviets would constantly try "to throw us off balance," but the U.S. had to plot a steady course. Crash measures would be militarily worthless in any case.[160] He did not even want to call the situation a "crisis." America was in for a very long period of tension, but the Soviets were not interested in a war, and thus there was no point now in taking "any sort of extreme military action, such as partial mobilization."[161] The U.S. was not in any event going to fight a massive ground war in Europe.

[157] John Eisenhower, Comments on Memorandum of Conclusions of White House Conference on Berlin, January 29, 1959, DDC 1983/2197.

[158] JCS to USNMR Paris, February 21, 1959, CCS 9172/9105 Berlin (21 Feb 1959)/JCS 1959/USNA.

[159] JCS to CINCPAC, CINCLANT, USCINCEUR, April 22, 1959, CCS 9172 Berlin/2000 (20 Mar 59)/JCS 1959/USNA. For naval measures in the North Atlantic, see also Brumly memo, March 24, 1959, FO 371/143677/ZP4/11, PRO.

[160] John Eisenhower, MCP, March 9, 1959, AWF/DDED/39/Staff Notes March 1–15, 1959 (1)/DDEL.

[161] Bryce Harlow memo of Eisenhower conversation with Congressmen McCormack and Halleck, March 26, 1959, DDC 1978/118C.

Eisenhower's policy during the Berlin Crisis is therefore not to be explained in terms of the weakness of American military strategy. Instead it seems he was thinking in long-range terms. Probably the United States could play for time and maybe get the Soviets to agree to some sort of temporary arrangement for Berlin. Even without an agreement, by taking a tough line the West might be able to force the Soviets to back down from their threats. But what good would it do? The problem would simply have to be faced again a few years later. The JCS and the CIA argued that while the U.S. still enjoyed military superiority, its position vis-à-vis the Soviets would probably deteriorate over the next few years. Eisenhower personally found this "hard to believe," but if there was any truth to it at all, it supported the conclusion that now was the best time to try to work out a settlement. The U.S. had to think in terms of the next ten years, and the Soviets, he implied, might not be "so generous" in the future.[162]

Eisenhower's general approach to the Berlin problem was in fact rooted in his administration's analysis of the basic long-term strategic problem facing the Western alliance. From the very outset, the assumption had been that the nuclearization of international politics would have a profoundly corrosive effect on the NATO alliance. It was taken for granted that in the long run the Europeans would not be able to stand up to Soviet nuclear power. Terrified by the prospect of nuclear war, the Europeans would drift away from the American policy of resistance to Soviet encroachments. The Americans might promise that any large-scale aggression would be met, in the final analysis, by an all-out nuclear attack. But the Europeans might some day begin to wonder what was worse, whether the Americans actually meant what they said, or whether NATO had come to rely on a strategy that at bottom was just pure bluff. In either case, an alliance whose central pillar was the threat of nuclear escalation would eventually be torn apart: NATO, at least in its present form, could not long survive the growth of Soviet nuclear capabilities and what was viewed as the inevitable loss of American nuclear superiority.

Dulles in particular often analyzed the basic strategic problem in these terms. As early as September 1953, he spoke about how the "NATO concept" was for these reasons "losing its grip" in Europe.[163] In 1955 he was

[162] JCS (Burke) to Secretary of Defense, on "Relative Military Capabilities in the 1959–1961/62 Time Period," July 13, 1959, CCS 9172 Berlin/9105 (13 July 1959)/JCS 1959/USNA; Gray, Memo of Meeting with the President, July 16, 1959, OSANSA/SA/P/4/Meetings with the President, June–December 1959 (6)/DDEL, for Eisenhower's incredulous reaction; Goodpaster, MCP, October 22, 1959, DDC 1982/2219. CIA memo, "U.S. Negotiating Position on Berlin—1959–62," July 13, 1959, MR 88-22403, DDEL.

[163] Dulles to Eisenhower, September 6, 1953, FRUS, 1952–54, 2, pp. 457–60. Note also Dulles's January 28, 1956 paper on nuclear weapons, esp. p. 3, DP/S/4/Paper on Nuclear Weapons/DDEL. For another copy: DDC 1982/802.

quite pessimistic about the future of the alliance: he seemed to view the "disintegration" of NATO as inevitable, the only question being how quickly it would unravel. The American goal, he said, should be "to see how much of the original NATO strategy can be salvaged."[164] In 1958, he said that unless basic American strategy were changed, the alliance could not be held together beyond another year or so. He thought that a strategy based on tactical nuclear weapons might be feasible; if not, he foresaw a "futile, brief effort" on the part of the Europeans "to become nuclear powers, followed by a trend toward neutralism." He in fact seemed to feel that these developments could not long be avoided.[165]

It was this general framework that was used to interpret events during the Berlin Crisis. What the crisis seemed to prove, in fact, was that the basic analysis had been essentially correct. In late January 1959, Dulles, for example, wrote a short "think piece" on Berlin. The Europeans, it seemed, were not willing to risk war over Berlin. Given this state of opinion, he wondered whether Western Europe was "really defensible at all." No amount of power could act as a deterrent unless there was "the will to use it." "So far as we are concerned, the will is present. If so far as Western Europe is concerned, the will is lacking, then I fear our entire NATO concept and US participation in it will require drastic review."[166]

What this suggested, first of all, was that the political burden placed on the alliance had to be eased if this were at all possible. With regard to Berlin, this implied that the U.S. should aim at some sort of settlement, if this could be achieved on reasonable terms, and not just at a postponement of the crisis for a few years.

The Berlin Crisis also forced the government to come to grips with the basic strategic problem. The issue was no longer abstract and theoretical, the sort of problem that the future could worry about. The question of the role that nuclear forces would play in NATO defense policy had suddenly become very real.

On August 16, 1960, President Eisenhower discussed the issue with Robert Bowie, who was working on a report on this general question. The two men agreed that tactical nuclear weapons offered no real solution to the problem. Was a conventional buildup the answer? Bowie had argued for increased emphasis on conventional forces, but Eisenhower at first disagreed. He could not "see any chance of keeping any war in Europe from becoming a general war. For this reason he thought we must be ready to throw the book at the Russians should they jump us." We

[164] Notes of NSC meeting, July 28, 1955, p. 7, AWF/NSC/7.

[165] Goodpaster, Memorandum for the Record, April 9, 1958, SS/S/A/21/Nuclear Exchange [Sept. 1957–June 1958] (3)/DDEL; Notes of high-level conference, June 17, 1958, DDC 1982/1578.

[166] "Thinking Out Loud," January 26, 1959, DDC 1987/1378.

would be "fooling ourselves," he argued, "if we said we could fight such a war without recourse to nuclear weapons. If massive land operations such as the Ludendorff offensive in early 1918 in World War I were to occur, he was sure that nations would use every weapon available to them."

Bowie did not dispute the President's point about the way a war would be fought. He argued instead that the real problem was "psychological and political more than military. If the Europeans think they are in a situation where they cannot resist at all if they do not use all-out nuclear attack, the probability becomes great that they would not resist and accordingly could not prevent Soviet encroachment. What he is suggesting is that we should be careful that we would not end up deterring ourselves."

The striking thing here is that Eisenhower, after some further discussion, admitted "that perhaps there has been a gap in his own thinking regarding this question." Since Bowie's argument was not really new, it seems that the reason that Eisenhower was receptive to it now probably had a good deal to do with the way these issues were coming to a head at this time, especially as a result of the Berlin Crisis.[167]

The argument about conventional forces was taken a good deal further in the next administration, and here again the Berlin Crisis was a driving force.

THE BERLIN CRISIS UNDER KENNEDY

The Paris summit conference collapsed in May 1960. But no treaty with East Germany was signed. Instead, the crisis went into remission. Khrushchev was awaiting the outcome of the American presidential elections.[168] As soon as the returns were in, the Russians began making overtures to the president-elect, using Averell Harriman and Adlai Stevenson as intermediaries. The Soviets stressed that they wanted to make a fresh start. They wanted especially to work together with the Americans to prevent "the spread of nuclear weapons." Without an agreement of this sort,

---

[167] Goodpaster, MCP, August 19, 1960, SS/S/DoS/4/State Department—1960 (August–September) (1)/DDEL. For an earlier argument along these lines, see, for example, Dulles's suggestions on basic national security policy, November 15, 1954, FRUS, 1952–54, 2, p. 775.

[168] It seems in fact that he had very much wanted Kennedy to win: he had gone so far as to make a point, during the campaign, of criticizing Kennedy, after Harriman had told him that the surest way to swing the election to Nixon, whom he obviously disliked intensely, was for him to express approval of the Democratic candidate. Harriman to Kennedy, November 15, 1960, POF/125/USSR. General. 1960/JFKL.

Ambassador Menshikov said, "China and other countries would obtain nuclear weapons in a few years." On Berlin and Germany, the Soviets accepted the fact that the U.S. was not ready to recognize the East German regime; still, they wanted to formalize and give some common juridical basis to the existing status quo. On West Berlin, they still thought it should be made into a "free city," but even here they were willing to be flexible. It was clear that the Soviets were eager to move quickly. Their tone was extremely conciliatory.[169]

But on January 6, 1961, in another one of those sudden shifts of position that marked Soviet policy during the crisis, Khrushchev (as the new Secretary of State, Dean Rusk, wrote President Kennedy) reiterated "his threat to sign a separate peace treaty."[170] This was the first of a number of signs that the crisis was beginning to heat up again. The climax of this new campaign came during Khrushchev's meeting with Kennedy at Vienna in June. He again explicitly threatened war over the issue. Unless a settlement of the German question could be worked out within six months, the Soviets would sign a separate peace treaty of their own with East Germany, unilaterally "putting an end to the occupation regime in West Berlin with all its implications."[171]

Khrushchev wasted no time in spelling out in very blunt language exactly what this meant. An attempt by the West to use force to maintain its access rights would be viewed as a violation of East German sovereignty; the USSR would regard it as an act of "open aggression" leading to war. Khrushchev had made an "irrevocable" decision. One way or another, a treaty would be signed by the end of the year. The U.S. was invited to help negotiate a peace settlement along the lines the Soviets suggested, "but if you want war, that is your problem."[172]

Within the Kennedy administration, there was a sense that the time had come for the United States to take a tough line on Berlin. On April 4, McGeorge Bundy, the President's National Security Advisor, had argued for a firm stand: "Attempts to negotiate this problem out of existence have failed in the past, and there is none which gives promise of success

[169] Harriman to Kennedy, November 12 and November 15, 1960; Memorandum of Conversation with Ambassador Menshikov, November 21, 1960; Adlai Stevenson, Report of Conferences with Ambassador Menshikov, November 28 and 29, 1960; Stevenson to Kennedy, November 22, 1960; Conversation with Ambassador Menshikov, December 14, 1960; Freedman telegram, December 16, 1960. All in POF/125/USSR. General. 1960/JFKL.

[170] Rusk to Kennedy, January 28, 1961, POF/117/Germany. Security. 1/61–6/61/JFKL.

[171] Soviet Aide-Memoire handed to President Kennedy at Vienna, June 4, 1961, DG, p. 645.

[172] Theodore Sorensen, *Kennedy* (New York, 1965), pp. 584–86, and Arthur Schlesinger, *A Thousand Days* (Boston, 1965), pp. 370–74. The similarity of language in these two accounts suggests that both authors were closely following official notes of the meeting.

now." He enclosed for the President what he called a "first-rate interim memorandum on Berlin from Dean Acheson."[173]

Acheson had been called in by the new administration to help shape first NATO and then Berlin strategy, and he quickly came to play a leading role. In his memorandum for the President, Acheson laid out his basic assumptions. "All courses of action are dangerous and unpromising," he said, but "inaction is even worse." He felt that if a crisis was provoked, "a bold and dangerous course may be the safest." Since so much was at stake, "a willingness to fight for Berlin" was essential. "Economic and political measures" would not be effective, "nor would threatening to initiate general war be a solution. The threat would not carry conviction; it would invite a preemptive strike; and it would alienate allies and neutrals alike. The fight for Berlin must begin, at any rate, as a local conflict. The problem is how and where will it end. This uncertainty must be accepted."[174]

The Acheson strategy was based on the idea that a *conventional* buildup was the way to strengthen *nuclear* deterrence.[175] Conventional forces were like chips that one could add to the pot: the greater the stakes, the greater the risk that the war would go nuclear. This new rationale for conventional capabilities was quickly taken up by other people in the Kennedy administration.[176] The great attraction here was that it seemed the United States could have its cake and eat it too. As a result of a conventional buildup, it would be possible, according to a Defense Department memorandum, "to raise substantially the level of non-nuclear force which is applied, and to broaden the range of alternative ways to use it. The increased flexibility resulting should at the same time improve nuclear credibility and also raise the threshold of nuclear choice."[177]

---

[173] McGeorge Bundy, Memorandum for the President, April 4, 1961, NSF/84/JFKL; also DDC 1986/2903.

[174] Dean Acheson, Memorandum for the President, April 3, 1961, DDC 1985/2547.

[175] Acheson had, in a rather informal way, made similar points in the past, but the argument was made explicitly and with characteristic analytical elegance by Thomas Schelling in an unpublished paper entitled "On the Problem of NATO's Nuclear Strategy," dated March 7, 1961, which can be found in the files Acheson kept when he was working on NATO strategy in early 1961: AP/85/State Department and White House Advisor, 1961. March/ HSTL. Schelling's theme here, as stressed on the first page, was "that a main consequence of limited war, and main reason for engaging in it, is *to raise the risk of general war.*" (Emphasis his.) This paper might have had a certain influence on Acheson's thinking at the time.

[176] For a typical example, see a memorandum of May 26, 1961 (n.a., but almost certainly written by Henry Owen), designed to brief President Kennedy for a meeting with de Gaulle, DDC 1986/2928: the president might argue that "the threat of nuclear war is more credible if it appears that we will first create a substantial level of non-nuclear violence, over Berlin or any other issue, than if we merely threaten to initiate general nuclear war *ab initio*."

[177] Draft paper on "Military Planning and Preparations toward a Berlin Crisis," p. 4,

This line of argument determined the path along which Berlin policy would now develop. But how far along this path would the new administration actually go? After Kennedy returned from Vienna, there was a vigorous debate within the administration about how sharp a response to make. Acheson and his allies wanted to take a series of measures, including a declaration of national emergency, that struck many others as too extreme.[178] The President finally decided on a more moderate program than Acheson had called for, but it was still quite dramatic.

Kennedy outlined his program in a televised speech to the nation on July 25. The government, he said, was taking a series of measures designed mainly to build up America's conventional military power.[179] Civil defense was also mentioned in the speech, even though there was evidently not much that could be done in this area that would be effective in reducing casualties if war broke out at the end of the year.[180] The President also referred to the fact that important steps had been taken in March and May to strengthen America's strategic nuclear forces. There had indeed been a striking increase in the size of the alert force in the past few months. From April 1 to July 15, the number of weapons committed to the alert force under the SIOP—the Single Integrated Operational Plan, the nation's basic plan for general nuclear war—increased from 1,108 to 1,530, representing an increase in megatonnage from 1,798 to 2,880.[181]

This effort conveyed a powerful message: to the U.S. government, a general war was a real possibility. "Our own plans," Bundy's aide Carl Kaysen noted, "emphasize that we must face the risk of war."[182] It was not that policy was built on the assumption that the President might *choose* to launch a nuclear attack; instead, the operative assumption was that a nuclear war was something that might well *happen*. As it turned

enclosed in McNamara to JCS Chairman, July 27, 1961, NSF/82/Germany. Berlin. General 7/27/61/JFKL.

[178] Bundy, Memorandum for the President, July 19, 1961, NSF/81/Germany. Berlin. General. 7/19/61–7/22/61/JFKL. See also Sorensen, pp. 583–92, and Schlesinger, pp. 380–92. Acheson must have been annoyed by the fact that both Secretary Rusk and the President's close advisor Theodore Sorensen used his own words against him in this debate. Sorensen, Memorandum to the President, July 17, 1961, POF/116a/Germany. General. 7/61/JFKL; Bundy, Memorandum of Discussion in the National Security Council on July 13, 1961, NSF/82/Germany. Berlin. General. 7/23/61–7/26/61/JFKL.

[179] DG, pp. 696–97.

[180] Kaysen to Bundy, "Berlin Crisis and Civil Defense" (with appendix), July 7, 1961, NSF/81/Germany. Berlin. General. 7/7/61–7/12/61/JFKL.

[181] This is based on a table found in the Fred Kaplan Papers/File 51/National Security Archive, Washington. The original tables are in the Lyndon Johnson Library in Austin, Texas.

[182] Kaysen to Bundy, "Berlin Crisis and Civil Defense," July 7, 1961, NSF/81/Germany. Berlin. General. 7/7/61–7/12/61/JFKL.

out, nothing more was needed. The new thrust of American policy had an enormous impact on the USSR.

The Soviet reaction to the President's speech was one of horror. What was the matter with these Americans? Were they actually contemplating thermonuclear war? Khrushchev had been misled by the Eisenhower policy of playing down the crisis into thinking that he could exercise sole control over the level of tension—that he could make his threats with impunity. But clearly things were getting dangerous, and on August 7 he pleaded for an easing of tension. "There should be a conference," he said; "let us not create a war psychosis, let us clear the atmosphere, let us rely on reason and not on the power of thermonuclear weapons." He would, for the moment at least, take no new military measures of his own. On Berlin itself he took a much milder line than he had taken at Vienna: "we do not intend to infringe upon any lawful interests of the Western Powers. Any barring of access to West Berlin, any blockade of West Berlin, is entirely out of the question."[183]

On August 11, with even more passion, he hammered away at the same themes. "Come to your senses, gentlemen." It was "madness" to threaten war. "War hysteria," he said, would "lead to nothing good. There must be a sense of proportion and military passions must not be fanned. If the feelings are let loose and they predominate over reason, then the flywheel of war preparations can start revolving at a high speed. Even when reason prompts that a brake should be put on, the flywheel of war preparations may have acquired such speed and momentum that even those who had set it revolving will be unable to stop it." He seemed to feel that things were moving out of control, and pleaded with the U.S. to behave in a reasonable fashion. "Let us not try to intimidate each other," he said, and added: "we propose to sit down at a conference table and discuss calmly, without inflaming passions and in a businesslike way, what is to be done to prevent the seeds of new conflicts from taking root in the soil left over from the last war."[184]

It is hard to read these speeches today without coming to the conclusion that Khrushchev felt he was getting in over his head—that he was deeply afraid that things were beginning to move out of control, and that now was therefore not the time to take a tough line and to affect, for bargaining purposes, anything like a willingness to go to war. But how much of this actually registered on the minds of policymakers in the United States? The available documentation is still too thin to try to give a definitive answer to this question, but a preliminary impression is that American officials, and indeed the attentive public as a whole, were not

[183] For the text, see the *New York Times*, August 8, 1961, p. 8.
[184] DG, pp. 718–20.

nearly as sensitive to evidence of Soviet anxiety as one might have expected. There was an image of the Soviets as made of steel, both willing and able to push things very close to the brink of war. Evidence to the contrary was simply screened out. The story in the *New York Times* on Khrushchev's August 7 speech, for example, portrayed the Soviet leader as "warning" the United States of a "Soviet troop build-up." This account thus missed the real point here, which was that Khrushchev was deliberately *not* responding in kind to the moves Kennedy had made on July 25: Khrushchev had announced that no additional military measures would be taken for the time being, noting only that "perhaps subsequently" additional measures might be necessary.[185]

Within the administration, there seems to have been a certain fear that the Soviets might not be deterrable. This was closely linked in the minds of at least some high officials to a set of strongly held beliefs about the role that nuclear weapons could play in international politics.

Secretary of Defense McNamara, for example, had decided very early on that the United States would never strike first with nuclear forces.[186] It seemed to follow that the possession of nuclear forces simply prevented an enemy from using them; they essentially neutralized each other, leaving the conventional balance as the politically decisive factor. The logic was so powerful and the conclusions so self-evident to people like McNamara that it was taken for granted that the Soviets would be able to see right through official pronouncements on nuclear strategy and grasp what the real situation was. In a basic policy document composed in late 1962, McNamara in fact argued that "the threat of a U.S. first-strike has long since been shown to be ineffective in deterring limited provocations and aggression."[187]

This was simply accepted as an article of faith. It ignored such key evidence as Khrushchev's frank admission, in his August 11 speech, that the Soviets had had to accommodate to American strategic superiority in the past. "There was a time," he said, "when American Secretary of State Dulles brandished thermonuclear bombs and followed a position of

[185] "Khrushchev asks Parley on Berlin but Warns U.S. of Soviet Troop Build-up," *New York Times*, August 8, 1961, p. 1. Note also the account in the *Times* of Khrushchev's August 11 speech, "Khrushchev Says Prestige Compels a German Treaty" (another headline suggesting continuing Soviet toughness), August 12, 1961, p. 1.

[186] McNamara to JCS Chairman, February 10, 1961, appendix A, enclosed in JCS 2101/408, CCS 3001 Basic National Security Policy (10 February 1961), RG 218, USNA. I am grateful to David Rosenberg for providing me with a copy of this document.

[187] Draft Memorandum for the President, November 21, 1962, on "Recommended FY 1964–FY 1968 Strategic Retaliatory Forces," p. 9, available from Freedom of Information Office, Office of the Secretary of Defense, Department of Defense, Washington. It is of course not clear who drafted this document, but it certainly reflected McNamara's basic thinking.

strength policy with regard to the socialist countries. . . . This was bare-faced atomic blackmail, but it had to be reckoned with at the time because we did not possess sufficient means of retaliation, and if we did, they were not as many and not of the same power as those of our opponents."[188]

Today, Khrushchev said, things were different, and implied that this was because the Soviets had achieved nuclear parity with the United States. This whole line of argument, however, left him vulnerable, at least in his own mind, to American suggestions in late 1961 that the United States still enjoyed clear strategic superiority. Deputy Secretary of Defense Gilpatric gave a speech on October 21 outlining how vast and how well-protected America's strategic nuclear forces actually were. According to Roger Hilsman, at the time a high official in the State Department, "the Gilpatric speech was followed by a round of briefings for our allies—deliberately including some whom we knew were penetrated, so as to reinforce and confirm through Soviet intelligence channels the message carried openly in the Gilpatric speech."[189]

The deterrent strategy seems to have been highly effective in late 1961, but one of the puzzles of the Berlin Crisis is that American officials did not seem to be aware of how well it was working. The most striking example of this was the Berlin Wall episode. The wall went up on August 13, just two days after Khrushchev's August 11 speech. If one were looking for something that would express Soviet acceptance of the status quo in Europe—of a divided Berlin and a divided Germany—what better symbol could there be than the Berlin Wall? Indeed, the direct purpose of the Wall was to help consolidate the status quo by putting an end to the great exodus from East Germany of many of its most skilled citizens. Even at the time, some of the most perceptive American observers understood that the closing of the border was something that would have to happen if the Soviets were to respect the status quo in West Berlin. "If we expect Soviets to leave Berlin problem as is," Ambassador Thompson had cabled from Moscow as early as March 16, "then we must expect East Germans to seal off sector boundary in order to stop what they must consider intolerable continuation of refugee flow through Berlin."[190]

Nevertheless, the sealing off of the border was interpreted at the highest political level not as the Soviets abandoning a policy which ultimately aimed at taking over all of Berlin, or which at least sought to exploit the threat of doing so, but rather as a serious escalation of the crisis, fore-shadowing further, and even more dangerous, Soviet moves in the near

[188] DG, pp. 718–19.

[189] Roger Hilsman, *To Move a Nation* (Garden City, N.Y., 1967), pp. 163–64.

[190] Thompson to Rusk, March 16, 1961, DDC 1977/46D. Note also the last paragraph of Bundy to the President, August 14, 1961, DDC 1986/910.

future. This was in spite of the fact that the Soviets had repeatedly gone out of their way to assure the Western Powers that "there would be no interference with allied traffic in and out of Berlin."[191] On August 14, the President fired off a couple of memoranda to Secretary McNamara. In light of the recent events in Berlin, he wanted to accelerate military preparations, and in particular urged that "we move ahead as quickly as possible on Civil Defense." McNamara then sent the following memo to the service secretaries: "As you know, our present Berlin military build-up is directed toward developing a capability to deploy to NATO up to six additional divisions, plus the associated air units, by January 1. The present closing of the East Berlin border may indicate that the Soviet Union is advancing its timetable. What can we do to accelerate our readiness date from January 1 to November 15?"[192]

Why this sense of crisis? Although there is no direct evidence to support this point, it is hard to avoid thinking that the reaction to the Wall in certain American circles, those most committed to an eventual reunification of Germany, had something to do with it. An undivided Berlin had come to symbolize this goal; the closing of the border was therefore an attack that needed to be resisted. This seems, for example, to have been behind Acheson's reaction. He was evidently willing to use force to bring about a return to "the *status quo ante* the wall." Only if the Russians were convinced that the U.S. was willing to go to the limit on this question, he said, could we "hope to go ahead toward the unity of the West and the reunification of Germany within it."[193] General Norstad also believed that military action should have been taken to tear down the Wall (although bizarrely he thought this was a decision for the local military commander in Berlin, and that no government could issue "orders to take such action").[194]

In any event, in late 1961 the United States continued with, and in some respects accelerated, its military preparations. In the earlier part of the year, the JCS had begun to study "non-nuclear military actions to reopen access to Berlin."[195] The existing plans for unilateral military action, Secretary McNamara pointed out in this context, were based on policy guid-

[191] Paul Nitze, *From Hiroshima to Glasnost: At the Center of Decision* (New York, 1989), p. 199.

[192] The two Kennedy memoranda: DDC 1985/1965, and NSF/82/Germany. Berlin. General, 8/11/61–8/15/61/JFKL. McNamara to service secretaries, August 18, 1961, CCS 9172 Berlin/3100 (9 Aug 61) sec 1/JCS 1961/USNA.

[193] Acheson to Clay, January 4, 1962, AP/65/State Department and White House Advisor 1962. January–December/HSTL.

[194] Memo of conversation between Johnson, Gavin, Finletter, and Norstad, September 30, 1961, DDC 1978/144B.

[195] JCS (Burke) Memorandum for the Secretary of Defense, April 28, 1961, NSF/81/Germany. Berlin. General. Report by the Joint Chiefs of Staff. Part 1. 5/5/61/JFKL.

ance left over from the Eisenhower period, and therefore did "not reflect new developments in U.S. strategic thinking."[196]

The 1961 plans put the emphasis on large-scale conventional operations, at least in the opening phases of a conflict. At some point, Soviet intentions might have to be tested with a small-scale probe of some sort. If this were resisted, the U.S. would not have to take further military action right away; a certain period of mobilization might be necessary. The important thing was that any military measures taken initially not be "irreversible."[197]

Was the ultimate goal to provide a totally non-nuclear defense of Europe—that is, to generate through mobilization whatever level of conventional military power was needed to meet any situation in which nuclear weapons were not used? This certainly was not the view of the military. The JCS, for example, thought the fundamental aim of the conventional buildup was to raise the nuclear threshold. Partial mobilization, as they understood it, had three basic goals:

a. Provide to USCINCEUR/SACEUR the capability to initiate military measures to reopen access to Berlin.

b. Provide sufficient forces to wage non-nuclear warfare on a scale which will indicate our determination and provide for some additional time to begin negotiation before resorting to nuclear warfare.

c. Provide increased readiness for the use of nuclear weapons should escalation to this level become necessary.[198]

The views of the civilians on this fundamental issue were more ambiguous.

What everyone agreed on, however, was that great emphasis should be placed on the deterrent effect of U.S. military preparations.[199] Information about these preparations leaked out to the press; in what may or may not have been a deliberate ploy, these reports were given additional credibility by the fact that the government appeared to be disturbed by the leaks and launched an FBI investigation.[200] Since information gathered

[196] Robert McNamara, Memorandum for the President, May 5, 1961, NSF/81/Germany. Berlin. General. Report by the Joint Chiefs of Staff. Part 1. 5/5/61/JFKL.

[197] This is based on a conversation with Paul Nitze, March 13, 1984. See also Nitze, *From Hiroshima to Glasnost*, pp. 203–4.

[198] Quoted in "The Defense Department Recommended Program Force Increases and Related Actions," [March 1961], pp. 2–3, DDC 1979/360A.

[199] See esp. the JCS Report of May 5, 1961, NSF/81/JFKL, and JCS to Norstad, May 30, 1961, CCS 9172/9105 (29 May 1961)/JCS 1961/USNA.

[200] See Don Cook, "De Gaulle to ask if Kennedy would fight for Berlin," *New York Herald Tribune*, May 29, 1961, and especially, "If You Want Peace . . . ," *Newsweek*, July 3, 1961. Note also "Factual Rundown on Newsweek Story," July 3, 1961, POF/117/Germany. Security 1/61–6/61/JFKL. For an argument that the FBI investigation was a tactic designed

through covert channels is often more credible than that derived from
open sources, there again seems to have been an attempt to exploit the
fact that Soviet intelligence had penetrated certain NATO governments.
Bringing the allies into U.S. contingency planning was thus, among other
things, a way to exert pressure on the Soviets. "For reasons which I cannot specify," Secretary Rusk later wrote, "we assumed that the Soviet
Union would become fully informed of these contingencies and would
take such possibilities into full account in their decisions about the follow
up to Chairman Khrushchev's ultimatum at Vienna about Berlin."[201]

By the end of 1961, a whole series of steps had been taken in preparation for an escalation of the crisis. These included certain moves in the
nuclear as well as the conventional area. Over State Department objections, Secretary McNamara decided to deploy 171 Davy Crocketts—a
very small nuclear weapon for infantry use—to Europe in December. He
felt that "these weapons may be urgently needed by our forces in the
event the Berlin crisis comes to a head and that short-run military considerations are overriding."[202] A certain amount of attention was given to
the selective use of nuclear weapons in Europe as part of a strategy for
the controlled manipulation of risk. Thomas Schelling, incidentally,
played a certain role in the policy process in 1961, although how much
of an impact his ideas had on operational strategy is very unclear.[203]

---

to "generate additional publicity," see Montague Kern, Patricia Levering, and Ralph Levering, *The Kennedy Crises: The Press, the Presidency and Foreign Policy* (Chapel Hill,
1983), pp. 80–81. These authors point out that prior to the *Newsweek* story, U.S. military
preparations "had been discussed before a large audience at a State Department briefing."

[201] Rusk to the author, January 25, 1984.

[202] Kohler to Nitze, October 27, 1961, and Nitze to Kohler, December 6, 1961, CCS 4712
Ground to Ground (10 Oct 1961)/JCS 1961/USNA.

[203] Schelling had written a short paper called "Nuclear Strategy in the Berlin Crisis," arguing that if nuclear weapons were to be used at all, their use should be thought of in
bargaining, as opposed to traditional military terms. This paper grew out of conversations
he had had in the spring of 1961 with Bundy and Henry Rowen. The paper was dated July
5; in a handwritten document called "JFK's Berlin Agenda," undated, but located in the
Berlin file for July 19–22, there is a reference to "Nuclear War—its flexibility (Schelling
Memo)." And on July 21, in a memo Bundy sent the President commenting on a series of
documents that he was enclosing for Kennedy to read over the weekend, there is the following passage: "A very intelligent paper from Thomas Schelling on nuclear strategy in Berlin.
If you find this paper at all persuasive, you will wish to start work on these problems in the
Defense Department where there is still a hideous jump between conventional warfare and
a single massive all-out blast." The Schelling paper is located in NSF/81/Germany. Berlin.
General. 7/1/61–7/6/61/JFKL. "JFK's Berlin Agenda" is in NSF/81/Germany. Berlin. General.
7/19/61–7/22/61. Bundy's comment on the Schelling paper is in NSF/318/ Index of Weekend
Papers 1/61–12/61. On the origins of the paper, see Schelling to the author, November 23,
1983.

On the question of operational content, the evidence is quite thin, as one might expect.
There is, however, a reference in one document to the FAST CAT command and control sys-

What was going on at the level of general war planning was also quite important. It is clear that the President and his chief advisors were not satisfied with the way the military had been dealing with this subject. If the Berlin Crisis escalated beyond the level of theater warfare, the only general war option the military had was the "one-shot response with all our nuclear forces" outlined in the SIOP.[204] Bundy and his aides Carl Kaysen and Henry Owen all agreed that the "current strategic war plan" was "dangerously rigid"; it "may leave you very little choice," Bundy told the President, "as to how you face the moment of thermonuclear truth."[205]

An alternative plan, which Kaysen worked on with Henry Rowen of the Defense Department, outlined an attack on Soviet strategic forces, mainly on long-range bomber bases and on the handful of ICBMs the Soviets then had. This "plan" was simply a rough calculation of what was possible. The project was evidently then taken up elsewhere in the Defense Department, and the planning effort became much more detailed. It was apparently expanded to include, for example, attacks on those Soviet nuclear forces that threatened Western Europe. It is hard to tell, however, what effect all of this had, and in particular whether, by the end of the year, the Air Force was prepared in operational terms to launch an attack of this sort.[206]

As for the crucial question of the President's own attitude, the available evidence does not support strong conclusions one way or the other. Even in the most extreme circumstances, should any sort of nuclear attack be launched? Kennedy was advised not to reveal his thinking on this issue, and he appears to have taken this advice to heart.[207] It is true that the instructions to General Norstad, approved by the President on October 20 or shortly thereafter, stated that "before any transition from non-nuclear to nuclear," he would "receive specific directives," and that "such transition would probably occur when Soviet forces sufficient to defeat

tem, which would permit "the instantaneous alert and release of selected nuclear delivery units assigned tasks under SACEUR's Nuclear Strike Plan." Enclosure B to JCS 2242/384, CCS 9050/4900 (26 Sept 1961)/JCS 1961/USNA. There is also a reference, almost certainly in October, to a letter that was to be sent to General Norstad. Norstad was "to spell out for President 'with particularity' operational concepts for command and control of selective nuclear attacks and limited tactical employment of nuclear weapons." Legere notes, Maxwell Taylor Papers/34/Items for Cable to Gen. Taylor/National Defense University, Washington. I am grateful to David Rosenberg for providing me with a copy of this material.

[204] Kaysen to Bundy, July 3, 1961, NSF/Germany. Berlin. General. 7/1/61–7/6/61/JFKL.

[205] "Covering note on Henry Kissinger's memo on Berlin," July 7, 1961, NSF/81/Germany. Berlin. General. Kissinger Report/JFKL.

[206] There is a brief account of this effort in Fred Kaplan, *The Wizards of Armageddon* (New York, 1983), but my understanding of this episode is based mainly on conversations with Kaysen himself.

[207] See, for example, a handwritten note from Rusk to the President at an NSC meeting, July 13, 1961, JFK Personal Papers/41/KP100-105.

non-nuclear efforts are brought into play."[208] But this may mainly have been for deterrent effect.[209]

While all this was going on in late 1961, important developments were also taking place on the political side. As with Eisenhower, the most striking thing here was the movement toward an accommodation with the Soviets, although the focus now was no longer Berlin itself, but rather Germany as a whole. Another major difference was that the Kennedy administration seemed much less inclined than its predecessor to defer to allied opinion.

At no point in the crisis was the idea of a negotiation with the Soviets simply ruled out. As Secretary Rusk put it in a conversation with Adenauer in August, General de Gaulle's view that "we are in Berlin and that if the Soviets disturb us we will shoot" was "not an adequate position in the sixties when we are considering a nuclear war." President Kennedy, he said, felt that if it did eventually come down to a decision to use military force, "it must be clear to all that every reasonable effort was made to find peaceful solutions, and that war was forced on us by the other side."[210]

In terms of substance, the shift in U.S. policy was dramatic. President Kennedy and his closest advisors were moving toward a position based on acceptance of the status quo in central Europe. In the NSC on June 29, Kennedy wondered "whether really it was to our advantage to press the argument for unification." Bundy a month earlier had broken with State Department orthodoxy and referred to "such items as the Oder-Neisse line and a de facto acceptance of a divided Germany" as open issues warranting "further discussion." By August 28, things had advanced consid-

---

[208] See the Legere notes cited at the end of n. 203. A draft of one of the documents referred to in Legere's notes, labeled simply "Meeting—Cabinet Room—Oct. 20, 1961," is in POF/116a/Germany. General. 8/61–10/61/JFKL.

[209] See the discussion in Nitze, *From Hiroshima to Glasnost*, pp. 203–4. Nitze here says that he thought at the time that "it would be best for us, in moving toward the use of nuclear weapons, to consider most seriously the option of an initial strategic strike of our own," in the sense of a limited preemptive attack on a small number of Soviet air bases. This conflicts somewhat with the account he gave me in 1984, when he said that he had discussed the issue with McNamara in some depth, but that the two of them in the final analysis ruled out the nuclear attack as too risky. Instead of a nuclear attack, he said, a naval blockade of the Soviet Union evidently struck them as the least unappealing option for dealing with the situation after a massive American defeat on the continent. I am inclined to believe the 1984 account (which does not strictly speaking absolutely contradict the account in his published memoir), because it seems to fit in better with Nitze's general approach, which was in the final analysis to accept defeat in Berlin rather than go to war, but not to "legitimize the act through a negotiated agreement." Ibid., pp. 196–97; see also Nitze to Lippmann, October 26, 1959, Box 23, Folder 295, Acheson Papers, Yale University Library, New Haven.

[210] Notes of U.S.-West German meeting, August 10, 1961, NSF/82/Germany. Berlin. General 8/9/61–8/10/61/JFKL.

erably: "the main line of thought among those who are now at work on the substance of our negotiating position," he wrote the President, "is that we can and should shift substantially toward acceptance of the GDR, the Oder-Neisse line, a non-aggression pact, and even the idea of two peace treaties."[211]

The President, at about this time, was very eager to move ahead. On August 21, he sent a memo to Secretary Rusk:

> I want to take a stronger lead on Berlin negotiations. Both the calendar of negotiation and the substance of the Western position remain unsettled, and I no longer believe that satisfactory progress can be made by Four-Power discussion alone. I think we should promptly work toward a strong U.S. position in both areas and should make it clear that we cannot accept a veto from any other power. We should of course be as persuasive and diplomatic as possible, but it is time to act.

"We should this week," he said, "make it plain to our three Allies that this is what we mean to do and that they must come along or stay behind." Again, it is clear he wanted to distance himself from the old U.S. line on German reunification. The American negotiating position, he said, should "protect our support for the *idea* of self-determination, the *idea* of all-Germany, and the *fact* of viable, protected freedom in West Berlin." With regard to the city itself, he thought we should "*not* insist on maintenance of occupation rights if other strong guarantees can be designed." And he also thought that the "option of proposing parallel peace treaties"—an idea which of course represented a certain movement toward acceptance of the East German regime—should be seriously considered.[212]

The State Department, however, seems to have dragged its feet in this area. Secretary Rusk's basic goal, it seems, was to play for time.[213] The

[211] Memorandum for Record, Discussion at NSC meeting June 29, 1961, NSF/313/NSC Meetings 1961. No. 486/JFKL; Bundy, Memorandum to the President, May 29, 1961, POF/126/USSR. Vienna Meeting. Background Documents (A); "The United States Position on Berlin" (State Department views), enclosed in Battle to Bundy, May 30, 1961, NSF/81/Germany. Berlin. General. 5/61; Carl Kaysen, "Thoughts on Berlin," August 22, 1961 (a strong, sustained argument for breaking with orthodoxy), NSF/82/Germany. Berlin. General. Kaysen Memo; Bundy to Kennedy, "Issues to be settled with General Clay," August 28, 1961, NSF/82/Germany. Berlin. General. 8/26/61–8/28/61.

[212] Kennedy to Rusk, August 21, 1961, NSF/82/Germany. Berlin. General. 8/21/61/JFKL. Emphasis in original text.

[213] See, for example, the first paragraph in Rusk to Kennedy, September 7, 1961, NSF/82/Germany. Berlin. General. 9/4/61–9/8/61/JFKL. Rusk (according to his later account), together with the British Foreign Secretary "decided that we would talk just as long and just as repetitively as the Russians were accustomed to doing and, over a period of time, we managed to talk most of the fever out of that situation." Rusk to the author, January 25, 1984.

margin for compromise with the Soviets, he thought, "had been ex-
hausted." There was "little meat on the bone." Khrushchev's prestige was
involved "and it would be difficult to save his face." A real solution was
just not in the cards. "His greatest ambition," he said, was "to pass the
Berlin question on to his successor."[214]

Given the way views on Berlin policy were developing, it is not surprising that top officials in the White House were increasingly dissatisfied
with the State Department.[215] Nor is it surprising that there was a certain
interest in bypassing Rusk and dealing with the problem more directly.
On September 12, Bundy raised for the President the problem of how to
reach the goal of a peace conference and parallel treaties with the two
German states, and proposed dealing directly with Adenauer through a
special presidential envoy.[216] (The German Chancellor was now not opposed to negotiations, provided they were held after the West German
elections scheduled for that month.) And on October 24, Bundy urged the
President to try to bring Adenauer around in a face-to-face meeting. The
meeting might be "crucial in winning the Chancellor's genuine and enthusiastic support." The U.S., he added, could "probably browbeat him into
acceptance of a reasonable negotiating position, but what we want is his
leadership, not his surrender."[217]

Did any of these efforts come to fruition, at least in some informal or
even tacit way? Soviet Foreign Minister Gromyko discussed these issues
with Kennedy, Rusk, and Thompson; there were other high-level U.S.-
Soviet contacts as well. But according to the standard accounts, "no real
progress was made"; the talks were "inconclusive," and simply served to
give Khrushchev a face-saving way to disengage; nothing was resolved,
but instead the crisis simply "faded away."[218]

Given the way American policy had been moving, and Kennedy's increasing unwillingness to defer to the allies, was it possible that these diplomatic exchanges were not as devoid of substance as these accounts suggest? After all, it seems the President was willing to go some way toward
meeting Soviet concerns. At Vienna he told Khrushchev that the U.S. "opposed any military buildup in West Germany that might threaten the Soviet Union"; what he objected to, it seems, was the Soviet demand that
the current situation be changed "overnight."[219] In fact, government

[214] Notes of U.S.-West German meeting, August 10, 1961, NSF/82/Germany. Berlin. General. 8/9/61–8/10/61/JFKL.

[215] This is reflected in the standard accounts: Sorensen, p. 596, Schlesinger, pp. 435–37.

[216] Bundy memo, September 12, 1961, NSF/82/Germany. Berlin. General. 9/9/61–9/12/
61/JFKL.

[217] Bundy to Kennedy, October 24, 1961, POF/117/Germany. Security. 8/61–12/61/JFKL.

[218] Sorensen, p. 598; Schlesinger, pp. 397–400.

[219] Schlesinger, p. 372.

opinion during this period had turned very dramatically against the whole idea of nuclear sharing; and with the introduction of permissive action links in the early 1960s, there was a de facto withdrawal from de facto sharing.[220] The U.S. also maintained its interest in the idea of a "security zone"—perhaps a zone of limited armaments—in central Europe. When Adenauer, as usual, objected vociferously to this idea, and in particular to the notion of a "special military status" for West Germany, Kennedy, in reply, agreed that the Federal Republic should not be singled out, but did make it clear that he wanted to keep the general issue open: "We think it would be worthwhile to see how the confrontation in Central Europe might be reduced."[221]

All of this meant that there was some basis for at least tacit understandings with the Soviets that could be reached in these bilateral talks. Indeed, Nitze's account of the proposal the Americans presented to Gromyko shows how far U.S. policy had evolved in the course of the crisis. Rusk, he says, "held out the prospect of an agreement that would prevent the spread of nuclear weapons"—something presumably which would, in particular, prevent West Germany from acquiring a nuclear capability. There would also be a "nonaggression pact between NATO and the Warsaw Pact," a measure that would tend to legitimate the existing political order in Europe. There would be "committees to be composed of equal numbers of East and West Germans" to deal with ostensibly " 'technical' contacts between the two Germanies," and an international access authority for West Berlin, on which East Germany would be represented. All of these positions ran directly counter to Adenauer's policy, and the West German government was very unhappy with the American proposal.[222]

There is not much hard evidence on the U.S.-Soviet Berlin negotiations,

[220] These shifting attitudes do not appear to have been a direct consequence of the Berlin Crisis: it was not as though people had realized that Soviet concerns about the nuclearization of West Germany lay at the heart of the crisis and therefore needed to be met in some way. If the Berlin Crisis played a role, it was by making issues of nuclear strategy less abstract, and of greater immediate concern, than they would otherwise have been; and this in turn led to the idea that if nuclear weapons had to be used, it was important that they be used in a controlled and discriminate way. This implied in turn that use should be governed by a single, central authority. This argument was for example laid out very explicitly for the allies in Secretary McNamara's (then secret) Athens speech in early 1962; a copy of this speech is available from the OSD Freedom of Information office in the Pentagon.

[221] Adenauer to Kennedy, October 4, 1961, DDC Retrospective/326F; Kennedy to Adenauer, October 13, 1961, POF/11/Germany. Security. 8/61–12/61/JFKL.

[222] Nitze, From Hiroshima to Glasnost, pp. 206–7. One should note that the records of these U.S.-Soviet negotiations are still highly classified. Since the Soviet government already knows what went on in these talks, one assumes that the U.S. government resists declassification because it does not want its allies, and especially the Germans, to know how far it was willing to go at the time.

but there is some material in the Acheson papers that strongly suggests that something serious was in the works in late 1961. On September 21, Acheson wrote a very private note to Truman to warn him about "developments which neither you nor I can prevent, but which neither one of us should support or condone." "I believe," he said, "that sometime this autumn we are in for a most humiliating defeat over Berlin." It seems clear that what he had in mind was a diplomatic settlement with the Communists: "The worst of it is not that eight years of Eisenhower inaction and one of Kennedy may have made the result inevitable, but that it will probably be dressed up as statesmanship of the new order, a refreshing departure from the bankrupt inheritance of the Truman-Acheson reliance on military power."[223]

On November 21, Acheson met with Adenauer, who, he wrote, was in a defeatist mood. Nuclear weapons, the German Chancellor felt, must not be used; the Soviets had clear conventional superiority; "therefore, we must negotiate." "The Germans," he said, "will leave it to us and not criticise if it turns out badly."[224]

At the end of the year, he still took a very somber view. General Clay had written him on December 29 that we were "facing the ultimate challenge now" and that the military balance was going to shift against us. "If we do not have the courage," Clay wondered, "or if we are deterred by Allied weakness in the short remaining period in which military odds are in our favor, what will we do when this is no longer true?" He thought therefore that "we should seek the confrontation sooner rather than later." Acheson fully agreed with this analysis, but took a darker view of the prospects. The allies, he wrote, were probably "scared to death" of a really tough military stand and would not cooperate. "But, even so, it is better to have the followers desert the leader, than to have the leader follow the followers. Who then picks up the pieces? Who is trusted to lead in a new start?"[225]

All of this has to be interpreted in the light of the fact that Acheson himself was by no means in favor of a totally rigid policy. He was willing, for example, to allow the East Germans to stamp allied documents, and was flexible on such issues as the Oder-Neisse line, a central European security zone, and German nuclear weapons.[226] It is hardly conceivable

[223] Acheson to Truman, September 21, 1961, AP/166/Acheson-Truman Correspondence, 1961/HSTL.

[224] Acheson memo, November 21, 1961, and Acheson to Marshall Shulman, November 23, 1961, AP/65/State Department and White House Advisor, 1961. October–December/ HSTL.

[225] Clay to Acheson, December 29, 1961, and Acheson to Clay, January 4, 1962, AP/65/ State Department and White House Advisor 1962. January–December/HSTL.

[226] See especially the Acheson Report of August 1, 1961, NSF/81/Germany. Berlin. Gen-

that he would condemn with such force a policy whose elements he himself had supported. It therefore seems that something was in the air in late 1961 that led Acheson to think that the Kennedy administration was willing to go a good deal further.

No arrangement, however, was worked out, and in 1962 Khrushchev, President Kennedy said, went "back to the same only Soviet position on Berlin." In fact, when the President saw Gromyko on October 17, the day after he had been informed that missiles had been discovered in Cuba, the Soviet foreign minister took a "very belligerent" line on Berlin—something, of course, which was bound to affect the way the U.S. government interpreted Soviet motives during the Missile Crisis.[227] Although the linkages are still very unclear, it seems in fact that the Cuban missile affair should be interpreted as the final phase of the Berlin Crisis: it was only after that episode that Berlin appears to have faded away as an issue.

THE MEANING OF THE BERLIN CRISIS

The world at the end of 1962 was very different from the world of November 1958. In the 1950s, the German question was still an open issue. In the 1960s, the division of Germany was accepted as a fact of life. In the late 1950s, it seemed West Germany was well on its way to acquiring nuclear weapons. By the early 1960s, it had become clear that the Federal Republic was not going to control nuclear forces of its own. By this time, it was also evident that American forces were in Europe on a permanent basis, whereas under Eisenhower the goal had been to bring the U.S. troops back home in the not-too-distant future. In general, it had seemed in the 1950s that events were in flux, but by the 1960s, the system of great power relations in Europe had acquired a certain permanence, and a certain stability.

Had anyone predicted that a system of this sort would emerge, and that it would provide the basis for a very durable peace? The predictions that were made pointed as a rule in the opposite direction: that Germany could not be kept down forever; that the Federal Republic would ultimately insist on not being so totally dependent on American nuclear protection, but would probably someday want nuclear forces of her own;

---

eral. Acheson Report 8/1/61/JFKL. Part of the package he called for (p. 9) was "a declaration by the Federal Republic indicating its intention not to produce or acquire nuclear warheads." Note also the reference in Bundy to Kennedy, October 24, 1961, to Acheson's approval of the "negotiating position that is emerging at the staff level." POF/117/Germany. Security. 8/61–12/61; also DDC 1986/2905.

[227] Memorandum of conversation between Kennedy and the Danish foreign minister, December 4, 1962, DDC 1984/2428.

that U.S. troops could not be expected to remain in Berlin, or even in Europe as a whole, on an indefinite basis; that NATO was bound to fall apart sooner or later; that the partition of Europe could not provide the basis for a stable peace. Yet all these predictions—every single one— turned out to be wrong.

How did it happen that a durable peace emerged in Europe? It was not an immediate by-product of the division of Europe between Western and Soviet armies in 1945: it took twenty years for a stable system to take shape. Nor was it a direct and automatic consequence of the nuclear revolution. Many people have claimed that nuclear weapons are the ultimate source of stability and that only they have kept the peace, but the real story is not nearly that simple. The idea that the basic effect of the coming of nuclear weapons was direct and overwhelming—that they served as a kind of deus ex machina bringing stability to a system that otherwise would have been quite unstable—is quite misleading. It is not just that nuclearization had complex effects that cut in many different directions, and that some of them were quite destabilizing in nature. The more basic point is that in the nuclear age as in the prenuclear past, the stability of the system is essentially a function of the structure of power, in a way that is largely (although obviously not entirely) independent of the particular form that power takes.

Instead, the emergence of a stable system has to be understood as the outcome of a long historical process. The system that took shape—where U.S. power balanced Soviet power, where both of these great states came finally to accept this status quo, and where no other state, especially not Germany, had any room to maneuver for basic change—did not come into being by design. Neither America nor Russia had originally wanted anything of the sort.

In this process the Berlin crisis played a central role. The crisis was the climax of a story that went back to 1945. This story revolved around the issue of power: what would be the structure of power in Europe? How in particular would the German question be resolved? On the military side, the key issue had to do with the role of nuclear weapons: were nuclear forces an effective instrument of statecraft, or did they essentially cancel each other out and play no real role beyond "deterring their use by others"?

The crisis served in effect to answer these questions. Policies were tested; difficult decisions had to be made. The result was to force a clarification—to lay bare the basic structure of the system. For the West, the crisis helped bring about what was in effect an acceptance of the status quo in central Europe. Perhaps the most striking thing to emerge from a study of the new evidence on this period is the degree to which both the Eisenhower and the Kennedy administrations had moved in this direction. By the end of 1961, German reunification had become a mere "idea" that one still had to pay lip service to, but nothing more. Hence Acheson's bitter reaction, which culminated in his extraordinary campaign in 1963 for an aggressive policy on the German question.[228] As far as the Germans themselves were concerned, the crisis had the effect of discrediting the rigid Adenauer line of the 1950s, and thus paved the way for the more flexible strategies of the late 1960s.

What limits did the nuclear revolution place on international politics? At what point would great powers like the United States and the Soviet Union draw the line and refuse to be pushed any further in a political dispute? Clearly the threat of nuclear war was not so overwhelming that both sides were too frightened to push forward at all. It is in fact striking how far the Soviets were able to go with what amounted to a crude strategy of just keeping the pot boiling and giving it a stir from time to time—and this during a period when the Americans clearly had the upper hand in terms of the strategic nuclear balance.

This did not, however, mean that there were no limits at all: as soon as the Soviets got their first real whiff of war, in July 1961, they quickly shifted course: the threatening tone at least temporarily disappeared, the deadline was again abandoned. This was based not so much on a calculation about what the Americans might *do*, but rather on a sense of what might *happen*—a visceral sense that things were moving to a point where perhaps no one would be able to control the situation. Nuclear weapons, therefore, had not simply neutralized each other, allowing international politics to proceed as though they did not exist at all. If Khrushchev had ever felt that he could proceed with total impunity, that he could push the West as far as he liked, because even a modest Soviet retaliatory capability completely canceled out American nuclear power, then he was rudely disabused of this misapprehension in 1961. The crisis had again clarified things. It had revealed something about the way international politics works in the nuclear age. While there was still a certain room for maneuver, there were also limits beyond which even a great power like the Soviet Union proved unwilling to go.

The Berlin Crisis, of course, was not the sole cause of all these changes. The argument here is simply that it played an important role in this basic historical process. It functioned partly as a catalyst, speeding up developments that probably would have taken place in any case, and partly as an independent cause, forcing people, for example, to deal with problems that they would otherwise have very much preferred to avoid.

[228] See especially his speech at the annual meeting of the Institute of Strategic Studies in September 1963, published in Adelphi Paper No. 5, *The Evolution of NATO*. The term "aggressive" is used advisedly. One passage in the speech boiled down to a call (in guarded language) for a policy of armed intervention in East Germany.

It was as though the system was coming to terms with its own basic structure. In the 1950s, a series of problems relating both to nuclear weapons and the German question had been building up. With the Berlin Crisis, these problems came to a head. The crisis might have led to war. If each side had dug in its heels and reacted to each hostile move by its adversary by toughening its own position, the crisis could easily have gotten out of hand. But neither side behaved in this way, and there was no war. Instead the storm had served to clear the air: the end of the Berlin Crisis marked the beginning of a new era.

CHAPTER SIX

The Influence of Nuclear Weapons in the Cuban Missile Crisis

WHAT ROLE did nuclear weapons play in the Cuban missile crisis, and what does the episode tell us about the broader problem of the political utility of nuclear forces? In 1983, a number of veterans of the Kennedy Administration were brought together to look back and reflect on the affair, and in their minds these questions had very clear answers. What the crisis showed, according to Robert McNamara, who had been Secretary of Defense at the time, was that America's superiority in numbers of nuclear weapons "was not such that it could be translated into usable military power to support political objectives."[1] Dean Rusk, the Secretary of State under Kennedy, made an even stronger claim: "The simple fact is that nuclear power does not translate into usable political influence."[2] And indeed the argument is often made that the crisis demonstrates the political insignificance of the nuclear balance—or even the political irrelevance of nuclear weapons in general.[3]

On the other hand, there have always been those who maintained that America's "overwhelming strategic superiority," or simply the American

---

This article originally appeared in *International Security* in the summer of 1985. I am grateful to the editors and to MIT Press for permission to republish it here.

[1] Transcript of Discussion about the Cuban Missile Crisis, June 28, 1983, pp. 1–2, Alfred Sloan Foundation, New York; hereinafter cited as "Sloan transcript, June 28, 1983." I am grateful to Arthur Singer for allowing me to view the videotapes of these discussions. McGeorge Bundy, who in 1962 had been Kennedy's national security adviser, elaborated the point: America's superiority, it was felt at the time, "was not a usable superiority in the sense that we would ever want to go first because if even one Soviet weapon landed on an American target, we would all be losers." Sloan transcript, January 27, 1983, reel 6, take 1, p. 7.

[2] Sloan transcript, January 27, 1983, reel 6, take 1, p. 40.

[3] See, for example, the joint statement by six veterans of the crisis (McNamara, Bundy, Rusk, Sorensen, Gilpatric, and Ball) in *Time* magazine, September 27, 1982: "The Cuban missile crisis illustrates not the significance but the insignificance of nuclear superiority in the face of survivable thermonuclear retaliatory forces" (Rusk et al., "The Lessons of the Cuban Missile Crisis," p. 85). See also Walter Slocombe, *The Political Implications of Strategic Parity*, Adelphi Paper no. 77 (London: Institute for Strategic Studies, May 1971), pp. 18–20 (although his Appendix 2, where he sets out his argument in greater detail, is more modest in tone); and Benjamin Lambeth, "Deterrence in the MIRV Era," *World Politics*, vol. 24, no. 2 (January 1972), pp. 230–34.

willingness to risk nuclear war, had a good deal to do with the course that the crisis took.[4] Bernard Brodie, for example, took it for granted that America's "nuclear superiority" had been crucial in 1962. It was, he said, "a mischievous interpretation" of the crisis "to hold that its outcome was determined mostly by our conventional superiority."[5]

In the twenty years that have passed since the confrontation took place, claims about the Cuban missile crisis have played an important role in the discussion of strategic issues. Theories are tested by events, and people have looked to the sharpest crisis of the nuclear age for answers: how much of a political shadow do nuclear weapons cast? These debates, however, have always had a rather abstract and speculative character. But thanks to the release in the last few years of an extraordinary series of documents on the crisis, it is now possible to study these issues on the basis of hard empirical evidence.[6]

What does the missile crisis tell us about the way nuclear weapons affect international politics? The problem will be approached here by examining three schools of thought—about the crisis, and about the political utility of nuclear forces in general.

There is first the thesis that nuclear weapons played no political role at all in 1962—that is, that their sole function was to deter their use by others. Thus General Maxwell Taylor, the Chairman of the Joint Chiefs of Staff at the time, once flatly stated that "the strategic forces of the United States and the U.S.S.R. simply cancelled each other out as effectual instruments for influencing the outcome of the confrontation."[7] And

[4] See, for example, Arnold Horelick, "The Cuban Missile Crisis: An Analysis of Soviet Calculations and Behavior," World Politics, vol. 16, no. 3 (April 1964), pp. 387–88; and Jerome H. Kahan and Anne K. Long, "The Cuban Missile Crisis: A Study of its Strategic Context," Political Science Quarterly, vol. 87 (December 1972), esp. pp. 579–81, 586; and especially Thomas C. Schelling, Arms and Influence (New Haven: Yale University Press, 1966), pp. 95–96.

[5] Bernard Brodie, "What Price Conventional Capabilities in Europe?," Rand Paper P-2696 (Santa Monica, Calif.: Rand Corporation, February 1963), pp. 24–25; also published in The Reporter, May 23, 1963. Note also Brodie's comment in a letter to the French strategist Pierre Gallois of July 21, 1965: "I do not think gross superiority matters as little as you suggest. The Cuban affair of 1962 does not bear you out. . . . The reasons are several, but it is mostly that neither side threatens the other with total war. Instead they simply threaten actions which could escalate" (Box 1, Brodie Papers, UCLA).

[6] Some of the most interesting material—extracts from the transcript of two secretly taped meetings held at the White House on October 16, and the minutes of two ExCom meetings held on October 27—was reproduced in International Security, vol 10, no. 1 (Summer 1985). But the recently declassified material represents only a small portion of the Kennedy Library's holdings on the crisis. And there are important, but still unavailable, sources in other archives, and in private hands as well—for example, the extensive, almost verbatim notes that Paul Nitze took of meetings during the crisis.

[7] Maxwell D. Taylor, "The Legitimate Claims of National Security," Foreign Affairs, vol. 52, no. 3 (April 1974), p. 582. Taylor here denied that America's "strategic superiority"

claims of this sort are often linked to more general arguments about the "uselessness" of nuclear forces. "Nuclear weapons," McNamara recently argued, "serve no military purpose whatsoever. They are totally useless— except only to deter one's opponent from using them."[8] From this point of view, it was the balance of conventional forces that was decisive.

A second major school of thought argues that nuclear weapons did matter, because the *risk* of nuclear war was bound to affect political behavior. This argument takes two basic forms. On the one hand, there is the notion of "existential deterrence": the mere existence of nuclear forces means that, whatever we say or do, there is a certain irreducible risk that an armed conflict might escalate into a nuclear war. The fear of escalation is thus factored into political calculations: faced with this risk, states are more cautious and more prudent than they would otherwise be.

On the other hand, there is the notion that risk is not simply an inescapable fact of life. The level of risk is instead seen as something that can be deliberately and consciously manipulated. As Thomas Schelling laid out the argument: international politics in the nuclear age often takes the form of a "competition in risk taking, characterized not so much by tests of force as by tests of nerve." The "manipulation of risk" was therefore the means of getting the upper hand in what was ultimately a kind of bargaining situation.[9] The missile crisis was Schelling's prime example: "The Cuban Crisis was a contest in risk taking, involving steps that would have made no sense if they led predictably and ineluctably to a major war, yet would also have made no sense if they were completely without danger."[10]

A third school of thought claims that it was the balance of nuclear capabilities, and not the balance of resolve or conventional capabilities, that proved decisive. This interpretation is not logically inconsistent with the approach that emphasizes risk, since a government's ability to manipulate risk might depend largely on the military power at its disposal. But those who emphasize the strategic balance tend to assume that its effects are virtually automatic: the Soviets were outgunned in 1962, and they had no choice but to accept the terms the United States insisted on.

---

played a meaningful role in the crisis. But at the time he had taken a radically different line: "We have the strategic advantage in our general war capabilities," he wrote McNamara on October 26, 1962. ". . . This is no time to run scared." Quoted in John Lewis Gaddis, *Strategies of Containment* (New York: Oxford University Press, 1982), p. 229n.

[8] Robert S. McNamara, "The Military Role of Nuclear Weapons: Perceptions and Misperceptions," *Foreign Affairs*, vol. 62, no. 1 (Fall 1983), p. 79. Note also his comments on the role of nuclear forces in the missile crisis in Gregg Herken, *Counsels of War* (New York: Knopf, 1985), p. 167.

[9] Schelling, *Arms and Influence*, p. 94.

[10] Ibid., p. 96.

NO ROLE AT ALL?

Is it true that the strategic forces of the United States and the Soviet Union "simply cancelled each other out" during the crisis? This claim is generally based on the notion that nuclear weapons are "unusable" weapons—that they are good only for deterring their use by others. This implies, with regard to the crisis, that nuclear forces neutralized each other and thus had no real effect on either side: it was as though they had been simply swept off the board, and that matters proceeded as though they did not exist. The effect of this line of argument, therefore, is to emphasize the importance of conventional forces—that is, of America's conventional predominance in the Caribbean.

The notion that nuclear forces cannot be harnessed to political purpose is thus often based on the assumption that the President of the United States would never deliberately start a nuclear war.[11] But if war could come without such a deliberate and conscious decision on the part of either the President or his Soviet counterpart, then the risk of war would be real and would therefore inevitably affect political behavior. The evidence in fact shows that: (1) leading officials believed that nuclear war could come without either side having to make a cold-blooded decision to start one; (2) these officials were willing during the crisis to accept a certain risk of nuclear war; and (3) the risk of nuclear war was consciously manipulated in order to affect Soviet options in the crisis.

First, McNamara, for example, in the postmortem he gave to a Congressional committee in February 1963, demonstrated a clear grasp of the logic of escalation—that is, of how one's actions could set off a chain of events over which one could exercise only limited control. If America had invaded Cuba, he said, thousands of Soviet soldiers would have been killed, and the Soviets "probably would have had to respond." Some of the Soviet missiles in Cuba might have been armed and operational, and if they were, "they might have been launched," so there was a danger of nuclear war. "In any event," he continued, Soviet leader Nikita Khrushchev "knew without any question whatsoever that he faced the full military power of the United States, including its nuclear weapons." McNamara's conclusion was chilling: "we faced that night the possibility of

---

[11] Note, for example, the logic of McGeorge Bundy's argument in "To Cap the Volcano," *Foreign Affairs*, vol. 48, no. 1 (October 1969), pp. 9–11—how he moves from the point about the impossibility of "any sane political authority" consciously starting a nuclear war to the conclusion about the irrelevance of the strategic balance; or the kind of argument McNamara makes in the Sloan transcript, June 28, 1983, pp. 1–2.

launching nuclear weapons and Khrushchev knew it, and that is the reason, and the only reason, why he withdrew those weapons."[12]

The general point that a nuclear war was possible because events could have a momentum of their own, quite apart from the conscious intent of statesmen, has been a staple of the strategic literature since the late 1950s. Even those who base claims about the irrelevance of the nuclear balance on the argument that no rational government would ever deliberately start a nuclear war have frequently argued along these lines. "The gravest risk in this crisis," according to McGeorge Bundy, McNamara, and four other former members of the Kennedy Administration, "was not that either head of government desired to initiate a major escalation but that events would produce actions, reactions or miscalculations carrying the conflict beyond the control of one or the other or both."[13]

Second, the highest officials in the American government clearly recognized that a confrontation with the Soviet Union would entail a certain risk of nuclear war. But they felt that this was a risk that simply had to be accepted. As Rusk put it on October 16: "I think we'll be facing a situation that could well lead to general war." The case of Secretary McNamara is again particularly interesting in this connection. On October 16, he argued that an attack on Cuba, after any of the missiles there were operational, would pose too great a risk: some of those missiles might survive an attack and be launched, and this could lead to a thermonuclear holocaust. But by October 27—that is, after the CIA had reported that some of the missiles on the island were indeed operational—McNamara declared that "we must now be ready to attack Cuba. . . . Invasion had become almost inevitable." In other words, even he, who was quite conservative in this regard, was willing by this point to accept what by his own reckoning was a serious risk of nuclear war.[14]

---

[12] U.S. Congress, House of Representatives, Committee on Appropriations, Subcommittee on Department of Defense Appropriations, "Department of Defense Appropriations for 1964," February 6, 1963, p. 31. Note also the discussion of the escalation problem on pp. 152–56 below.

[13] For the point about the strategic literature, see Bernard Brodie, *Strategy in the Missile Age* (Princeton: Princeton University Press, 1959), p. 355; and Albert Wohlstetter, "Nuclear Sharing: NATO and the N + 1 Country," *Foreign Affairs*, vol. 39, no. 3 (April 1961), pp. 378–79. Note also Bundy, "To Cap the Volcano," p. 18; and his "Strategic Deterrence After Thirty Years: What Has Changed?," *Atlantic Community Quarterly*, vol. 17, no. 4 (Winter 1979–80), p. 486. The quotation is from Rusk et al., "Lessons of the Cuban Missile Crisis," p. 86.

[14] For Rusk, see Presidential Recordings, Transcripts, Cuban Missile Crisis Meetings, October 16, 1962, first meeting (11:50 a.m.–12:57 p.m.), p. 10, President's Office Files, John F. Kennedy Library, Boston. Henceforth this source will be cited as "October 16 transcripts, I" (for the 11:50 meeting) or "II" (for the second meeting, which lasted from 6:30 to 7:45 p.m.). For McNamara, see October 16 transcripts, I, pp. 11, 13; "Summary Record of NSC

Finally, there is the point that the specter of nuclear war was deliberately manipulated to support American objectives in the crisis. McNamara, for example, pointed out on October 16 that American military action would probably lead to a Soviet military response "some place in the world." The United States, he argued, should recognize that possibility "by trying to deter it, which means we probably should alert SAC, probably put on an airborne alert, perhaps take other s-, alert measures. These bring risks of their own, associated with them."[15] (McNamara here was probably referring to the danger that too much might be read into these preparations, and that they might touch off a Soviet preemptive attack. The fear of preemption was widely viewed at the time as lying at the heart of a semiautomatic process of escalation.)

Note that McNamara's assumption was that nuclear preparations would serve to deter Soviet responses *in general*; that is, the implied nuclear threat was not directed simply at the possibility that the USSR might consider using its *nuclear forces*. If the missiles in Cuba were attacked, the Soviets would very much want to take some kind of counteraction—in Berlin, most probably, or against Turkey, or maybe even in Iran or Korea—and the United States had to take "a whole series of precautionary measures. . . . All of our forces should be put on alert, but beyond that, mobilization, redeployment, movement and so on."[16] The threat of general war—in fact, the threat of any U.S.-Soviet war, because of the risk of escalation it would inevitably entail—would be the means of dealing with these possible Soviet countermoves. These deterrent threats, by reducing the probability of any direct Soviet retaliation, would thus increase America's freedom of action in Cuba.

It is clear, therefore, that the risk of nuclear war did play a role. Indeed, this risk was overtly and deliberately exploited. But this was a deadly

Executive Committee Meeting No. 8, October 27, 1962, 4:00 PM," p. 5, Box 316, National Security Files, John F. Kennedy Library (and also published below)—cited hereinafter as "ExCom Minutes" with number and date; CIA Report, "Major Consequences of Certain U.S. Courses of Action in Cuba," October 20, 1962, reporting that 16 MRBMs were then operational, and arguing that it was "prudent to assume" that nuclear warheads for them would be available, Declassified Documents Collection, 1975, 48E.

[15] October 16 transcripts, II, p. 10; see also Dillon's remarks, ibid., I, p. 27. The same kind of point might be made about the effect of American military preparations during the Berlin crisis the previous year. In a letter to Chancellor Adenauer of October 13, 1961, President Kennedy remarked cryptically, "The Soviets have been warned and they appear to have taken cognizance of the warning that our present course is dangerous to them" (Box 117, Folder "Germany. Security. 8/61–12/61," President's Office Files, John F. Kennedy Library). Note, finally, General Burchinal's remarks, quoted below, p. 157.

[16] October 16 transcripts, II, pp. 49–50. For discussion of the measures that were in fact taken, see Scott D. Sagan, "Nuclear Alerts and Crisis Management," *International Security*, vol 9, no. 4 (Spring 1985), pp. 106–22.

game, played reluctantly and without any trace of enthusiasm. Political necessity—the logic of the confrontational situation—prevailed over the government's horror of nuclear war and led it to adopt tactics of this sort.

THE BALANCE OF RESOLVE

The specter of nuclear war influenced both Soviet and American policy. But did these nuclear fears and anxieties simply make both sides equally cautious, or were the effects uneven?

The fear of a Soviet countermove against Berlin weighed heavily on American policy during the crisis. This was what McNamara wanted to prevent by taking his "series of precautionary measures." But why was it assumed that the prospect of nuclear war would have such a one-sided effect? The Soviets would be deterred from moving against the city (even though their forces in the Caribbean might already have been attacked); but the Americans presumably would not be deterred by the same threat of war from following through with their policy of defending the city. It was taken for granted that the same risk would have unequal effects.

The situation in the Caribbean was the mirror image of the situation around Berlin. The Americans had conventional predominance, but (given that the missiles had already been put in) the United States was the power that was threatening to alter an existing situation. If the nuclear threat had perfectly symmetrical effects, American power should have been as stalemated around Cuba as Soviet power was around Berlin. But the fact that this was not the case shows that fears and anxieties were not perfectly in balance: the balance of resolve favored the United States.

Thus an invasion of Cuba might lead to a general war. This put pressure on the Soviets to head off that invasion and accept terms. The Americans, for similar reasons, were also under pressure to settle the crisis before matters came to a head. But the pressures were not equal: if a settlement had not been reached, the United States, in spite of the risks that U.S. leaders themselves recognized, would almost certainly have invaded Cuba at the end of October.

How much of an imbalance was there? And what determines the level of tolerable risk? One way to test this issue is to examine the case of the Jupiters—that is, the question of an arrangement involving the withdrawal of the American Jupiter missiles from Turkey in exchange for a withdrawal of the Soviet missiles from Cuba.

Kennedy, according to his close adviser Theodore Sorensen, was "quite amazed" when Treasury Secretary Douglas Dillon (who had also served under Eisenhower) told him during the crisis that "everyone knows that those Jupiter missiles aren't much good anyway. We only put them in there during the previous Administration because we didn't know what else to do with them, and we really made the Turks and the Italians take them."[17] Could the Jupiters therefore be removed in exchange for a withdrawal of the Soviet missiles in Cuba? It is well known that the idea was seriously considered by American officials during the crisis, well before the Soviet government even formally proposed a "deal" of this sort.[18]

What has not been clear, however, is the degree to which the President was personally in favor of such an arrangement. In fact, there were from the outset very precise assurances to the contrary. When McNamara, for example, was asked during his congressional testimony in February 1963 about a trade involving the missiles in Turkey, he said that "the President absolutely refused to discuss it at the time, and no discussion took place."[19] Taking such claims at face value, historians and political scientists have constructed many arguments on the basis of President Kennedy's supposed refusal to consider a trade.[20]

On the other hand, a number of scholars have argued, essentially on the basis of Robert Kennedy's memoir on the crisis, that there is fact was a "deal."[21] According to Robert Kennedy, the Soviet Ambassador was told on October 27 that the President "had been anxious to remove those missiles from Turkey and Italy for a long period of time. He had ordered their removal some time ago, and it was our judgment that, within a short time after this crisis was over, those missiles would be gone."[22] On the basis of these assurances, so the argument goes, the Soviets agreed to withdraw their missiles from Cuba. And within the space of a few months, the Jupiters were in fact dismantled. Did this mean that a "bargain" had been struck?

There are two ways in which the documents throw some light on this issue. First of all, the Executive Committee minutes show very clearly that

[17] Transcript of oral history interview of Theodore Sorensen, by Carl Kaysen, March 26, 1964, pp. 65–66, Kennedy Library.

[18] See *The New York Times*, December 6, 1962, p. 3:1; Arthur M. Schlesinger, Jr., *Robert Kennedy and His Times* (Boston: Houghton Mifflin, 1978), p. 515; and Abram Chayes, *The Cuban Missile Crisis* (New York: Oxford University Press, 1974), pp. 81–82, 98–99.

[19] U.S. Congress, "Department of Defense Appropriations for 1964," p. 57; see also p. 74. Note also the passage in Theodore Sorensen, *Kennedy* (New York: Harper & Row, 1965), p. 714.

[20] See for example Jack Snyder, "Rationality at the Brink: The Role of Cognitive Processes in Failures of Deterrence," *World Politics*, vol. 30, no. 3 (April 1978), esp. pp. 354–55; and Barton J. Bernstein, "The Cuban Missile Crisis: Trading the Jupiters in Turkey?," *Political Science Quarterly*, vol. 95, no. 1 (Spring 1980), pp. 97–125.

[21] Graham T. Allison, *Essence of Decision: Explaining the Cuban Missile Crisis* (Boston: Little, Brown, 1971), p. 218, 228–30; Chayes, *The Cuban Missile Crisis*, p. 98; and Schlesinger, *Robert Kennedy*, pp. 520–24.

[22] Robert F. Kennedy, *Thirteen Days* (New York: W. W. Norton, 1969), pp. 108–9.

at the peak of the crisis, on October 27, with an invasion of Cuba imminent, President Kennedy was in fact the strongest advocate of a trade in that high policy-making group. Repeatedly, he returned to the theme that some kind of trade involving the Jupiters would eventually be necessary. What he plainly wanted was to get the Russians to stop working on the missile sites in Cuba and maybe also make the missiles there inoperable; this would then be followed by a negotiation involving the missiles in Turkey. But he was opposed on this issue by all of his chief advisers. Rusk, Bundy, and his brother Robert all came out against the idea. Even McNamara was arguing by this point that an invasion of Cuba, which the President was then defining as the only alternative to a trade, was "almost inevitable."

The second point is that what Robert Kennedy told the Soviet Ambassador that very evening was not quite accurate: although the government had been interested in withdrawing the Jupiters for some time, their removal had not actually been *ordered* prior to the crisis.[23] What Dobrynin was told was thus not just a simple statement of fact: a concession of sorts was being made, but it was a disguised concession. In view of the President's attitude about a trade and the more hostile attitude of his advisers, what all this implies is that the settlement that emerged after the assurances were given to Dobrynin should probably be understood as the conflation of a negotiation—as an "imposed negotiated solution," so to speak.

Thus Kennedy had not ruled out an arrangement involving the Jupiters, and McNamara's recent comment about the President's attitude rings true: "I recall him saying very well, 'I am not going to go to war over worthless missiles in Turkey. I don't want to go to war anyhow, but I am certainly not going to go to war over worthless missiles in Turkey.' "[24]

But the implication here is that it was taken for granted that the level of risk should be commensurate with the political importance of the issues in dispute. If ultimately the issue came down to whether America was willing to withdraw the "worthless" Jupiter missiles from Turkey,

---

[23] Roger Hilsman, a high State Department official at the time, claimed in his memoirs that the President had "ordered—in August 1962—that steps be taken immediately to remove the American missiles from Turkey." *To Move a Nation* (Garden City, N.Y.: Doubleday, 1967), p. 203; repeated in Schlesinger, *Robert Kennedy*, p. 519, and Allison, *Essence of Decision*, p. 226. But the document Hilsman evidently had in mind, National Security Action Memorandum 181 of August 23, 1962, merely stated that "in the light of evidence of new bloc activity in Cuba," the President had directed that the Defense Department study the question of "what action can be taken to get Jupiter missiles out of Turkey?" (Box 338, Folder "Cuba(4). 8/23/62." National Security Files, Kennedy Library). On the myth of the presidential "order," see in particular Bernstein, "Trading the Jupiters," pp. 102–4, and esp. n. 24.

[24] Sloan transcript, June 28, 1983, p. 63.

then, no matter what the strategic balance was, the President was not going to dig in his heels and risk a nuclear holocaust over that. Kennedy's eagerness for something like a political settlement was therefore rooted not in a conviction that nuclear forces were politically impotent, but rather in the notion that the main obstacle to a solution was too trivial to warrant any serious risk of nuclear war. The same logic, however, implies that his attitude about the kind of risk worth running might have been very different if the political issues at stake had been viewed as basic—as in fact they had been during the Berlin crisis the previous year.

Thus one is struck, on the one hand, by the President's aversion to risk: he certainly did not view the crisis as a "contest in risk taking" in which the goal was to outbid the other side. But on the other hand, Kennedy's aversion to risk was by no means absolute: during the crisis, the Soviets were after all under enormous pressure. In fact the new evidence about the final settlement supports the idea that the basic situation was not one of simple parity. If the settlement was not tantamount to a Soviet capitulation, it was not really a bargain either—and above all, not a bargain between equals.

THE ROLE OF THE STRATEGIC BALANCE: THE AMERICAN SIDE

Political concerns therefore played an important role in determining the kind of risk the American government was willing to take on. But how did military factors affect the course of the crisis? Would it in particular have made a difference in 1962 if "the relative strategic positions of the Soviet Union and the United States had been reversed"? In 1969 Mc-George Bundy said no: "A stalemate is a stalemate either way around."[25] But what does the historical evidence suggest?

In theory, the strategic balance could have played a role by influencing either American policy or Soviet policy or both. This section will be concerned mainly with how the Americans might have been affected; the Soviet side will be examined in the next section. Three issues in particular will be considered here: (1) did people at the time think that America's strategic superiority would be decisive? (2) how did people deal with the narrower problem of the military significance of the Soviet missiles in Cuba? (3) how was the problem of escalation handled, and how does this bear on the problem of the strategic balance?

To begin with the crudest way in which the balance might have played a role: was the American government more willing to face the prospect of general war with the Soviet Union because it knew that damages, even in the worst case, could be limited to a certain "tolerable" level of dev-

[25] Bundy, "To Cap the Volcano," p. 11.

astation? Actually, there is no evidence that President Kennedy and his advisers counted missiles, bombers, and warheads, and decided on that basis to take a tough line. The veterans of the crisis have often denied that any calculation of that sort had been made, and there is no reason to dispute them on this point.[26] Few assumed at the time that the strategic balance in itself meant that the USSR would almost automatically back down; and there is no evidence at all in the documents that anyone believed that the United States could face a war with confidence because of its vast nuclear power.

In fact, one of the most striking things about the transcript of the secretly taped October 16 meeting between Kennedy and his main advisers is that no one even touched on the issue of what exactly would happen if the crisis escalated to the level of general war—although of course everyone might have learned all they felt they needed to know about the issue in some other way. But one does come away from the transcript with the sense that even rough calculations of this sort were not terribly important. No one discussed what American counterforce capabilities were—that is, how well the United States might be able to "limit damage" in the event of an all-out war. It was as though all the key concepts associated with the administration's formal nuclear strategy, as set out for example just a few months earlier in McNamara's famous Ann Arbor speech—in fact, the whole idea of controlled and discriminate general war—in the final analysis counted for very little. One of President Kennedy's remarks on October 16 seems to capture this feeling: "What difference does it make? They've got enough to blow us up now anyway."[27]

But the absence of a crude belief in the decisiveness of the strategic balance does not in itself mean that the issue was not present in less direct ways. People were in fact concerned with the problem of whether the deployment of missiles in Cuba would make an important difference in military terms. The positions taken on this question reflect, in a rather crude and imperfect way to be sure, basic attitudes about the significance of shifts in the strategic balance. They thus can function as something of a surrogate for more direct notions about the role of the nuclear balance.

It is sometimes claimed that the general belief among high administration officials was that the deployment would not count for much from a strictly military point of view. And the chief document used to support this argument is a Sorensen memorandum of October 17, which claimed that it was "generally agreed that these missiles, even when fully operational, do not significantly alter the balance of power—i.e., they do not

---

[26] See, for example, Rusk in Sloan Transcript, January 27, 1983, reel 6, take 1, p. 40; or Paul H. Nitze, "Assuring Strategic Stability in an Era of Détente," *Foreign Affairs*, vol. 54, no. 2 (January 1976), pp. 214–16.

[27] October 16 transcripts, II, p. 15.

significantly increase the potential megatonnage capable of being unleashed on American soil, even after a surprise American nuclear
strike."[28] But Sorensen was simply wrong on this point: there was in fact
no consensus on the issue of whether the deployment of the missiles really
mattered on strategic terms. The transcript of the October 16 discussions
makes this very clear. "What," Bundy asked, "is the strategic impact on
the position of the United States of MRBM's in *Cuba*? How gravely does
this change the strategic balance?" And McNamara answered as follows:
"Mac, I asked the Chiefs that this afternoon, in effect. And they said,
substantially. My own personal view is, not at all."[29]

What the military, and for that matter the CIA as well, were worried
about was that the missiles currently in Cuba might just be an opening
wedge, preparing the way for a more massive buildup there. The larger
the force, the more the Soviets would be able, in the words of the CIA
assessment, "to blunt a retaliatory attack,"[30] and thus to threaten the

[28] In Box 48, Folder "Cuba. General. 10/17/62–10/27/62." Sorensen Papers. Kennedy
Library. This document is the basis for Bernstein's claim, in "Trading the Jupiters," that the
missiles "did not alter the strategic balance" (p. 118). In an earlier article, he developed this
point at greater length, arguing, on the basis of the Sorensen memorandum, that most
ExCom members agreed (among other things) that the development of the missiles in Cuba
"did not add to the likelihood of a Soviet first strike." But there is *nothing at all* in the
Sorensen document that even remotely deals with this question. Bernstein's claim was made
in his "The Week We Almost Went to War," *Bulletin of the Atomic Scientists*, vol. 32, no.
2 (February 1976), p. 16. It is of course odd that Sorensen in this document takes megatonnage as the basic index of strategic power—and this a couple of years after the total megatonnage of the American nuclear arsenal had begun its long and dramatic decline. The Kennedy Administration, in fact, wanted other things besides sheer destructive power from its
strategic forces. In one typical document, Rusk called for improvements in the American
strategic force "which would increase its survivability, its flexibility, and its ability to be
used under a wide range of contingencies" (Rusk to McNamara, enclosed in Rusk to Bundy,
October 29, 1961, Box 275, Folder "Department of Defense. Defense Budget FY 1963. 1/
16–10/61," National Security Files, Kennedy Library). A shift in the strategic balance could
be meaningful if it affected any of these things; and Rusk later recalled that in 1962 "we
were concerned on the military side that substantial numbers of missiles in Cuba . . . could
knock out our Strategic Air Command bases with almost no advance warning—they were
so close" (Sloan transcripts, January 27, 1983, reel 1, take 1, p. 18).

[29] October 16 transcripts, II, p. 12.

[30] Gen. Taylor in October 16 transcripts, II, p. 13; CIA Report, "Soviet Reactions to Certain US Courses of Action on Cuba," October 19, 1962, Annex B ("Military Significance of
Ballistic Missiles in Cuba"), Declassified Documents Collection, 1975, p. 48D. Note also
Raymond Garthoff's analysis, written at the end of the crisis: his memorandum on "The
Military Significance of the Soviet Missile Bases in Cuba" of October 27, 1962 was published (with commentary) in his article "The Meaning of the Missiles," *Washington Quarterly*, vol. 5, no. 4 (Autumn 1982), pp. 78–79, and again in his "A Retrospective Look at a
1962 Evaluation of the Soviet Missiles in Cuba," an addendum to *Intelligence Assessment
and Policymaking: A Decision Point in the Kennedy Administration* (Washington, D.C.:
Brookings, 1984), pp. 32–33. In his commentary, Garthoff asserted that the question of

United States with a first strike. Neither President Kennedy nor anyone else at the meeting, however, seemed much concerned with how such a deployment would affect the vulnerability of America's strategic forces. But Kennedy did seem concerned that the initial deployment might be followed by a more massive one. He in fact linked this point to Mc-Namara's argument about how the United States could not contemplate military action against the island once the missiles there were operational. No one could be sure an air strike would destroy all the missiles, and if any remained, some of them might be launched against America:

> Let's just say that, uh, they get, they get these in there and then you can't, uh, they get sufficient capacity so we can't, uh, with warheads. Then you don't want to knock 'em out ['cause?], uh, there's too much of a gamble. Then they just begin to build up those air bases there and then put more and more. I suppose they really. . . . Then they start getting ready to squeeze us in Berlin, doesn't that. . . . You may say it doesn't make any difference if you get blown up by an ICBM flying from the Soviet Union or one that was ninety miles away. Geography doesn't mean that much.[31]

The President was clearly thinking out loud: he was not really sure how he stood on this issue. A little later in the meeting, he veered toward the McNamara line. The real issue now, he said, was a political or psychological one. He had said the previous month that we would not tolerate the deployment of Soviet missiles in Cuba, and now he had to follow through: "Last month I said we weren't going to. Last month I should have said . . . that we don't care. But when we said we're *not* going to and then they go ahead and do it, and then we do nothing, then . . . I would

---

how the deployment affected the military balance was not "an issue of contention," and that in fact "it was not even fully analyzed in the hectic week of initial decisions" (*Intelligence Assessment*, p. 28; with some minor variations of wording, also in "The Meaning of the Missiles," p. 76). But the evidence just cited shows that these claims have to be taken with a grain of salt. There is additional evidence as well. The issue of the "effect of the missiles on the overall balance of power" was, for example, considered by the "main policy group" at its meeting at the White House on October 18, according to p. 46 of the recently declassified Sieverts Report, "The Cuban Crisis, 1962," an in-house history written mainly on the basis of interviews and completed in mid-1963 (Box 49, National Security Files, Kennedy Library). Indeed, the issue of the military significance of missiles in Cuba had been around ever since the administration had begun to worry about a possible deployment during the summer. For example, National Security Action Memorandum No. 181 of August 23, 1962 specifically requested an analysis "of the probable military, political and psychological impact of the establishment in Cuba of either surface-to-air or surface-to-surface missiles which could reach the U.S." (Box 338, National Security Files, Kennedy Library). It is unclear whether such a study was ever written; an attempt to locate it via the Freedom of Information Act proved unsuccessful.

[31] October 16 transcripts, II, p. 13 (for JFK), and I, p. 11 (for McNamara).

think that our risks increase."[32] What perhaps made this line attractive was that it freed him from the need to agonize over the more difficult problem of whether the deployment was militarily important. It provided a straightforward rationale for the American decision to resist the deployment of the missiles, sparing the President from any need to resolve the perplexing issues of nuclear strategy.

At other times, however, Kennedy's remarks point in the other direction: "In his view the existence of fifty planes in Cuba [the IL-28 bombers] did not affect the balance of power, but the missiles already in Cuba were an entirely different matter."[33] Or, on October 27, when he was making a case for a trade involving the Jupiters: "The President recalled that over a year ago we wanted to get the Jupiter missiles out of Turkey because they had become obsolete and of little military value. If the missiles in Cuba added 50% to Soviet nuclear capability, then to trade these missiles for those in Turkey would be of great military value."[34]

One of the ways that President Kennedy tried to get a handle on the issue of the military significance of the missiles was by raising the question of Soviet motivation. If they did not matter strategically, why would the Russians put them in? Were they unhappy with their ICBMs? Khrushchev was running a major risk. What did he think he could get out of deploying these missiles in Cuba? "It's just as if we suddenly began to put a major number of MRBMs in Turkey," he said. "Now that'd be goddam dangerous, I would think." "Well, we *did*, Mr. President," Bundy replied. "Yeah, but that was five years ago."[35] They had been warned, the President said, and still they put the missiles in: "I don't think there's any record of the Soviets making this direct a challenge, ever, really . . . since the Berlin blockade."[36] But then Bundy placed this issue in its proper perspective by pointing out that the Soviets had made their decision *before* the President had issued his warning; they could have drawn back later, of course, but proceeding with a decision that had already been made was not quite the same as an outright act of defiance.

One therefore has the sense that President Kennedy's feelings on this issue had not really taken definite shape: it was as though he was groping for answers. Indeed, it seems that the administration in general, ever since it took office, was being pulled in two opposite directions: by intellectual argument, and by its extreme distaste for the idea of massive retaliation,

[32] Ibid., II, p. 15.

[33] Schlesinger, *Robert Kennedy*, pp. 510–11. Since one of the basic differences between bombers and missiles relates to warning time, this quotation suggests that by this point Kennedy was concerned with how the missiles might affect Soviet first strike capabilities.

[34] ExCom Minutes No. 7, October 27, 1962, p. 4.

[35] October 16 transcripts, I, p. 13, and II, p. 26.

[36] Ibid., II, p. 32.

it was drawn toward notions of discriminate and controlled war-fighting, and in fact nuclear war-fighting, strategies; but revolted by the very idea of nuclear war, and convinced that matters would in all probability very quickly get out of hand as soon as nuclear weapons began to be used in a major way, the most important people in the Kennedy Administration found it hard to take such notions seriously. As a result, the nuclear strategy of "controlled response" never really cut very deep under Kennedy;[37] and a certain ambivalence about these basic issues was very characteristic of that administration's approach to military policy.

Thus the administration was still sorting out its views on this issue: it was unclear exactly what the strategic significance of the Soviet deployment was, and people's attitudes were so uncertain, and so divided, that the discussion tells us very little about more fundamental beliefs about the political meaning of the strategic balance.

But views about escalation throw a much sharper light on the problem. What is striking here is the sense that peace was hanging on a thread, that it did not take much to touch off a nuclear holocaust—attitudes that would have been inconceivable if the sense was that the Soviets were simply out-gunned and would have to back down, or even if the assumption was just that they were desperately anxious to avoid war and would draw back in a simple test of will. General David Burchinal, the Director of Plans on the Air Staff in 1962, later recalled how during the crisis an American U-2 spy plane had gotten lost and turned up over Soviet territory. Word of this "came into the 'tank' where McNamara and the Chiefs were meeting: 'We've got a U-2 at 75,000 feet over the Kola Peninsula.' " McNamara, he said, "turned absolutely white and yelled histerically, 'This means war with the Soviet Union. The President must get on the hot line to Moscow.' And he ran out of the meeting in a frenzy."[38]

Whether this story is true or not, it is clear from other sources that McNamara was very sensitive to the danger of things spinning out of control. But President Kennedy also, in some comments on the crisis he gave to the National Security Council in January 1963, stressed the importance of having time to work out policy: if the Russians had had to

[37] It is now well known that the influence of declaratory strategy on actual planning for general war is much slighter than many people used to assume. Note in this connection the testimony, for example, of Air Force General Bruce K. Holloway. What role did McNamara's strategy of "assured destruction" play in the elaboration of the Single Integrated Operational Plan (SIOP)—the basic plan for general war? "This is one place I can certainly say something nice about McNamara," Holloway remarked. "He never reversed us to my knowledge while I was STPS on the SIOP as it was presented to the ICS and as it was approved" (Holloway oral history interview, August 16–18, 1977, p. 359, Office of Air Force History, Bolling Air Force Base, Washington, D.C.).

[38] Transcript of oral history interview of General David Burchinal, April 11, 1975, pp. 114–15. Office of Air Force History, Bolling Air Force Base, Washington, D.C.

react in only "an hour or two, their actions would have been spasmodic and might have resulted in nuclear war."[39]

Fears of this sort had an important effect on policy: there was in particular a great concern about the risk of escalation within the Cuban theater. With regard to the air strike option, Taylor and McNamara argued on October 16 that it was crucial to take out every target that might have any nuclear capability. The Joint Chiefs, Taylor said, unanimously believed that an attack should not be limited to the missile sites:

> It would be a mistake to take this very narrow, selective target because it invited reprisal attacks and it may be detrimental. Now if the, uh, Soviets have been willing to give, uh, nuclear warheads to these missiles, there is every, just as good reason for them to give nuclear capability to these [air] bases. We don't think we'd ever have a chance to take 'em again, so that we lose this, the first strike surprise capability. Our recommendation would be to get complete intelligence, get all the photography we need, the next two or three days, no, no hurry in our book. Then look at this target system. If it really threatens the United States, then take it right out with one hard crack.[40]

McNamara fully accepted the basic argument about the risk of retaliation from surviving forces on the island, and in fact developed it in a number of ways. One point was that if military action was to be undertaken, it had to be done quickly, before the missile sites became operational. Otherwise, since there was no guarantee a strike would destroy all the missiles, some of the surviving ones might be launched against American cities: once any missiles became operational, he argued, the risk of an attack would be too great.[41] Another point was that there could be no warning: "if you are going to strike, you shouldn't make an announcement."[42] If you went the political route, that meant giving a warning, and hence a chance for an adversary to prepare his missiles for launch, thus effectively preventing the U.S. from taking military action: the political approach "almost *stops* subsequent military action"; "once you start this political approach, I don't think you're gonna *have* any opportunity for a military operation."[43]

Note how this kind of reasoning thus tends to draw one to the extremes: either a full-scale surprise attack or no direct military action at all, but not the brandishing of threats to coerce an adversary. Military power is viewed primarily as a way of affecting an enemy's capabilities

[39] "Notes on Remarks by President Kennedy before the National Security Council, Tuesday, January 22, 1963," National Security Files, Box 314, Kennedy Library.

[40] October 16 transcripts, II, p. 8.

[41] Ibid., I, pp. 11, 13, 14.

[42] Ibid., II, p. 17.

[43] Ibid., pp. 9, 44.

rather than as a means of influencing his will. And this is based on the notion that once the ball starts rolling, things may very well become uncontrollable; the enemy cannot be counted on to behave rationally and control his own behavior.

But it was precisely this set of assumptions that was attacked by Rusk and Bundy. There were great political advantages to limiting the attack to the missile sites; there was no reason to assume that the Soviets would retaliate with whatever they had left, since such behavior would be suicidal for them. Rusk, for example, did not believe that "the critical question" was whether, in the event of an attack, every missile could be destroyed before it went off, because if the remaining missiles were launched, "we are in general nuclear war": "In other words, the Soviet Union has got quite a different decision to make."[44] And Bundy refuted the notion that if the United States attacked the missiles, the other side would retaliate with bombers, some of which might have nuclear capability: if their bombers attacked America in retaliation, then *they* were opting for general war—"it then becomes much more *their* decision."[45] President Kennedy himself saw both sides of the argument—one again has the sense that he was thinking out loud—but on balance it seems he favored the more limited form of attack: he just did not believe that if the missiles were destroyed, there might be a reprisal with nuclear weapons dropped from bombers, "because obviously why would the Soviets permit nuclear war to begin under that sort of half-assed way?"[46]

This argument turned to a certain degree on the technical issue of Soviet command and control: how automatic retaliation would be would depend to a considerable extent on whether the decision to strike back would be made in Moscow or by some low-level Soviet commander in charge of a missile battery in Cuba. McNamara's disagreement with Rusk focused on this point: "We don't know what kinds of communications the Soviets have with those sites. We don't know what kinds of control they have over the warheads."[47]

The problem of command and control thus relates to the broader question of whether the deployment of nuclear missiles in a given country deters all forms of attack on that country—an issue that bears on the current debate over the deployment of intermediate-range missiles in Europe. The deterrent effect in 1962 seems real enough, even if in the final analysis the presence of operational missiles would not in itself have been sufficient to prevent an American attack on Cuba. But was this effect rooted solely in assumptions about the possible looseness of an enemy's

---

[44] Ibid., I, p. 13.
[45] Ibid., II, p. 18. See also I, p. 25, and II, p. 43.
[46] Ibid., I, p. 25. See also I, p. 17, and II, pp. 10, 17.
[47] Ibid., I, p. 13.

control apparatus? While the evidence of this point is not very strong, it does seem that a sense for the danger of attacking Cuba after nuclear weapons were deployed there had a somewhat broader issue base than uncertainty about Soviet command and control. For one thing, one is struck by the casual way in which people referred to *Cuban* control over the missiles.[48] And this was linked to a visceral fear that the missiles might be *deliberately* launched if, for example, the United States sent troops to Venezuela: Robert Kennedy was worried about an implicit Cuban threat "that if you go there, we're gonna fire it."[49]

From McNamara's point of view, the air strike option clearly had its problems: for political reasons, a "bolt from the blue" was obviously unattractive, but to give warning would allow the other side to take actions that could effectively paralyze the United States. He therefore proposed a blockade as an alternative. The missiles in Cuba posed, to his mind, not a military problem, but rather a "domestic political problem."[50] America had said it would act if missiles were brought in, and now it had to do something—not necessarily enough to force the withdrawal of the missiles, but measures that would prevent their use: a continuous surveillance of Cuba and a permanent naval blockade to prevent any more missiles from coming in. The United States would declare to the world that, "if there is ever any indication that [the missiles in Cuba were] to be launched against this country, we will respond not only against Cuba, but we will respond directly against the Soviet Union with, with a full nuclear strike." This was not "a perfect solution by any means," and he said he did not want to argue for it; but if this alternative did not seem very acceptable, "wait until you work on the others."[51]

The fear of escalation thus went a long way toward neutralizing whatever advantages might have accrued to the United States by virtue of its "strategic superiority"—at least from the point of view of the American government. This was most true in the case of McNamara, but to one degree or another, these fears were shared by most of his colleagues, and the American government was very cautious during the crisis.[52] The Ken-

[48] Ibid., II, pp. 14, 46.

[49] Ibid., pp. 14–15.

[50] Ibid., pp. 46, 48.

[51] Ibid., pp. 46–48.

[52] Note in this context General Burchinal's later account of how the blockade was actually implemented: "So about that time, also, we decided to impose a blockade, and we put our naval vessels out on picket—no more ships coming into Cuba. They would be challenged on the high seas regardless of flag, and they'd be searched, and if they had anything that falls under war materiel they will be turned around or they will be sunk. So, we set it up. And, there was control in detail, so there was a phone from the Secretary of Defense's office right to the deck of the damn destroyer on patrol in this blockade. So, the first ship comes up to the blockade line. He's a Swede. They give him the signal 'heave-to.' 'Standby,

nedy Administration did not plunge eagerly into the poker game of risk manipulation, encouraged by a sense that strategically it had the upper hand.

But it is also important to remember that its fear of escalation did not drive the threshold of acceptable risk down to zero. On both the air strike and the blockade, McNamara's initial views were not accepted. The blockade did in fact eventually function as a political instrument—that is, as a "first step," raising the prospect of further, more extreme steps if a settlement was not reached. If the blockade did not "achieve the removal of the missiles," the President seemed ready, on October 20, to approve an air strike "against a minimum number of targets to eliminate the main nuclear threat."[53] And of course at the peak of the crisis, the United States was ready to invade Cuba, even though some of the missiles there were by then considered operational: even McNamara at that point thought that an invasion was "almost inevitable."

THE STRATEGIC BALANCE: THE SOVIET SIDE

There were two possible ways in which the strategic balance could have influenced the course of the crisis: through its effect on American policy or through its effect on Soviet behavior. We have already seen that its direct effect on the United States was apparently minimal. But a strong, although somewhat speculative, case can be made that Soviet policy was very much influenced by the strategic balance. This case rests on a study of what was going on in the area of military preparations during the crisis.

One of the most striking features of the Cuban missile crisis, in fact, is an extraordinary asymmetry in the area of general war preparations. On October 22, President Kennedy announced the presence of the missiles

---

what is your cargo?' And he said, 'Go to hell!' Full steam ahead and right through the damn blockade and right on into Havana. Nobody stopped him. He just said, 'The hell with you—nobody tells me what to do on the high seas with my ship.' So, they just looked at each other, these people who were now learning to 'manage crises' and run wars. 'That didn't work very well. What do we do now?' And so our signal caller had said, 'Don't shoot,' and the destroyer had said. 'I'm ready to stop him.' 'No, no, let him go.' So the next ship comes along and he's Lebanese—he's flying a Lebanese flag. So, they challenge him. And he said, 'Oh, I'm very happy to comply. I'll stop, come aboard, here I am, I'm just a poor Lebanese out here running my ship into Cuba.' So they went aboard and opened up his hatches, and he's got a bunch of military electronic gear, and they shut the hatches down, pretended it wasn't there, and said, 'Pass friend.' And he steamed merrily into Havana. That was our naval blockade. And that's the way it was being run under the kind of civilian control we had." Burchinal oral history, pp. 116–17.

[53] Sieverts Report, p. 75.

and the measures the United States was taking to force their removal, and every day, from that point on, the Central Intelligence Agency prepared a memorandum outlining the military measures the Soviet Union was taking in response. The first order of business at each morning ExCom meeting was a briefing by the CIA Director, John McCone, essentially summarizing the latest intelligence memorandum. Day after day, the theme was the same: the USSR was not making preparations for war. Thus, the CIA, on October 24, did not believe that "measures to achieve a higher degree of action readiness for Soviet and bloc forces are being taken on a crash basis." The same point was made in the October 25 memorandum; and still on October 27, at the climax of the crisis, the CIA said it simply had not been able to detect any "significant redeployment" of Soviet forces.[54]

The United States, on the other hand, was making very serious preparations for a general nuclear conflict: America's ICBMs were put on alert, and the Strategic Air Command as a whole, as one writer put it, was "fully mobilized for war."[55] "We increased the airborne alert force of B-52's up to a third of the force," General Burchinal recalled. "We had SAC bombers on nuclear alert with weapons in the bomb-bays on civilian airfields all over the US. We dispersed the air defense force, with nuclear weapons, also on civilian airports all over the country." But the point that Burchinal stressed was that "all these moves were signals the Soviets could see and we knew they could see them. We got everything we had, in the strategic forces, nuclear forces, counted down and ready and aimed and we made damn sure they saw it without anybody saying a word about it."[56]

How is Soviet inaction to be understood, and what inferences from the disparity between Soviet and American military measures might have plausibly been drawn at the time? Military preparations, of course, strengthen one's bargaining position. They are an indication of resolve, a hint of what one might actually do, a means perhaps of preventing the enemy from making certain countermoves and thus of preemptively increasing one's own freedom of action. It is clear that these bargaining advantages of preparing for war were understood at the time.[57] But if taking these measures can have such effects, it is even clearer that a *refusal* to make serious preparations during a confrontation, when one's adversary has put his strategic forces on full alert, can have important political

[54] Both the CIA memoranda and the Executive Committee minutes are in Boxes 315 and 316, National Security Files, Kennedy Library.

[55] See David Detzer, *The Brink: Cuban Missile Crisis. 1962* (New York: Thomas Crowell, 1979), p. 164.

[56] Burchinal oral history, p. 115.

[57] October 16 transcripts, I, p. 27, and II, p. 10.

effects. It is a question here not just of the Soviets' reluctance to declare an official alert of their own. This might be explained by the specific character of what an alert might have meant in the Soviet system. For instance, the Soviets might have been unable for technical reasons to hold their strategic force on alert for more than a short period of time, and therefore might have been reluctant to place their forces on alert unless they were certain a war was coming.[58] The more important point is that the Soviets evidently did nothing, even in the way of major ad hoc measures (such as putting some of their bombers on strip alert), to reduce the vulnerability of their strategic forces. A national leader like Khrushchev may take a tough position in diplomatic contacts, in effect threatening war if his opponent perseveres with his policy; but how seriously can such threats be taken if what is going on in the military sphere is giving exactly the opposite signal?[59]

It can be taken for granted that the Soviet Union of Nikita Khrushchev was not oblivious to considerations of this sort. Khrushchev had tried over the past few years to extract political advantages by brandishing the specter of nuclear war. If anything, he had tended to overestimate the bluff value of nuclear weapons, and to overlook the ways in which the tactic of exploiting the nuclear threat could backfire.[60] But during the Cuban crisis, the Soviets backed away from a strategy of bluff: something more compelling had intervened, leading them to pay the price, in bargaining terms, of not seriously preparing for war.

It is reasonable to suppose that their view of the United States had a good deal to do with the choices they made. For they saw a country whose whole way of thinking about nuclear issues had focused on the question of how much an advantage there might be to getting in the first blow; where responsible officials, from the President on down, had stressed how the United States would not rule out the option of striking first in certain circumstances; and where the logic of preemptive action—of semi-unin-

---

[58] The Soviet missile guidance system evidently used gyroscopes with metal ball bearings that would fail if they were subject to continuing stress—that is, if the missile were held ready for launch over a prolonged period. See Robert P. Berman and John C. Baker, *Soviet Strategic Forces: Requirements and Responses* (Washington, D.C.: Brookings, 1982), p. 88.

[59] See the Khrushchev-Kennedy correspondence published in the Department of State *Bulletin*, November 19, 1973, and republished in Ronald R. Pope, ed., *Soviet Views on the Cuban Missile Crisis: Myth and Reality in Foreign Policy Analysis* (Washington, D.C.: University Press of America, 1982), pp. 28–67. Note also the account of Khrushchev's interview with the American businessman W. E. Knox in Hilsman to Rusk, October 26, 1962, Box 36a. Folder "Cuba. General. 10/15/62–10/23/62," National Security Files, Kennedy Library.

[60] Arnold L. Horelick and Myron Rush, *Strategic Power and Soviet Foreign Policy* (Chicago: University of Chicago Press, 1966), is the classic study.

tended war, resulting from the fear of surprise attack—was very widely recognized.[61]

The important volume on *Soviet Military Strategy* (1962), edited by Marshal Sokolovskii, shows just how sensitive the Soviets were at this time to the American emphasis on the logic of preemption. The Americans, the Soviet authors pointed out, understood that "the one who strikes first will undoubtedly gain an important advantage." This was why the United States was so afraid of surprise attack. But the Americans assumed that the fear of surprise attack—and here the Soviet authors were quoting directly from a U.S. Senate document—"gravely increased the temptation to strike first in a nuclear war." The Americans thought they might have to attack simply because they felt their enemy was about to strike: "a pre-emptive blow ... is defensive, according to American military theorists, since it is dealt to an enemy who is ready to attack (to initiate a preventive war or deal a first blow). It is considered to be the final and only means of avoiding disaster."[62]

It is clear that the Soviet authors understood some of the basic arguments American strategists were making during the period; official doctrine, and the capabilities with which it was linked, would naturally be viewed in this context. The most disturbing thing here, from their point of view, would be the notion of "damage limitation" and the American counterforce capabilities that supported it. "Damage limitation," whatever official attempts were made to rationalize it in "second-strike" terms, must have struck them as a code term for preemption. This certainly was how Carl Kaysen, Bundy's aide during the Kennedy administration, explained it a few years later: "Should sufficient warning of preparations for a Soviet strike or actual launching of one be available, U.S. missiles could be launched against Soviet missiles sites and airfields, thus limiting to an extent depending on warning time the damage the Soviet strike would inflict."[63]

Given all this, Soviet leaders might have viewed war preparations as very dangerous—and quite possibly because of the disparity in force levels and in degrees of force vulnerability, risky in a way that the corre-

[61] See especially Khrushchev's July 10, 1962 speech, published in *Pravda* the next day, and in English in the *Current Digest of the Soviet Press*, vol. 14, no. 28 (August 8, 1962), esp. pp. 3–4, for the Soviet leader's reaction to President Kennedy's refusal to rule out a first strike option. Kennedy's remarks were originally made in an interview with Stewart Alsop, "Kennedy's Grand Strategy," *Saturday Evening Post*, March 31, 1962, p. 14. See also Michael Brower, "Nuclear Strategy of the Kennedy Administration," *Bulletin of the Atomic Scientists*, vol. 18, no. 8 (October 1962), esp. pp. 38f.

[62] V. D. Sokolovskii, ed., *Soviet Military Strategy* (Englewood Cliffs, N.J.: Prentice Hall, Rand edition, 1963), pp. 160–62. The original Soviet edition was published in 1962.

[63] Carl Kaysen, "Keeping the Strategic Balance," *Foreign Affairs*, vol. 16, no. 4 (July 1968), p. 668.

sponding American alert simply was not. Indeed, the famous remark of
Soviet Deputy Foreign Minister Kuznetsov to John McCloy shortly after
the crisis—"You Americans will never be able to do this to us again"—
suggests that the Soviets drew back because of a relative, but remediable,
weakness, and obviously their conventional inferiority in the Caribbean
was not what Kuznetsov had in mind.[64]

But however the asymmetry in military preparations is to be explained,
the important thing to note is that people in Washington were aware of it
during the crisis. What conclusions might they have realistically drawn
from it? Could they have felt that the lack of parallelism reflected a Soviet
sense of their own strategic inferiority? This is why speculation about the
Soviet motivation for the deployment can be so revealing: did anyone feel
that the Soviets had made what was assumed to be the very risky move of
introducing missiles into Cuba out of weakness—for example, because
they had been so uncomfortable with the existing strategic balance during
the Berlin crisis the previous year? And what conclusions were drawn
from the fact that the deployment had been carried out in such a furtive
and deceptive fashion, tactics of this sort being traditionally associated
with the weak?[65]

These certainly are the kinds of things to look out for as more evidence
is released. It is already clear that some people close to the crisis did in
fact draw these sorts of inferences. General Burchinal, for example, later
stressed that Khrushchev "never alerted a bomber or changed his own
military posture one bit. We had a gun at his head and he didn't move a
muscle"; and Burchinal implied that this issue was discussed at the time
with his civilian superiors.[66] One would like to see how the arguments
were played out and what effect they had on policy. In any event, the mere
fact of asymmetry does not seem consistent with the picture that Bundy
painted in 1969. It suggests in itself that the nuclear situation was not one
of simple "stalemate" in 1962.

What then was the role of the strategic balance in 1962? America's
"superiority" apparently did not have much of a direct effect on Ameri-

---

[64] The quotation is from Charles E. Bohlen, *Witness to History, 1929–1969* (New York:
W. W. Norton, 1973), pp. 495–96. There is also the related question, about which there has
been so much conjecture, of the connection between the Cuban missile crisis and the development of Soviet strategic capabilities after 1962. It is hard to believe there is no connection
at all, but it is still too early for firm conclusions on this subject.

[65] This is no accident, since everyone knows that one pays a price for deceptive or devious
behavior: the risk of embarrassment if one is found out, a discrediting of one's future claims
and promises, possibly increased self-righteousness on the part of one's adversary and the
bargaining advantages this gives him. For these reasons it is pointless to lie or cheat without
sufficient cause: the disadvantages have to be offset by some other consideration, and the
most natural candidate is a sense of one's own relative weakness.

[66] Burchinal oral history, p. 116.

can policy during the crisis—or at least this is what the limited evidence now available seems to indicate. But with regard to the Soviets, the evidence points in the opposite direction: their strategic "inferiority" appears to have had a profound effect on their behavior in the crisis.

CONCLUSIONS

What role did nuclear forces play during the Cuban missile crisis? We began by considering three different lines of argument: (1) the claim that nuclear weapons played no role at all, that they just cancelled each other out; (2) the set of arguments that emphasize the notion of risk; and (3) the strategic balance interpretation, which asserts that America's nuclear superiority played a crucial role in determining the course and outcome of the crisis. How well have each of these interpretations held up in the light of the evidence examined here?

There is first the argument that nuclear forces simply neutralized each other—that nuclear forces were "unusable," and that because they were militarily useless, they could not be harnessed to any political purpose, beyond simply deterring their use by others. Of all the arguments considered here, this is the most difficult to sustain. It is obvious that the fear of nuclear war affected both Soviet and American behavior in the crisis; and indeed these fears were consciously manipulated, most notably by the American strategic alert. For such anxieties to have a real effect on political behavior, there was no need for the President to decide consciously that he would under certain circumstances start a nuclear war: escalation could be largely inadvertent. It was sufficient, as Brodie pointed out in a 1963 talk on the crisis, that the government was able simply to "threaten the next in a series of moves" that seemed to tend in the direction of general war.[67]

The risk of nuclear war could therefore affect behavior. But the threshold of acceptable risk could vary, and nuclear anxieties in fact did not have an equal effect on both sides. The "balance of resolve" was therefore crucial. The balance was not so completely lopsided that the crisis was ended by a total Soviet capitulation. Nor, on the other hand, was the final arrangement a bargain negotiated between equals. The balance was unequal, but not so unequal that it makes sense to view the crisis as a simple "contest" with a clear victor.

It would therefore be a bit too extreme to view the crisis as a "competition in risk-taking" à la Thomas Schelling. "Until we can manipulate

---

[67] Bernard Brodie, "AFAG Talk: Political Impact of U.S. Force Postures," May 28, 1963, p. 7 (recently released by Rand).

the risk of general war and engage in competitive risk-taking with the Soviets," Schelling said a few months after the crisis, "I don't think we are going to learn to take care of Berlin, much lesss to take care of Indonesia and Finland, when the time comes."[68] But this kind of attitude is really not reflected in the documents on the Cuban crisis. To be sure, people felt they had to act. Both for foreign policy reasons—the Soviet deployment was in direct defiance of an American warning—and for reasons of domestic politics as well, the administration knew that it could not sit this one out. But no one wanted to keep upping the ante, to keep outbidding the Soviets in "resolve," as the way of triumphing in the confrontation.

As for the argument about the strategic balance, the evidence at this point suggests that it did not have an important direct influence on American policy. The Kennedy administration's fears of escalation substantially cancelled out, in its own mind, whatever benefits it might have theoretically been able to derive from its "strategic superiority." The American ability to "limit damage" by destroying an enemy's strategic forces did not seem, in American eyes, to carry much political weight. Thus in practice the more subtle official theories about nuclear war-fighting evidently did not have much of an effect on American policy.

But the Soviets seem to have been profoundly affected by their "strategic inferiority." The ironic thing is that they probably took American ideas about "damage limitation" and "discriminate and controlled general war," and the capabilities with which they were linked, far more seriously than the Americans did. And this was in spite of the fact that just a few months earlier, after the Ann Arbor speech, they had contemptuously dismissed the McNamara strategy as absurd. It really does seem that "we had a gun to their head and they didn't move a muscle"—that their failure to make any preparations for general war was linked to a fear of provoking American preemptive action. And this meant that it was more essential than it otherwise might have been to head off an invasion of Cuba through a political settlement. The danger of provoking an American preemptive strike tended to rule out countermeasures—or even the serious threat of countermeasures, around Berlin or elsewhere—that would significantly increase the risk of war. The effect therefore was to tie their hands, to limit their freedom of maneuver, and thus to increase their incentive to settle the crisis quickly.

This implies that the strategic balance mattered in 1962. Does this conclusion have "hawkish" or "pro-nuclear" implications? Its real meaning is more complex: the point that nuclear forces can carry political weight

[68] David Abshire and Richard Allen, eds., *National Security: Political, Military, and Economic Strategies in the Decade Ahead* (New York: Praeger, 1963), p. 646.

in itself tells us very little about basic issues of policy—about whether, or in what ways, nuclear power *should* be used to support political objectives. The lessons of history are rarely clear-cut.

The historical analysis of the Cuban missile crisis is still in its infancy. The new documents on the crisis, as revealing as they are, represent just the tip of the iceberg. It is only as more material is released that the full meaning of the crisis can begin to unfold. If this material is approached correctly—if questions are framed so that answers turn on what the archival evidence shows—the historical study of the crisis can be of real value. It is one of the best ways we have of bringing the problem of the political utility of nuclear forces into focus—of going beyond speculation and reaching some solid conclusions about one of the most basic problems of the nuclear age.

CHAPTER SEVEN

Making Sense of the Nuclear Age

In 1955 Bernard Brodie published an article in *Harper's Magazine* called "Strategy Hits a Dead End." With the coming of the hydrogen bomb, he argued, the strategy of unrestricted warfare had become obsolete; indeed, "most of the military ideas and axioms of the past" no longer made sense in a world of thermonuclear weapons. But it was not enough to allow these "old concepts of strategy" to "die a lingering death from occasional verbal rebukes." What was needed, he said, was a whole new set of ideas, a comprehensive and radically different framework for thinking about strategic issues.[1] And over the next decade that was exactly what took shape. Strategy as an intellectual discipline came alive in America in the 1950s. A very distinctive, influential and conceptually powerful body of thought emerged. But by 1966 or so, this intellectual tradition had more or less run its course. Strategic discourse, it seemed in the 1970s and early 1980s, had become stale, even sterile.

Was the problem that strategic studies had too narrow a focus? The argument was made that the field had to reach out to new disciplines, to psychology, to history, and to more exotic areas as well. What kind of impact can this effort hope to achieve? In particular, what sort of contribution can historical study make to the analysis of strategic issues, and to the intellectual reinvigoration of the field?

By "historical study" I do not mean simply learning more about the past. That, of course, has an obvious value. Even a single document can set the mind of an intelligent observer moving in all sorts of unexpected directions. But historians try to do more than just present the facts in an easy-to-digest fashion. Historical analysis also has a conceptual dimension. A historian and a political scientist might be studying the same subject, and might even end up using the same sources. But the products of their work will almost certainly be very different from each other. It is a mistake to assume that this is because the political scientist is interested in problems of theory, while the historian, obsessed with detail and factual accuracy, has sunk into a kind of mindless empiricism. Historians are

A version of this paper was originally presented at a conference on nuclear threats held in 1985 at Columbia University's Institute of War and Peace Studies.

[1] Bernard Brodie, "Strategy Hits a Dead End," *Harper's Magazine* (October 1955), pp. 33–37.

also concerned with conceptual problems—in this field, above all with the problem of war and peace—albeit in a more indirect and less overt way. It is rather that the *sensibility* is different: the kind of intellectual baggage a historian takes with him to the analysis of the subject is going to produce work of a very different sort, in substance as well as in form.

It is hard to describe in any detail what this historical sensibility amounts to. Basically it is a sense that what has happened in the past is not to be understood as a series of discrete episodes strung together over time, but rather that the course of events has a logic to it—not as tight as the logic of a mathematical theorem, of course, but a logic that can be understood through careful historical study. People at the time might have only dimly understood what was going on at the most basic level of international politics; the way they conceptualized international conflict might have been very crude. But looking back, one can see how events have a momentum of their own—that what happens is only to a limited extent the product of design—and one can begin to understand the past. The key thing here is a sense of *process*. The basic logic unfolds *over time*, and therefore the causal structure of the past is reflected in its chronological structure. Studying in detail exactly what happened and when is therefore crucial if the larger picture is to be understood: hence the almost obsessive belief in the importance of factual accuracy that is one of the formal values of the historical profession.

The question I am concerned with here is whether history in this sense—as a scholarly discipline, as a field with an intellectual personality of its own, as something more than a mere source of information about the past—is of any real value to strategic studies. Can history help bring about a fundamental rethinking of the basic problems of foreign and military policy in the nuclear age?

It would be easy, if ultimately not very rewarding, to talk about these questions in general terms. But a real sense for the value of historical research, in this area especially, emerges only as the work is being done. I want therefore to approach the question indirectly by talking on a more concrete level about how this kind of work actually proceeds and the sort of insight that develops from it, and here I will be relying mainly on personal experience.

There are two other reasons for looking more deeply than is usually done into the question of how historical interpretation takes shape. First of all, it is only by understanding the way a piece of history is constructed that one can know what to make of it. The idea here, in other words, is to throw open the doors of the workshop so that those who use the product can see how it is put together and will thus be in a better position to judge its value.

Finally, I want to give some sense for the fact that there is nothing mysterious about historical analysis. This is not to say that anyone can walk in off the street and do essentially the same kind of work that professional historians do. There is a set of skills involved, but they are by no means arcane or in any way difficult to acquire. My personal feeling is that a minimal mastery of these skills should be part of the intellectual equipment of anyone seriously interested in the study of security issues, and the first step toward developing this mastery is to understand what these skills and techniques in fact are.

DRAWING MEANING FROM THE SOURCES

The aim of historical analysis is to understand the past by reducing it to a story—by showing how one thing leads to another. But how does a story get constructed? How do you go beyond a mere narrative of events and develop a sense for what the central dynamic of historical change in the period in question really was?

"Learn the facts," George Smiley was told in a Le Carré novel, "then try on the stories like clothes." When doing historical work, however, the procedure is rarely that simple. It is only when you begin to get a rough idea for what the overall story is that the raw facts begin to take on their full meaning. Your antennae have to be continually sensitized: you do not simply immerse yourself in the sources like a sponge, passively absorbing any documents that happen to be in the files. The research effort has to be active and directed; you have to begin to develop a "feel" for the subject in order to know what to focus in on, and how to draw full meaning out of the documents you read.

As a rule, a research strategy takes a long time to develop. The effort has to become systematic at some point, but there is a danger in trying to impose too tight a structure on the project prematurely. It is as though the process of sorting things out has a life of its own, and no one can tell at the outset exactly where things will lead or what form the story will take. If an attempt is made to force things into some kind of preconceived mold—if the *organic* nature of the research process is not respected—something very important is going to be lost. The spark of inquiry, the thing that gives life to the whole project, will be snuffed out.

What this means, however, is that the initial effort is going to be somewhat haphazard, and in all likelihood will be moving in a number of directions at once. First of all, the secondary literature—accounts written by historians, political scientists, journalists, and others—has to be identified and then read critically. But at the same time, it is a good idea to start looking at documents, at least at those sources that are most easily available. The archival evidence is always full of surprises; reading the documents, it is as though new lights are constantly being turned on. That tends to generate a sense of excitement which helps drive the whole research effort.

Every research project has its own character. Sometimes the evidence available to a historian is relatively complete. You can go through the archives volume by volume, file by file, box by box; it may take a bit of effort, but basically the story just emerges before your eyes. At other times, the archives are like a black hole: nothing worth looking at ever makes its way out. But for the history of the nuclear age, the situation lies about halfway between these two extremes. For the 1950s and 1960s especially, it is as though only bits and pieces of evidence have made their way through our rather erratic declassification process. Many of these fragments are too minor in themselves ever to be cited in a formal academic book or article, but they reveal something about tone or attitude, and the more of them you see, the better you are able to shade the picture correctly.

Thus, for example, during the Kennedy period, one of the ways that policy was coordinated was for drafts of speeches to be sent to the White House for comment. In early 1963, Paul Nitze, then a high official in the Defense Department, sent over a draft which contained the following passage:

> Communists demonstrate a proclivity for bold political actions against a background of impressive military force, but also a calculation of risks and a scrupulous interest in keeping events under their own control. Because they do not seem to like high risks of nuclear war or events leading to it, their military actions against the West at any one moment are likely to be controlled in magnitude and aimed at limited objectives. It is difficult to believe that an appropriate initial NATO response to most of such lower levels of aggression would involve the use of nuclear weapons.[2]

McGeorge Bundy, the President's National Security Advisor, commented on this as follows. At this point in the speech, he wrote Nitze,

> I would avoid calling the Russians scrupulous even in the special sense of [the third line quoted above], and I would suggest that the last sentence be written in somewhat different terms, perhaps like this: "In such circumstances, NATO will surely wish to have the choice of avoiding immediate use of nuclear weapons; it would be neither wise nor credible for us to build our doctrine and our forces on the premise that every pinprick must be met by nuclear war." I hold no brief for this language—I am simply trying to leave open the sharp tactical nuclear response if in fact at a given moment that should be

[2] Draft of Nitze speech, February 28, 1963 (to be delivered in Cleveland, March 2, 1963), National Security Files, Box 274, Folder "Department of Defense, 1/63–6/63," JFK Library.

the least of the evils, and still more I want to leave that thought open for the friendly Germans at the moment.[3]

This document certainly throws some light on the Kennedy administration's attitude toward tactical nuclear weapons. Note how different the impression would be if the final phrase (about the "friendly Germans") had been deleted—if Bundy, that is, had not given the argument this particular twist.

The document may not be terribly important in itself, but it adds something to the broader picture. The more documents of this sort you see, the better sense you have for the overall texture of policy. What makes all this important is that issues of interpretation often cannot be resolved through direct analysis of the sources. To resolve a problem, one therefore often has to resort to indirect reasoning—to inferences drawn from what one has learned about the larger picture.

To give an important example, there is the general problem of how the Eisenhower strategy is to be interpreted. There are those who argue, for instance, that the threat of massive retaliation was in the final analysis a gigantic bluff. The most important test is the first phase of the Berlin Crisis, in 1958–1959. When I deal with the issue, as in the Berlin paper published above, I quote some remarks Eisenhower made to a congressional delegation in March 1959:

> Senator Russell expressed dismay at the prospect of fighting on the ground where we have no chance.
>
> Here the President expressed his basic philosophy of the necessity for the U.S. to be willing to "push its whole stack of chips into the pot" when such becomes necessary. He expressed the conviction that the actual decision to go to all-out war will not come, but if it does come, we must have the crust to follow through.[4]

Why, however, are these comments to be taken at face value? Why shouldn't we assume that the President was taking this line simply to manipulate perceptions? Of course, you never know for sure what was in other people's minds, but often you can read enough material to enable you to form an opinion on this kind of problem. An assessment of this sort is based on such things as the *tone* of the documents, whether you can detect real feeling; *consistency* between what is said and what is done, and overall coherence of policy; and *persistence* of a point of view over

---

[3] McGeorge Bundy, "Memorandum for the Honorable Paul Nitze," March 1, 1963, National Security Files, Box 274, folder "Department of Defense, 1/63–6/63," JFK Library.

[4] "Memorandum of Conference with the President," March 6, 1959, Declassified Documents Collection, 1981/598a.

time, in this case even after President Eisenhower had left office.[5] The basic point is that meaning does not emerge directly and automatically out of the reading of the sources, but rather takes a certain intellectual effort.

Sometimes this applies even to the interpretation of specific documents. Here, for example, is an extract from the record of a meeting between Dulles and Eisenhower in the middle of the second Taiwan Straits crisis in 1958. The Secretary of State was discussing a "memorandum summarizing factors involved in the Taiwan Straits situation, prepared following consultation with State, Defense and intelligence officials": "Mr. Dulles directed attention to the point regarding atomic weapons, recalling that we have geared our defense to the use of these in case of hostilities of any size, and stating that, if we will not use them when the chips are down because of adverse world opinion, we must revise our defense setup. The memorandum undertook to bring out this point."[6]

Was this an argument *for* using nuclear weapons if war broke out in the Taiwan Straits? This is what the conventional interpretation of Dulles, as the supposed architect of the strategy of massive retaliation, might lead one to think. But in fact there are a number of documents, dating even from the early Eisenhower period, where Dulles explicitly argued

[5] On the question of *tone*, let me give an example from the end of 1956. The Net Evaluation Subcommittee gave a presentation to the NSC at this time on the effects of a nuclear war, and Eisenhower commented on it in part as follows: "The President indicated that the Subcommittee's presentation prompted several observations on his part. He queried as to why we should put a single nickel into anything but developing our capacity to diminish the enemy's capacity for nuclear attack." "Discussion at the 206th Meeting of the National Security Council, Thursday, December 20, 1956," Dwight D. Eisenhower: Papers as President of the United States, 1953–61 (Ann Whitman File), NSC Series, Box 8, Eisenhower Library, Abilene, Kansas. This document is also in the Declassified Documents Collection, 1981/500A.

One also sometimes stumbles across anecdotes that contribute to the general picture. In December 1952, Eisenhower urged his son, then serving on the front in Korea, to kill himself rather than allow himself to be captured; during World War II, German commandos, the President-Elect said, would never have been able to take him prisoner because he would have shot himself first. Bob Considine, *It's All News to Me* (New York, 1967), pp. 363–67. This sort of soldierly ethic could easily be projected to the level of whole societies. Note in this context his obvious admiration for the Norwegians, who, he said, would "resist to destruction rather than give in to the Russians." "Notes on a meeting at the White House, January 31, 1951," *Foreign Relations of the United States*, 1951, vol. 3, p. 452.

For an example of how Eisenhower's views remained intact even after he left office, see the record of his comments when he was briefed on how his successors were handling the Berlin Crisis in 1961: Allen Dulles, Memorandum for the President, August 22, 1961, National Security Files, Box 82, folder "Germany. Berlin. General. 8/22/61," Kennedy Library, Boston, esp. pp. 5–7.

[6] "Memorandum of Conference with the President," September 4, 1958, Declassified Documents Collection, 1984/2760.

against massive retaliation—even documents where he took what amounted to an antinuclear line.[7] Any single such document might be dismissed as simply an anomaly, a mere flash in the pan; but when you see a series of such documents, you have to conclude that they might tell you something fundamental about Dulles's point of view. Taken as a whole, they imply that the Dulles comment referred to above perhaps should be interpreted as an argument *for* revising "our defense setup" and for moving away from such a great reliance on nuclear forces, or at the very least that it reflected a certain ambivalence about the nuclear question.

These then are some of the techniques used to process basic information, and in particular to understand what policy at different points in the past in fact was. The next goal is to try to piece this information together, to extrapolate and interpolate, until you come up with some plausible version of at least part of the overall story.

It must be stressed that even when the sources are mined systematically, the available evidence is often extremely fragmentary. Of course an archaeologist can reconstruct a good deal of what a prehistoric society was like on the basis of the few shards and other remnants that have survived, and an astronomer can learn a great deal about the origins of the universe from barely detectable vestiges of cosmic events that took place "billions and billions" of years ago. With history, the same sort of thing is possible: every document is a window into what is basically the same reality. The view from just one window, however, or even from a small number of windows, can be very misleading. The goal therefore is to keep adding evidence until you have gone well beyond the point where new documents point in essentially the same direction as old ones—where what you find becomes almost predictable in advance. You may never be able to get the whole truth, but the real goal is simply to reach a point where you are

[7] See, for example, the Dulles Memo of December 22, 1954, John Foster Dulles Files, White House Memoranda Series, Box 1, file "Meetings with the President," Eisenhower Library, Abilene, Kansas, and the "Discussion at the 363rd Meeting of the National Security Council, April 24, 1958," in Eisenhower: Papers, 1953–1961 (Ann Whitman File), NSC Series, Box 10, Eisenhower Library; also in Declassified Documents Collection, 1980/384B. And note especially Dulles's comments at the next NSC meeting: "The massive nuclear deterrent was running its course as the principal element in our military arsenal, and very great emphasis must be placed on the elements which in the next two or three years can replace the massive nuclear retaliatory capability. In short, the United States must be in a position to fight defensive wars which do not involve the total defeat of the enemy." "Discussion at the 364th Meeting of the National Security Council, Thursday, May 1, 1958," in the same file as the document just cited; also in Declassified Documents Collection, 1980/384C. Finally, the "anti-nuclear" thrust of the argument in a paper Dulles wrote on the nuclear issue dated January 22, 1956, should also be cited in this context: it is in the John Foster Dulles Papers, Subject Series, Box 4, Seeley G. Mudd Library, Princeton; also in Declassified Documents Collection, 1982/802.

confident that the essential lines of the story have been understood correctly.

That is the goal, but of course historical works often fall short of achieving it. When the documentation is limited, the temptation is to read too much into the evidence that is available. A finished work of history is supposed to be neat and tidy, which means that loose ends are often hidden from view. People tend to make their accounts appear more definitive and more conclusive than they in fact are, and to impute a tighter logic to the course of events than their evidence really warrants, because work of this sort is what the historical profession generally expects and rewards. It is important to be aware of these sources of bias, because they get added to other kinds of bias, especially the kind that comes from having a political axe to grind.

THE CONSTRUCTION OF A STORY

Reading the secondary accounts, and going through some of the primary sources, you are not just learning things about the past and filing them away in the back of your mind. You are also trying to sort things out—to understand why things were developing the way they were. This means that you have to try to construct a story out of what you have learned, and you begin with what are essentially conjectures about important parts of the story. Many of these guesses turn out to be contradicted by additional evidence, and they therefore have to be dropped. But a number of conjectures begin to ring true, and indeed start to fall into a pattern.

The pattern does not emerge in a completely unsystematic way out of a reading of the sources. It is driven by a sense for the overall structure of the problem—that is, the series of interrelated questions that the larger problem breaks down into. The core of the problem is understanding how military policy relates to political behavior—within a state, within an alliance, and between rival blocs of powers. The issue is complex: for any given power, military and foreign policy are each partly autonomous, and partly bound up with each other; for any two powers, the foreign and military policies of each affect both the foreign and military policy of the other. Policy as a whole is embedded in a domestic political system, and may be heavily influenced by the structure of bureaucratic power within a government. There is also the intellectual side of the problem—the kind of thinking that went on, both inside and outside the government, and how this was related to what actually was done. Understanding how the broader problem breaks down into its component parts provides a framework for thinking about specific issues: it directs your attention to the sorts of things you need to examine.

The idea that political context is important in explaining military policy, for example, almost automatically leads to certain conjectures. You learn something about the New Look—what the Eisenhower strategy was, when it came into being, what the formal rationales were, and how it changed over time. You also know something about the Korean War, and especially about Eisenhower's feelings about the role that nuclear weapons should have played in Korea, and the role that nuclear threats played in ending the war. Knowing what the chronology was leads to the hypothesis that the two things are linked, that in some important way Korea led to the New Look: the Eisenhower strategy was rooted in the conviction that the United States was not going to fight another major war on the ground, above all with its principal instrument of military power left unused—that America was not going to allow itself, as Richard Nixon put it at the time, to be "nickeled and dimed to death" by Korea-style aggression in the future. The conjecture is not a product of evidence suggesting a link—for example, references to the Korean War in the records of the meetings in which the New Look strategy was worked out. It turns out that there are certain documents which suggest a connection, but you only realize the significance of these documents once the conjecture takes root in your mind.[8] The real source for this idea is a conviction that for a major policy move of this sort, the particular historical context is always important,[9] and that you can conceive of a certain logic tying these things together.

Similarly, there is the problem of interpreting the Berlin Crisis of 1958–61. The Soviet "ultimatum" that led to the crisis is explained by scholars like Adam Ulam and Jack Schick in terms of Soviet anxiety about West Germany becoming a nuclear power. What makes it plausible to assume a linkage of this sort? You make assumptions about political behavior being in some way a function of what really matters: because of the size,

[8] See, for example, an undated memorandum from early 1953, not signed but clearly written by Dulles himself, Dulles Papers, White House Memoranda Series, Box 8, folder "General Foreign Policy Matters (3)," Eisenhower Library, Abilene, Kansas. The memo has no title, but can be identified by its mandatory review number, MR 85-413 #12.

[9] This is one of those areas where the historian's instincts diverge from those of the political scientist. I remember being amazed in graduate school by E. E. Schattschneider's classic study of the making of the Hawley-Smoot tariff, *Politics, Pressures and the Tariff* (New York, 1935). In spite of the fact that the author drew all kinds of general conclusions from this case study, not once did he even mention that this tariff was worked out after the United States had been hit by the worst depression in its history, and that the case he studied might therefore be somewhat atypical. It is also worth noting that Desmond Ball's important analysis of the American strategic arms decisions of 1961, *Politics and Force Levels* (Berkeley and Los Angeles, 1980), made almost no mention of the Berlin Crisis, although it was bound to be on everyone's mind at the time, and thus almost certainly had an important bearing on the kinds of decisions that were made.

the history, the geographical position, and the industrial and technological capabilities of the German nation, the fate of Germany is bound to be a matter of enormous concern to the Soviet Union. One assumes, in other words, that Soviet policy is not indiscriminately expansionist—that it does not aim mechanically at filling "every nook and cranny in the basin of world power"—but rather that some concerns are far more salient than others. This is linked to the general idea that fear is a more powerful emotion than greed, which in turn lies at the heart of a set of more specific arguments relating to Soviet fears about Germany. There is the key point that while the German nuclear issue was important, it was not an isolated issue, but was rather embedded in a whole complex of related problems— what people at the time still called the "German question." In particular, there was the fact that the West German government viewed itself as the only legitimate government for all of Germany, that it refused to accept even the eastern borders of East Germany, that it spoke of changing the situation by creating positions of strength (the term itself was apparently picked up from Acheson), that its new army was led by veterans of the Wehrmacht that had invaded Russia scarcely more than a decade earlier, and so on. The West German alliance with America raised the prospect that the Germans, especially if they acquired nuclear weapons of their own, might be able to manipulate and exploit the risk of a great U.S.-Soviet war for purposes of their own, purposes which their allies by no means fully shared.

The idea here is that by the mid-1950s, with regard to Europe at any rate, the Soviet Union had become essentially a status quo power. During the Stalin period, the USSR could scarcely bring itself to accept the division of Germany as permanent, let alone as desirable, but under Khrushchev, the Soviet attitude appears to have undergone a radical change. "We will not agree to a united Germany that is not socialist," Khrushchev told Harriman during the extraordinary ten-hour meeting they had in June 1959. "In fact, no one wants a united Germany. De Gaulle told us so; the British have told us so; and Adenauer himself when he was here said he was not interested in unification. Why, then do you insist on talking about it?"[10]

This sort of thinking leads to the idea that the Soviets by this time would not have welcomed even a unified Communist Germany. It was hard enough, the argument would be, for them to keep their little Slavic (and non-Slavic) brothers in Eastern Europe under control; how could they hope to exert permanent control over a great nation like Germany? And if a powerful Communist state were truly independent, this might

[10] Owen to State Department, June 26, 1959, President's Office File, Box 126, folder "USSR. Vienna Meeting. Background Documents 1953–61 (D)," Kennedy Library, Boston.

lead to very serious problems, as their experience with China was then very vividly demonstrating. Why on earth, then, should they take any serious risk of war in order to bring about a basic change in the status quo—to disrupt the NATO alliance, to eject American power from Europe—if that would ultimately lead to German unification under Communist auspices?

This kind of argument is of course simply an interpretation; the fact that one can speculate along these lines in itself proves nothing. Even if you think that this type of thinking makes perfect sense in power political terms, that is no reason to assume that it adequately explains what actually happened. There is no guarantee that the behavior of any state is ever fully guided by rational analysis of this sort. But the assumption of rationality, in history as in other areas of scholarship, generally serves as a good basis for a first approximation. Thinking along these lines conflicts with conventional interpretations on a number of key points; these differences generate specific problems that help define and operationalize the research strategy.

In particular, the idea, as rough and as tenuous as it is, that the Berlin Crisis was at its heart related to the German nuclear weapons issue acts as a kind of engine driving the research effort. First, one would like to know what German policy on nuclear weapons in fact was. The first step here is a careful reading of Catherine Kelleher's book, and also the contemporary information reported in the very well indexed *New York Times*.[11] Then there is the question of the interpretation of the mid-1950s—the period of the Austrian State Treaty, the Geneva Summit, the Rapacki Plan. Were the Soviets trying to head off a nuclearized Germany by means of a "soft" policy, and was it the failure of this policy that led them to opt for the tougher strategy of using Berlin as a lever? But the more basic problems have to do with the German question as a whole. How, first of all, is West German policy—the "policy of strength"—to be understood? Was the Adenauer government really completely committed to reunification, or did it—did Adenauer himself—view the issue more ambivalently? Here it helps to know something about German history, and in particular about the way the Catholics, especially in the Rhineland, had felt about the traditional German state; it helps to know something about Adenauer's role in Rhenish politics in the troubled period after World War I. The issue is worth pursuing, if only because questions of this sort played a central role in German politics in the 1950s.

---

[11] Note especially articles like "Adenauer Favors Nuclear Weapons" and "Bonn House Backs Nuclear Weapons," *New York Times*, March 21 and 26, 1958; Catherine Kelleher, *Germany and the Politics of Nuclear Weapons* (New York, 1975). See also Gordon Craig, "Germany and NATO: The Rearmament Debate, 1950–1958," in Klaus Knorr, ed., *NATO and American Security* (Princeton, 1959), pp. 243–49.

And what about the other Western Powers? Did they really *want* a unified Germany of any sort—or did they even know what they wanted? Was there any chance for a negotiated solution to the problem of German reunification, and if so, why was it allowed to slip away? And again, what exactly did the policy of creating "positions of strength" mean in this regard? What kind of strategy of effecting change in central Europe did people have in mind, and how seriously is it to be taken?

All these issues go right to the heart of the story. The German question was salient because what was at stake here was the overall structure of power in Europe; and the question of German nuclear weapons had such great importance because it was so closely bound up with the German question as a whole.

What has all this amounted to so far? Two tentative links in a causal chain have emerged. You can see how things might have gone from *a* to *b*—from Korea to the New Look—at the beginning of the Eisenhower period, and from *c* to *d*—from the German nuclear weapons issue to Berlin—toward its end. This partial framework almost automatically raises the question of whether there was any connection between *b* and *c*—that is, whether the New Look led to the projected nuclearization of West Germany. To raise the question is virtually to answer it, at least at the highly speculative level we are still working on. The New Look, by degrading the importance of conventional forces, by practically guaranteeing that any major war in Europe would be nuclear, gave the Germans a tremendous incentive to think seriously about developing nuclear forces of their own, which evidently was the only kind of military power that would carry real political weight. It was (as James King once pointed out) like a military equivalent of Gresham's Law: the "bad currency" of nuclear weaponry was driving the "good" conventional currency out of circulation.

Again, the basic function of all this is to give some focus and direction to the research effort. Assuming that there was a linkage of this sort between the New Look and German military policy in the late 1950s, how much of it was "pull" from the German side, as opposed to "push" from the American? What in fact was American policy on nuclear sharing, and how did it run its course? Every now and then you come across a document that makes these issues come alive.[12] And the relevance of other issues suddenly becomes much clearer—British and French nuclear weapons policy, for example.

[12] For example, see the "Memorandum of Conference with the President," February 8, 1960, Declassified Documents Collection, 1985/529: "This means that there will be no monopoly on possession of nuclear weapons. The President said that it is because of this possibility that he has always strongly favored the sharing of our weapons. It makes little sense not to share them when nations can, with facility, provide them for themselves."

This focusing function also works in another somewhat different way. Looking at the emerging schema as a whole, there are basic facts which just do not fit. These now become especially salient. To take the most important case: why did the Soviets revive the Berlin issue in 1961 after the Americans—or so it seems at first glance—had begun to move rather dramatically away from the whole idea of nuclear sharing? Could the answer have anything to do with their relations with China, obviously their other great concern at the time? Did they want to show the Chinese how tough they were with the West, and thus maybe salvage their alliance? Or perhaps the goal was to clear the decks in the West, while the facade of the Chinese alliance was still intact.

The general idea is hardly new: similar arguments about China play a major role in Adam Ulam's highly speculative interpretation of Soviet foreign policy in this period.[13] Ulam, in fact, argues that Soviet relations with China were behind even the first phase of the Berlin Crisis in 1958–59: "The growing trouble with China was to precipitate the Khrushchev regime into another crisis with the West."[14] Claims of this sort help bring some basic problems into focus: what exactly happened in Sino-Soviet relations at this time to set off the Berlin Crisis? Did it have anything to do with the Taiwan Straits affair that had taken place a little earlier in the year? But if the Taiwan Straits Crisis of 1958 led to the Berlin Crisis, why had the previous Taiwan Straits Crisis of 1954–55 been followed by a period of U.S.-Soviet detente?

Moreover, just thinking about the possible role of China links up with certain other lines of thought. One is rooted in certain reactions to the older American strategic literature from the 1950s and 1960s. It was the conventional wisdom at that time among critics of the Eisenhower strategy that one of the problems with massive retaliation was that it tended to cement relations between the Soviet Union and China, whereas America's primary goal should have been to drive a wedge between these two powers. "One of the basic indictments of an excessive emphasis on a strategy of all-out war," Henry Kissinger wrote in *Nuclear Weapons and Foreign Policy*, "is that its inability to differentiate and graduate its pressures may actually contribute to the consolidation and the unity of the Soviet bloc." Thomas Schelling argued along similar lines a decade later in *Arms and Influence*: "We came at last to treat the Sino-Soviet split as a real one; but it would have been wiser not to have acknowledged their fusion in the first place. In our efforts to dramatize and magnify the Soviet

---

[13] Adam Ulam, *Expansion and Coexistence: The History of Soviet Foreign Policy, 1917–67* (New York, 1968), chap. 9.

[14] Ibid., p. 619.

threat, we sometimes present the Soviet Union with a deterrent asset of a kind we find hard to create for ourselves."[15]

A "deterrent asset" pure and simple? Hadn't we also imposed on them a huge liability? In reacting to passages like these, one is led naturally to the opposite hypothesis that the Eisenhower policy—the policy of treating the Communist world as a single, monolithic bloc, and the military strategy associated with it—might actually have been one of the chief factors leading to the Sino-Soviet schism. After all, if the United States got into a major war with China, this policy meant that there was a risk that it might attack the Soviet Union as well, and this gave the Soviets a tremendous incentive to distance themselves from the Chinese, or at least to try to rein them in and keep them from pursuing a provocative policy. So massive retaliation might have tended to create tensions between the two great Communist powers.

Thus a hypothesis begins to take shape, and it directs research into particular areas: how exactly did the American government view Sino-Soviet relations, and how, if at all, did it try to influence them? This line of thought creates a certain sensitivity, a sharpening of antennae, so that documents that you might have otherwise paid little attention to now assume new importance. Consider, for example, the following extract from a recently declassified CIA memo of July 1, 1955:

> *If indeed the Soviets are now more keenly aware of the dangers of nuclear war, they must have regarded recent mounting tensions in the Formosa Straits with real apprehension.* Despite the many ties between Peiping and Moscow, the USSR must be worried about the possible unpredictability of their Chinese ally, and the chances of its taking action which would undesirably involve the USSR. Even local hostilities in the Formosa Strait might require greater material support from the USSR and might involve great danger of embroiling the USSR itself.[16]

The implication was clear: conflict in the Taiwan Straits area could lead to real friction between the Russians and the Chinese. Did a sense that this kind of effect was likely have any impact on American policy? Considerations of this sort might not have played any role at the beginning of the Eisenhower period when the New Look was adopted. But perhaps they were factored into policy calculations in the late 1950s, when the Eisenhower strategy was under attack both within and outside the administration. In any case, basic facts that you already know—that the Sino-Soviet split emerged so sharply in the course of the Eisenhower period,

[15] Henry Kissinger, *Nuclear Weapons and Foreign Policy* (New York, 1957), p. 148; Thomas Schelling, *Arms and Influence* (New Haven, Conn., 1966), p. 62.

[16] "Intelligence Comments on NSC 5524," July 1, 1955, Declassified Documents Collection, 1985/848. Emphasis in original.

and that nuclear issues played a central role in the developing tension—are suddenly seen in a new light.

The same thing is true of evidence that you come across virtually by accident. Consider, for example, the following quotation from Secretary Dulles, cited in John Gaddis's *Strategies of Containment*: "the best hope for intensifying the strain and difficulties between Communist China and Russia would be to keep the Chinese under maximum pressure rather than by relieving such pressure."[17] This certainly relates to the issue, but I had only realized its importance when I was rereading the book for a class after I had already begun to think along these lines; the relevance and broader meaning of the quotation had completely escaped me the first time I had read it.

Moreover, the idea that the German and Chinese issues are not totally autonomous, but were related to each other in some fundamental way, makes you perk up and pay special attention whenever the documents show the Soviet leadership saying anything of this sort. Take, for example, the minutes of the Camp David summit of September 1959. Khrushchev, on September 15, took a very reasonable line on Berlin, and in fact on Germany as a whole:

> It would be desirable [he said] if we could work out common language, recognizing the fact of the existence of two German states, and confirming that neither side would try to bring about either a Socialist or a Capitalist solution by force. If we could make that point clear, then we would remove the danger from the situation. If we were to speak of our sympathies, then we both know where the sympathies of the other lie. American sympathies lie with West Germany and the system existing there. Soviet sympathies are with East Germany and the system prevailing on that side. It would be well to recognize the facts. That doesn't mean that the United States would accord juridical recognition to the GDR, but would accept the state of fact as it exists.[18]

---

[17] John Lewis Gaddis, *Strategies of Containment* (New York, 1982), p. 143. The document Gaddis cites has now been published: U.S. Department of State, *Foreign Relations of the United States*, 1952–54 series, vol. 5, p. 1809. There are a number of other documents that point in this same general direction. See especially Eisenhower to Churchill, February 19, 1955, p. 3, Ann Whitman File, International Series, Box 17, folder "President—Churchill, 1/1/55–4/7/55 (4)," Eisenhower Library, and also the report of Task Force B on the Solarium Study, July 16, 1953, p. 17, Office of the Special Assistant for National Security Affairs, NSC Series, Subject Subseries, Box 9, Eisenhower Library. See finally David Mayers, "Eisenhower and Communism: Later Findings," in R. A. Melanson and D. Mayers, eds., *Reevaluating Eisenhower* (Urbana, Ill., 1987), esp. pp. 89, 92., and an important article by Gaddis: "Dividing Adversaries: The United States and International Communism, 1945–1958," in his *The Long Peace: Inquiries into the History of the Cold War* (New York, 1987).

[18] Memorandum of Conversation, September 15, 1959, p. 9, in President's Office Files, Box 126, folder "USSR. Vienna Meeting. Background Documents, 1953–61 (C)," John F. Kennedy Library, Boston.

But then, on September 27, Khrushchev brought up the issue of China, attacking the American policy of supporting the Nationalist government on Taiwan. When Eisenhower laid out the standard American position,

> Mr. Khrushchev said that he had to respect the President's statement. He merely would point out that he considered that there was a lack of consistency in our policy. The President said that if the two German states remained, they would be an indefinite hot bed of conflict. If this statement was true with respect to Germany, then it was true with respect to China, too. The President agreed that it was possible to make such a comparison. However, he commented that human affairs got very badly tangled at times and that we would simply have to try to straighten them out. Mr. Khrushchev replied that he realized this but that he had just wanted to point out the inconsistency of our policy. . . . The President said he wanted to add that while he admitted the comparison between the German and Chinese situations, he wished to point out that the U.S. seeks peaceful settlements in both instances.[19]

Now, what inferences can be drawn from this discussion? The basic point is that in drawing the analogy between China and Germany, Khrushchev was opening himself to some obvious counterarguments: "You say we must respect facts and accept the reality of two states in Germany. Given the parallel which you yourself draw, doesn't the same point also apply to China? Or, alternatively, if a unified state is the only solution in the Chinese case, why doesn't the same argument also apply with regard to Germany?" This rejoinder is so obvious that you have to wonder if Khrushchev was expecting something of this sort—if he was in fact broaching some kind of a deal.[20] Or perhaps this taunting of Eisenhower about American inconsistency on a pair of issues where Soviet policy was at least as inconsistent reflected Khrushchev's sense of what he could get away with because of Eisenhower's obtuseness.[21] You sometimes get the

---

[19] Memorandum of Conversation, September 27, 1959, pp. 5–6, in President's Office Files, Box 126, folder "USSR. Vienna Meeting. Background Documents, 1953–1961 (C)," JFK Library.

[20] Note in this context some remarks the Chinese made a few years later: "Back from the Camp David talks, [Khrushchev] went so far as to try to sell China the U.S. plot of the 'two Chinas' . . ." Quoted in Ulam, pp. 628–29.

[21] Note, along these lines, the comments he made during the extraordinary ten hours he spent with Harriman a few months earlier: "Speaking most confidentially, he [Khrushchev] stated it was embarrassing if not unpleasant to note the manner in which Mr. Eisenhower had behaved at Geneva, not as a maker of policy but as an executor of Mr. Dulles' policies. Mr. Dulles, sitting on his right during the conference, had simply passed Eisenhower notes which the latter had then read out without contributing anything of his own"; "Comparing him [Harriman] to Eisenhower, he stated, 'You talk with authority and not as a lackey, and that is why we have been so glad to receive you.' " Owen to Department of State, June 26, 1959, pp. 6, 11, in President's Office Files, Box 126, folder USSR. Vienna Meeting. Background Documents, 1953–61 (D), JFK Library.

impression that the Soviets viewed the Americans, and Eisenhower in particular, as not too bright: the danger, as they saw it, was not American
aggressiveness as such, but that the United States because of its childish
approach to international politics, might get drawn into a war in support,
for example, of an aggressive West German policy.[22]

The time has come now to stand back and look at what has been going
on here. The basic aim was to construct a story, and the first rough
schema to emerge was a simple linear model: Korea leads to the New
Look, which leads to the nuclearization of NATO and the projected nuclearization of the Bundeswehr, and that in turn leads to the Berlin Crisis.
But now, with the addition of these ideas about China, the central logic
of the story is broadening out. A new element is being added: the New
Look—and one could as well add the Korean War itself[23]—also affects
the course of Sino-Soviet relations, and this in turn may have had an important bearing on the course of the Berlin Crisis.

This, however, is just the beginning. There are many other causal cross-
currents that have to be worked into the basic model. Take, for example,
the question of the link between American military policy and foreign
policy in this period. We now associate a heavy nuclear emphasis with the
political right; it is the left that wants to move away from nuclear weapons toward a greater reliance on conventional forces. But in the late
1950s and early 1960s things were not so simple. For someone like Dean
Acheson, for example, a conventional buildup was linked to political
goals, especially with regard to Germany, that went beyond the mere
maintenance of the status quo: conventional forces were "useable" in a
way that nuclear forces were not.[24] This is typical of the sort of linkage

[22] Note in this context Ambassador Thompson's general impressions about Soviet policy
in early 1961: "I believe Soviet interests as such lie rather in German problem as whole than
Berlin. Soviet Union interested in stabilization their western frontier and Communist re-
gimes in Eastern Europe, particularly East Germany which probably most vulnerable. Soviets also deeply concerned with German military potential and fear West Germany will
eventually take action which will face them with choice between world war or retreat from
East Germany." Thompson to Secretary of State, February 4, 1961, Declassified Documents
Collection, 1977/74B.

[23] See Mineo Nakajima, "The Sino-Soviet Confrontation: Its Roots in the Background of
the Korean War," *Australian Journal of Chinese Affairs*, 1979; Roy U. T. Kim, "Korea and
the Sino-Soviet Dispute," unpub. diss., University of Pennsylvania, 1969; and Roger Kanet
comment in Francis Heller, ed., *The Korean War: A 25-Year Perspective* (Lawrence, Kansas,
1977), p. 84. The origins of the conflict between the Chinese and the Soviet Communist
parties go back to the 1920s, and even in the immediate aftermath of the Chinese Revolution, it does not take too much reading between the lines to detect evidence of Soviet dis-
comfort. Note especially Molotov's extraordinary remark, in a speech he gave on Stalin's
birthday on December 21, 1949: "One cannot help but admit the world-wide significance
of the formation of the Chinese People's Republic." Quoted in Ronald L. Letteney, "Foreign
Policy Factionalism under Stalin," unpub. diss., Johns Hopkins University, 1971, p. 297.

[24] See especially Acheson's September 1963 speech to the Institute for Strategic Studies

that emerges in the course of normal research, and that has to be worked into the basic analytical framework.

Or consider an argument that can be made about the purely military side of the interaction process. The New Look, it seems, had an important influence on Soviet military policy in the late 1950s: the extraordinary decline of Soviet military manpower that took place during this period probably should be understood, at least in large part, as a reaction to the Eisenhower strategy: given that the Americans, in the event of major war in Europe, were going to escalate in any case, what was the point of maintaining a massive conventional war–fighting capability? And it was this, it seems, that brought conventional parity within reach by the end of the Eisenhower period, thus making an American conventional buildup a plausible military option under Kennedy. This in turn affected what America actually did when the Berlin Crisis reached a climax in 1961.

These conjectures represent just a handful of those that will have to be made and tested; the hypotheses and arguments about causal linkages sketched out in this section are just the tip of the iceberg. Even if they all turn out to have some validity, they capture only part of a very complex story. The key thing to bear in mind, however, is that the goal of historical analysis is not simply to identify these different strands and study them in isolation from each other. The aim is to get a sense for how they all interact so that you can weave them together into a story. This can take time and there are dangers en route—especially the danger of falling in love with one's own pet theories and giving an interpretation that goes far beyond what the evidence really warrants. It is for this reason that the test of evidence is so crucial: speculation may be essential as an engine of analysis, but only a deep respect for the evidence as final arbiter can keep it under control.

MACRO-LOGIC, MICRO-ANALYSIS

Since it is impossible to study everything in equal detail, you have to develop a sense of priorities. It is necessary to focus on specific problems

published in Adelphi Paper No. 5; note Brodie's comments on this in his book *War and Politics* (New York, 1973), p. 402. Acheson, in his well-known report on Berlin of August 1, 1961, had called for the "de-Sovietization of East Germany" as a long-term American goal. National Security Files, Box 82, Kennedy Library.

Note also in this context Henry Kissinger's argument for a limited war capability in order to support such "positive goals" as the reunification of Germany and the relaxation of Soviet control over Eastern Europe in *Nuclear Weapons and Foreign Policy* (New York, 1957), esp. pp. 13, 37, 39, 42; and also Thomas Schelling's argument for conventional forces as the only way of supporting an interventionist policy in Eastern Europe in David Abshire and Richard Allen, eds., *National Security: Political, Military, and Economic Strategies in the Decade Ahead* (New York, 1963), pp. 626–27, 735.

where close analysis of the sources can have an important payoff in terms of the light it sheds on the overall story. And in fact one of the basic rationales for trying to develop a rough sense for the broader story is to get some feel for what these areas are—for which particular episodes played a key role in shaping the course of events.

In this respect, the history of the nuclear age is to be approached in much the same way as the history of earlier periods. After the First World War, for example, the structure of power in Europe—how much freedom of maneuver Germany was to have, and what the limits on French power would be—was worked out in the conflict over German reparations in the early postwar years. The conflict culminated in the Ruhr Crisis of 1923, the great test of will and of strength between France and Germany in this period. Studying these events (which I spent about ten years doing), you get the sense of something very basic coming to a head. This was no arcane dispute over a mere technical problem; it was because the structure of power in Europe was at stake that this whole business really mattered and was thus worth examining in detail.

Similarly, for the period after World War II, you can look back and see how the basic structure of world power was worked out. The German question was clearly of central importance in this regard, and once again crises played an important role in this larger process. Studying the Berlin Crisis of 1958–61—the crisis itself, its origins and its consequences—you again get a strong sense that something fundamental was building up to a kind of climax: the underlying structure of the system was being tested and clarified. It was almost as though the system was coming to terms with its own basic structure. Certainly what happened during the crisis, especially in 1961, was to have very important consequences for how things were to develop from that point on. It thus makes sense to focus on the Berlin crisis as a central part of a general research strategy.

A political scientist, of course, would have no trouble accepting this conclusion. The Berlin Crisis would obviously make an interesting "case study." As opposed to other areas of the world where geographical conditions were such that conventional military strength could be quite effective as a means of exerting power, the isolation of West Berlin within the Soviet bloc meant that nuclear aspects of defense policy had an unusual salience. Because of the sharp way the nuclear problem was defined during the crisis, a study of this episode lends itself to an analysis of basic theoretical problems having to do with the role that nuclear forces play in international political life. One could argue, moreover, that the fact that there were two distinct phases to the crisis—the Eisenhower phase in 1958–59 and the Kennedy phase in 1961 (or three phases if we include the Berlin Blockade affair of 1948–49)—provides us with something as close to a controlled experiment as is ever found in the history of international politics.

These are all perfectly valid rationales for studying the crisis. But they are not really *historians'* arguments. The whole idea of producing a series of "case studies"—of generating the elements of a sample, which can then be analyzed via the method of structured comparisons in order to produce insights of a theoretical nature—simply runs counter to the historian's sensibility. The crisis is treated as an isolated event, as an episode that could have happened at any point in time for all it matters to the analysis, and not as something whose real meaning derives from the fact that it is embedded in, and plays an important role in, a broader historical process.

This is, however, not to imply that the sorts of concerns the political scientist takes to the study of the crisis are foreign to the historian. In fact, the basic problem of the political role of nuclear forces is bound to be a focus for analysis, no matter who is studying the crisis. Were nuclear weapons really "unusable" in 1961? What kind of relation was there between nuclear planning and political behavior?

No historian working on the crisis can avoid having to come to grips with issues of this sort. It follows, therefore, that in studying the episode, a basic aim is to get some feel for what would have happened if the crisis had erupted into armed conflict. This is obviously a question that no one can answer with any certainty. The closest you can come to it is to explore how people dealt with this problem at the time, what kind of contingency planning was done, who was involved in it, and how seriously it was taken. What kind of light do the sources in the Kennedy Library throw on this issue?

There is little direct evidence, but one document—marked "Meeting—Cabinet Room—Oct. 20, 1961—10 a.m."—was very suggestive:

> First: What I want is a sequence of graduated responses to Soviet/GDR actions in denial of our rights access. The purpose is to maintain our rights and preserve our alliance. The responses should begin with the non-military and move to the military in the sequence outlined below. We cannot plan in advance the exact time each response should be initiated; for one reason, because we cannot now predict the date of Soviet/GDR response, for another because we cannot foresee the duration or the consequences of each response. But there are some principles applicable to this matter of timing. The earlier responses should be thoroughly prepared in advance and the purpose should be to initiate them and keep them going long enough so that the next response may, if necessary, come in when needed. This requires vigor in preparation, readiness for action, and caution against going off half-cocked.
>
> The military sequence should begin with the air action outlined in IIIB and every effort in preparation and execution should be made to achieve success.

The rewards of success would be great indeed. The next steps, if needed, should be those outlined in IIA and C, executed for the reasons given nearly simultaneously. This will require the timely movement of considerable forces to your command, and appropriate dispositions on your central front.

Should it appear that Soviet forces sufficient to crush the ground action are being brought into play the response must be that contained in Paragraph II and must be decisive.[25]

How is this document to be interpreted? The speaker is not identified, but one judges from the tone that President Kennedy was doing the talking. Clearly, a high military commander was being addressed: the document refers to "the timely movement of considerable forces to *your* command" and "*your* central front." Who, aside from the President himself, could lay down the law to such a commander the way this document evidently does?

What were the military measures to which the document referred? There was obviously a companion document in which they were outlined, but which a mandatory declassification request could not pry loose. One therefore once again has to fall back on inference. The options are obviously becoming increasingly serious as you go along. What is left, at the end of the document, when the Soviets are about to crush this large-scale ground action? What remaining option could possibly be "decisive"? Doesn't this suggest rather strongly that this final response involved nuclear forces? It in fact does seem from other sources that the term "decisive" then had a nuclear connotation.[26]

This string of inferences, however, is too fragile to support the basic conclusion that if forced to make the ultimate decision, the President would have gone for some kind of nuclear option in 1961 rather than accept a massive defeat. A conclusion as fundamental as that should never rest on a single document in any case. An obvious next step, therefore, was to try to check this interpretation against the memories of those who took part in the meeting. What was striking here was that not a single person still alive who took part in the meeting remembered President Kennedy saying anything of the sort. In fact, and regardless of where they stand politically today, a number of them stressed the point that the President deliberately refrained from giving any clear indication of what his ultimate decision would be. It was also important to note that there was another copy of this document in the same file where the crucial final paragraph had been crossed out.

What is to be made of all this? One possibility is that the President had

[25] President's Office Files, Box 116a, folder "Germany. General. 8/61–10/61."

[26] See the reference to a speech given by Gen. Norstad in Brodie, *Strategy in the Missile Age*, p. 341.

dictated the document for possible use at the meeting, but was uncertain about the point suggested in the final paragraph, and decided in the final analysis not to make this sort of statement at all. The document is too interesting to ignore completely, but it is very hard to know how to assess it.

The point of the story is not simply that the research effort often takes you down blind alleys. It also tells you something about how the research process proceeds. You do not just absorb documents passively, assuming that in some mechanical way they will add up to an interpretation. The process is much more active and directed. The broad goal of trying to understand how things ran their course in the period as a whole leads inevitably to the more specific question of trying to understand the role nuclear forces played in the story, and in particular how nuclear forces affected political behavior. The question of political utility is obviously linked to (although of course not identical with) the issue of military usability; both can best be studied by looking at periods of crisis. The issue is narrowed down still further to a study of the Berlin Crisis in 1961; and ultimately, the problem ends up focusing on the interpretation of a particular document.

Finally, this episode also throws a certain light on the organic character of historical research. Secretary of State Dean Rusk had attended the October 20 meeting, and he was therefore one of the people I asked to comment on the document. He wrote back that

> this was a discussion of contingency plans in the event the Soviets and the East Germans took action against West Berlin or the access routes thereto. The underlying idea was that the lowest level of force would be used at any particular time to maintain our access to West Berlin and that movement through additional phases of the contingency would depend upon Russian and East German reaction. Literally no one can say what would have been done in fact because only the President and the chiefs of the governments in NATO could have made those decisions and the situation did not reach that point.
>
> For reasons which I cannot specify, we assumed that the Soviet Union would become fully informed of these contingencies and would take such possibilities into full account in their decisions about the follow up to Chairman Khrushchev's ultimatum at Vienna about Berlin.[27]

This latter point was certainly a very intriguing comment. It seemed to imply that some sort of conduit—perhaps an espionage conduit—had been discovered, and that instead of rooting it out, the American govern-

---

[27] Rusk to the author, January 25, 1984. See also Norman Gelb, *The Berlin Wall* (New York, 1987), p. 143.

ment had decided to exploit it. If this was true, the whole issue of contingency planning, difficult to interpret in the first place, would have to be seen in a very different light. In any case, Rusk's comment stimulated a certain interest in the whole problem of intelligence and counterintelligence, especially as it related to the highest political level. Do we ever want the enemy to be able to eavesdrop on us? Can we effectively manipulate perceptions in this way? If we can, does our knowledge that this can be done ever get factored into basic policy decisions? Issues of this sort are then added to the research agenda: this is another part of the larger story that in some way has to be taken into account.

THE VALUE OF HISTORICAL ANALYSIS

To return now to the question we started out with: all this may be very interesting, but what difference does it make? The whole interpretation sketched out here is tentative and subject to change, but even if it were absolutely accurate, why should anyone care? What conceivable impact should any of this have on the way we deal with strategic issues?

The basic point to be made in response is that, whether we like it or not, the way the recent past is understood is always going to lie at the heart of our thinking about policy. These interpretations may never be laid out explicitly, and they may be naive or amateurish in the extreme; they are nonetheless going to carry enormous political weight.

Basic assumptions about policy often translate directly into particular interpretations of recent history. There is the idea, for example, that nuclear weapons are inherently unusable—that is, they cannot be used to support any purpose beyond simply "deterring their use by others"—and that nuclear forces, from a political point of view, therefore essentially cancel each other out. On the other hand, people often claim that nuclear weapons are the bedrock of international stability in Europe, that without them there would almost certainly have been another great war. Or, to take a final example, the common belief that arms control is of fundamental importance rests on the idea that the nuclear arms race is a basic source of international tension—that it has played a destabilizing role in global politics. Each of these claims rests on a particular interpretation of history—and, to a certain extent, on a *testable* interpretation of history. Historical analysis therefore can function as a kind of arbiter, or at least as a control, on ideas that lie at the heart of the nuclear debate.

This is, however, an essentially negative argument about the value of historical analysis. The real question is whether the historical approach has anything positive to contribute. What is distinctive about this approach is its emphasis on *process*. For example, it is not simply particular crises, taken as discrete episodes, that we historians are interested in studying. Our more basic interest is seeing how they fit into a larger scheme of things. When thinking about the role of nuclear weapons, the most important question for us is not *whether* they proved decisive in various crises, but rather *how* they influenced the course of events, in normal times as well as in periods of high tension. The *indirect* effects, the things that happen other than by design, are of particular interest when a story is being put together. But what do we gain by approaching the issue in this way? Why is a sense of process important?

The answer becomes obvious as soon as the problem is translated into more concrete terms. Does it matter, for example, whether the deployment of Soviet missiles in Cuba in 1962 is seen as an act of aggression pure and simple, or if, on the other hand, the Missile Crisis is viewed as a kind of aftershock of the Berlin Crisis? One could argue, for example, that the United States had taught the Soviets in 1961 that the strategic balance mattered politically, and that by deploying missiles in Cuba, the Soviets did not have any specific purpose in mind, but were simply trying to improve their general position as quickly and as cheaply as possible. At the very least, this is an interpretation worth considering; and if it turns out to be correct, the point would clearly have broad implications. Similarly, it certainly makes a difference if the Berlin Crisis itself is attributed solely to Soviet aggressiveness, or if it is understood as part of a process whereby the fate of Germany and the structure of power in Europe were worked out—a process wherein Western policy was by no means solely reactive. More generally, the idea, as Eisenhower put it in 1959, "that the Soviets are engaged in confronting the U.S. with a series of crises," that these tense situations have nothing to do with American policy but are simply laid on by the adversary, has a profound effect on the way both military and political issues are approached.[28]

In particular, if international politics is not to be viewed essentially in interactive terms, if, from the American standpoint, important challenges

---

[28] For the Eisenhower quotation: "Memorandum of Conference with the President," March 6, 1959, 5 p.m., p. 3. Declassified Documents Collection, 1981/598a.

Reading the documents, especially from the early 1950s, you get the sense that many people in the government assumed that dealing with the Soviet Union was almost like dealing with a force of nature: what the Soviets did—not just in foreign policy, but in military policy as well—was essentially beyond American control. See, for example, the Joint Chiefs of Staff memorandum of October 22, 1951: "The degree of the Soviet threat in each instance depends on the plans and intentions of the USSR, its willingness to engage in general hostilities, and/or its estimate as to the lengths to which it could go without provoking general hostilities. Inasmuch as these factors are not subject to control or determination by the United States or its allies, the initiative as to further hostilities on the part of the USSR and/or its satellites presently rests with the USSR." *Foreign Relations of the United States*, 1951, vol. 1, p. 240.

simply emerge in a kind of arbitrary way out of the other side's aggressiveness, then the test of military policy is what puts the country in the
best possible position for dealing with these situations once they arise.
The issue, that is, boils down to how something might influence behavior
during periods of crisis, and not how it would affect the normal course of
political relations among states. The test, in other words, is whether a
given move would "strengthen deterrence"—that is, how it might affect
the calculations of a potential aggressor, especially in crisis situations.

But if international conflict, now as in the prenuclear past, does not
revolve essentially around the threat of aggression, then it follows that
military policy should not be based so narrowly on the concept of deterrence—since it is aggression, and only aggression, that one seeks to deter.
If international conflict is seen in terms of an interactive process, it is that
process itself that we should try above all to control. And to control
something, you first have to understand how it works, what the basic
mechanisms are—and especially how the political and military sides of
the story interact with each other. We tend to think of this form of interaction in very crude terms—in terms of overt deterrent threats restraining
a potential aggressor when political disputes come to a head—but in reality the interaction process is a good deal more subtle and more complex.
The indirect effects play a central role: things often develop, for good or
for ill, in ways that nobody wanted or even anticipated.

What this suggests is that the historical approach can lead to arguments
and insights that might be of basic importance. At this point, the claim
does not have to be any stronger. It is in fact difficult to know exactly
how things will develop in this field of scholarship. Many of the people
involved in this work, both historians and historically minded political
scientists, have the sense that something important is beginning to happen
in this area, but it is hard to see where it will all lead.

What is clear, though, is that certain problems—problems of professional identity—will have to be faced and worked out as this area of
scholarship starts to develop. Historians in particular are under pressure
to show explicitly how their work bears on broader issues of foreign and
military policy. This is something we are reluctant to do, since one of the
basic values of the profession is to avoid being judgmental—to avoid taking too explicit a stand on theoretical, let alone on policy issues. The idea
is that clarity of vision depends on a kind of Olympian detachment—that
getting too involved with policy questions tends to limit your ability to
analyze things objectively.

Whatever force there is to this argument, it is evident that historians
are being drawn in this direction—that is, toward articulating explicitly
what there is to be learned from the study of the past. Academic political
scientists, for their part, have been reaching out in the past few years,

sometimes to the point where they are in effect doing history themselves. A process of cross-fertilization and intellectual interaction is just beginning to get off the ground, but already the people involved have the sense that this sort of thing is tremendously valuable. It may be odd for a historian to try to predict the future, but even now you can feel a certain momentum: clearly something important is taking shape on that border area where history and political science meet.

Appendix

Key to Abbreviations in Chapter Five

THE CITATIONS in general take the form: collection/series (if any)/subseries (if any)/box or volume/folder (unless obvious)/repository. Often for folder titles abbreviated versions are used. In the case of a series of citations from the same repository in a single note, the repository as a rule will only be cited once.

Archival Sources

HSTL: Harry S Truman Library, Independence, Missouri
  AP Dean Acheson Papers
DDEL: Dwight D. Eisenhower Library, Abilene, Kansas
  AWF Papers of Dwight D. Eisenhower as President (Ann Whitman File)
    A Administration Series
    AWD Ann Whitman Diary Series
    DDED Dwight D. Eisenhower Diary Series
    I International File
    NSC National Security Council Series
    DH Dulles-Herter Series
  SS White House Office. Office of the Staff Secretary
    I International Series
    ITM International Trips and Meetings Series
    S Subject Series
        A Alphabetical Subseries
        DoS Department of State Subseries
        DoD Department of Defense Subseries
        WH White House Subseries
  OSANSA Office of the Special Assistant for National Security Affairs
    NSC National Security Council Series
        PP Policy Papers Subseries
        S Subject Subseries
    SA Special Assistants Series
        P Presidential Subseries
        S Subject Subseries
  DP John Foster Dulles Papers
    GCM General Correspondence and Memoranda Series
    S Subject Series
    TC Telephone Conversations Series
    WHM White House Memoranda Series
  HP Christian Herter Papers

JFKL: John F. Kennedy Library, Boston, Massachusetts
 NSF National Security Files
 POF President's Office Files
USNA: United States National Archives, Washington, D.C.
 DSCF Department of State Central (or Decimal) Files, Diplomatic Branch.
 The citation is by decimal number only.
 PPS Records of the Policy Planning Staff, Diplomatic Branch
 JCS (date[s]) Papers of the Joint Chiefs of Staff, series for given date(s), Military Records Branch. The citation is by CCS number (and if necessary section number) only.
 JCS Twining JCS Chairman's Papers, Twining, Military Records Branch. Again, the citation is by CCS number (and if necessary section number).
PRO: Public Record Office, Kew (Great Britain)

Published Sources

FRUS United States Department of State, *Foreign Relations of the United States.* Citations are by series, volume, and page number.

DG United States Senate, Committee on Foreign Relations, *Documents on Germany, 1944–1961*, reprinted version (New York: Greenwood Press, 1968).

FMM United States Department of State, *Foreign Ministers Meeting, May–August 1959, Geneva*, International Organization and Conference Series, no. 8 (Washington, D.C., 1959).

DDC Declassified Documents Collection. Available on microfiche at a number of university libraries and from the Center for Research Libraries in Chicago (to member institutions). Citations are by year and number. For example, DDC 1985/336 refers to document number 336 in the microfiche series for 1985. Because of its accessibility, the DDC number given here is preference to archival citations for the same documents.

Other Abbreviations

MCP Memorandum of Conference with the President
GDR German Democratic Republic
SACEUR/CINCEUR Supreme Allied Commander, Europe/Commander in Chief, U.S. European Command

Index

Acheson, Dean, 107–9, 111, 112n, 114n, 120n, 125–26, 159, 173, 175n, 217–18, 222, 230, 233
Adenauer, Konrad, 175n, 176, 176n, 177–83, 188n, 191, 197–98, 198n, 200–201, 205, 207, 226, 228–30, 233, 240n, 271
Albertini, Luigi, 50–51, 63, 75–76, 78–79, 81–85, 89–91, 94, 98
Allison, John, 122
Anderson, Orvil, 105, 117–18
arms control, 200, 207, 229. *See also* stability theory
Attlee, Clement, 120n, 163n

Baruch, Bernard, 124n
Bedell Smith, Walter, 116, 132n
Berchtold, Count Leopold von, 80, 82
Berlin, U.S. strategy on, 1948–53, 130–31, 130n, 131n, 209–10; crisis expected, 1950–53, 150–51, 150n, 151n; under Eisenhower, 209–12, 265; under Kennedy, 217, 222–26
Berlin crisis (1958–62), 169–234, 269–73, 279–82. *See also* Cuban missile crisis
Bethmann Hollweg, Theobald von, 53n, 56–59, 61–62, 75, 78, 80, 83–92, 97
Blackett, P.M.S., 5n
Bohlen, Charles, 104, 114
Bowie, Robert, 143n, 189, 207n, 214–15
Bracken, Paul, 47, 72
Bradley, Omar, 119, 122, 125, 130–31, 156n, 157
Brodie, Bernard, vii, ix, 3, 28, 33–34, 44–46, 261; and Cuban missile crisis, 236, 236n, 258; and economists, 12n–13n; and Herman Kahn, 39n; and inadvertent escalation, 17n; inconsistency, 18, 32–33; and limited war thinking, 4–11; and nuclear coercion, 7–11, 15–16, 27; and outbreak of World War I, 58; and preventive war, 21, 21n, 103–4; and stability theory, 33, 44; and strategic force vulnerability, 10, 18–19, 20, 44; and tactical use of nuclear weapons, 10, 18, 33–34; and the military, 11–12

Bruce, David, 184, 197, 207
Bülow, Prince Bernard von, 61
Bundy, McGeorge, 216, 224n, 225, 235n, 238n, 239, 243–44, 251, 264–65
Burchinal, David, 249, 252n–53n, 254, 257
bureaucratic politics paradigm, origins of, 28–31

China, U.S. policy toward, 125, 125n–26n, 127, 131, 148–49; and Berlin crisis, 205–7, 206n–7n, 216, 266, 273–76, 277n
Churchill, Winston, 105, 140, 204–5
city-avoidance. *See* coercion
civil defense, 218, 222
civil-military relations, 58–62, 89–91
Clausewitz, Carl von, 7, 45, 134n, 138
Clay, Lucius, 230
coercion, as the "business of war," 38; and city-avoidance in nuclear war, 8, 10, 11, 27–29, 31, 33, 37; in Cuban missile crisis, 237, 240–41, 244; and risk manipulation, 15–17, 27, 36–37; technique of threat-making, 132n, 212, 221, 224, 282; and "threat value" of nuclear forces, 4, 7–11, 15–16, 27, 31, 33, 37
Collins, J. Lawton, 124, 156n, 161
Conrad von Hotzendorf, Baron Franz, 80, 82
counterforce, 22, 26–29, 31, 33–38; during Berlin crisis, 225, 226n; during Cuban missile crisis, 246, 246n, 256. *See also* preemption, stability theory, strategic balance
Couve de Murville, Maurice, 172–73
Craig, Gordon, 58, 61, 75, 89
Cuban missile crisis, 235–60; Eisenhower predicts, 203–4

"danger zone" thinking, 112, 114–15, 114n, 115n, 121
Dean, Gordon, 135–36
De Gaulle, Charles, 166–67, 179, 184n

deterrence theory, criticized as premised on near-perfect rationality, 17; as influencing U.S. policy in Vietnam, 43–44, 43n; as nonchalant about nuclear war, 39; as too based on game theory, 14n

Dillon, Douglas, 203–4, 241–42

Dulles, John Foster, and surprise attack, 24n; and basic U.S. policy, 136, 144–46; and Berlin crisis, 194–99, 204; and China, 206, 206n–7n; and future of NATO, 139, 213–14; and German question, 174n, 175–76, 178, 185; and limited war, 40–41, 211n; and nuclear weapons, 182, 266–67, 267n; and U-2 overflights, 208n

economists and strategy, 12–15

Eisenhower, Dwight, and NATO strategy (1951), 160–61; and aggressive strategies, 139–41, 144, 145, 150, 175n; and alliance politics, 166–67; and basic strategy ("New Look"), 40–43, 137–39, 138n, 147, 162, 214–15, 265–66, 269, 284; and Berlin crisis, 170, 171, 176, 194–97, 201–9, 212–13; Berlin strategy, 209–12; and Britain, 186, 187, 198–201; and France, 186, 198; and German question, 175n, 176; and nuclear sharing, 185–90; and preemption, 134n, 162, 163n, 209, 266n; and "redeployment," 168, 185, 185n, 186; and U.S. vulnerability to surprise attack, 24n

Falkenhayn, Erich von, 88, 96

Fellner, William, 15

FIG (France-Italy-Germany) agreement, 184n

Fischer, Fritz, and origins of World War I, 49–57, 85–86, 91n

Forrestal, James, 154

forward Defense, 153, 157, 159; and nuclear-based strategy, 159–60

François-Poncet, André, 175n, 178n

Gaither Committee, 24n, 146n

game theory, role of, 14, 14n

Gates, Thomas, 41

Geneva Foreign Ministers' Meeting, 172–73, 195, 200, 202

German nuclear weapons question, 164, 172, 172n, 173, 180–83, 182n, 184n,

187–91, 189n, 201, 207, 216, 228–29, 269–72

German question (1949–59), 148, 150–52, 163, 173–80; and France, 177n, 178–79, 198; and Great Britain, 176n, 177n, 178, 198–201; and USSR, 179–80

Germany. See Adenauer, Berlin crisis, German question, German nuclear weapons issue, World War I

Gilpatric, Roswell, 221

Grey, Sir Edward, 72, 79, 81, 85–86, 97

Gromyko, Andrei, 173, 228–29, 231

Groves, Leslie, 100, 103

Gruenther, Alfred, 159

Harmon, H. R., 119, 156

Harriman, Averell, 179, 202, 215

Herter, Christian, 176, 193, 196–97, 205

Hilsman, Roger, 221

Hitch, Charles, 6, 12–13, 28, 37

Holstein, Baron Friedrich von, 60–62

Howard, Michael, 48, 81

Hoyos, Count Alexander, 53n, 69n

Hull, John, 119, 156

inadvertent war, defined, 48; and Cuban missile crisis, 238–39, 255–56, 258; Khrushchev's fear of (1961), 219; and mobilization system in 1914, 72–73, 76, 81; and World War I, 47, 48, 51, 55–56. See also preemption, security dilemma, stability theory

Indochina, 43n–44n, 131, 144n, 145

interservice conflict, 90n–91n, 123n, 153–60

IRBMS (Intermediate Range Ballistic Missiles), 202, 202n, 203; in Cuban missile crisis (Jupiter missiles), 241–43, 243n, 248

Jagow, Gottlieb von, 54, 62, 81, 84n, 92

Jervis, Robert, 64, 72

Joffre, Joseph, 66

Johnson, Louis, 117

Kahn, Herman, 39, 75

Kaufmann, William, 24n, 26n, 34n

Kaysen, Carl, 5n, 12, 218, 225, 256

Kennan, George, 104, 110, 114n, 173–75

Kennedy, John, military policy, 43, 248–49; and Berlin crisis, 216, 218, 222, 225–31, 281; and Cuban missile crisis, 241–53; and Europe, 166–67

Kennedy, Robert, 242–43, 252

Khrushchev, Nikita, and German question, 179, 205–6; and Berlin crisis, 171, 172, 191, 193–94, 199, 215–16, 219–21, 228, 233; and China, 206n, 275–76, 276n; and Cuban missile crisis, 238, 255, 257; and Dulles, 151n, 276n; and Kennedy, 215n

Kiderlen-Wächter, Alfred von, 67

Kissinger, Henry, 34n, 99, 152n, 208–9, 273, 278n

Knowland, William, 149

Korean War, and "window" thinking, 101, 112–30, 132; and limited war question, 115, 125; and New Look, 14, 269

Laurence, William, 102–3

Lebow, Richard Ned, 48, 76

Leites, Nathan, 20

LeMay, Curtis, 106, 134n

Lichnowsky, Prince von, 54, 85–86

limited war, thinking, origins of, 4–11; and Dulles, 40–42, 211n, 266–67; and Kissinger, 208–9; U.S. capabilities for, 41, 41n. See also Korean War, coercion

Lippmann, Walter, 176

Lloyd George, David, 98

Loftus, Joseph, 5n, 28–30

Lovett, Robert, 109

MC-48. See NATO, nuclear sharing

McCloy, John, 181, 257

McCone, John, 254

McElroy, Neil, 187, 203–4

McMahon, Brien, 103

Macmillan, Harold, 176n, 199–202, 202n, 207

McNamara, Robert, 220, 222, 229n, 235, 237–53, 259

Marshall, Andrew, 8n, 28–30, 36

Marshall, George, 122n, 126

massive retaliation. See New Look, Eisenhower

Matthews, Francis, 117–18

Mikoyan, Anastas, 195

Moltke, Helmuth von, (the elder), 60, 63, 66

Moltke, Helmuth von, (the younger), 58–60, 72, 75, 82, 83, 88–91, 96

Murphy, Robert, 192

Mutual Assured Destruction (MAD). See stability theory

NATO (North Atlantic Treaty Organization), strategy, 159–63, 181–82; and control of nuclear forces, 188n, 190; and nuclear question, 213–14; politics within, 165–68. See also Dulles, Eisenhower

NSC (National Security Council) doc. 68, 107–12

Naumann, Victor, 51–52

Neumann, John von, 103–4

New Look (Eisenhower strategy), 137–39, 161–62; and "redeployment," 164–65, 167–68. See also Eisenhower

Nicholas II, Tsar, 76–80, 93

Nitze, Paul, 36, 107–12, 121–22, 135n, 152n, 173, 226n, 229, 236n, 264

Nixon, Richard, 132, 269

Norstad, Lauris, 188n, 191, 192n, 194, 196, 207, 222, 225

nuclear sharing, 164, 182, 182n, 184–90, 189n, 229, 229n, 272n; and NATO strategy, 181–82. See also German nuclear weapons question

nuclear war-fighting, 25–29, 31–40. See also coercion, counterforce, preemption, warfare

Paris summit, 208, 215

peripheral strategy, 153, 159, 166

Poincaré, Raymond, 67n

Pourtalès, Count Friedrich von, 78–79

preemption, vii–viii; and Berlin crisis, 193, 209, 226n; and Cuban missile crisis, 240, 255–56; and Eisenhower strategy, 134n, 162, 163n, 209, 266n; and escalation, 17–25, 26n; during first Taiwan Straits crisis, 128n; in Korean War, 127–28; Liège issue, 68, 92n; in 1914, 61n, 68–69, 72, 75, 87–96; in 1941, 96–97; and nuclear weapons, 108, 134–35, 134n; and preventive war, 134–35, 147; and Truman, 134

preventive war and "window" thinking, viii, x; before 1914, 51–52, 54, 56–57, 61, 65, 69–70, 92; after 1945, 100–107, 112–15, 117–18, 123–24, 132–46, 148

Quester, George, 72

Radford, Arthur, 143, 148

RAND Corporation, 3, 5n, 6, 8, 11, 17, 20, 21, 26, 27, 28, 31, 40, 104

Renouvin, Pierre, 50
Ridgway, Matthew, 127, 138n, 144n, 165, 206n
Riezler, Kurt, 57
risk manipulation. *See* coercion
Ritter, Gerhard, 60–61, 89
Roosevelt, Franklin, 204–5
Rosenberg, David, 134, 158n
Rowen, Henry, 34–35, 224n, 225
Rusk, Dean, 123, 216, 224, 226–28, 227n, 235, 239, 243, 246n, 251, 282
Russell, Bertrand, 103

Sazonov, S. D., 53, 72, 75, 78, 80, 83–92, 97
Schelling, Thomas, 3; and arms control, 25; and Brodie, 34n; and controlled counter-city warfare, 37–38; and counterforce, 27n, 35–36; and Cuban missile crisis, 237, 258–59; and game theory, 14n; influence on policy, 39, 43, 217n, 224, 224n–25n; and intervention in Eastern Europe, 278n; and logic of preemption, vii–viii, 23–25; and manipulation of risk, 15–17, 23, 27, 37, 45; and origins of World War I, 47–48; and Sino-Soviet split, 273–74
Schlesinger, James, 39
Schlieffen, Count Alfred von, 58, 60–61, 66n; Schlieffen Plan, 58–63, 68–69, 73, 82, 90
Schmitt, Bernadotte, ix, 50, 80, 82
security dilemma, viiin, 64–65, 114n
SIOP (Single Integrated Operational Plan), 39–40, 218, 225, 249n
Sokolovskii, Marshal, 256
Solarium, Project, 132, 136–37, 141, 142, 148
Sorensen, Theodore, 241, 245–46
Spaak, Paul-Henri, 188n, 190, 196
Sprague, Robert, 146n
stability question, in 1952, 108, 134–35
stability theory, origins of, 20–25; applied to 1914, 95–96; and arms control, 25, 31; and counterforce, 33–36, 38. *See also* preemption
strategic balance, and Korean war buildup, 128–30; role in Cuban missile crisis, 235–37, 244–59, 246n, 247n; U.S. first strike capabilities, 28–29, 192–93. *See also* counterforce, preemption, preventive war

strategic intelligence, 28–30, 117n, 208, 208n
strategy, as "tactics writ large," 12, 45; as "how-to-do-it" study, 45–46; as "manipulation of risk," 15–17, 23, 45; as target selection, 11–12, 33
Strauss, Franz-Josef, 183–85, 188
Symington, Stuart, 123–24, 124n
Szilard, Leo, 21, 103

tactical nuclear weapons, 10, 26, 33, 214, 264
Taylor, A.J.P., 73
Taylor, Maxwell, 236, 236n–37n, 250
Teller, Edward, 119, 133
thermonuclear revolution, 132–36; and American strategic thought, 4–15
Thompson, Llewellyn, 171, 172, 174, 176n, 178, 191, 198n, 207, 221, 228
Truman, Harry, 106, 116–17, 120, 124, 126n, 134, 158n
Tuchman, Barbara, 72
Twining, Nathan, 106, 149–50, 195

Ulam, Adam, 273

Vandenberg, Arthur, 146
Vandenberg, Hoyt, 123, 128, 154–55
Van Evera, Stephen, 65–71
Vienna Summit, 216, 218

warfare, in early atomic age (1945–52), 4–8, 107, 119–21, 132–33, 154–64. *See also* thermonuclear revolution
White, Thomas, 34
William II, Emperor, 51–52, 56, 58–59, 62, 84, 87
"windows" of vulnerability and of opportunity. *See* preventive war, Korean War
Wohlstetter, Albert, 3, 17n, 239n; and counterforce, 27–28, 34–35, 37–38; and stability theory, 22–25; and vulnerability question, 17–25
World War I, origins of, 47–99; and "cult of the offensive," 64–72; and military plans, 48, 57–64; and mobilization system, 47, 72–95; and prewar arms race, 97n

Zimmermann, Alfred, 53